POPULATION AND ECONOMIC CHANGE IN EAST ASIA

POPULATION AND ECONOMIC CHANGE IN EAST ASIA

C. Y. Cyrus Chu
Ronald Lee
Editors

POPULATION AND DEVELOPMENT REVIEW

A Supplement to Volume 26, 2000

POPULATION COUNCIL
New York

Library of Congress Cataloging-in-Publication Data
Population and economic change in East Asia / C.Y. Cyrus Chu, Ronald Lee, editors.
    p. cm.
    Based on papers from a workshop entitled Economic aspects of demographic transition: the experience of Asian-Pacific countries in Asia, held at the Academia Sinica in Taipei, June, 1998.
    "Population and development review, a supplement to volume 26, 2000."
    Includes bibliographical references.
    ISBN 0-87834-101-3 (pbk. : alk. paper)
    1. Demographic transition--East Asia--Congresses. I. Chu, C. Y. Cyrus. II. Lee, Ronald Demos, 1941- III. Population and development review. Vol. 26 (Supplement)
HB887 .P658 2001
304.6'2'095--dc21

ISSN 0098-7921

ISBN 0-87834-101-3

00-066875

Printed in the United States of America.

CONTENTS

ACKNOWLEDGMENTS

We would like to thank a number of people and institutions for supporting the activities leading to the publication of this volume. This volume grows out of a workshop on Economic Aspects of Demographic Transition: The Experience of Asian-Pacific Countries in Asia, held at the Academia Sinica in Taipei in June of 1998, organized by Cyrus Chu and Ronald Lee. The individual chapters are based on selected presentations at the workshop. Funding for the workshop was provided by the National Institute of Aging through the University of California at Berkeley's Center for the Economics and Demography of Aging, and by the National Science Council and Academia Sinica of Taiwan. Financial support for publication of this volume was provided by the United Nations Population Fund (UNFPA). Finally, we extend our thanks to Sandra Ward and to the staff of *Population and Development Review* for their assistance in preparing this book for publication.

C. Y. Cyrus Chu

Ronald Lee

Introduction

RONALD LEE

C. Y. CYRUS CHU

FERTILITY TRANSITIONS SINCE World War II have typically been very fast, with fertility reaching replacement level in 20 to 30 years after the onset of the decline for those countries that have completed the transition. Fertility transitions in East Asia have been especially early and rapid within the context of overall demographic transition. Fertility transition is a narrower concept than demographic transition; the latter also incorporates the decline in mortality (which typically begins earlier than fertility decline) and the changes in a population's age distribution caused by the changing vital rates. Demographic transitions take more than a century to complete, starting with the decline in mortality and ending after the surge of population aging. The chapters in this volume investigate the causes of fertility transition in a selection of Asian countries, assessing the relative contributions of social and economic change and of state-sponsored family planning programs. They also investigate the economic consequences of demographic transition, including the consequences of aging.

In the first phase of the demographic transition, mortality begins to decline, perhaps a few decades before fertility does so, causing an increase in the proportion of children in the population and raising child-dependency ratios. Next fertility begins to decline, initiating a long period of declining child-dependency ratios and declining total dependency ratios. This second phase may last 40 or 50 years. It culminates in a third phase, characterized by rapid increase of the elderly population and rising old-age dependency ratios and total dependency ratios. At the end of that phase the total dependency ratio is similar to the level that existed before the demographic transition began, but with a quite different composition: child dependency is low, and old-age dependency is high. Presumably mortality will continue to decline during the twenty-first century, so that the process of population aging will continue, but at a gradual pace. We mark the end of the demographic transition when this process of gradual aging begins.

In a number of Asian countries (for example, in Japan, South Korea, Taiwan, and perhaps China) the total fertility rate has fallen well below replacement. Whether fertility will remain below replacement in such countries or will instead return to replacement level is unknown and depends in part on the extent to which their currently low levels are a transitory consequence of women's rising average age at childbearing.

In the middle phase of the demographic transition, labor force growth is rapid and the dependent age groups grow more slowly, particularly the youngest age groups. Therefore the age-distributional changes of this middle phase are conducive to rapid growth in per capita incomes. These changes in age distribution may also lead to higher saving rates, which could contribute to economic growth, and increasing life expectancy could add to this effect. Whether these economic benefits actually ensue depends on the factors that influence saving behavior and on the institutional context. Is consumption in old age supported by the family or, alternatively, by an unfunded public-sector pension system? Is the family system of support eroded by state action or by the processes of development themselves? This phase in the demographic transition may also be both cause and consequence of rapid increases in educational investment per child, further boosting economic growth. The growth-enhancing forces of this middle phase have been referred to as the "demographic bonus" and the "demographic gift."

In the third phase, although child-dependency ratios remain low, the old-age dependency ratio rises sharply. Some models of saving behavior suggest that aggregate saving rates may drop sharply as a result, as the elderly tend to dissave (spend) as they live off their assets. This point is controversial. But even if saving rates fall, with slower labor force growth the amount of capital per worker may nonetheless rise. The consumption possibilities of the working-age population will depend on whether the elderly support themselves out of savings or are supported by transfers from their families or an unfunded public-sector pension program. Despite these uncertainties about saving and capital in the third phase, per capita investment in education is likely to remain high, since fertility is expected to remain low.

In Asia, Japan has entered the third phase, while a number of other countries such as Taiwan are on the threshold of population aging, and many others will enter it in the next few decades. Although discussions of the demographic transition and economic development have usually concentrated on either the middle phase of improved total dependency ratios, or on the first two phases together, such discussions are incomplete. Population aging is an integral part of the demographic transition. The buoyant middle phase is transitory and inevitably leads to a reversal.

In some parts of Asia the demographic transitions have been distinctively early and rapid, whereas in others they have started late and proceeded slowly. Although the causes of these transitions are still debated after many decades of research, the debate focuses not so much on the factors that account for the transitions as on the relative importance of each factor. Those factors include the decline in mortality and particularly improvement in child survival; socioeconomic development, including rising incomes, urbanization, industrialization, and increasing work opportunities for women in the market economy; the wish of parents to invest more in the health and education of each child and the consequent need to reduce the number of children they have; and state-run family planning programs. It is noteworthy that the onset of fertility decline often lags behind mortality decline and socioeconomic development; but once the fertility decline starts, it proceeds far more rapidly than these other processes, often reaching a level of two children per woman in only two to three decades. This sequence has led many observers to conclude that a process of diffusion must be involved—diffusion of information about the changes, of attitudes, or of contraceptive knowledge.

For the study of demographic transition and its consequences, the experience of some Asian countries is particularly pertinent. In many European countries and Japan, the process of mortality decline was closely related to the development of medical technology and public health measures, which occurred gradually. Similarly, their economic development was gradual. For these reasons the demographic transitions in those countries were slow. But many Asian countries have been able to adopt the medical and industrial technologies from the advanced countries all at once. Their mortality declined sharply, contributing to the speed of the demographic transition. Such a condensed transitional experience conveys advantages for academic research, because irrelevant shocks are fewer and social impacts are easier to observe. Moreover, the experience of Asian countries provides sharp contrasts. Some failed to reduce their fertility, whereas others had highly effective family planning programs or rapid fertility declines for other reasons.

Corresponding to these massive and sweeping demographic changes are economic, social, and institutional changes that are part cause and part consequence. For instance, parents with fewer children are able to invest more in each child. This well-known quantity–quality tradeoff may be one of the reasons why they reduced their fertility to begin with. Parents with fewer children and longer life expectancy may save more and invest to support their old age. The increased availability of financial institutions that facilitate this process may also be one of the causes of fertility decline. In addition, new institutions such as public pension systems may help support the increasingly numerous elderly, as traditional family-support mechanisms are weakened by development. The demographic transition and the age-distributional changes that accompany it may in these ways foster increased human-capital accumulation, physical-capital accumulation, and favorable dependency ratios, thus boosting economic development. But each of these possible links to more rapid development may fail. Public education systems may be overwhelmed by the increasing numbers of children, or rates of return to education may fall, discouraging further investment in schooling. Longer life and fewer children may not encourage private saving behavior to an appreciable extent. Rapidly increasing labor supply may lead only to declining capital-to-labor ratios and increasing unemployment, rather than to proportional increases in output. In any event, the demographic transition and economic development are closely connected.

Part One, containing three chapters by Hirschman and Young; Poston; and Molyneaux and Gertler, reviews and analyzes the transition experience in various Asian countries. Part Two is concerned with institutional arrangements to accommodate the increasing proportion of the elderly in Asian societies. The chapters by Benjamin, Brandt, and Rozelle and by Hu, Chen, and Chen discuss the experiences of China and Taiwan. Part Three focuses on the changing pattern of saving behavior, giving particular attention to the case of Taiwan, which had an unusually rapid and early demographic transition and an unusually high saving rate. Examining this topic are three chapters by Deaton and Paxson; Tsai, Chu, and Chung; and Lee, Mason, and Miller. Finally, Part Four focuses on the relationship between demographic transition and economic development. From different perspectives, the chapters by Montgomery, Arends-Kuenning, and Mete and by Bloom, Canning, and Malaney examine the effects of the quantity–quality tradeoff in family size, the age-composition effect, and other demographic influences on economic development. In the last chapter, Fogel provides a historical overview of the demographic transition, emphasizing the role of improved nutrition and longer life.

All three chapters in Part One address the debate over the respective roles of socioeconomic development, mortality decline, and family planning programs in the fertility transition. Investigating the causes of fertility decline in four Asian countries, Hirschman and Young have found that the core theory of demographic transition can be supported, but that the relative weights of its determinants vary widely across time and location. Poston compares the cases of Taiwan and China, focusing on the diverging patterns of fertility decline caused by the gradual and voluntary adoption of family planning in Taiwan in contrast to China's imposition of its family planning program by fiat. His results indicate the strong influence of socioeconomic factors on fertility behavior. Molyneaux and Gertler assess the role of family planning programs in Indonesia's fertility decline over the period 1986 to 1994. They confront an old problem in assessing the impact of programs: if program resources are allocated to areas with high or steady fertility, then the impact of the resources may be underestimated; if, on the other hand, resources are allocated to areas of high demand for contraceptive services, then the impact may be overestimated. By carefully modeling and estimating the process by which program inputs are allocated, they have devised a strategy for avoiding these pitfalls. They conclude that, properly estimated, program inputs do matter along with educational expenditures, but that some matter much more than others.

In the 1980s a widely held view emerged that population growth was not a major deterrent to economic development (e.g., Kelley 1988; National Research Council 1986). This view contrasted strongly with an earlier one, that the rapid population growth in developing countries after World War II was a serious impediment to development, and that without development, rapid population growth was likely to continue (Coale and Hoover 1958; National Academy of Sciences 1971). The earlier literature emphasized the adverse effects of capital dilution resulting from rapid labor force growth, and it stressed the dangers of growing unemployment in economies with surplus labor. More recently a new literature has reemphasized the potential economic consequences of the changes in age structure that accompany the demographic transition, changes that we described above. Although population growth rates may matter relatively little in themselves, the same growth rate could result either from high fertility and high mortality, or from low fertility and low mortality; and that difference is vital. Furthermore, it matters a great deal whether it is the working-age population that is growing rapidly or the population of children, so that the details of age and timing are important. These ideas are not new; indeed, they were contained in some classic studies. But for various reasons they have received less attention than they might have in subsequent work. The chapter by Bloom, Canning, and Malaney addresses these issues in a broad, cross-national framework that examines the interrelations between growth in per capita income and demographic change over the period 1960 to 1995. Although there are ambiguities in sorting out cause from effect, these authors argue that the initial phases of the fertility transition lead to accelerated growth in income per capita, which in turn leads to further fertility decline and further economic growth. The estimated effects are somewhat larger than can be explained by changing dependency ratios alone, but the mechanisms through which this sequence of events occurs are not clear. Bloom, Canning, and Malaney suggest that the age-distribution changes caused by the transition can explain most of the unusually rapid economic growth in East Asia during recent decades.

The chapter by Benjamin, Brandt, and Rozelle focuses on the economic position of the elderly in rural northern China, examining that age group's family composition, incomes, and work patterns. It shows that the role of private, family-based social security was weakened during the era in which community support was intended to replace that of the family. Today, while community support is being withdrawn as the market economy grows in China, the family system may not be able to perform its former role. In Taiwan, which faces a rapidly aging population, the pressing need is to find new ways to provide old-age social security, as the extended family becomes less prevalent. Introducing an unfunded public pension system may undermine private savings and hence retard economic growth. Hu, Chen, and Chen apply simulation to a standard growth model to examine the influences of several social security designs on Taiwan's saving rate, including pay-as-you-go and fully funded programs. On the basis of their simulation results, they propose some policy solutions.

Each of the three chapters on saving and capital accumulation examines the possibility that the aforementioned demographic changes boost rates of saving, which is one route through which the demographic transition may affect economic development. All three study the experience of Taiwan, which has unusually good data for this purpose.

Deaton and Paxson build on their earlier work in two respects: by estimating the influence of individuals of different ages on household saving, and by using the resulting estimates to simulate the effects of nonstable transitional demographic dynamics on aggregate saving. Although they find that the effects of changing demographic dynamics depend on the rate of economic growth, it appears that the changing age distributions caused by the transition in Taiwan did indeed boost savings. The amount of the increase, however, is only a fraction of the total rise in savings, and Deaton and Paxson do not view their findings as supporting the idea that the transition may have boosted savings sufficiently to have had much of a role in recent growth.

Lee, Mason, and Miller address the same question from a different methodological perspective. They assume that adults provide for their old age through savings and investment, and that they have always done so. Under these assumptions, they ask, how would the demographic transition, with its outcome of fewer children and longer life, have affected aggregate saving rates? On the basis of their macrosimulation model, they conclude that the effects on aggregate savings would be quite large, more than twice as large as those found by Deaton and Paxson, but with similar timing. Like Deaton and Paxson, they conclude that if the rate of economic growth slows in the early twenty-first century, then population aging will lead to lower saving, even though the amount of wealth per worker and the wealth-to-income ratio will remain high. The patterns of consumption and saving they simulate by age of household head seem broadly consistent with patterns observed in the microdata for Taiwan, and with patterns found by Deaton and Paxson.

Tsai, Chu, and Chung take yet another approach. They model and estimate the effect of longer life on household savings, using a structural model fitted to household data. Their idea is to characterize explicitly the "cohort" effect emphasized by Deaton and Paxson, and the theoretical structure they adopt is based on the model of precautionary savings developed by Ehrlich and Lui (1991). Using a pseudo panel data set, they conclude that longer life has in fact motivated higher saving rates. Thus all three of these chapters find evidence that the demographic transition has stimulated savings, albeit at quite different magnitudes, at the household level.

The chapter by Montgomery, Arends-Kuenning, and Mete investigates the interaction between declining fertility and rising investments in human capital. These two processes are interlinked because the desire to invest in children's human capital is one of the causes of the fertility transition. High rates of return to investment in education at primary, secondary, and higher levels of learning provide a strong incentive. But why do these high levels of investment not decline as educated workers flood the labor market? This is one of the puzzles investigated by these authors.

In the past, attention has focused appropriately on the causes of the transitions in fertility and mortality, and on the economically beneficial middle phase of the demographic transition, in which the labor force grows more rapidly than the numbers of young or old. As we noted at the outset, however, it would be misleading to view this phase in isolation or as one that could continue indefinitely. Consequences of the initial phase of the transition, in which child dependency ratios rise as mortality declines, are rarely considered, but they set the stage for the dramatic changes in the middle phase. It is also important to realize that the machinery of demographic dynamics links the promising middle stage inevitably to subsequent population aging, which has both positive and negative aspects. This volume provides a fresh look at some old questions surrounding the fertility decline, as well as exploring a new and more comprehensive terrain that includes the third phase of the demographic transition—population aging—as an integral and inevitable part of the population–development nexus. The studies it contains help place the demographic transition within an integrated, fully rounded framework. Their examination of the consequences of the second and third phases of the transition is helpful for a comprehensive understanding of demographic transitions and their implications in specific contexts.

References

Coale, Ansley J. and Edgar M. Hoover. 1958. *Population Growth and Economic Development in Low Income Countries*. Princeton, NJ: Princeton University Press.

Ehrlich, I. and F. T. Lui. 1991. "Intergenerational trade, longevity, and economic growth," *Journal of Political Economy* 99(5): 1237–1261.

Kelley, Allen. 1988. "Economic consequences of population change in the Third World," *Journal of Economic Literature* 36(4): 1685–1728.

National Academy of Sciences. 1971. *Rapid Population Growth: Consequences and Policy Implications,* 2 vols. Baltimore: Johns Hopkins University Press for the National Academy of Sciences.

National Research Council. 1986. *Population Growth and Economic Development: Policy Questions.* Working Group on Population Growth and Economic Development, Committee on Population. Washington, DC: National Academy Press.

PART ONE

THE ASIAN DEMOGRAPHIC TRANSITION AND ITS CAUSES

Social Context
and Fertility Decline
in Southeast Asia:
1968–70 to 1988–90

CHARLES HIRSCHMAN
YIH-JIN YOUNG

THEORETICAL DEBATES CONTINUE on how best to explain both the historical record of fertility declines in developed countries and the ongoing fertility transitions in the developing world (Hirschman 1994; Kirk 1996; Mason 1997). Demographic transition theory has guided empirical research over the past 40 years, but consistent empirical evidence has not always been available to affirm every proposition from the theory. These anomalies have sparked a number of revisionist and "new" theories and approaches that have been introduced or reintroduced to explain fertility change—for example, intergenerational wealth flows (Caldwell 1982), demand and supply models (Bulatao and Lee 1983), ideational theory (Lesthaeghe 1983), and diffusion and interaction interpretations (Bongaarts and Watkins 1996; Rosero-Bixby and Casterline 1993).

These new theoretical formulations, however, have not yet replaced demographic transition theory as the dominant perspective in the field. In several cases the new ideas represent only partial theoretical frameworks and do not offer a comprehensive account of how social change affects demographic processes. In other cases the new theories are promising, but the core hypotheses have not been empirically confirmed and perhaps may not be testable with available data. A major limitation of most empirical research on fertility from all theoretical perspectives has been a reliance on cross-sectional data from a single country. In this chapter we test several core hypotheses from demographic transition theory with a longitudinal and comparative research design that is appropriate to the theory.

This study extends research comparing the fertility declines in four Southeast Asian countries based on multilevel models with microlevel census data from 1970, 1980, and 1990. In earlier work we described patterns of fertility decline in Southeast Asia and tested cross-sectional and lagged multilevel models of fertility determination (Hirschman and Guest 1990a and 1990b) and tested a preliminary model of fertility change for one country (Hirschman et al. 1998). Here we broaden the empirical analyses of this framework to test several key hypotheses from classical demographic transition theory on the causes of fertility change, using data from three rounds of censuses for four countries.

Southeast Asian societies in transition

With a combined population of more than 500 million (about 9 percent of the world's total), Southeast Asia encompasses a great diversity of religion, language, colonial history, and current political and economic structures.[1] Despite its diversity, it has some common cultural features—specifically, bilateral kinship and a relatively high status for women—that distinguish the region from the more patriarchal societies of South and East Asia (Hirschman 1992; Reid 1988).

For the present analysis we use microdata census files to focus on Thailand, Malaysia, Indonesia, and the Philippines. For three of these countries the files are samples of their entire national populations. For Malaysia, however, the microdata census file is limited to Peninsular Malaysia. Indonesia is by far the most populous of the four countries, with an estimated population of 212 million in 2000. The Philippines and Thailand are also populous by world standards, with estimated populations in 2000 of 76 million and 61 million, respectively. Malaysia is smaller, with an estimated population of 22 million in 2000; more than 80 percent of the population is in Peninsular Malaysia (United Nations Population Division 1999).

Although slowed by the Asian economic crisis that began in 1997, Southeast Asia has been a region of impressive socioeconomic development. Malaysia had a per capita gross national product (GNP) of US$3,480 in 1994, which put the nation into what the World Bank calls "upper middle income" economies (World Bank 1996: Table 1). The other three countries are ranked in the "lower middle income" category in the World Bank's classification. Economic growth in these countries has also been rapid, with average annual growth rates of 4 percent or higher in per capita GNP from 1965 to 1986 in Malaysia, Indonesia, and Thailand. The Philippines has been less successful, but it still attained a respectable 1.9 percent per capita average annual growth rate over the two decades (World Bank 1988: Table 1). During the decade of the last half of the 1980s and the first half the 1990s (the latter largely beyond the empirical focus of this study), the rapid economic growth characterized as the "East Asian economic miracle" was thought to be spreading from East to Southeast Asia (World Bank 1993).

Other socioeconomic measures, including school enrollment, occupational patterns, and infant mortality, show comparable gains for these years. Recently the four countries have experienced major setbacks from the Asian economic crisis. Our empirical analysis, based on census data from 1970, 1980, and 1990, focuses on the period preceding the recent economic downturn.

Theories and models of fertility decline

The central thesis of demographic transition theory is that economic and social modernization leads to an initial decline in mortality, which reduces incentives for large families and eventually leads to low levels of fertility (Davis 1963; Notestein 1953). One of the primary criticisms of demographic transition theory has been the weak relationship between measures of modernization and fertility (Cleland 1985; Cleland and Wilson 1987; Knodel and van de Walle 1979). Indeed, cases can be cited of fertility beginning to decline in rural rather than in urban areas and of fertility decline preceding socioeconomic development or following it after a long period (Watkins 1987).

Although anomalies tend to generate more interest than replications, a significant body of research supports many of the central propositions from classical demographic transition theory (Friedlander, Schellekens, and Ben-Moshe 1991; Lee, Galloway, and Hammel 1994). Over the long term, socioeconomic modernization and declines in mortality and fertility move together, but short-run trends often reveal a variety of anomalous patterns (Mason 1997).

To resolve the current debate over demographic transition theory, it is important to develop a cumulative research tradition based on an explicit conceptualization of how the many and varied dimensions of socioeconomic development are linked to each other and to lowered fertility. On the basis of observations from a number of developing countries, Freedman (1979) posits that various subsets of the conventional predictors may be sufficient to lead to lower fertility, but that none of the variables seems to be a necessary condition for a fertility decline. Perhaps some of the debate over the determinants of fertility change arises from the plethora of empirical research that assumes that all indicators of socioeconomic status are interchangeable and that multivariate research should include all available variables (Hirschman 1994).

In this study and in prior work, we have been guided by a general theoretical model of fertility behavior presented schematically in Figure 1 (Hirschman and Guest 1990b; Hirschman et al. 1998). This model draws upon the central hypotheses of demographic transition theory but makes a significant distinction between macro- and microlevel determinants of fertility. Classical demographic transition theory specifies that changes in so-

FIGURE 1   Multilevel model of contextual and individual-level effects on current fertility

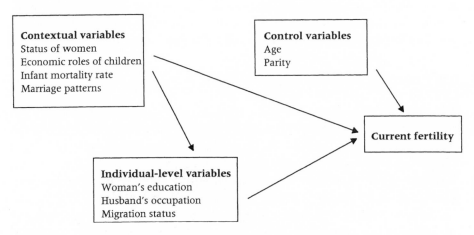

cial institutions and social structure are the fundamental causal forces that shape human fertility (Smith 1989). These institutional factors, which we have labeled as contextual variables in Figure 1, are only indirectly reflected in the individual-level survey data that are typically used in cross-sectional analyses of fertility. The assumption guiding the current study is that fertility behavior, like all individual behavior, is influenced by the social, economic, and cultural context as well as by individual circumstances. Changes in social structure—opportunities, constraints, and normative context—are not simply exogenous variables to be held constant in order that individual-level relationships can be examined. Our premise is that change in fertility behavior is a product of large-scale changes in the organization of societies that are filtered through changes in individual characteristics and the opportunities that individuals face.

On the basis of demographic transition theory and past research, the four specific structural characteristics we have selected for this study as the most likely institutional factors to influence fertility are the status of women, the economic roles of children, infant and child mortality, and marriage patterns. Although these factors are correlated with other aspects of social structure that may influence fertility, they capture several of the central hypotheses of demographic transition theory.

Social structure may influence the fertility of individuals directly through economic incentives and normative pressures, or indirectly by modifying the characteristics of individuals. To cast the net as broadly as possible, the model portrayed in Figure 1 contains several individual-level characteristics, including a woman's educational attainment, her migration status, and her husband's occupation. These individual-level characteristics serve as intervening variables between socioeconomic context and fertility outcomes, and also as important causal variables in their own right because there is considerable individual heterogeneity in all institutions, places, and social contexts. Age and parity are included as control variables because fertility is also dependent on the stage a woman has reached in the reproductive life cycle.

Although this is a general theoretical framework, the choice of particular variables to represent key concepts reflects the availability of data. Our analysis is based upon data files that pool microdata samples from three successive census rounds (1970, 1980, and 1990). With individual women of ages 15–44 as the units of analysis, the dependent variable is a measure of current fertility for the periods 1968–70, 1978–80, and 1988–90, and is based on the presence of children between the ages of 0 and 2 who can be linked with a mother in the same household.

The contextual variables are created from census data assembled for the province or district of residence for each woman respondent in the sample. The major limitation of census data is the lack of the full range of individual-level variables that are usually considered in fertility research. Moreover, some possibly significant determinants of fertility change, such as family planning programs, the availability of contraceptive services, and informal social networks that may diffuse fertility norms, cannot be measured with census data. In spite of these limitations, our focus on social structural determinants of fertility change within a multilevel analytical framework, measured across two time intervals and four countries, represents a more comprehensive approach to the study of modern fertility transitions than is typical in the research literature.

The major determinants of fertility change identified in this model are fairly similar to those that might be presented in an economic theory of fertility. The concepts of the status of women, the economic roles of children, and infant mortality could be reconceptualized to be consistent with a supply-demand framework for children (Easterlin and Crimmins 1985). From an economic perspective, the status of women might well be conceptualized as the value of a woman's time, and the concept of the economic roles of children is analogous to the "price" of children. The major omission in our formulation of the demographic transition framework is income. Income is a central element in economic theory, but the impact of income on fertility in demographic theory is secondary to the institutional structure of society and the family. Moreover, a microeconomic framework would posit individual-level variables as the primary causal factors, whereas the aggregate characteristics of social contexts would be considered only as environments that shape preferences or condition individual-level relationships.

The basic difference between our social demographic model of fertility, based on the demographic transition literature, and the economics of fertility model is the primacy of the community versus that of the individual. We assume that individuals are socialized as members of specific communities, in which they learn norms of appropriate behavior and face the collective constraints and opportunities in specific geographical settings shaped by social institutions and the level of technological development. Therefore, our theoretical perspective specifies that contextual variables should be considered as the prime explanatory variables, and that individual-level variables can be introduced as mediators of the community-level influences and as potentially independent determinants in their own right. Economic theory would posit that individual-level variables should be considered as the fundamental causal variables for explaining fertility and fertility change; then, and only then, should contextual variables be considered for their marginal explanatory power. Given that the validity of these contrasting assumptions cannot be empirically determined, but only evaluated with data, our analysis compares models with alternative sequences of contextual and individual-level variables.

Measuring fertility change and testing hypotheses

With pooled census data from the 1970 and 1980 censuses, the baseline model is the regression of current fertility on a dummy variable representing the census year (1980 = 1, 1970 = 0). The year coefficient can be interpreted as the absolute decline in period fertility over the decade. We elaborate this baseline equation in subsequent models with the introduction of additional independent variables. The change in the year coefficient from the baseline to the more complex models is a measure of our ability to "explain" fertility change in a multilevel model of socioeconomic change. We conduct this analysis for the first intercensal decade (1970–80) and then repeat the analysis for the second decade using pooled data from the 1980 and 1990 censuses.

Following the order of the variables in Figure 1, we first add the set of structural variables (provincial-level contextual variables) in the second model. The third model includes only the individual-level characteristics as independent variables; the fourth model includes both the macro- and microdeterminants of fertility. One of our objectives is to compare the explanatory power of the contextual variables and the individual variables. Both sets of variables, macro and micro, represent a demand model of fertility. Unfortunately, census data do not contain measures of "supply" (fecundity, breastfeeding, spouse absence), nor are indicators of family planning services available for the geographic areas and time periods considered here. Consequently, our emphasis is on the potential explanatory power of macro- or structural characteristics of geographic areas, coded as contextual variables in multilevel models of fertility change.

The individual-level variables may be mediators of the structural or contextual variables and may also have independent explanatory power. An important question is whether individual characteristics mediate the influences of the contextual variables on fertility. In other words, is the impact of modernized areas just the weighted sum of the impact of "modernized" persons in those areas? Caldwell (1980) argues that the community level of educational attainment can have a stronger influence on individual fertility behavior than individual characteristics. The primary substantive hypotheses to be examined are whether the three primary contextual variables of women's status, children's economic roles, and infant mortality can explain the observed fertility declines in the four countries over the 1970s and 1980s. These factors may affect fertility by postponing marriage or may affect marital fertility directly.

The theme of women's status and roles encompasses an array of issues ranging from women's participation in economic life to their relative power in household decisionmaking (Mason 1987). Our focus here is on the relative balance of women's involvement in traditional (family and household) versus modern (nonhousehold) roles. To the extent that significant proportions of women in the community are active in the modern sector, there should be some legitimation and freedom to break with traditional roles, including high fertility. We suggest that much of the effect of socioeconomic development on fertility is mediated by the structure of women's roles inside and outside the family. From the census data on educational attainment, we have constructed a contextual indicator of women's status at the provincial level: the proportion of women aged 15–34 who have attained schooling beyond the primary level. The age boundaries 15–34 identify women in the peak childbearing years whose behavior might serve as a model for the normative context of appropriate fertility behavior.

In a similar fashion, social and economic structure may influence fertility by modifying the roles of children, especially their economic contribution to the family. The typical illustration of demographic transition theory describes how the shift from an agricultural economy to an urban, industrial economy transforms children from economic assets to economic liabilities. From this hypothesis has come a considerable body of research that attempts to measure the actual and perceived value of children to the household economy (Caldwell 1983; Darroch, Meyer, and Singarimbun 1981; Mueller 1976; Nag, White, and Peet 1978). The variable identified here is the labor force activity of children aged 10–14; for the Philippines the youngest age group possible is 15–18.

Infant and child mortality, in addition to being an important index of socioeconomic development, also has a well-developed theoretical link to the motivation for childbearing. If parents lack institutional-based pensions, they see their adult children as providers of old-age assistance. Under conditions of high infant and child mortality, parents are likely to "insure" themselves with extra births. When mortality begins to decline, however, parents may begin to see large families as an impediment to social mobility or status maintenance (Davis 1963).

The contextual variables may affect fertility directly by influencing marital fertility, or indirectly via the postponement of marriage. The status-of-women variable is most likely to influence the incidence of very early marriage. We therefore include an indicator of the level of marital postponement, the percentage of women aged 15–24 in the province who have never married, as an additional contextual variable.

At the individual level, a large body of research has shown that a woman's education is the most powerful individual-level predictor of fertility (Cochrane 1979). It seems that higher levels of education lead to lower fertility, not only because of improved employment prospects but also because educated women's ideas about family life and childbearing are different from those of uneducated women (Cleland 1985: 239). Migration status is generally thought to have a negative influence on fertility. The basic assumption is that the act of migration is an innovative behavior that is correlated with other innovative behavior such as lower fertility. Migration, however, is not always an independent activity of the individual. By comparing the place of birth and the current place of residence, we measure lifetime migration across administrative boundaries, but the migration decision may have been made by a woman's parents or spouse. For married women living with a spouse, the husband's occupation is a crude measure of social class. The standard expectation is that the wives of agriculturalists will have the highest fertility, whereas women married to men of higher status, in white-collar occupations, will have the lowest fertility. In every model we enter the age of the woman as a covariate to serve as a partial control for exposure.

Data and measurement

We base our analysis on microdata samples from three population censuses in each of the four countries—those of 1970 (1971 for Indonesia), 1980, and 1990 (1991 for Peninsular Malaysia). The samples were constructed by the national statistical office in each country to be representative of the national population. The one exception is Malaysia, where the microdata sample covers only Peninsular Malaysia and excludes the states of Sabah and Sarawak on the island of Borneo (containing about 20 percent of Malaysia's population). Throughout the subsequent analysis presented here "Malaysia" refers to Peninsular Malaysia only.

The sampling fractions and sample designs varied across the 12 data files. In some instances the sample was a straightforward systematic random sample of the master census file. In others the microdata sample was drawn from the "long-form" (detailed census questionnaire) sample. Some sample designs were based on disproportionate geographic areas, and therefore it was necessary to apply weights to adjust such samples to the total census-enumerated population. For each entire census population, our estimated models use the sample weights in order to have a representative sample of the population, but the weights are "deflated" so that each weighted sample size is equal to that of the original unweighted sample.

Although the weighted microdata samples are representative of the complete census-enumerated populations, they are not, with the exception of Malaysia, simple random samples of all households in the country. In some cases the census offices administered the long-form questionnaire to all persons within a random sample of geographic areas. That procedure means that the standard errors estimated by statistical packages, which assume simple random samples, may be in error. This bias is partially offset by the large sample sizes of the census microdata files and our conservative criterion for reporting results having statistical significance at the .001 level. For the subsamples of women aged 15–44, the sample sizes range from 35,000 observations for the 1970 Malaysian sample to more than 1.5 million cases for the 1980 Indonesian sample. For the largest of the sample files we took random subsamples to make computation more manageable (e.g., sampling fractions are .67 for the 1970 Philippine census, .50 for the 1980 Philippine census, and .18 for the 1980 Indonesian census). Further details on each microdata census sample are presented in the Appendix Table.

The dependent variable is an index of current fertility, specifically the number of surviving children aged 0–2 of each woman. Using the own-children methodology (Cho, Retherford, and Choe 1986), we matched each child with his or her mother in the household. In earlier work we based the index of current fertility on surviving children of ages 1–4 to minimize the effect of the underenumeration of infants (Cho et al. 1980: 31). This bias seems to be limited to the 1971 Indonesian census, and in this analysis we rely on the more conventional measure of own-children below age 3. The index is weighted to represent the number of children a woman would eventually have if current fertility continued for her entire reproductive career (i.e., it is akin to a total fertility rate), and it is adjusted for the proportion of unmatched children in the sample. The current-fertility indexes are presented (and analyzed separately) for women in two age groups, 15–29 and 30–44. Our assumption is that the factors that shape "early" fertility behavior are somewhat different from those that determine fertility at older ages (Hirschman 1985: 35–36). At younger ages the timing of marriage, the postponement of the first birth, and the intervals between early births strongly influence variation in fertility. Our analysis of early fertility is based on the sample of all women (married and unmarried) in the 15–29 age group. For older women, fertility decisions center on the completion of childbearing, or "stopping" behavior. The sample is restricted to ever-married women in the 30–44 age range, which includes almost all women in that age range for these years.

The own-children method is subject to a number of measurement problems, but it has the virtue of being an indicator of recent behavior. An alternative indicator, children-ever-born, measures cumulative fertility more accurately than the own-children method, but it includes births that may have occurred 10 or 20 years in the past. Additional analyses, not reported here, using the number of children ever born as the dependent variable, have yielded results generally consistent with those reported here. (For more discussion of the concept and measurement of current fertility, see Hirschman and Guest 1990a.) Own-children fertility estimates for areas are usually adjusted for variations in areal levels of infant and child mortality. For studies, including this one, that use own-children techniques to estimate fertility at the individual level, there is no reliable method of adjustment for infant mortality (Rindfuss and Sweet 1977; Swicegood et al. 1988). The lack of adjustment for infant mortality means that current fertility is underestimated, and it is underestimated most for women in areas with higher infant mortality, such as Indonesia. The provincial level of infant mortality is one of the central independent variables in our analysis. Moreover, other aggregate and individual-level variables are probably correlated with the infant mortality rate (the number of infant deaths per 1,000 births). The consequence is a bias in the estimated relationships between these independent variables and our index of current fertility that is opposite to our theoretical expectations. This may be one of the reasons for some of the counterintuitive findings of the study.

We have measured contextual variables for the smallest geographic units for which the necessary data are available, adjusting them for consistency across censuses and combining some units to ensure a minimum number of cases in each area. In Indonesia the units are regencies (*kabupaten* or *kotamadya*, $N = 246$); in Malaysia the standard geographic units are districts ($N = 70$); in the Philippines and Thailand the units are provinces ($N = 67$ and 71, respectively). Although the constraints of available data have greatly influenced our choice of geographic units, the units seem to offer a reasonable balance between small communities and very large heterogeneous states or regions.

We have estimated the contextual variables from the original microdata census samples. The great advantage of census files is their large size, which makes it possible to reliably estimate the characteristics of subnational areas, including the provinces and districts. Most of the contextual variables were estimated in a relatively straightforward fashion. The one exception was infant mortality. Only for Malaysia were published and reliable vital statistics available for each areal unit (district). For the other countries we had to estimate provincial levels of infant mortality (q_x values) using Brass-type methods based on the number of children ever born and children surviving. If independent estimates for regional values of infant mortality were available, we attempted to follow precedents in methods of estimation. We do not yet have measures of infant mortality for the late 1980s, and so our analysis of the effect of infant mortality on fertility declines is limited to the first intercensal interval. Additional information on the estimation of infant mortality levels is available from us.

In the multivariate analysis that follows, the age of a woman is included as a covariate in all models. In all models containing microlevel variables, current parity (measured by the number of children ever born minus current fertility) is included as an additional covariate. Our objective is to measure the total effects of contextual variables and their direct effects, after including intervening individual-level variables in the models.

Descriptive analysis

Table 1 presents summary measures of fertility and fertility change for the four countries. Age-specific fertility rates are computed by dividing the average annual number of births for the three years prior to the census (based on the number of surviving children of ages 0–2) to women of age (x) by the number of women of age (x). The total fertility rates are simply the sum of the age-specific fertility rates computed on a per woman basis. The fertility indexes in Table 1 are lower than those reported in other sources for the same countries and times, primarily because the own-children estimates have not been adjusted for infant and child mortality. The rates are also somewhat lower than those reported in our own prior publications using these data (Hirschman and Guest 1990a); the lower rates are due to the different reference period and, in the case of Indonesia, the underenumeration of infants in the 1971 census. The very low figure for the 1990 Thai total fertility rate is biased downward by the lack of correction for infant mortality and perhaps by other factors (Hirschman et al. 1994; Knodel et al. 1996). We do not claim that these figures are the best estimates of fertility for these dates, but rather that they are fairly reasonable indicators based on a common measurement strategy across countries and time periods.

Table 1 reveals that fertility declined in all four countries during the 1970s and 1980s. In Thailand the rapidity of the decline is astonishing—a reduction of more than 2.6 births per woman in the 1970s and of an additional 1.1 births in the 1980s. Even with a generous allowance for an underestimate of fertility in the 1990 census, fertility in Thailand had probably reached replacement level by the late 1980s. In Malaysia the pace of fertility decline was slower in the 1980s than in the 1970s, dropping by 0.4

TABLE 1   Age-specific fertility rates, total fertility rates, and change in rates: Thailand, Indonesia, Malaysia, and Philippines, 1968–70 to 1988–90

Country and age at midpoint of interval	Age-specific fertility rates per 1,000 women			Change	
	1968–70	1978–80	1988–90	1970–80	1980–90
Thailand					
15–19	89	55	49	−34	−6
20–24	247	152	100	−95	−52
25–29	263	141	90	−122	−51
30–34	228	104	53	−124	−51
35–39	180	68	27	−112	−41
40–44	79	41	13	−38	−28
Total fertility rate	5.43	2.81	1.66	−2.63	−1.14
Indonesia[a]					
15–19	112	104	67	−8	−37
20–24	205	200	143	−4	−57
25–29	189	179	136	−10	−42
30–34	140	132	99	−8	−33
35–39	83	75	55	−8	−20
40–44	32	28	20	−5	−8
Total fertility rate	3.81	3.59	2.60	−0.22	−0.99
Peninsular Malaysia[b]					
15–19	80	48	27	−31	−21
20–24	219	162	130	−56	−32
25–29	249	200	178	−48	−22
30–34	206	148	145	−58	−2
35–39	125	90	86	−35	−4
40–44	51	36	33	−15	−4
Total fertility rate	4.65	3.43	3.00	−1.22	−0.43
Philippines					
15–19	84	80	59	−5	−21
20–24	221	219	175	−1	−44
25–29	244	238	197	−6	−41
30–34	202	194	156	−8	−38
35–39	133	131	103	−2	−28
40–44	55	57	44	3	−13
Total fertility rate	4.69	4.60	3.67	−0.09	−0.93

NOTES: Fertility is measured by the own-children method, based on the number of children, ages 0–2, matched to their mothers. The estimated number of births is adjusted for the proportion of children not matched (less than 10 percent in every census) but is not adjusted for infant and early childhood mortality or the under-enumeration of infants and children. Ages of women are indexed to the reference interval (1968–70, 1978–80, and 1988–90): age = age at census −2. Total fertility rates are expressed per woman.
[a] In Indonesia, where the 1970 census round was conducted in 1971, the first interval is 1969–71.
[b] In Malaysia, where the 1990 census round was conducted in 1991, the third interval is 1989–91.
SOURCES: Census microdata samples (machine-readable data files) from the 1970, 1980, and 1990 census rounds.

births per woman compared with a decline of 1.2 births in the first interval. Almost all of the decline in Malaysia in the 1980s was among younger women, perhaps reflecting a continuing desire for moderate-size families among married women in their 30s.

In contrast to Malaysia, the pace of fertility decline accelerated in Indonesia and the Philippines in the 1980s. After only slight declines during the 1970s, the total fertility rate fell by almost one birth per woman during the following decade in both countries.

The primary explanatory variables for these fertility changes, changes in contextual variables at the provincial level, are displayed in Table 2. The figures shown there are summary statistics (means and percentages) of the contextual variables for the two samples of women—all women of ages 15–29 (hereafter called "younger women") and married women of ages 30–44 (henceforth called "older women")—for each country in 1970, 1980, and 1990. Individuals are the units of analysis for both sets of independent variables, but the contextual variables can be interpreted as the social environment of each individual respondent. The average or mean social context in Table 2 is not a simple average of the provinces in the country, but rather a weighted average with the total population in each province as the weight.

The contextual measure of women's status—the percentage of women aged 15–34 in the province having attained secondary schooling—rose sharply in every country during both intercensal intervals. In Thailand the figure rose from 11 percent in 1970 to 29 percent in 1980, then rose again to 59 percent in 1990. In Indonesia the figure doubled from 7 percent in 1971 to 14 percent in 1980 and doubled again, reaching 31 percent in 1990. In Malaysia the index of women's status doubled from 25 percent to 50 percent between 1970 and 1980, then rose to 75 percent by 1991. Comparable figures for the status of women in the Philippines were 38 percent in 1970, 53 percent in 1980, and 66 percent in 1990.

Our indicator of children's economic roles, the percentage of children between ages 10 and 14 in the labor force, did not show a consistent pattern of change across countries. The average level dropped significantly in both Thailand and Indonesia between 1970 and 1980, but somewhat less so in Malaysia, where few children were reported to be in the labor force. The reported increase in child labor in the Philippines probably reflects a change in the measurement of labor force activity between the two censuses rather than a real change in behavior. There were only modest changes in this index from 1980 to 1990 in the three countries for which data are available. With fewer than 10 percent of children aged 10–14 working in Malaysia and Indonesia in 1980, there was almost no room for further change in the more recent decade. For Thailand the proportion of children working seems to have leveled off at about 40 percent during the 1980s.

TABLE 2 Changes in contextual variables: Thailand, Indonesia, Malaysia, and Philippines: 1970–80 and 1980–90

Country and variable	All women, ages 15–29			Change		Married women, ages 30–44			Change	
	1970	1980	1990	1970–80	1980–90	1970	1980	1990	1970–80	1980–90
Thailand										
% of women with secondary ed.	11	29	59	18	30	10	27	58	17	31
% of children in labor force	67	47	43	-20	-4	67	49	45	-18	-4
Infant mortality rate	58	41	u	-17	u	59	42	u	-17	u
% of single women, ages 15–24	63	67	71	4	4					
Indonesia										
% of women with secondary ed.	7	14	31	7	17	7	13	30	6	17
% of children in labor force	18	7	6	-11	-1	18	7	6	-11	-1
Infant mortality rate	142	105	u	-37	u	141	105	u	-36	u
% of single women, ages 15–24	30	36	58	6	22					
Peninsular Malaysia										
% of women with secondary ed.	25	50	75	25	25	24	48	75	24	27
% of children in labor force	8	7	1	-1	-6	9	6	1	-3	-5
Infant mortality rate	42	27	u	-15	u	42	28	u	-14	u
% of single women, ages 15–24	67	74	80	7	6					
Philippines										
% of women with secondary ed.	38	53	66	15	13	37	52	65	15	13
% of children in labor force	19	26	29	7	3	19	26	29	7	3
Infant mortality rate	80	59	u	-21	u	82	61	u	-21	u
% of single women, ages 15–24	65	67	73	2	6					

NOTES: The contextual variables are "average" provincial characteristics for the two samples (all women, ages 15–24, and married women, ages 30–44). The percentage of women with at least some secondary education is based on the percentage of women, ages 15–34, in the province with more than primary-level education. (In Thailand this is more than four years of schooling.) Except in the Philippines, the variable for economic roles of children is the percentage of children, ages 10–14, in the labor force; in the Philippines the age group is 15–18. The infant mortality rate is the number of deaths before age 1 per 1,000 births, estimated by indirect techniques. The marital-status variable is the percentage of women, ages 15–24, who have never married.
u = unavailable.
SOURCES: See Table 1.

Infant mortality (measured only for the 1970–80 interval) fell substantially, with absolute declines of between 15 and 37 deaths before age 1 per 1,000 births and relative declines from 26 to 36 percent. The average contextual level of infant mortality remained highest in Indonesia and lowest in Malaysia. As noted earlier, data on infant and child mortality for 1990 are not currently available.

For the final contextual variable, the average percentage of young (15–24), single (never-married) women, a ceiling effect was beginning to emerge over the two decades in Thailand, Malaysia, and the Philippines, where some 70 to 80 percent of young women were not yet married. Only modest change was reported in these countries in either period. In Indonesia, where age at marriage was considerably younger, marital postponement increased substantially during the more recent period.

Multilevel models of fertility change

For our multilevel analysis of fertility change, we use four basic equations (or models) suggested by the order of variables shown in Figure 1. Model 1 includes only "year" as an independent variable, with the year coefficient representing the observed change in fertility over the intercensal decade.[2] Model 2 adds the contextual variables as covariates. Model 3 includes only the individual-level variables, and Model 4 includes both the contextual and the individual-level independent variables. Because of the large volume of results from these equations for two intervals and two populations (younger and older women) for each country, only selected coefficients for each equation are shown in Tables 3 and 4, which present the results for the 1970–80 interval and the 1980–90 interval, respectively. The complete tables of results from every equation are available from us.

Table 3 presents the results of the multilevel models of fertility decline from 1968–70 to 1978–80 for the four countries based on the pooled data from the 1970 and 1980 census rounds. Only the coefficients for the year and contextual variables are shown for each model. The results for the sample of younger women are shown in the left-hand panel, and those for the sample of older women are shown in the right-hand panel. Above each set of equations are summary measures of the dependent variable, current fertility, for the two samples.

The 1970s

The mean fertility for younger Thai women (ages 15–29) in 1968–70 was 2.65 births.[3] Subtracting the comparable figure for 1978–80, 1.64 births, yields the measured decline in fertility, 1.01 births, over the decade of the 1970s for women aged 15–29. The comparable exercise for the sample of older Thai women shows a decline of almost 1.7 births over the same pe-

TABLE 3 Models of fertility change for all women, ages 15–29, and for married women, ages 30–44: Thailand, Indonesia, Malaysia, and Philippines, 1968–70 to 1978–80

Country and variable	All women, ages 15–29				Married women, ages 30–44			
	Model 1	Model 2	Model 3	Model 4	Model 1	Model 2	Model 3	Model 4
Thailand								
Gross fertility change (1980 – 1970) (Grand mean of fertility)	(1.64 – 2.65 = –1.01) (1.94)				(1.24 – 2.93 = –1.69) (2.37)			
Year coefficient (1970 = 0, 1980 = 1)	–1.05	–0.53	–0.85	–0.50	–1.62	–1.04	–1.51	–1.20
Contextual variables								
Women's status (% postprimary)		–0.08		n.s.		–0.06		0.08
Children's economic roles		0.11		0.12		–0.21		–0.20
Infant mortality rate		–0.02		–0.02		–0.04		–0.05
% of single women, ages 15–24		–0.28		–0.27				
R-squared (percent)	10.5	12.0	13.6	14.6	11.0	12.3	14.5	14.9
(N)	(145,240)				(77,676)			
Indonesia								
Gross fertility change (1980 – 1970) (Grand mean of fertility)	(2.33 – 2.48 = –0.15) (2.38)				(1.42 – 1.72 = –0.30) (1.52)			
Year coefficient (1970 = 0, 1980 = 1)	–0.12	n.s.	–0.13	n.s	–0.21	–0.16	–0.35	–0.29
Contextual variables								
Women's status (% postprimary)		–0.05		n.s.		0.10		0.05
Children's economic roles		–0.06		n.s.		–0.07		–0.06
Infant mortality rate		0.04		0.04		0.05		0.04
% of single women, ages 15–24		n.s.		0.03				
R-squared (percent)	4.3	4.4	5.5	5.6	6.4	6.7	8.5	8.7
(N)	(257,567)				(128,513)			

Peninsular Malaysia

	(1.93 − 2.51 = −0.58) (2.19)				(1.62 − 2.30 = −0.68) (1.95)			
Gross fertility change (1980 − 1970) (Grand mean of fertility)	Model 1	Model 2	Model 3	Model 4	Model 1	Model 2	Model 3	Model 4
Year coefficient (1970 = 0, 1980 = 1)	−0.67	n.s	−0.18	0.25	−0.61	n.s.	−0.41	n.s.
Contextual variables								
Women's status (% postprimary)		−0.28		−0.15		−0.23		−0.12
Children's economic roles		n.s.		n.s.		n.s.		n.s.
Infant mortality rate		n.s.		n.s.		n.s.		n.s.
% of single women, ages 15–24			−0.13	n.s.				n.s.
R-squared (percent)	9.9	11.0	15.2	15.5	8.8	9.3	10.4	10.5
(N)	(46,331)				(23,161)			

Philippines

	(2.56 − 2.59 = −0.03) (2.57)				(2.33 − 2.42 = −0.11) (2.37)			
Gross fertility change (1980 − 1970) (Grand mean of fertility)	Model 1	Model 2	Model 3	Model 4	Model 1	Model 2	Model 3	Model 4
Year coefficient (1970 = 0, 1980 = 1)	n.s.	0.32	0.17	0.34	n.s.	0.25	−0.12	0.12
Contextual variables								
Women's status (% postprimary)		−0.18		−0.06		−0.23		−0.17
Children's economic roles		n.s.		n.s.		n.s.		n.s.
Infant mortality rate		−0.15		n.s.		−0.30		−0.19
% of single women, ages 15–24			−0.34	−0.30				
R-squared (percent)	9.5	10.5	13.4	13.7	8.6	9.1	9.9	10.1
(N)	(302,261)				(133,542)			

NOTES: Categories with missing data are coded as dummy variables and included in each model, but the coefficients are not reported here. Model 1 includes only the year and age-group variables; Model 2 includes year, age-group, and the contextual variables; Model 3 includes year, age-group, and the individual-level variables; and Model 4 includes year, age-group, the contextual variables, and the individual-level variables. n.s. = not significant at p = 0.001.

riod. Explaining these observed changes is the objective of this analysis. Below the headings with the observed changes in fertility are the grand means of current fertility for the combined samples in the two census years. The pooled sample of younger women from the 1970 and 1980 Thai censuses (for the three-year periods prior to each census) had an overall mean of 1.94 births (N = 145,240 women), and the comparable pooled sample for older women (N = 77,676) had a mean fertility of 2.37 births.

The first equation, Model 1, contains only the dummy variable for the year (1980 = 1, 1970 = 0) and age as independent variables. The year coefficient in this equation is the decline in current fertility over the decade. This coefficient should be the same as the gross change computed by subtracting the 1980 mean fertility from the 1970 mean. The Thai coefficient is, however, slightly different (–1.05 compared with –1.01) because age composition is held constant in the regression equation. Since the current fertility measure is weighted to approximate the total fertility rate, these coefficients can be interpreted as declines in the average level of childbearing over the decade for the age range included in the model.

In Model 2 the four contextual variables are added as predictors of fertility. All four structural variables have significant effects on fertility, but our primary interest is observing the change in the year coefficient from Model 1 to Model 2. The direct effect is reduced from –1.05 to –0.53 births. This means that changes in the four contextual variables can explain about half of the observed change in fertility among younger Thai women from 1968–70 to 1978–80.

The contextual variables for women's status, the economic roles of children, and marital structure are coded so that a unit change in the unstandardized regression coefficients represents an effect of 10 percentage points in the provincial characteristic. The effect of infant mortality is coded so that a unit change is 10 points in the infant mortality rate. All these variables have the expected net effects on fertility, with the exception of infant mortality. Except for changes in proportions married, the contextual variable of the economic roles of children has the largest absolute effect on fertility, and change in this variable has the largest effect on the reduction in Thai fertility over the decade.

Introducing individual-level variables (coefficients not shown) in Model 3 also mediates the overall trend by reducing the Model 1 year coefficient by about 20 percent (compared with a 50 percent reduction in Model 2). It seems that changes in context have been more important than changes in the composition of the individual variables (as measured here) in explaining fertility decline during the 1970s. Nevertheless, there are important direct effects of individual variables, as indicated by the increment to variance explained (R-squared) from 10.5 percent to 13.6 percent from Model 1 to Model 3. The contextual variables and the individual variables are, of course, correlated.

Model 4 shows the effect of introducing both the contextual and the individual variables in the model. The joint effect of both sets of variables on the year coefficient is about the same as with the contextual variables alone. The effect of the contextual variable for women's status is entirely mediated by the educational distribution of individual women. The introduction of individual-level covariates, however, has no effect on the economic roles of children.

The patterns for the sample of older Thai women are roughly comparable to those for the sample of younger women. About one-third of the observed fertility decline of 1.6 births over the decade can be explained by changes in the contextual variables, primarily the economic roles of children. Changes in the composition of individual characteristics (at least those measured here) play almost no role in explaining the decline over the 1970s in marital fertility of women above age 30. The combined model (Model 4) of both contextual and individual variables explains only slightly more of the variance in fertility change than does Model 2, which includes only the contextual variables. The importance of changes in the economic roles of children for the Thai fertility decline corroborates a similar explanation reported in qualitative research (Knodel, Chamratrithirong, and Debavalya 1987).

The next panel of Table 3 presents a comparable analysis of Indonesian fertility change for the first intercensal interval. The modest reduction in Indonesian fertility during the 1970s is confounded by problems of measurement in our analysis and provides little demographic change to be explained.[4] Taking the results at face value, we find there was a decline of 0.12 births for younger women and of 0.21 births for older women between the late 1960s and the late 1970s. Adding the contextual variables in Model 2 reduces the year coefficient among younger women to zero (technically it is not significantly different from zero), but there is little reduction in the effect of year on fertility decline in the equations for older women. From additional analyses (not shown here), in which each contextual variable is tested individually, it appears that the most significant contextual factor is the decline in infant mortality. Interestingly, changes in the individual-level variables do not account for any reduction in the year coefficient. The increase in the year coefficient for older women when the individual-level variables are added (see Model 3) may be due to some particular compositional shifts into categories having a positive relationship to fertility.

For Malaysia the basic patterns are very similar to those of Thailand. During the 1970s Malaysia experienced a substantial reduction in measured fertility of about two-thirds of a birth per woman among both younger and older women. These fertility declines can be "explained" entirely by changes in the contextual variables, in particular the status of women. Changes in the composition of the individual variables work in the same direction, but they do not account for the changes in fertility as completely as do the contextual variables. These results suggest a "suppressed" trend toward higher fertility in the 1970s, net of the changes in context and composition for younger women.

Fertility in the Philippines declined by a small amount during the 1970s, but the year coefficients in Model 1 for the samples of younger and older women are not significant—effectively equal to zero. An interesting pattern emerges, however, when the contextual variables are entered as covariates in Model 2. The year coefficient becomes significant, but in a positive direction. This equation is a "statistical experiment" that represents the counterfactual, wherein the passage of time witnesses changes in statistical relationships but context (as measured here) is held constant; that is, no change occurs during the decade. According to this model, fertility would have risen over the decade if there had been no change in the contextual variables.

The potential increase in fertility, as implied by the year coefficients in Model 2, is relatively modest: a third of a birth among younger women and a quarter of a birth among older women. What is important is that the provincial variables (the status of women is the key variable in the Philippines) play a similar role in societies where fertility is declining rapidly (as in Thailand) and in societies where fertility is stagnant (as in the Philippines). In Thailand, change in the contextual variables was a key mechanism that mediated a substantial share of the trend in rapidly declining fertility. In the Philippines the underlying trend was one of rising fertility (by about one-half of a birth over the decade); but changes in social structure, as indexed by the contextual variables, held the observed fertility change to almost zero.

The change in the composition of the measured individual variables did not have consistent effects on fertility change. Among younger women, changes in female education and other microvariables worked in the same fashion as the macrovariables, though to a lesser extent. Among the sample of older married women the opposite pattern prevails. The changes in composition actually favored increased fertility; had there been no changes in the individual-level variables, fertility would have decreased over the decade.

The 1980s

The fertility transition continued at an impressive pace in Thailand during the 1980s, and the relative importance of changes in contextual variables remained broadly similar (Table 4). Changes in the structural variables accounted for about one-half of the observed fertility decline between the late 1970s and the late 1980s for both younger and older women. (Compare the year coefficients in Models 1 and 2 in both the left-hand and right-hand panels of Table 4.) Individual-level characteristics are important as predictors of fertility, but changes in the composition of individuals over time do not explain fertility decline as much as do changes in structural characteristics. The fertility decline in Thailand has been largely completed in little more than two decades, and one of the major reasons for this striking social change appears to have been changes in the economic roles of children, as measured by the contextual variable.

The second panel of Table 4 shows a comparable analysis of the accelerating pace of the Indonesian fertility transition during the 1980s—about two-thirds of a birth among younger women and about one-third of a birth among women above age 30. The structural variables in Model 2, as measured here, provide a slightly better explanation for the Indonesian fertility decline in the 1980s than for that in the 1970s, but at a fairly modest level. The structural variables mediate only about one-third of the observed fertility decline for younger women during this period. Nonetheless, in comparison with the lack of explanatory power (in mediating the year coefficient) of the individual-level variables, there is some basis for claiming that changes in social structure explain a significant fraction of the Indonesian fertility decline. The addition of infant mortality to the model may strengthen this interpretation when measures for the 1980s become available.

The analysis of the slowdown of the Malaysian fertility decline in the 1980s, shown in the third panel of Table 4, reveals some new twists to our previous account for the 1970s. The entire decline of about 0.4 of a birth occurred among younger women in the 1980s, perhaps as part of the process of increasing marital postponement. This change can be entirely accounted for by the changes in the structural variables (the year coefficient is insignificant in Model 2). For older women the observed levels of fertility showed no change during the decade, but this stability is the product of countervailing forces. Changes in both structural forces and individual composition were working to lower fertility. Were it not for the "social change," as indexed by these measures, fertility among women above age 30 would have increased by one child per woman, or more than 60 percent.

As we noted earlier, the Philippine fertility transition accelerated in the 1980s, resulting in a decline of nearly one-half of a birth among both younger and older women. Almost all of the decline among younger women and about half of the decline among older women can be "explained" by changes in the structural variables, particularly in the status of women. In comparison, changes in the composition of individual characteristics did not mediate the observed fertility decline among younger Filipino women (Model 3). When the macro- and microvariables are both included as independent variables (Model 4), there is less mediation of the observed fertility decline coefficient than when the macrovariables are included alone (Model 2). The microvariables, however, do have strong direct effects on fertility, as indicated by the increase in variance explained when the indi-

TABLE 4 Models of fertility change for all women, ages 15–29, and for married women, ages 30–44: Thailand, Indonesia, Malaysia, and Philippines, 1978–80 and 1988–90

Country and variable	All women, ages 15–29				Married women, ages 30–44			
	Model 1	Model 2	Model 3	Model 4	Model 1	Model 2	Model 3	Model 4
Thailand								
Gross fertility change (1990 – 1980) (Grand mean of fertility)	(1.10 – 1.64 = –0.54) (1.33)		(0.59 – 1.23 = –0.64) (0.84)					
Year coefficient (1980 = 0, 1990 = 1)	–0.58	–0.24	–0.39	–0.20	–0.68	–0.38	–0.67	–0.36
Contextual variables								
Women's status (% postprimary)		–0.90		0.59		–0.72		–0.47
Children's economic roles		0.43		0.33		–0.33		–0.31
Infant mortality rate		u		u		u		u
% of single women, ages 15–24		–1.78		–1.43				
R-squared (percent)	4.2	5.6	6.4	7.1	4.9	5.0	5.5	5.5
(N)	(128,040)				(64,474)			
Indonesia								
Gross fertility change (1990 – 1980) (Grand mean of fertility)	(1.72 – 2.32 = –0.60) (2.08)				(1.12 – 1.42 = –0.30) (1.30)			
Year coefficient (1980 = 0, 1990 = 1)	–0.65	–0.45	–0.60	–0.55	–0.35	–0.35	–0.44	–0.43
Contextual variables								
Women's status (% postprimary)		–0.14		–0.09		n.s.		n.s.
Children's economic roles		–0.19		–0.13		–0.08		n.s.
Infant mortality rate		u		u		u		u
% of single women, ages 15–24		n.s.		0.04				
R-squared (percent)	5.4	5.6	6.7	6.7	6.4	6.4	7.5	7.5
(N)	(293,355)				(146,244)			

Peninsular Malaysia

	(1.67 – 1.93 = -0.26) (1.78)				(1.64 – 1.62 = -0.02) (1.63)			
Gross fertility change (1990 – 1980) (Grand mean of fertility)	Model 1	Model 2	Model 3	Model 4	Model 1	Model 2	Model 3	Model 4
Year coefficient (1980 = 0, 1990 = 1)	-0.38	n.s	-0.47	0.33	n.s.	0.49	0.86	1.06
Contextual variables								
Women's status (% postprimary)		-0.14		-0.06		-0.21		-0.08
Children's economic roles		-0.34		-0.19		n.s.		n.s.
Infant mortality rate		u		u		u		u
% of single women, ages 15–24		-0.42		-0.16				
R-squared (percent)	9.4	10.7	27.8	28.0	7.1	7.5	14.6	14.6
(N)	(61,791)				(34,805)			

Philippines

	(2.05 – 2.52 = -0.47) (2.12)				(1.89 – 2.33 = -0.44) (1.96)			
Gross fertility change (1990 – 1980) (Grand mean of fertility)	Model 1	Model 2	Model 3	Model 4	Model 1	Model 2	Model 3	Model 4
Year coefficient (1980 = 0, 1990 = 1)	-0.50	-0.03	-0.51	-0.31	-0.48	-0.22	-0.29	-0.22
Contextual variables								
Women's status (% postprimary)		-0.15		-0.04		-0.19		-0.07
Children's economic roles		-0.02		0.01		0.03		0.05
Infant mortality rate		u		u		u		u
% of single women, ages 15–24		-0.41		-0.26				
R-squared (percent)	8.4	9.4	20.7	20.9	6.8	7.4	13.1	13.2
(N)	(975,086)				(469,567)			

NOTES: Categories with missing data are coded as dummy variables and included in each model, but the coefficients are not reported here. Model 1 includes only the year and age-group variables; Model 2 includes year, age-group, and the contextual variables; Model 3 includes year, age-group, and the individual-level variables; and Model 4 includes year, age-group, the contextual variables, and the individual-level variables.

u = unavailable.

n.s. = not significant at p = 0.001.

vidual-level variables are added as independent variables (Model 3). Among older women, changes in either the contextual variables or the individual-level variables mediate roughly the same proportion of the observed fertility decline, but the contextual variables alone (Model 2) provide the most parsimonious explanation.

Conclusions

For many decades demographic transition theory was the standard theoretical template for studies of fertility around the world. In many ways it was an ideal framework, with a plausible hypothesis about the modernization of societies and the resulting decline of fertility; but it remained loose enough to incorporate novel ideas. Before the 1970s the evidence in support of demographic transition theory consisted of parallel societal trends in fertility and socioeconomic development in Western societies. Although there were some notable exceptions (e.g., France) to the standard account, transition theory seemed to be a reasonable framework for explaining the historical trend from high to low fertility in Europe and North America. Before the 1970s, as well, there were so few cases of fertility decline in developing countries that fertility research was largely limited to the examination of cross-sectional fertility differentials.

Beginning in the 1970s, demographic transition theory was challenged, first by empirical evidence and then by rival theoretical interpretations. Research findings from the Princeton European Fertility Project raised fundamental questions about the applicability of transition theory to fertility declines in Europe (Coale 1973; Coale and Watkins 1986; Knodel and van de Walle 1979). At about the same time the World Fertility Surveys significantly expanded data from developing countries. Although there was clear evidence of declining fertility in many Asian and Latin American countries, the correlations between socioeconomic variables and fertility were often only modest. Without a viable theoretical alternative, transition theory remained the standard, although increasingly criticized, perspective in the field.

By the 1980s, several new ideas and reworkings of older ideas began to vie with transition theory as alternatives to explain the decline of fertility. Perhaps most influential has been ideational theory, which postulates that cultural values are the most important determinant of cross-national variation in fertility levels and fertility declines (Cleland and Wilson 1987; Lesthaeghe 1983; Lesthaeghe and Surkyn 1988). The evidence for ideational theory is primarily the association between regional and cultural areas and fertility decline. This is clearly a significant contribution, and there appears to have been rapid diffusion of innovative fertility behavior within culturally homogeneous areas. But there has not yet been a convincing theoretical argument that would explain the origins and spread of cultural values that shape fertility behavior.

Much of the support for ideational theory and other new theories of fertility is based on the empirical weaknesses of socioeconomic hypotheses (demand theory) of fertility. The lack of empirical support for demographic transition theory, in our judgment, is due in large part to the lack of formal specification of key hypotheses and clear operationalization of important concepts. Treating every socioeconomic variable as equally important and testing hypotheses with bivariate relationships have failed to produce a strong body of empirical generalizations and theoretical cumulation in the research literature (Hirschman 1994).

In this study we have tested propositions from demographic transition theory in a different way than is generally the case. Most important, we have specified a multilevel model that incorporates the key hypotheses from demographic transition theory as structural or contextual variables that influence the fertility behavior of individuals. Although the record of multilevel or contextual models of fertility has not always been encouraging (Casterline 1985), we believe that analyses in which fertility change—rather than simply differences in cross-sectional fertility—is the dependent variable will lead research in more promising directions.

The findings from our analysis of own-children census data provide evidence in support of hypotheses drawn from demographic transition theory, although the patterns vary substantially across time and space. Fertility declines were reported in both intercensal decades in all four countries we studied, although the declines were modest in Indonesia and the Philippines during the 1970s. Simple regression standardization models show that a significant share—up to 50 percent or more—of the fertility declines in these countries can be "explained" (or mediated) by temporal shifts in women's status, the economic roles of children, and infant mortality. These results can be interpreted as statistical experiments using the method of regression standardization. The question is how much of the measured decline in fertility would have occurred if other factors had remained constant. It seems that the changes in the structural environment have been a critical factor in accounting for the decline of fertility. Our results show that if there had been no changes in women's status, children's roles, or infant mortality, then much of the observed declines in fertility in these countries would not have happened.

These findings are the more striking because we compared the relative explanatory power of models with (1) changes in only contextual variables, (2) changes in only individual variables (composition), and (3) changes in both the contextual and individual variables. In almost every case, the model with changes in the contextual variables alone proved to be a more powerful explanation of the observed fertility decline than the model with changes in the individual variables, or even the model with both contextual and individual variables. The individual-level variables have strong associations with fertility levels, but the changes in the macrovariables worked much better in explaining fertility declines over time.

The method of regression standardization, used here, holds the values of the covariates constant at a weighted average of the different populations in the sample. In these equations the weighted values are intermediate between the 1970 and 1980 populations for the first period and between the 1980 and 1990 populations for the second period. If there are interactions between the covariates, year, and fertility, then the estimates of fertility decline (the year coefficient) in these models could be unstable, depending on the values of the covariates. To investigate this possibility, we tried other forms of regression standardization. We substituted 1980 values of the contextual variables in the 1970 regression equation. We also did the reverse by substituting 1970 values of the contextual variables in the 1980 regression equations. The results, not presented here, confirm the essential findings of our regression analysis.

As with any study, the results reported here have many important qualifications. First, the geographic areas used for the construction of the contextual variables were generally very large provinces and for that reason may not be characteristic of the local social spheres and institutions that shape reproductive norms and behavior. And the variables available for our study are limited to those collected in the censuses. The set of individual variables in this analysis does not include some of the important determinants of fertility, most notably family planning programs. For these reasons our results are suggestive, not definitive.

In spite of these limitations, the findings provide encouragement for new directions of research and the development of a comprehensive theoretical framework to study fertility transitions. We have identified several key structural variables that appear to be important in explaining the fertility decline in several Southeast Asian countries during the 1970s and 1980s. There may well be systematic variations in the pathways of fertility decline among societies and over time with different forces appearing more important in some contexts than others. These findings do not necessarily invalidate the ideas from alternative theories of fertility decline. In most cases, arguments about the causes of fertility decline are not mutually exclusive. Another lesson from this study is the importance of testing hypotheses with comparative research designs that follow demographic transitions from their onset to their completion.

APPENDIX TABLE   Characteristics of the microdata sample from the 1970, 1980, and 1990 census rounds: Thailand, Indonesia, Malaysia, and Philippines

Country and year	Sampling fraction	Unweighted sample size, all persons	Adjusted sample size, women 15–44[a]	Percentage of children age 0–2 matched to mothers
Thailand				
1970	0.020	772,251	161,246	96
1980	0.010	388,080	91,081	92
1990	0.012	485,096	186,475	96
Indonesia				
1971	0.038	634,647	139,112	92
1980	0.050	7,234,962	1,611,093	96
1990	0.005	912,554	204,932	97
Peninsular Malaysia				
1970	0.020	176,287	35,706	95
1980	0.016	182,593	41,954	90
1991	0.020	347,982	62,120	98
Philippines				
1970	0.050	1,651,506	357,846	96
1980	0.050	2,260,602	501,614	96
1990	0.100	6,013,913	1,287,473	98

NOTES: The census microdata samples were constructed with varied sampling designs, and consequently we used different weighting procedures. The analyses reported here are based on the weighted data, but the weights have been deflated so that the weighted sample size equals the original unweighted sample size. The Malaysian microdata samples are not weighted (all three censuses are systematic random samples). To minimize computation, we drew random samples of the largest files: 0.18 of the 1980 Indonesian file, 0.67 of the 1970 Philippine file, and 0.50 of the 1980 Philippine file.

[a]These figures have been adjusted by the sample weights and deflated to the unweighted sample size; however, they do not reflect the sampling for computational purposes, as noted above.

Notes

This research was supported by a grant, "Fertility and Fertility Change" (HD21267), from the National Institute of Child Health and Human Development.

1 Mainland Southeast Asia includes Burma, Thailand, Peninsular Malaysia, Singapore, Cambodia, Vietnam, and Laos. Insular Southeast Asia includes the huge Indonesian and Philippine archipelagoes, the two Malaysian states of Sabah and Sarawak on the island of Borneo, and Brunei, a microstate on Borneo.

2 Age group, measured as a series of dummy variables for each five-year age group, is also included as an independent variable in Model 1 and in every other equation. Since fertility change may be due to changes in age composition, the inclusion of the age covariate allows us to focus on explaining the change in "age-standardized" measures of fertility.

3 This measure of current fertility is coded with the logic of a total fertility rate, which can be expressed as the number of births a woman would have from age 15 to age 30 implied by the current fertility in this period. The mean number of births (own children, ages 0–2) for this sample of women is divided by 3 to give an annual measure and then multiplied by 15 to represent the 15 years of exposure from age 15 to age 30.

4 Infants (children under age 1) were disproportionately underenumerated in the 1971 Indonesian census. Moreover, the lack of adjustment in the own-children estimates of fertility for infant and child mortality is a more serious problem in Indonesia than in the other

three countries because of the higher mortality levels there, especially in 1971. And if the underestimation problem is greater for the 1971 census than for the 1980 census, then we have underestimated the 1971–80 fertility decline.

References

Bongaarts, John and Susan Cotts Watkins. 1996. "Social interactions and contemporary fertility transitions," *Population and Development Review* 22(4): 639–682.

Bulatao, Rodolfo A. and Ronald D. Lee (eds.). 1983. *Determinants of Fertility in Developing Countries*, 2 vols. New York: Academic Press.

Caldwell, John C. 1980. "Mass education as a determinant of the timing of fertility decline," *Population and Development Review* 6(2): 225–256.

———. 1982. *Theory of Fertility Decline*. London: Academic Press.

———. 1983. "Direct economic costs and benefits of children," in *Determinants of Fertility in Developing Countries*, eds. Rodolfo A. Bulatao and Ronald D. Lee. New York: Academic Press, pp. 370–397.

Casterline, John B. (ed). 1985. *The Collection and Analysis of Community Data*. Voorburg, Netherlands: International Statistical Institute.

Cho, Lee Jay, Robert D. Retherford, and Minja Kim Choe. 1986. *The Own-Children Method of Fertility Estimation*. An East-West Center Book. Honolulu: University of Hawaii Press.

Cho, Lee Jay et al. 1980. *Population Growth of Indonesia: An Analysis of Fertility and Mortality Based on the 1971 Population Census*. Honolulu: University of Hawaii Press.

Cleland, John. 1985. "Marital fertility decline in developing countries: Theories and the evidence," in *Reproductive Change in Developing Countries: Insights from the World Fertility Survey*, eds. John Cleland and John Hobcraft. Oxford: Oxford University Press, pp. 223–252.

Cleland, John and Christopher Wilson. 1987. "Demand theories of the fertility transition: An iconoclastic view," *Population Studies* 41(1): 5–30.

Coale, Ansley J. 1973. "The demographic transition," in *International Population Conference*, Vol. 1. Liège: International Union for the Scientific Study of Population, pp. 53–73.

Coale, Ansley J. and Susan Cotts Watkins (eds.). 1986. *The Decline of Fertility in Europe*. Princeton: Princeton University Press.

Cochrane, Susan Hill. 1979. *Fertility and Education: What Do We Really Know?* Baltimore: Johns Hopkins University Press.

Darroch, Russell K., Paul A. Meyer, and Masri Singarimbun. 1981. *Two Are Not Enough: The Value of Children to Javanese and Sundanese Parents*. Country Studies on the Value of Children, No. 60. Papers of the East-West Population Institute. Honolulu: East-West Center.

Davis, Kingsley. 1963. "The theory of change and response in modern demographic history," *Population Index* 29(4): 345–366.

Easterlin, Richard A. and Eileen M. Crimmins. 1985. *The Fertility Revolution: A Supply-Demand Analysis*. Chicago: University of Chicago Press.

Freedman, Ronald. 1979. "Theories of fertility decline: A reappraisal," *Social Forces* 58(1): 1–17.

Friedlander, Dov, Jona Schellekens, and Eliahu Ben-Moshe. 1991. "The transition from high to low marital fertility: Cultural or socioeconomic determinants?" *Economic Development and Cultural Change* 39(2): 331–351.

Hirschman, Charles. 1985. "Premarital socioeconomic roles and the timing of family formation: A comparative study of five Asian societies," *Demography* 22(1): 35–59.

———. 1992. "Southeast Asian studies," in *Encyclopedia of Sociology*, Vol. 4, eds. Edgar F. Borgatta and Marie L. Borgatta. New York: Macmillan, pp. 2037–2041.

———. 1994. "Why fertility changes," *Annual Review of Sociology* 20: 203–233.

Hirschman, Charles and Philip Guest. 1990a. "The emerging demographic transition of Southeast Asia," *Population and Development Review* 16(1): 121–152.

———. 1990b. "Multilevel models of fertility determination in four Southeast Asian countries: 1970 and 1980," *Demography* 27(3): 369–398.

Hirschman, Charles et al. 1994. "The path to below replacement-level fertility in Thailand," *International Family Planning Perspectives* 20(3): 82–87, 107.

———. 1998. "Explaining the rapid fertility decline in Thailand." Unpublished paper, Center for Studies in Demography and Ecology, University of Washington, Seattle.

Kirk, Dudley. 1996. "Demographic transition theory," *Population Studies* 50(3): 361–387.

Knodel, John, Aphichat Chamratrithirong, and Nibhon Debavalya. 1987. *Thailand's Reproductive Revolution: Rapid Fertility Decline in a Third-World Setting.* Madison: University of Wisconsin Press.

Knodel, John and Etienne van de Walle. 1979. "Lessons from the past: Policy implications of historical population studies," *Population and Development Review* 5(2): 217–246.

Knodel, John et al. 1996. "Reproductive preferences and fertility trends in post-transition Thailand," *Studies in Family Planning* 27(6): 307–318.

Lee, Ronald D., Patrick R. Galloway, and Eugene A. Hammel. 1994. "Fertility decline in Prussia: Estimating influences on supply, demand, and degree of control," *Demography* 31(2): 347–373.

Lesthaeghe, Ron. 1983. "A century of demographic and cultural change in Western Europe: An exploration of underlying dimensions," *Population and Development Review* 9(3): 411–435.

Lesthaeghe, Ron and Johan Surkyn. 1988. "Cultural dynamics and economic theories of fertility change," *Population and Development Review* 14(1): 1–45.

Mason, Karen Oppenheim. 1987. "The impact of women's social position on fertility in developing countries," *Sociological Forum* 2(4): 718–745.

———. 1997. "Explaining fertility transitions," *Demography* 34(4): 443–454.

Mueller, Eva. 1976. "The economic value of children in peasant agriculture," in *Population and Development: The Search for Selective Interventions,* ed. Ronald G. Ridker. Baltimore: Johns Hopkins University Press, pp. 98–153.

Nag, Moni, Benjamin White, and Robert C. Peet. 1978. "An anthropological approach to the study of the economic value of children in Java and Nepal," *Current Anthropology* 19(2): 293–306.

Notestein, Frank W. 1953. "Economic problems of population change," in *Proceedings of the Eighth International Conference of Agricultural Economists.* New York: Oxford University Press, pp. 13–31.

Reid, Anthony. 1988. *Southeast Asia in the Age of Commerce, 1450–1680,* Vol. 1 of *The Lands Below the Winds.* New Haven: Yale University Press.

Rindfuss, Ronald R. and James A. Sweet. 1977. *Postwar Fertility Trends and Differentials in the United States.* New York: Academic Press.

Rosero-Bixby, Luis and John B. Casterline. 1993. "Modelling diffusion effects in fertility transition," *Population Studies* 47(1): 147–167.

Smith, Herbert L. 1989. "Integrating theory and research on the institutional determinants of fertility," *Demography* 26(2): 171–184.

Swicegood, Gray et al. 1988. "Language usage and fertility in the Mexican-origin population of the United States," *Demography* 25(1): 17–33.

United Nations Population Division. 1999. *World Population Prospects: The 1998 Revision,* Vol. 1, *Comprehensive Tables.* New York: United Nations.

Watkins, Susan Cotts. 1987. "The fertility transition: Europe and the third world compared," *Sociological Forum* 2(4): 645–673.

World Bank. 1988. *World Development Report, 1988.* New York: Oxford University Press.

———. 1993. *The East Asian Miracle: Economic Growth and Public Policy.* Washington, DC.

———. 1996. *World Development Report, 1996.* New York: Oxford University Press.

Social and Economic Development and the Fertility Transitions in Mainland China and Taiwan

DUDLEY L. POSTON, JR.

THE PEOPLE'S REPUBLIC of China and Taiwan have experienced remarkable reductions in their fertility rates during the past 40 years. Time-series data indicate that total fertility rates, which exceeded 6 children per woman in the early 1950s in both countries,[1] had declined to less than 2 by 1997 (Figure 1). China's fertility has followed a somewhat different course from that of Taiwan, however. A few areas of China, namely Beijing, Shanghai, and some other cities, experienced earlier fertility transitions and changes very similar to those observed in Taiwan (Lee and Wang 1999: Fig. 7), whereas the transition in China as a whole began some 20 or so years later than in Taiwan. Nevertheless, it is striking that in the early 1950s and again in the late 1990s the two countries had about the same fertility levels.

The question addressed in this chapter is to what degree the fertility reductions in China and Taiwan may be viewed as responses to social and economic development. It is thought that Taiwan's fertility decline resulted mainly from voluntary reductions in family size, induced in large part by social and economic development (Feeney 1994; Sun 1984), whereas the fertility reduction in China has been the result in part of social and economic development (e.g., Poston and Gu 1987; Tien 1984) and in part of "direct and forceful government intervention" in family planning (Wolf 1986: 101; see also Feeney and Wang 1993). Family planning programs were also influential in Taiwan, but participation in them was voluntary (Freedman 1998).

In this study I examine how factors associated with social and economic development in Taiwan and China have operated independently and together to influence fertility change. I address this issue cross-sectionally,

FIGURE 1   Total fertility rates: China and Taiwan, 1950–97

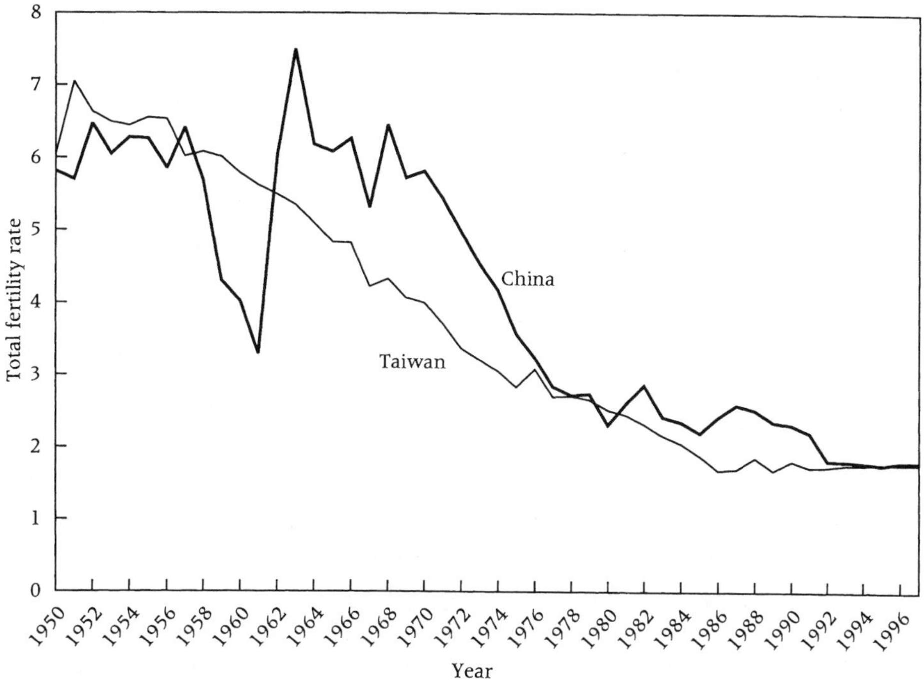

SOURCES: Poston (1992); China Population Information and Research Center (1994, 1996, and 1997); China, Republic of, Ministry of the Interior (1996).

using subregional data for a few points in time. One reason for taking this route is that annual time-series data are not available for either country in the kinds of descriptive detail necessary. Therefore, I examine the relationship between development and fertility by using data for the counties and provinces of China for 1982, 1990, and 1995; and for the counties and cities of Taiwan for 1980, 1990, and 1995. Even though the cross-sectional investigation is based on data starting with 1980 and 1982, that is, after the fertility transitions in both countries had begun, the analysis will be instructive because of its subregional focus. Most cross-sectional investigations of development and fertility have been conducted at the national level (e.g., Donaldson 1991; Hernandez 1984; Livi-Bacci 1997: Chap. 5; Mauldin and Berelson 1978; Mauldin and Ross 1991; Tsui and Bogue 1978).

Finally, there are methodological reservations about the extent to which an essentially diachronic relationship, such as that between social and economic development and fertility, may be investigated with cross-sectional data (Alker 1969; Lieberson and Hansen 1974). The results of the current study should provide some insight into the mechanisms and processes of fertility change in general, and the degree to which social and economic factors play a role in that change.

Rationale for this study

Social and economic development is typically viewed as providing an aggregate setting that influences fertility directly. Blake (1973) has noted that social and economic structures and institutions tend to influence reproductive motivation and fertility by specifying the reward structures related to childbearing. The institution of the family, for instance, may emphasize pronatalist norms. And the institution of the economy may have employment norms proscribing the employment of women (see also Hernandez 1984: 11–13). Analyzing Chinese fertility patterns, Tien (1984: 385) observes that among those subareas experiencing the greatest fertility decline, "profound changes in socioeconomic structure may have occurred at the same time." Birdsall and Jamison (1983) and Poston and Gu (1987) have made similar arguments. Sun (1984) found comparable patterns in his cross-sectional analysis of Taiwan (see also Poston 1988).

Social and economic development may also influence fertility indirectly through family planning programs and behaviors and through other variables more proximate to fertility (see, e.g., Hernandez 1984: 101–102). In this context family planning programs and services are seen as facilitating an already preeminent relationship. Without the prior effects of social and economic development on reward structures, however, family planning programs would have little or no effect on fertility. Many of the analyses of the respective roles of development and family planning programs on fertility have shown that the effects of development are usually stronger than those of such programs (Gertler and Molyneaux 1994; Hirschman and Young in this volume; Molyneaux and Gertler in this volume; Pritchett 1994a and 1994b; Schultz 1971, 1980, and 1994).

The notion that fertility rates, as well as mortality rates, fall in response to increases in social and economic development is central to the classic theory of demographic transition, as originally described by Notestein (1953). As Mason (1997: 444) has noted, "this theory attributes fertility decline to changes in social life that accompany, and are presumed to be caused by, industrialization and urbanization. These changes initially produce a decline in mortality, which sets the stage for—or by itself may bring about—fertility decline by increasing the survival of children, and hence the size of families."

Demographic transition theory has been the subject of critical debate among demographers in recent years. Hirschman (1994), for example, has questioned its overall utility. He has correctly observed that "over the past few decades intensive research on demographic change in historical and contemporary societies has revealed complex patterns that do not fit neatly into [the] earlier theoretical schema" (1994: 204). The extensive publications originating from the European Fertility Project (see Coale and Watkins 1986 for a synopsis) have shown many exceptions to the general theory. In some European countries, for instance, fertility change was rapid, whereas in others it was gradual. Moreover, the initial declines in fertility were not always responses to prior changes in urbanization, literacy, agricultural production, or labor force activity (Kertzer and Hogan 1989: Chap. 8; Knodel and van de Walle 1979). So extensive have been the criticisms of demographic transition theory that some observers have pronounced its imminent or actual demise (Alter 1992: 13; Greenhalgh 1990: 86; Hirschman 1994: 213). Perhaps the ultimate embarrassment for demographers is Fricke's (1997: 825) observation: "Wielding the hammers that drove the nails into its coffin were demographers themselves."

These criticisms notwithstanding, some of the ideas of demographic transition theory "are hard to ignore and...live on" (Mason 1997: 444). This is due in part to the fact that, according to Hirschman (1994: 214), "there is no consensus on an alternative theory to replace demographic transition theory." More important in my view is McNicoll's (1992: 92) point that some of its ideas persist because "at least in general terms, many of the [theory's] associations are quite well substantiated—though allowing ample scope for dispute over emphasis."

I agree with many scholars (e.g., Leete 1987; Teitelbaum 1975) that the characteristics of the demographic transition in developing countries, especially in China and Taiwan, differ from those of the transition in many European countries. And I concur with Hirschman's (1994: 220) observation that "the basic flaw in demographic transition theory...is the assumption that there is a single monolithic pattern of modernization that could be indexed by any socioeconomic variable.... The real theoretical challenge is to specify more clearly what aspects of modernization are linked to fertility change." This is precisely my objective in conducting the analyses of fertility change in China and Taiwan described below.

In analyzing the aggregate relationship between development and fertility, I consider four specific factors to have particularly influential effects on fertility: (1) advances in economic development, specifically increases in economic productivity and participation in the nonagricultural labor force; (2) improvements in general health conditions, especially reductions in infant mortality; (3) improvements in social conditions and livelihood, particularly in educational attainment; and (4) absolute and relative improvements in female status. A number of studies show one or more of these social and economic development factors to be influential in accounting for fertility trends in China (e.g., Birdsall and Jamison 1983; Gu 1989; Poston and Gu 1987; Poston and Jia 1990; Tien 1984) and in Taiwan (e.g., Easterlin and Crimmins 1985; Feeney 1994; Jia 1991; Poston 1988; Robey 1991; Sanchez 1993; Schutjer and Stokes 1984; Sun 1984). A contribution of this chapter is the separation of specific aspects of social and economic development and the analysis of their individual effects on fertility.

Fertility trends in China and Taiwan

Figure 1 traces the similar declines in fertility in China and Taiwan between 1950 and 1997. In Taiwan the fertility decline mirrored changes in economic development, which, Feeney (1994: 518) has argued, affected the economic costs and social value of children. Sun (1984: 49) has pointed out the strong effects of urban industrial development on Taiwan's fertility in the early stages, but not necessarily the later stages, of its fertility transition. In China the trends in fertility since 1950 reflect both the effects of social and economic factors and the influences of a compulsory family limitation policy (Feeney and Wang 1993; Poston 1992). The dramatic fall in the total fertility rate from the late 1950s to the early 1960s was caused by the famine experienced in China during and immediately after Mao's Great Leap Forward. The program and the famine led to serious conditions of subfecundity as well as to disruptions for numerous couples in their patterns of normal married life (Chen 1984; Coale 1984; Poston 1992). The marked increases in the fertility rate in the early 1960s occurred in conjunction with the economic recovery in China and resulted as well from "the restoration of normal married life, from an abnormally large number of marriages, and from the unusually small fraction of married women who were infertile because of nursing a recently born infant" (Coale 1984: 57). By the mid-1970s, China's fertility rate had returned to about the same level as Taiwan's.

The rapid decline in total fertility rates occurred in both countries despite the fact that in the 1970s China instituted a coercive fertility control program whereas Taiwan did not. Both countries, however, experienced significant increases in social and economic development, which, it has been argued, were responsible in large part for the fertility declines. It is those factors, and their effects on fertility, that I examine below in a series of cross-sectional analyses.

The analyses focus on the subregions of China and of Taiwan at two time points, the early 1980s and 1990. There is considerable heterogeneity among the countries' subregions in fertility and in social and economic development. I postulate that cross-sectional analyses of the relationships between development and fertility among the subregions can clarify those relationships in ways that would not be evident from analyses based on national-level data for the two countries. In the following analyses I investigate the relationship between development and fertility first among the counties of China, then among its provinces, and finally among the counties and cities of Taiwan.

The counties of China

To investigate changes in fertility patterns in the counties of China, I conduct two cross-sectional analyses, one for 1982 and the other for 1990, the two most recent years for which census data are available. The 1982 analysis is concerned with the fertility patterns of the 2,300 counties of China for which I have fertility and social and economic development data. According to the 1982 census, Mainland China had 2,378 counties in that year. The fertility and social and economic data used here, however, were not gathered for all the counties; most of the counties with missing data are in the Xizang (Tibet) Autonomous Region. The 1990 analysis of fertility focuses on 2,349 counties. I have omitted about 100 counties because they have incomplete or missing data for one or more variables. About 80 new counties were created in China between 1982 and 1990, when the government took territory away from various counties in existence in 1982. However, I am not yet able to link the 1982 set of counties with the 1990 set because I lack the requisite boundary files. Hence it is not possible to estimate county-level equations dealing with fertility change between 1982 and 1990.

For both periods the dependent variable is the general fertility rate: the number of births in the year preceding the census per 1,000 women in the 15–49 age group. Among the 2,300 counties of China for which 1981 data are available, the general fertility rate has an average value of 98, varying from a low of 36 in Shihezhi City in Xinjiang Province to a high of 233 in Butuo County in Sichuan Province (Table 1). These rates indicate substantial variability in fertility. Shihezhi City's low rate of 36 approximates the rate of 37 reported by West Germany in 1986 (United Nations 1988), the country then with one of the lowest general fertility rates in the world. Conversely, Butuo County's high rate of 233 is close to the rates reported recently by Rwanda and Nigeria, two countries with general fertility rates among the highest in the world. Thus the variation in fertility in 1981 among the counties of China parallels the variation in fertility among the countries of the world during the mid-1980s.

The four social and economic measures used as independent variables in the analysis are (1) the per capita gross value of industrial and agricultural output (in yuan) in 1982; (2) the infant mortality rate in 1981; (3) the illiteracy rate, specifically the percentage of the population aged 12 and older in the county in 1982 who were illiterate or semi-literate; and (4) the percentage of the labor force in 1982 classified as industrial employees. These four variables reflect three of the four modernization and development factors identified earlier. The gross value of industrial and agricultural output and the percentage of the labor force in industrial employment represent the economic development factor, a low illiteracy rate represents social development, and the infant mortality rate represents the health dimension. County-level data were not available on women's status.

TABLE 1   Descriptive statistics for fertility rates and social and development
variables: 2,300 counties of China, 1982, and 2,349 counties of China, 1990

Variable	Mean	Standard deviation	Minimum value	Maximum value
General fertility rate				
1981	98.5	32.8	36.2, Shihezhi (Xinjiang)	232.6, Butuo (Sichuan)
1989–90	91.1	27.4	35.0, Jiading (Shanghai)	210.0, Cuoqin (Tibet)
Gross value of industrial and agricultural product per capita, 1982 (in yuan)	654.6	793.2	70.0, Haiyuan (Ningxia)	11,020.0, Beijing City
Gross value of agricultural product per capita, 1990 (in yuan)	973.6	1,140.8	222.1, Erguna-zuoqi (Inner Mongolia)	46,770.4, Manzhouli City (Inner Mongolia)
Infant mortality rate, 1981	39.1	29.1	6.0, Langfang City (Hebei)	319.0, Da-Qaidam (Qinghai)
Crude death rate, 1989–90	6.6	1.4	4.0, Dongying (Shandong)	16.4, Jiali (Tibet)
Percentage of population illiterate and semi-literate				
Ages 12+, 1982	34.2	13.8	2.7, Lianjiang (Guangdong)	85.0, Dongxiang (Gansu)
Ages 15+, 1990	26.8	15.3	5.2, Changsha City (Hunan)	94.2, Nierong (Tibet)
Percentage of labor force in industrial occupations				
1982	13.2	14.5	0.1, Jishishan (Gansu)	76.7, Beijing City
1990	12.3	12.1	0.4, Weixian (Hebei)	81.1, Jiujiang (Jiangxi)

1 yuan = US$1.93 in July 1982, $4.73 in July 1990.
SOURCES: Population Census Office of the State Council, PRC, and the Institute of Geography, CAS (1987); China Population
Information and Research Center (1997).

The variation in these four independent variables is as striking as the
variation in fertility. Per capita industrial and agricultural output, for example, ranges from 70 yuan to 11,020 yuan, and infant mortality ranges
from 6 to 319 deaths per thousand births. I anticipate negative relationships between fertility and the two economic measures, and positive relationships between fertility and the illiteracy and infant mortality variables.
All four of the independent variables are related to each other, although
none of the zero-order correlations is outside the range of –0.6 to +0.6.

In Table 2 the panel for 1982 presents the results of county-level multiple regression equation of the four independent variables with the general fertility rate. All four variables have unstandardized regression coefficients with signs predicted by the hypotheses, and all but one (gross
industrial and agricultural output) are statistically significant. An inspection of the standardized regression coefficients in the second column of
Table 2 shows that the infant mortality rate has the greatest effect on fertility, net of the effects of the other independent variables. Together the
four variables account for almost 43 percent of the variation in fertility.

The dependent variable in the analysis for 1990 is also the general
fertility rate, this time measured as of the second half of 1989 and the first

TABLE 2   Multiple regression coefficients for the general fertility rate on social
and economic development variables: Counties of China, 1982 and 1990

Independent variable	1982		1990 (Model 1)		1990 (Model 2)	
	Unstan-dardized	Stan-dardized	Unstan-dardized	Stan-dardized	Unstan-dardized	Stan-dardized
Gross output	−0.001	−0.035	−0.000	−0.006	−.000	−.001
Infant mortality	0.453*	0.401				
Illiteracy	0.483*	0.204	0.669*	0.373	0.547*	0.305
Industry	−0.436*	−0.192	−0.797*	−0.353	−0.751*	−0.333
Crude death rate					2.665*	0.141
Constant	71.040		83.196		68.271	
R^2 (adjusted)	0.429		0.378		0.392	

* Significant at p = <0.05.

half of 1990 (see Table 1). The rate has a mean value of 91 and ranges
from a low of 35 in Jiading District in Shanghai to a high of 210 in Cuoqin
County in Tibet. As in 1982, there is considerable variation in the rate among
the counties of China.

Two of the independent variables in the 1990 analysis are similar to
those used for 1982, namely the illiteracy rate and the percentage of the
labor force in industrial jobs. The numerator and denominator of the illiteracy rate in 1990, however, refer to the population aged 15 and older (as
compared with ages 12 and older in 1982). The economic productivity variable in 1990 is the gross value of agricultural output (in yuan) divided by
the agricultural population; for 1982 this variable included both agricultural and industrial output, and its denominator was the total county population. The variable used for 1990 is an imperfect economic measure because it is restricted to agricultural productivity, but it is all that is available.

Unavailable for the 1990 analysis of counties are data on infant mortality. The only available mortality measure or indicator of health conditions is the crude death rate. In 1982, however, there was a correlation of
0.79 between the infant mortality rate and the crude death rate among the
counties of China. Therefore, I estimate two regression equations for 1990,
one with no mortality independent variable, and a second using the crude
death rate as a rough proxy for the infant mortality rate.

The middle panel of Table 2 reports the results of a county-level multiple regression equation for 1990 of the general fertility rate on the three
social and economic development variables. All three show coefficients with
the expected signs, but the agricultural output variable is not significant.
The standardized effects of the illiteracy and industry variables on fertility
are of about the same magnitude. The three variables together account for
38 percent of the variation in fertility.

The right panel of Table 2 shows the results of a multiple regression equation for 1990 in which the crude death rate has been added as a fourth independent variable. This variable has a positive effect on fertility, but the illiteracy and industry variables retain their more substantial impacts. The results of this second equation for 1990 are similar to those of the first.

Overall, the results of the 1982 and 1990 models show more similarities than differences. The economic productivity predictor, either industrial and agricultural output or agricultural output alone, is never significant; but the other economic development variable, industry, measuring industrial participation in the labor force—to be sure, an expression of the overall state of the economy—is significant and influential. The infant mortality rate, a social and health-related variable, is the most important predictor in 1982, whereas the other social variable, illiteracy, along with the industrial labor force, is the most influential in 1990. Adding the crude death rate in 1990 as a proxy for infant mortality changes only slightly the results of an equation estimated without the crude death rate. The amounts of explained variance are similar in the three equations.

The provinces of China

Turning next to several cross-sectional analyses of fertility patterns in the provinces of China, I first analyze the effects of the social and economic development factors on fertility in 1982, then regress fertility in 1989 on the social and economic development variables in 1982. Next I perform a similar analysis for 1990 by looking first at the effects of the development variables on fertility in 1990, and then at their effects on fertility in 1995.

In 1982 Mainland China was divided into 29 provinces, municipalities, and autonomous regions; in 1990 and 1995 the number was 30. For 1982, detailed fertility and development data were not available for Tibet. Before the 1990 census was conducted, Hainan Island, formerly included in Guangdong Province, became a separate province. In the provincial-level analyses that follow, I use 28 provinces, excluding Tibet and treating Hainan as part of Guangdong.

The fertility variable for 1982 and 1990 is the total fertility rate, measured respectively in 1981 and 1989; for 1995 it is the crude birth rate as measured in 1995. I use the crude birth rate for 1995 because data on total fertility are not available for that year. Among the 28 provinces, however, the total fertility rate and the crude birth rate in 1981 and in 1989 are correlated with each other at 0.93 and 0.91, respectively, and so I assume that the variation in the crude birth rate in 1995 is very similar to the variation in the total fertility rate in 1995.

In 1981 and 1989 the total fertility rate has mean values of 2.7 and 2.3, respectively, and the 1995 crude birth rate has a mean value of 15.4 (Table 3). Shanghai has the lowest fertility values for all three time periods, with total fertility rates of 1.3 and 1.4 for 1981 and 1989, and a crude birth rate of 5.8 for 1995. The highest fertility values are in Guizhou (total fertility rate of 4.4 in 1981), Xinjiang (total fertility rate of 3.1 in 1989), and Qinghai (crude birth rate of 22.0 in 1995). Although fertility varies considerably among the provinces in the three years, it does so less than among the counties.

I use four social and economic development variables as predictors of fertility: per capita provincial income, the illiteracy rate, the ratio of female-to-male life expectation at birth, and the infant mortality rate. The income variable, an indicator of structural economic development in the province, refers to newly created value in yuan of labor engaged in production activities in agriculture, industry, construction, transportation, social services, and commerce (China Population Information and Research Center 1996: 110). It has a mean value of 547 yuan in 1982 and of 1,471 yuan in 1990. In both years Shanghai has the highest values and Guizhou the lowest. Illiteracy, a negative measure of social development, refers to the percentage of the population 12 years of age and older in 1982, or 15 years of age and older in 1990, who were illiterate or semi-literate. Beijing

TABLE 3   **Descriptive statistics for fertility rates and social and development variables: 28 provinces of China, 1982, 1990, and 1995**

Variable	Mean	Standard deviation	Minimum value	Maximum value
Total fertility rate				
1981	2.7	0.8	1.3, Shanghai	4.4, Guizhou
1989–90	2.3	0.5	1.4, Shanghai	3.1, Xinjiang
Crude birth rate, 1995	15.4	4.1	5.8, Shanghai	22.0, Qinghai
National income, per capita (in yuan)				
1982	546.8	465.2	235.0, Guizhou	2,518.0, Shanghai
1990	1,470.9	919.2	654.0, Guizhou	4,822.0, Shanghai
Percentage of population illiterate and semi-literate,				
Ages 12+, 1982	31.6	10.3	15.0, Beijing	49.3, Yunnan
Ages 15+, 1990	22.6	8.6	10.9, Beijing	40.0, Qinghai
Ratio of female/male life expectation at birth				
1982	1.04	0.02	1.01, Guizhou	1.07, Guangdong
1990	1.05	0.01	1.03, Gansu	1.07, Guangdong
Infant mortality rate				
1981	37.3	22.5	14.9, Beijing	108.1, Xinjiang
1989–90	28.7	16.7	8.8, Beijing	66.3, Qinghai

1 yuan = US$1.93 in July 1982, $4.73 in July 1990.
NOTES: For definition of variables see discussion in the text.
SOURCES: Poston and Gu (1987); China Population Information and Research Center (1996 and 1997).

has the lowest percentages in 1982 and in 1990; the highest values are in Yunnan in 1982 and Qinghai in 1990. The third independent variable, the ratio of female-to-male life expectation at birth, is a relative measure of women's status that is commonly used in international research (Sivard 1995). The higher the value of the ratio, the higher is women's status. This measure has mean scores of 1.04 and 1.05 in 1982 and 1990, respectively. The infant mortality rate, the fourth independent variable, is used here to represent overall health conditions. In 1981 the rate ranges from a low of 15 deaths per 1,000 births in Beijing to a high of 108 in Xinjiang; the range in 1989–90 is from 9 in Beijing to 66 in Qinghai.

The four panels of Table 4 report the results of the regressions. The regressions apply to (1) the dependent variable (the total fertility rate) and the four independent variables, all measured circa 1982; (2) the dependent variable, measured in 1989, and the independent variables, measured in 1982; (3) the dependent variable and the independent variables, all measured circa 1990; and (4) the dependent variable (the crude birth rate in this case), measured in 1995, and the independent variables, measured in 1990.

My hypotheses posit negative associations with fertility for the income and life expectancy variables, and positive relationships for the illiteracy and infant mortality variables. The results of all four equations are the same: income and infant mortality are signed in the hypothesized directions and are significant. The coefficients of the illiteracy variable are signed in the hypothesized direction but are not significant. The coefficients of the life expectancy variable are either not signed in the expected negative direction or are not significant. The income variable reports the highest coefficients in two of the equations, whereas the infant mortality variable has the highest coefficients in the other two.

Among the provinces of China in 1982 and in 1990, on the one hand, the measures of structural economic development (income) and health conditions (infant mortality) have consistently strong and significant effects on fertility, irrespective of whether fertility is measured at the same time as the two development variables or lagged five or more years later. On the other hand, the women's status variable and the illiteracy variable either have no effect on fertility in any of the equations, or an effect in the wrong direction. It may be that these two latter indicators of development should have been measured differently. I shall return to this issue in the discussion section.

The cities and counties of Taiwan

Next the analysis focuses on several cross-sectional investigations of the effects in 1980 and 1990 of social and economic development on fertility among the cities and counties of Taiwan. In 1980 there were 21 cities and

TABLE 4   Multiple regression coefficients for two fertility measures on social and economic development variables: 28 provinces of China, 1982 and 1990

Independent variable	1982 (TFR, 1981)		1982 (TFR, 1989)		1990 (TFR, 1989)		1990 (CBR, 1995)	
	Unstan-dardized	Stan-dardized	Unstan-dardized	Stan-dardized	Unstan-dardized	Stan-dardized	Unstan-dardized	Stan-dardized
Income	−0.001*	−0.316	−0.001*	−0.517	−0.001*	−0.541	−0.002*	−0.418
Illiteracy	0.015	0.183	0.001	0.126	0.001	0.016	0.110	0.231
Female/male life expectancy	13.012	0.253	9.956*	0.346	6.035	0.172	−14.400	−0.047
Infant mortality	0.024*	0.630	0.011*	0.509	0.012*	0.436	0.100*	0.407
Constant	−11.853		−8.327		−3.982		27.859	
R^2 (adjusted)	0.622		0.620		0.573		0.785	

NOTE: Dependent variable is identified in parentheses. TFR = total fertility rate; CBR = crude birth rate.
* Significant at $p = <0.05$.

counties *(hsiens)* in Taiwan. Five were cities or municipalities (hereafter referred to as cities), namely Kaohsiung Municipality, Keelung City, Taichung City, Tainan City, and Taipei Municipality; and 16 were counties, namely Changhwa, Chiayi, Hualien, Hsinchu, Ilan, Kaohsiung, Miaoli, Nantou, Penghu, Pingtung, Taichung, Tainan, Taipei, Taitung, Taoyuan, and Yunlin. Four of the counties have the same names as four of the cities and are contiguous to those cities. By 1990 the number of cities and counties had increased to 23. Chiayi County had split into Chiayi County and Chiayi City, and Hsinchu County had split into Hsinchu County and Hsinchu City. In my analyses for 1990, however, I return Chiayi County and Hsinchu County to their 1980 boundaries and thus use the same 21 cities and counties as in 1980.

The analysis strategy for Taiwan differs slightly from that for the counties and provinces of China. For at least two reasons I do not rely solely on multiple regression analysis to investigate the effects of social and economic development on fertility among the cities and counties of Taiwan. The first is that only 21 areal units are available for analysis; the second is that many of the social and economic development indicators are correlated with one another, usually at levels of +/–0.6 or higher. Therefore I first examine zero-order correlations between fertility and various indicators of social and economic development to gain a general view of the bivariate associations, then follow this with a series of multiple regressions. I begin by examining the zero-order effects on fertility in 1980 and 1990 of the social and economic development factors measured in 1980. Next I undertake a similar analysis of the effects of the development variables measured in 1990 on fertility measured in 1990 and then in 1995.

I use the total fertility rate for all three periods: 1980, 1990, and 1995. The total fertility rate has mean values for these years of 2.5, 1.8, and 1.8, respectively (Table 5). Taipei City has the lowest values for all three years, and three counties have the highest values. However, there is far less variation in fertility among the cities and counties of Taiwan than among the provinces of China. Miaoli County in 1990 and Yunlin County in 1995 have the highest fertility rates of all the cities and counties in Taiwan, but even these are replacement-level fertility values of 2.1. For all practical purposes the fertility transition was completed in Taiwan more than 20 years ago (Freedman, Chang, and Sun 1994; Weinstein et al. 1990), and fertility is quite low everywhere on the island.

For the analyses of fertility patterns among the Taiwan cities and counties, I use four social and economic development variables as predictors: the divorce rate (the number of divorces per 1,000 current marriages), the percentage of the labor force in professional occupations, the percentage of females who are illiterate, and the crude death rate. The divorce variable is a measure of secularization, and I use it here to represent social

TABLE 5 Descriptive statistics for fertility rates and social and development
variables: 21 cities and counties of Taiwan, 1980, 1990, and 1995

Variable	Mean	Standard deviation	Minimum value	Maximum value
Total fertility rate				
1980	2.5	0.3	1.9, Taipei City	2.9, Changhwa County
1990	1.8	0.2	1.5, Taipei City	2.1, Miaoli County
1995	1.8	0.2	1.4, Taipei City	2.1, Yunlin County
Divorce rate				
1980	3.7	1.5	1.6, Penghu County	6.4, Taipei City
1990	9.2	3.0	5.0, Changwa & Yunlin Counties	15.0, Hualien County
Percentage in professional occupations				
1980	6.0	1.8	3.4, Yunlin County	10.8, Taipei City
1990	8.0	2.5	4.6, Yunlin County	14.0, Taipei City
Percentage of females illiterate				
1980	29.3	10.0	11.6, Taipei City	50.0, Yunlin County
1990	12.9	4.4	4.7, Taipei City	21.6, Yunlin County
Crude death rate				
1980	6.1	1.3	4.3, Tainan City	9.5, Hualien County
1990	6.9	1.8	4.7, Taipei County	11.5, Taitung County

NOTE: For definition of variables see discussion in the text.
SOURCES: Poston (1988); Republic of China, Ministry of the Interior (1996).

development. My reasoning is that departures from traditional family forms
and patterns accompany development; divorce has an insignificant role in
traditional social systems. Among the cities and counties of Taiwan the mean
number of divorces per 1,000 current marriages increased from 3.7 in 1980
to 9.2 in 1990; the values for this variable range from 6.4 in Taipei City to
15.0 in Hualien County. The professional occupations variable is a proxy
for structural economic development. The kinds of economic productivity
data I used in the analyses of the Chinese subregions were not available
for Taiwan. Yunlin County has the lowest values for professional occupations in 1980 and 1990, and Taipei City the highest. The third independent
variable, female illiteracy, is a direct and negative measure of female status. It has mean scores of 29.3 in 1980 and 12.9 in 1990; Taipei City has
the lowest scores, and Yunlin County the highest. As the fourth independent variable in the analysis of the counties of China, I use the crude death
rate as a proxy for the infant mortality rate to represent overall health conditions. In 1980 Taiwan's crude death rate ranged from a low of 4.3 in
Tainan City to a high of 9.5 in Hualien; in 1990 it ranged from 4.7 in Taipei
County to 11.5 in Taitung County.

I hypothesize negative associations with fertility for the professional and divorce variables, and positive relationships for the illiteracy and crude death rate variables. In all cases these expectations are upheld. The first panel of Table 6 reports zero-order correlations in which both the independent variables and the total fertility rate are measured in 1980. In panel 2 the independent variables are measured in 1980 and the fertility rate is measured in 1990. Panel 3 shows the results for the independent variables and the total fertility rate both measured in 1990, and panel 4 shows the independent variables measured in 1990 and the total fertility rate measured in 1995. In all four panels the professional variable, indicating structural economic development, has the strongest (negative) relationship with fertility, ranging from –0.62 to –0.80. And in the first three panels of the table the crude death rate, representing overall health conditions, shows the lowest (positive) correlations with fertility. In the same three panels the social development variable (divorce) and the female status variable (illiteracy) have the second and third highest correlations, respectively, with fertility, in the expected directions. Only in the last panel is the order of the magnitude of the relationships with fertility of these three predictors reversed.

For the most part the development variables show strong correlations with fertility in all four panels. As I observed earlier, however, the independent variables are also correlated with one another. Some of those correlations are as high as 0.6. The illiteracy variable in particular is highly correlated with the other predictors, and so I do not use it in the multiple regressions.

Table 7 reports the results of four regressions. The first regression is for the three remaining independent variables and the dependent variable, all measured in 1980; the second is for the independent variables in 1980 and the dependent variable in 1990; the third is for the independent variables and the dependent variable in 1990; and the fourth is for the independent variables in 1990 and the dependent variable in 1995.

My hypotheses postulate negative associations between fertility and the professional and divorce variables, and a positive relationship between fertility and the crude death rate. The results indicate that in the first two

TABLE 6   Zero-order correlation coefficients for the total fertility rate and four social and economic development variables: 21 cities and counties of Taiwan, 1980 and 1990

Independent variable	1980 (TFR, 1980)	1980 (TFR, 1990)	1990 (TFR, 1990)	1990 (TFR, 1995)
Professionals	–0.796	–0.708	–0.621	–0.725
Divorce rate	–0.631	–0.600	–0.555	–0.387
Female illiteracy	0.566	0.465	0.456	0.588
Crude death rate	0.249	0.258	0.283	0.602

NOTE: Dependent variable is identified in parentheses. TFR = total fertility rate.

TABLE 7 Multiple regression coefficients for the total fertility rate on social and economic development variables: 21 cities and counties of Taiwan, 1980 and 1990

Independent variable	Total fertility rate, 1980 (Independ. variables: 1980)		Total fertility rate, 1990 (Independ. variables: 1980)		Total fertility rate, 1990 (Independ. variables: 1990)		Total fertility rate, 1995 (Independ. variables: 1990)	
	Unstandardized	Standardized	Unstandardized	Standardized	Unstandardized	Standardized	Unstandardized	Standardized
Professionals	−128.11*	−0.92	−63.54*	−0.75	−0.87	−0.01	−3.07	−0.04
Divorce rate	5.9	0.03	−1.86	−0.02	−34.38	−0.65	−33.72	−0.54
Crude death rate	−40.24	−0.20	−13.26	−0.11	38.18	0.43	74.58*	0.71
Constant	3,484.10		2,294.80		1,887.14		1,650.57	
R^2 (adjusted)	0.60		0.43		0.40		0.61	

* Significant at p = <.05.

regressions, only the professional variable is both signed in the hypothesized direction and statistically significant. None of the three social and economic predictors is significant in the third regression. In the fourth regression, only the crude death rate, representing overall health conditions, is signed in the hypothesized direction and significant.

The results of the analyses in Tables 6 and 7 indicate that despite the fact that by 1995 fertility in all the cities and counties of Taiwan was at or below replacement levels, there were still sizable zero-order relationships between the development measures and fertility. The multiple regressions show that in three of the four equations, one of the development variables is statistically associated with fertility in the direction expected. The finding that some of the social and economic predictors do not have statistically significant relationships with fertility is due in large part to the high collinearity among the predictors.

Discussion

With respect to levels of social and economic development, China lags considerably behind Taiwan. This is the case throughout the period examined. In 1990, for instance, the infant mortality rate was 37 in China and 17 in Taiwan (Population Reference Bureau 1990). Per capita gross national product in the late 1980s was just over $300 in China, and more than ten times higher ($3,750) in Taiwan (Encyclopaedia Britannica 1989: 574, 709). Yet the levels of fertility for China and Taiwan were nearly the same in 1990 and were almost identical in the late 1990s (see Figure 1).

One of the major differences between the fertility reductions in China and Taiwan is that the decline in China was due in part to a forceful and very effective intervention in family planning by the government of the People's Republic. Family planning programs were also influential in Taiwan, but participation in them was voluntary. Were it not for China's far-reaching fertility-control policies, it is unlikely that its fertility rate would have dropped as rapidly and precipitously as it did in recent decades, nor would it be as low today as Taiwan's. Nevertheless, despite the vastly different levels of social and economic development in China and Taiwan, the effects of development on fertility have been very similar in the two countries.

As expected, the results of the analyses provide general support for the relevance of social and economic development as an explanation for fertility decline. Although the results are not uniform regarding the influence of a single development variable, they support the hypothesis that, among the provinces and counties of China and Taiwan, higher levels of social and economic development are associated with lower fertility rates.

Tests of the development–fertility association could be significantly improved if it were possible to employ the same indicators of development in all cases. Since this was not possible, it is necessary to exercise caution in postulating that the effects of certain development factors are more influential than others. Nevertheless, the results of this study indicate that labor force measures of economic development appear to have greater effect on fertility than do indicators of economic productivity. Similarly, health-based indicators as represented by the infant mortality rate and crude death rate do not seem to be as influential as social indicators based on educational levels. To the extent that social and economic factors and contexts tend to influence reproductive motivation and fertility by specifying the reward structures related to childbearing, the more influential ones may well be those tied closely to such structures. Aggregate measures of economic productivity and health conditions could be argued to be less proximate than the more socially based indicators, and hence less effective predictors of fertility.

My choice of variables for analysis also requires comment. In several tests I used the illiteracy rate as a negative indicator of social development. And in another test I used the ratio of female-to-male expectation of life at birth as a measure of relative female status. Illiteracy may no longer be a sensitive indicator of social development, given the widespread increases in educational attainment in China since the late 1960s, particularly among women (Freedman et al. 1988; Lavely et al. 1990). Moreover, there have been such improvements in female and male life expectancy in China in the past few decades (Banister 1987) that, at the provincial level at least, only modest variability in this ratio was seen in both 1982 and 1990.

The finding that the ratio of female-to-male life expectancy was not related to fertility in the provinces of China does not necessarily mean that improvements in women's status are not associated with fertility decline. As one reviewer of this study pointed out, in some countries with high ratios of female-to-male life expectancy, women's social status is nevertheless low. The lack of an association established with fertility is likely the result of the use of a less-than-adequate indicator of women's status.

In a similar vein, the failure of this study to show any association between the divorce rate, an indicator of secularization, and fertility decline among the counties of Taiwan does not necessarily mean that secularizing trends in Taiwan are unrelated to fertility change. The same reviewer noted that in some countries more developed than either China or Taiwan the divorce rates are very low. The lack of an association found here may therefore be due in part, again, to an imperfect indicator of social development.

These observations notwithstanding, the results indicate clearly the strong influences of social and economic development factors on fertility. The cross-sectional examinations show consistent and pervasive negative associations between social and economic development and levels of fertility among the subregions of China and Taiwan. Indeed, the similarities of the experiences in the two countries are often more apparent than the dissimilarities. The similar associations between development and fertility are sustained irrespective of whether fertility is measured at the same time as development or five or ten years later. These results provide confirming evidence that a social and economic development–based theory of fertility decline, as represented by the broader theory of demographic transition, continues to have considerable relevance for understanding variation in fertility among the subregions of China and Taiwan.

Note

1 For ease of reference I refer in this chapter to the People's Republic of China as China, and to the Republic of China as Taiwan. For the same reason, I refer to the two entities as countries while acknowledging that Taiwan's political status is a contentious issue. My reference to Taiwan as a country does not represent a viewpoint about that status.

References

Alker, H. R., Jr. 1969. "A typology of ecological fallacies," in *Quantitative Ecological Analysis in the Social Sciences*, eds. M. Dogan and S. Rokkan. Cambridge, MA: MIT Press, pp. 69–86.

Alter, George. 1992. "Theories of fertility decline: A nonspecialist's guide to the current debate," in *The European Experience of Declining Fertility, 1850–1970: The Quiet Revolution*, eds. John R. Gillis, Louise A. Tilly, and David Levine. Cambridge, MA: Blackwell Publishers, pp. 13–25.

Banister, Judith. 1987. *China's Changing Population*. Stanford: Stanford University Press.

Birdsall, Nancy and D. T. Jamison. 1983. "Income and other factors influencing fertility in China," *Population and Development Review* 9(4): 651–675.

Blake, Judith. 1973. "Fertility control and the problem of voluntarism," in *Scientists and World Affairs*, Proceedings of the Twenty-second Pugwash Conference on Science and World Affairs, London, September, pp. 279–283.

Chen Shengli. 1984. "Fertility of women during the 42-year period from 1940 to 1981," in *Analysis on China's National One-per-Thousand Sampling Survey*. Beijing: China Population Information Center, pp. 32–58.

China, Republic of, Ministry of the Interior. 1996. *1995 Taiwan-Fukien Demographic Factbook, Republic of China*. Taipei, Taiwan.

China Population Information and Research Center. 1994. *Basic Data on China's Population*. Beijing: China Population Publishing House.

———. 1996. *Population and Socioeconomic Data of China by Province*. Beijing: China Population Publishing House.

———. 1997. *Chinese Population Census* (CD Containing Results of All Population Censuses and the 1995 Sampling Census). Beijing.

Coale, Ansley J. 1984. *Rapid Population Change in China, 1952–1982*. Washington, DC: National Academy Press.

Coale, Ansley J. and Susan Cotts Watkins (eds). 1986. *The Decline of Fertility in Europe*. Princeton, NJ: Princeton University Press.

Donaldson, Loraine. 1991. *Fertility Transition: The Social Dynamics of Population Change*. Cambridge, MA: Basil Blackwell Publishers.

Easterlin, Richard A. and Eileen M. Crimmins. 1985. *The Fertility Revolution: A Supply-Demand Analysis*. Chicago: University of Chicago Press.

Encyclopaedia Britannica. 1989. *1989 Britannica Book of the Year*. Chicago.

Feeney, Griffith M. 1994. "Fertility decline in East Asia," *Science* 266(5190): 518–523.

Feeney, Griffith M. and Wang Feng. 1993. "Parity progression and birth intervals in China: The influence of policy in hastening fertility decline," *Population and Development Review* 19(1): 61–101.

Freedman, Ronald. 1998. *Observing Taiwan's Demographic Transition: A Memoir*. Taichung: Taiwan Provincial Institute of Family Planning.

Freedman, Ronald, M. C. Chang, and Te-Hsiung Sun. 1994. "Taiwan's transition from high fertility to below-replacement levels," *Studies in Family Planning* 25(6): 317–331.

Freedman, Ronald et al. 1988. "Education and fertility in two Chinese provinces: 1967–1970 to 1979–1982," *Asia-Pacific Population Journal* 3(1): 3–30.

Fricke, Tom. 1997. "The uses of culture in demographic research: A continuing place for community studies," *Population and Development Review* 23(4): 825–832.

Gertler, Paul J. and John W. Molyneaux. 1994. "How economic development and family planning programs combined to reduce Indonesian fertility," *Demography* 31(1): 33–63.

Greenhalgh, Susan. 1990. "Toward a political economy of fertility: Anthropological contributions," *Population and Development Review* 16(1): 85–106.

Gu Baochang. 1989. "On the effects of socio-economic development and family planning on the decline of fertility in China," *Chinese Journal of Population Science* 1(2): 125–138.

Hernandez, Donald J. 1984. *Success or Failure? Family Planning Programs in the Third World*. Westport, Connecticut: Greenwood Press.

Hirschman, Charles. 1994. "Why fertility changes," *Annual Review of Sociology* 20: 203–233.

Jia, Z. 1991. "Socioeconomic development, family planning, and fertility in Taiwan," *Chinese Journal of Population Science* 3(2): 107–113.

Kertzer, David I. and Dennis P. Hogan. 1989. *Family, Political Economy, and Demographic Change: The Transformation of Life in Casalecchio, Italy, 1861–1921*. Madison: The University of Wisconsin Press.

Knodel, John and Etienne van de Walle. 1979. "Lessons from the past: Policy implications of historical fertility studies," *Population and Development Review* 5(2): 217–245.

Lavely, William et al. 1990. "The rise in female education in China: National and regional patterns," *The China Quarterly* 121: 61–93.

Lee, James and Wang Feng. 1999. "Malthusian models and Chinese realities: The Chinese demographic system, 1700–2000," *Population and Development Review* 25(1): 33–65.

Leete, R. 1987. "The post-demographic transition in East and South East Asia: Similarities and contrasts with Europe," *Population Studies* 41(2): 187–206.

Lieberson, Stanley and L. K. Hansen. 1974. "National development, mother tongue diversity, and the comparative study of nations," *American Sociological Review* 39(4): 523–541.

Livi-Bacci, Massimo. 1997. *A Concise History of World Population*, 2nd ed. Boston, MA: Blackwell Publishers.

Mason, Karen Oppenheim. 1997. "Explaining fertility transitions," *Demography* 34(4): 443–454.

Mauldin, W. Parker and Bernard Berelson. 1978. "Conditions of fertility decline in developing countries," *Studies in Family Planning* 9(5): 89–147.

Mauldin, W. Parker, and John A. Ross. 1991. "Family planning programs: Efforts and results," *Studies in Family Planning* 22(6): 350–367.

McNicoll, Geoffrey. 1992. "Changing fertility patterns and policies in the third world," *Annual Review of Sociology* 18: 85–108.

Notestein, Frank W. 1953. "Economic problems of population change," in *Proceedings of the Eighth International Conference of Agricultural Economists*. London: Oxford University Press, pp. 13–31.

Population Census Office of the State Council, People's Republic of China (PRC), and the Institute of Geography, Chinese Academy of Sciences (CAS). 1987. *The Population Atlas of China.* New York: Oxford University Press.

Population Reference Bureau. 1990. *1990 World Population Data Sheet.* Washington, DC.

Poston, Dudley L., Jr. 1988. "Childlessness patterns in Taiwan," *Journal of Population Studies* 11: 55–78.

———. 1992. "Fertility trends in China," in *The Population of Modern China,* eds. Dudley L. Poston, Jr. and David Yaukey. New York: Plenum Press, pp. 277–286.

Poston, Dudley L., Jr. and Gu Baochang. 1987. "Socioeconomic development, family planning, and fertility in China," *Demography* 24(4): 531–551.

Poston, Dudley L., Jr. and Jia Zhongke. 1990. "Socioeconomic structure and fertility in China: A county-level investigation," *Journal of Biosocial Science* 22(4): 507–515.

Pritchett, Lant H. 1994a. "Desired fertility and the impact of population policies," *Population and Development Review* 20(1): 1–55.

———. 1994b. "The impact of population policies: Reply," *Population and Development Review* 20(3): 621–630.

Robey, Bryant. 1991. *Economic Development and Fertility Decline: Lessons from Asia's Newly Industrialized Countries,* Asia-Pacific Population and Policy, No. 16. Honolulu: East-West Center.

Sanchez, L. 1993. "Women's power and the gendered division of domestic labor in the Third World," *Gender and Society* 7(3): 434–459.

Schultz, T. Paul. 1971. *Evaluation of Population Policies: A Framework for Analysis and Its Application to Taiwan's Family Planning Program.* Santa Monica, CA: The Rand Corporation.

———. 1980. "An economic interpretation of the decline in fertility in a rapidly developing country: Consequences of development and family planning," in *Population and Economic Change in Developing Countries,* ed. Richard A. Easterlin. Chicago: University of Chicago Press, pp. 209–288.

———. 1994. "Human capital, family planning, and their effects on population growth," *American Economic Review* 84(2): 255–260.

Schutjer, Wayne A. and C. Shannon Stokes (eds). 1984. *Rural Development and Human Fertility.* New York: Macmillan.

Sivard, Ruth Leger. 1995. *Women: A World Survey,* 2nd ed. Washington, DC: World Priorities.

Sun, Te-Hsiung. 1984. "Urban-industrial development as a force in rural fertility change: The case of Taiwan, Republic of China," in *Rural Development and Human Fertility,* eds. Wayne A. Schutjer and C. Shannon Stokes. New York: Macmillan, pp. 49–76.

Teitelbaum, Michael S. 1975. "Relevance of demographic transition theory for developing countries," *Science* 188(4187): 420–425.

Tien, H. Yuan. 1984. "Induced fertility transition: Impact of population planning and socioeconomic change in the People's Republic of China," *Population Studies* 38(3): 385–400.

Tsui, Amy Ong and Donald J. Bogue. 1978. "Declining world fertility: Trends, causes, implications," *Population Bulletin* 33(4): 2–56.

United Nations. 1988. *1986 Demographic Yearbook.* New York: United Nations.

Weinstein, Maxine A. et al. 1990. "Household composition, extended kinship, and reproduction in Taiwan: 1965–1985," *Population Studies* 44(2): 217–239.

Wolf, Arthur P. 1986. The preeminent role of government intervention in China's family revolution," *Population and Development Review* 12(1): 101–116.

The Impact of Targeted Family Planning Programs in Indonesia

JOHN W. MOLYNEAUX
PAUL J. GERTLER

REDUCING RAPID POPULATION growth, in particular by reducing fertility, is often cited as a key element in a country's ability to maintain and improve its economic and social welfare. Many governments have established explicit policies designed to slow population growth. Such policies range from aggressive family planning programs to efforts aimed at improving basic education and economic opportunities for women. From the 1994 United Nations International Conference on Population and Development, in Cairo, came a report stating that strong, publicly financed family planning programs were critical elements of most countries' population policies. The report recommended that global spending on family planning programs be tripled by the year 2010. Multilateral aid agencies such as the World Bank, the regional development banks, and the United Nations, and bilateral aid agencies such as the US Agency for International Development continue to provide large-scale funding for population programs and to emphasize their importance.

Yet debate continues over the importance of family planning programs in reducing fertility. The debate focuses on the following questions: When in the development process are family planning programs most effective? Which components of those programs are most effective? And how effective are family planning programs compared with other factors, especially improvements in women's educational and economic opportunities? (See, for example, Bulatao and Lee 1983; Demeny 1979; Freedman and Berelson 1978; Gertler and Molyneaux 1994; Hermalin 1975 and 1983; Mauldin and Berelson 1978; Schultz 1992; Tsui and Bogue 1978; Westoff, Moreno, and Goldman 1989.) In this chapter we contribute to the debate by investigating the effects on fertility of an array of public family planning programs in Indonesia—a relatively mature developing country—while controlling for economic growth and improvements in the status of women.

A major stumbling block in measuring the effects of family planning programs on fertility is that the programs are not randomly placed; instead, governments tailor their programs to the local needs of the populations they serve. In the case of nonrandom placement, ordinary least squares (OLS) regression coefficients reflect both the effects of government programs on fertility and the effect of fertility (and its proximate determinants) on governments' allocation decisions. Rosenzweig and Wolpin (1986: 476) explain that the direction of the bias introduced by nonrandom placement is not clear. On the one hand, it can have a downward bias on measured impacts in cross-sectional studies if governments target areas of greatest need. On the other hand, it can have an upward bias if government supplies of contraceptives are diverted to areas of greatest contraceptive demand—and they do not respond to local needs. Indeed, several cross-sectional studies using Indonesian data have found negative correlations between selected program inputs and contraceptive prevalence (Wirakartakusumah 1988; Lerman et al. 1989; Molyneaux et al. 1990). But nonrandom placement can also have an upward bias if government supplies of contraceptives are diverted only to areas of greatest demand. Because our study seeks to measure the effects of various types of family planning programs in Indonesia, including contraceptive subsidies (which are not delivered to regions where they will not be used) and other contraceptive-promoting activities (which, along with contraceptive subsidies, are routinely targeted to poorly performing areas), we explicitly deal with these limitations of OLS analysis.

With a few notable exceptions, previous studies of the impact of family planning programs on fertility have assumed that government programs are randomly allocated or allocated in a way that is uncorrelated with fertility or its proximate determinants. Only a few studies have tried to control for the nonrandom targeting of program inputs. Montgomery and Casterline (1993); Pitt, Rosenzweig, and Gibbons (1993); Schultz (1973); and we (Gertler and Molyneaux 1994) use panel data to estimate a fixed-effects model to control for this endogeneity. The model regresses changes in local birth probabilities on changes in the explanatory variables. The fixed-effects model controls for the endogeneity of program placement if a government allocates family planning program inputs on the basis of fixed characteristics of the population. The fixed-effects specification eliminates the effects of these fixed characteristics from the model and the error terms. As a result, changes in program variables are uncorrelated with changes in the error term.

Fixed-effects models may be appropriate for measuring the effects of government interventions that do not respond dynamically to changing demand characteristics. Our own application (Gertler and Molyneaux 1994) used a limited five-year time frame and focused on the roles of such relatively stable program interventions as clinics, distribution infrastructure, personnel, and contraceptive-promotion activities. However, the study was unable to assess the impact of contraceptive-subsidy allocations, which respond quickly to changing demands for contraceptives and account for more than half of all program costs (World Bank 1990). In Indonesia the allocation of contraceptive subsidies is based, in part, on contraceptive use and thus responds dynamically to program performance.

Angeles, Guilkey, and Mroz (1998) allow for more complex allocation rules than the fixed-effects models require. They model jointly the determinants of the geographic allocation of family planning programs and the determinants of fertility. They apply an efficient, semi-parametric, random-effects estimator that allows for correlation between unobservable factors that influence program placement and the fertility outcome. Excluding some of the determinants of program placement from the fertility equation, but not from the program-placement equation, identifies their model. The excluded variables include lagged national and regional health and family planning expenditures. Such an identification strategy does not work in the Indonesian context, where the government's dynamic process for allocating family planning resources revises the allocations on the basis of observed contraceptive use and fertility. In this case, lagged family planning program budgets are likely to be correlated with the error term in the fertility equation and are therefore not a valid identifying variable.

In this study we develop a method for estimating program impacts, despite this endogeneity. Our method depends on a model of decisionmaking for allocating family planning resources that is used by the Indonesian government. The Indonesian allocation process provides a set of valid instrumental variables for estimating program effects on fertility. Because provincial governments allocate resources across districts that are subject to an overall budget constraint, an increase in the allocation to one district reduces the amount that can be allocated to other districts. Therefore variables that shift contraceptive demand in competing districts are valid instruments.

In the following two sections we describe the institutional setting and data sources. Next we investigate the allocation of family planning program expenditures. We find not only that the government's allocation of family planning is not random, but also that it responds dynamically to contraceptive use. This implies that a simple fixed-effects estimator is insufficient to control for the endogeneity of program placement. However, our analysis of the allocation rule suggests a feasible identification strategy that allows us to estimate consistent effects of these endogenous contraceptive subsidies. In the subsequent section we investigate the effects of family planning program inputs on fertility, using a regression analysis based on this identification strategy. Finally, we summarize our findings and discuss their policy implications.

The institutional setting

Indonesia is the fourth most populous country in the world and has substantial ethnic, cultural, and economic diversity. It is well known for its dynamic and innovative family planning program, and it has recently achieved rapid fertility declines. Moreover, the government has invested heavily in education and infrastructure over the past two decades. During this study's time frame (1986–94), Indonesia experienced substantial macroeconomic shocks, stemming from booms and busts in oil prices, aggressive deregulation of capital markets, and rapid expansion of export-oriented manufacturing industries.

Over the period studied here, Indonesia's National Family Planning Coordinating Board, known by its Indonesian initials as BKKBN, has experimented aggressively with a variety of approaches to influencing fertility. Those approaches include extensive campaigns to educate couples about family planning and to promote contraceptive use, the development of contraceptive-delivery systems and training of personnel, and the procurement of contraceptives. Contraceptive use has grown rapidly and consistently over the last several decades, with a growing reliance on hormonal methods accompanied by a decline in the use of IUDs. The changing pattern of use probably reflects the compound effects of a maturing and increasingly well-informed clientele, increasing levels of disposable income, an improved transportation infrastructure, and a changing mix of contraceptive subsidies.

The years 1986–94 were a period of sustained but decelerating fertility decline and rapid economic growth in Indonesia. Although the study period preceded the 1997–98 monetary crisis and Indonesia's subsequent recession, our findings are relevant to the policy choices that the BKKBN has had to make in the face of the crisis. At the beginning of the analysis period, Indonesia's fertility transition had been underway for more than 15 years, though after 1986 the pace appears to have slackened. Total fertility rates declined 22 percent over the decade from 1970 through 1980 and declined another 25 percent during the next nine years, with much of the decrease occurring between 1980 and 1986 (Central Bureau of Statistics 1992). Moderate fertility declines continued from 1991 through 1994.

Historically, most of this fertility decline has been attributed to two proximate determinants: a sharp rise in contraceptive prevalence and an increase in age at marriage (Adioetomo, Kitting, and Taufik 1990; Hull and Hatmadji 1990). The proportion of married women of reproductive age practicing contraception increased from 27 percent in 1980 to 47 percent in 1987, then rose more gradually to 50 percent in 1991 and 55 percent in 1994 (Central Bureau of Statistics 1995). In addition, the mean age at marriage for women rose from 19.3 years in 1971 to 21.1 years in 1985 (Hull and Hatmadji 1990). Two institutional factors that are often cited as explanations for the changes in these proximate determinants of fertility are an expansion of economic welfare combined with improved opportunities for women, and a strong government commitment, both political and financial, to limiting population growth through family planning programs (Hull and Hatmadji 1990; Hull and Hull 1987; World Bank 1990).

Early improvements in economic welfare resulted from a rapid expansion of the education system in combination with occasional periods of strong economic growth. Primary school enrollment increased from 13 million in 1974 to 27 million in 1985, with enrollment rates reaching nearly 95 percent by 1994. The proportion of the population living in poverty fell from about 40 percent in the late 1970s to about 22 percent in the late 1980s (World Bank 1989), then declined further, to 13 percent, by 1993 (Central Bureau of Statistics 1994). National surveys on household expenditures indicate that price-adjusted nonfood expenditures rose by nearly 60 percent over the six-year period from 1978 to 1984 (Lembaga Demografi 1988). Real wage rates increased by 65 percent for women and by 40 percent for men between 1980 and 1987 (Ananta et al. 1990). More recently, wages have continued to rise, though at a slower pace. Over the period from 1985 to 1993, real wages for both men and women increased by roughly 20 percent.

The BKKBN has been widely cited as a model of government-sponsored fertility control in a developing country (Snodgrass 1979; Warwick 1986; World Bank 1990). Established in 1970, it developed a flexible family planning program that coordinates the activities of several ministries, local governments, and volunteers. Despite the faltering economy of 1986–87 and marked reductions in the Health Ministry's budget, the BKKBN's program budget continued to expand at a steady rate throughout the 1980s (World Bank 1990). Moreover, the manipulation of contraceptive procurements has become increasingly a key instrument in the BKKBN's array of interventions.

The BKKBN's main methods of encouraging contraceptive use are contraceptive subsidies and distribution networks. It purchases and directly distributes contraceptives, principally through the Ministry of Health's clinic system and through community-based outlets known as village contraceptive distribution centers. It also promotes contraceptive demand and encourages women to postpone marriage through its information, education, and communication activities. Most recently the BKKBN's family planning field workers have taken on an expanded role, promoting income-generating groups and managing small, group-based savings-and-loan facilities.

Indicative of the endogeneity of program placement is the fact that the BKKBN has introduced its activities neither uniformly nor randomly in Indonesia; rather, it has tailored them to local needs (BKKBN 1984; Snodgrass 1979). Provincial and district officials are given substantial incentives to increase contraceptive prevalence and have autonomy to tailor family planning program inputs to local needs and conditions. These officials negotiate method-specific prevalence targets and receive resources based on the negotiated targets and their prior record of target achievement.

Data

We make use of data from multiple sources, capturing fertility and its determinants for almost a decade across Indonesia's 27 diverse provinces. We use two Demographic and Health Surveys (DHS), disaggregated statistics on family planning program activities, and national labor force and employment surveys to track fertility and its determinants. The unit of observation in our data is the district. We have quarterly data on 286 districts for nine years. Altogether, we have 10,296 observations.

The Indonesian DHS of 1991 and 1994 provide historical data on respondents' fertility, marriage, and contraceptive use, as well as age and education. The quality of DHS retrospective birth-history data is well documented as highly accurate (Central Bureau of Statistics 1989). The 1991 DHS surveyed a nationally representative sample of 23,000 women from 1,100 sampling units; the 1994 DHS surveyed 28,000 women from 1,200 sampling units. Within sample units we aggregate data from individual women (about 20 women per sample unit) to produce district-level measures of fertility, several of its proximate determinants, the age distribution, and educational attainment.

Two measures of fertility and its proximate determinants are presented in Figure 1, which shows a slight decline in marriage rates (associated with continued increases in the age at marriage), along with a gradual increase in contraceptive prevalence. By contrast, the two measures of fertility, the overall hazard (births per person-year) and the birth rate among married, noncontracepting women, while declining over the period, are much more erratic than the proximate determinants.

Our data on family planning services, personnel, and infrastructure are from a wealth of program statistics available in Indonesia. Since 1982 the BKKBN has maintained computerized monthly records of the numbers of family planning clinics, summaries of their monthly activities, and detailed statistics on the numbers and types of subsidized contraceptives distributed. The strength of the BKKBN's programs can be measured from the monthly records of family planning activities within each district in Indonesia. The data allow the construction of measures of specific aspects of the national family planning program.

We capture program inputs in three variables, all of them measured at the district level. The variables are (1) the government's expenditures in 1996 rupiah on contraceptive supplies per eligible married couple in a district; (2) the number of Ministry of Health clinics, per thousand eligible couples, that distribute contraceptives in a district; and (3) the number of

FIGURE 1   Two measures of fertility (birth per person-year) and two measures of the proximate determinants of fertility: Women 15–49, Indonesia, 1985/86–1993/94

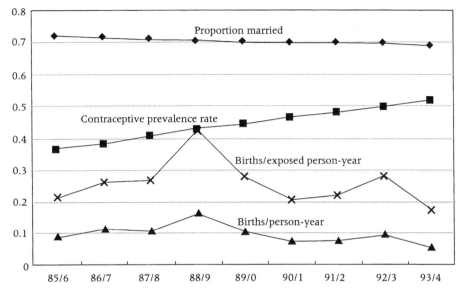

SOURCE: 1991 and 1994 Indonesian Demographic and Health Surveys, Contraception Calendars.

village contraceptive distribution centers per thousand eligible couples in a district. The numbers of clinics and distribution centers increased substantially over the period from 1986 to 1994. In contrast, the real value of per capita contraceptive expenditures peaked around 1988, declined through the remainder of the period covered by this study, then grew rapidly again until the 1997–98 monetary crisis. Thus, although contraceptive subsidies declined in importance over the period of the study, they continue to be an important policy instrument for the BKKBN.

To measure the economic status of the family, we use the wages that the husband and wife earn in the formal wage sectors. We calculate male and female hourly wages from the 1986 through 1994 SAKERNAS surveys. The SAKERNAS surveys are nationally representative enumerations of 50,000 to 60,000 households. Wages earned by all "employees"—that is, those not self-employed—and the hours they work are the data source. We predicted wages from regressions of individual real hourly wages on individual ages and levels of education. We estimated unique intercepts for each district, but assumed age and education coefficients to be equal across all districts within a province. These regressions were run separately for males and females, urban and rural populations, and provinces, as well as by year.

In sum, the data provide an eight-year history of fertility, contraceptive use, and economic development, along with the expansion of the family planning program inputs, at a nationally representative level. The length of the time frame has allowed us to document the joint roles of family planning programs and socioeconomic development in influencing Indonesia's fertility decline. The interesting time-series changes in fertility, contraception, economic conditions, and government programs provide important sources of variation in key factors influencing demographic behavior.

The allocation of family planning inputs

In Indonesia, family planning program inputs are allocated at three administrative levels. First, the BKKBN central office allocates its budget by category across the 27 provinces. Second, each province allocates its budget by category across its districts (300 nationally). And third, each district allocates its budget by category to delivery units that exist at the subdistrict level and lower. Nationally there are 4,000 subdistricts. At each level the lower administrative units negotiate with the higher administrative unit over their annual budget allocations.

These allocation decisions make use of routinely reported information from an annual planning and logistics system. In the beginning of a fiscal year, officials in each subdistrict are asked to estimate their method-specific contraceptive requirements for the coming year. These estimates are based on past contraceptive use and the forecasted number of eligible couples. The estimates are reported to the district offices. The district offices, in turn, compile the subdistrict requests along with other district information to generate a set of district-demand projections. These district-level estimates are forwarded to the 27 provincial offices, which aggregate them and report provincial-level estimates to the national office. At the national level the BKKBN compiles the provincial requests and compares them with the forecasts of demand from their demographic models. On the basis of the provincial requests, available resources, and input from the demographic models, the BKKBN modifies the provincial requests and proposes a draft set of provincial allocations. National and provincial planning officers then negotiate a revised set of allocations. The revised allocations are presented to the National Development Planning Body, which then negotiates another set of revisions to the allocations and an associated budget with the BKKBN. The final provisional allocations are submitted for approval to the President and Parliament as part of the national budget.

In practice, district, provincial, and central BKKBN planners establish projections of population growth, fertility, and contraceptive use based on projections of the number of eligible couples, past records of contraceptive use, shortages or excess stocks, and other location-specific information. At the national level this information is used to negotiate the allocation of the central budget across the competing demands of the 27 provinces. At the provincial level the same information is used to negotiate the allocation of the province's budget across the competing district demands; and at the district level it is used to allocate the district budget across the subdistricts and programs.

This process determines the annual targeted allocations at the beginning of the budget year and the fixed budgets allocated to the provinces. However, the allocations from the provinces to districts and in turn from the districts to subdistricts allow for real-time reallocations based on shortages or excess stocks in the field. Contraceptive supplies are shipped each month. If one area experiences a shortage, then the provincial or district BKKBN office can direct additional stock there from other areas' future shipments.

This budgeting process—of an initial allocation from the central government to the BKKBN, and from the BKKBN central office to provincial and lower levels of the national program, followed by adjustments made during the year in response to competing demands for inputs from the provinces, districts, and subdistricts—suggests a model of program input allocation across geographic areas. According to this process a district's allocations are a function of both its and its competitors' real and forecasted demand as well as the provincial budget constraint. We therefore specify a model of the provincial allocation of family planning expenditures to a district as:

$$E_{it} = \alpha_i + \beta_1 \hat{C}_{it} + \beta_2 \sum_{j \neq i} \hat{C}_{jt} + \beta_3 \left(C_{it} - \hat{C}_{it} \right) + \beta_4 \left(\sum_{j \neq i} C_{jt} - \sum_{j \neq i} \hat{C}_{jt} \right) + \gamma E_t + \tau_{it} ,$$

where E_{it} is the budget allocated to district i in period t, $\hat{C}_{it}$ is the forecasted contraceptive demand in district i in period t, and E_t is the provincial budget in period t.

This equation states that a district budget allocation is a fixed amount that is adjusted on the basis of the district's forecasted contraceptive use, the forecasted contraceptive use of competing districts, the difference between actual and forecasted contraceptive use in the district (i.e., shortage or surplus), the difference between actual and forecasted contraceptive use in the competing districts, the provincial budget constraint, and an error term.

If the government uses a simpler allocation rule based on fixed characteristics, then the district allocation will depend on just the fixed effect and the provincial budget, and the beta coefficients will be zero. In this case the fixed effects will control for the endogeneity of program placement. However, if the government allocations respond to current and lagged information about contraceptive use, then these beta coefficients will not be zero, and the allocations will be correlated with the nonfixed unobservables in the fertility equation. If this is the case, a fixed-effects model will not control for the endogeneity of program placement. The model provides a test of which approach is appropriate for estimating program impacts.

The dependent variable is the natural log of the quarterly district pro-curement expenditures per eligible couple. The independent variables are the forecasted number of eligible couples in the district and in competing districts, past contraceptive use in the district and in competing districts, and the provincial budget per eligible couple. The number of eligible couples and past contraceptive use are proxies for forecasted contraceptive demand. The higher the forecasted demand, the higher the allocation. The BKKBN targets subsidies to areas of contraceptive prevalence, however, and so we expect an overall negative effect of own-district lagged prevalence and a positive effect of lagged prevalence in competing districts. Similarly, the number of eligible couples in the district should have a positive effect and the number of eligible couples in competing districts should have a nega-tive effect on budget allocations. The difference between current contra-ceptive prevalence and forecasted demand is the shortage or surplus. There-fore, we expect own prevalence to be positively and competing prevalence to be negatively related to budget allocations.

We estimated the model using district and quarterly fixed effects. The results, presented in Table 1, reject the hypothesis that the allocations are made only on the basis of fixed factors subject to an overall budget con-straint. Information on current contraceptive use and population changes affects the allocations, and that suggests that the government dynamically allocates contraceptive subsidies in response to changes in contraceptive prevalence. In this case subsidies respond positively, in the short run, to contraceptive prevalence surprises. This finding is consistent with the BKKBN's practice of reallocating monthly allotments from districts with excess stocks of contraceptives to districts that can absorb them. How the BKKBN responds in the long run is more strategic; regions with little need for support are to be gradually weaned from their subsidies, while poorly performing areas are brought under more careful scrutiny and perhaps pro-vided with additional inputs. Thus, according to the BKKBN's strategy, the long-term response should differ from the short-term. Indeed, the very long-term response determines the correlation between the district-level fixed effects (i.e., the average contraceptive prevalence rate) and contraceptive subsidies—a correlation that is overwhelmingly positive. These results im-ply that a fixed-effects model will not sufficiently control for the endogeneity of program placement in analyses that measure the effect of family plan-ning programs on fertility.

This analysis also suggests a set of valid instruments. Recall that a valid instrument is one that is correlated with the program inputs but uncorrelated with the error term in the fertility equation. In other words, a valid instrument is a right-hand side variable in the program input equa-tions, but not in the fertility equation. The model developed in this section implies that variables that shift contraceptive demand in competing dis-tricts affect the allocation of contraceptive subsidies to other districts, but

TABLE 1　Fixed-effects model of allocations for family planning contraceptive subsidies: Indonesia

Independent variable	ln (subsidy per eligible couple)
District population	0.037
	(1.05)
Lagged district contraceptive prevalence	−0.037
	(0.90)
Current district contraceptive prevalence	0.104
	(2.55)
Average population of competing districts	−0.008
	(3.64)
Average lagged contraceptive prevalence of competing districts	0.549
	(3.73)
Average current contraceptive prevalence of competing districts	−0.312
	(2.24)
ln (provincial budget)	0.001
	(95.57)
District fixed effects	Yes
Quarterly fixed effects	Yes
R-squared	0.77

do not directly affect fertility. Therefore, we use current and lagged male and female wage rates, along with the age and education distribution of eligible couples in competing districts, as instruments.

The impact of family planning program inputs

Given our primary goal of evaluating the contribution of government family planning program inputs to fertility decline in Indonesia, our conceptual framework is illustrated by Figure 2, which depicts the relationships among fertility, its proximate determinants, and exogenous factors. According to the proximate-determinants model, four factors are the most important determinants of fertility: marriage, contraceptive use, postpartum amenorrhea, and induced abortion (Bongaarts and Potter 1983).

The four proximate determinants are choice variables that are determined by observed and unobserved exogenous factors. Observable individual and household characteristics that affect the proximate determinants include age, education, and income. Community-level variables such as prices, wages, infrastructure, and the availability of contraceptive information and supplies also affect the choice variables. In addition to observable factors, unobservable determinants such as a woman's underlying prefer-

FIGURE 2   Determinants of fertility: Conceptual framework

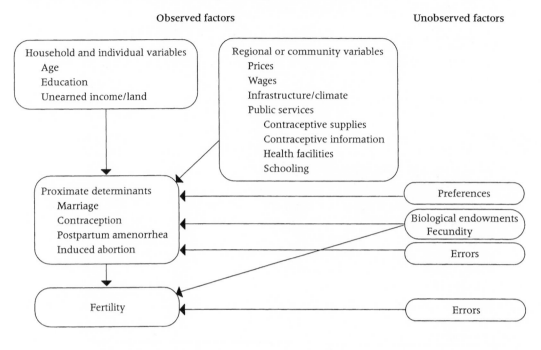

ences and her fecundity (the biological ability to conceive and bear children) also play a role in determining fertility outcomes.

We model the demand for children by regressing fertility directly on the exogenous factors. The results of such an analysis reveal the net effect of the exogenous variables on fertility (as well as their relative importance), but do not identify the mechanisms through which they work. As Figure 2 indicates, these factors influence fertility through the mediating influence of the proximate determinants. The parameters implied by this relationship reflect the net effects of programmatic, household, and individual characteristics, through all of the proximate determinants, on fertility. In this specification the mechanisms through which these factors influence fertility are not explicitly modeled. This summarizing specification is the reduced-form model.

Estimation of the reduced form is complicated by the fact that the BKKBN introduced program inputs in a dynamic, nonrandom fashion. This implies that program inputs are correlated with both observed and unobserved determinants of fertility. Consequently, the inputs may be correlated with the error terms in the reduced-form model, rendering inconsistent both OLS and fixed-effects coefficient estimates. We use an instrumental-variable, fixed-effects method to control for this endogeneity. The specific set of instruments was discussed in the previous section.

Because of the need to specify a fixed-effects model of fertility and its proximate determinants, we conduct the subsequent analyses at the community level. We aggregate the demographic data—birth probabilities, age distributions, and educational attainment—to the district level from an average of four enumeration areas per district, each composed of roughly 30 households. Government program inputs and wage data are also measured at the district level.

The dependent variable is the community-level quarterly birth hazard. It is calculated as the proportion of women aged 15–49 who gave birth in an enumeration area over a three-month period. Quarterly birth hazards were measured nine months early, at the approximate date of conception, to facilitate the match between births and the factors influencing conceptions. Although observations on births, contraception, and marriage provide 34 quarterly intervals starting from the first quarter in 1986 through the second quarter in 1994, fewer observations can be used for the analyses; the first three quarterly birth hazards do not match up with measured influencing factors. This leaves us with 31 quarterly intervals, starting with births resulting from conceptions occurring in the third quarter in 1986 through the third quarter in 1993.

We selected exogenous variables on the basis of the standard model of demand and supply of births as depicted in Figure 2. Because we use a fixed-effects estimator, only time-varying variables are included. These are the age distribution, to account for changes in fecundity associated with aging; women's economic opportunities, reflected by their educational attainment and mean real wages; household economic resources and the value of time captured by male and female real wages; and measures of family planning programmatic inputs.

We aggregated the individual age and education data from the DHS to district proportions. From Table 2 we can see that there were roughly 10 percent increases in the proportion of women aged 25–34, and comparable declines in the proportion aged 40–49. The remaining changes were all much smaller. The changes in educational attainment of women aged 15–49 reflect marked shifts in primary school enrollment over the past several decades. As new cohorts enter our analysis and old cohorts leave, we see substantial shifts in educational attainment. As can be seen in Table 2, the proportion of women with no schooling declines by 20 percent over the period, and the proportion with completed primary education increases similarly.

Mean levels of log male and female wages are also reported in Table 2. Female real hourly wages increased by 17 percent over the analysis period; similarly, male wages increased by 19 percent. The wage growth was not uniform throughout Indonesia. Due to regional differences in economic growth, caused by localized effects of oil shocks, regional growth of industries, and other export growth, important differences exist in the rates of wage growth across the major regions of Indonesia.

TABLE 2 Descriptive statistics used in the analysis, by fiscal year: Indonesia, 1985/86 to 1993/94

Statistic	85/86	86/87	87/88	88/89	89/90	90/91	91/92	92/93	93/94	Total mean	Std. dev.
Quarterly birth hazard[1]	0.094	0.114	0.11	0.166	0.106	0.076	0.078	0.095	0.076	0.101	0.519
Contraceptive prevalence[2]	0.365	0.380	0.405	0.428	0.443	0.464	0.48	0.496	0.516	0.453	0.928
Predicted eligible couples (ECs)[3]	156209	158184	161208	164291	166669	169985	173157	176624	179893	168832	737927
Contraceptive subsidy per EC (Rp)	431.02	634.69	816.86	796.64	510.52	527.79	512.46	537.01	516.72	630.35	1870.63
Village distribution centers per 10,000 ECs	0.332	0.345	0.355	0.380	0.380	0.409	0.435	0.452	0.477	0.401	0.333
Clinics per 10,000 ECs	2.889	3.035	3.266	3.506	3.714	3.909	3.687	3.390	3.162	3.331	2.690
Proportion of women by level of education[4]											
No schooling	0.187	0.182	0.174	0.165	0.157	0.151	0.144	0.137	0.132	0.155	0.836
Some primary school	0.327	0.322	0.315	0.306	0.298	0.292	0.284	0.275	0.269	0.295	0.721
Primary school completed	0.236	0.240	0.244	0.250	0.256	0.259	0.265	0.270	0.272	0.257	0.669
Some secondary school	0.106	0.110	0.118	0.128	0.133	0.144	0.143	0.151	0.166	0.137	0.470
Secondary school completed	0.144	0.147	0.149	0.151	0.155	0.154	0.163	0.167	0.160	0.156	0.843
Proportion of women by age group[4]											
15–19	0.235	0.228	0.229	0.23	0.222	0.217	0.211	0.208	0.206	0.219	0.269
20–24	0.223	0.217	0.209	0.201	0.199	0.19	0.184	0.184	0.18	0.195	0.258
25–29	0.184	0.180	0.179	0.183	0.185	0.183	0.185	0.178	0.171	0.181	0.258
30–34	0.150	0.153	0.150	0.148	0.153	0.153	0.156	0.159	0.157	0.154	0.230
35–39	0.108	0.107	0.111	0.114	0.118	0.121	0.125	0.127	0.127	0.119	0.203
40–44	0.100	0.112	0.100	0.089	0.093	0.090	0.09	0.093	0.095	0.094	0.208
45–49	0	0.003	0.022	0.035	0.03	0.046	0.049	0.051	0.064	0.038	0.189
Predicted log hourly wage (1986 Rp)											
Males	6.39	6.38	6.37	6.36	6.40	6.46	6.49	6.50	6.56	6.44	1.37
Females	5.94	5.94	5.91	5.91	5.95	5.99	6.04	6.06	6.11	5.99	2.07

NOTES: N = 10,296.   Rp = rupiah. In 1991, Rp 1,000 = approximately US$0.50.
[1] Quarterly birth hazard is defined as the number of births in three months divided by the number of all women aged 15 to 49.
[2] Contraceptive prevalence is the proportion of currently married women aged 15–49 using any contraceptive method.
[3] Number of eligible couples, based on Indonesian Central Bureau of Statistics population projections.
[4] Proportions of DHS respondents in each education and age group.
SOURCES: See data section.

The family planning program inputs are captured in quarterly district-level procurement expenditures per eligible couple (materials only), clinics per eligible couple in the district, and village distribution centers per eligible couple in the district. We treat all three of these variables as endogenous and use the set of instruments described in the previous section to control for their endogeneity.

The regression results are reported in Table 3. The specifications are all linear probability models so that coefficients are interrelated directly as effects on the birth hazard. We estimated the model using several procedures. The first column reports the results using OLS; the second, using district fixed effects and time fixed effects; and the third, using instrumental variables and district and time fixed effects (IVFE). In the IVFE model the three first-stage regressions for contraceptive subsidies, clinics, and village distribution centers demonstrate that the instruments have sufficient power for identification. Most of the identifying variables are significant in each of the regressions. The F-statistics are 73.32, 68.46, and 20.19, respectively. The R-squares are 0.38, 0.37, and 0.14, respectively.[1]

The results on the non–family planning variables are consistent with expectations. More-educated women have fewer births. The birth hazard first rises with age and then falls. Female wages are weakly and negatively correlated, whereas male wages are weakly and positively correlated, with fertility.

The first three rows of Table 3 report the estimated coefficients on the family planning program variables: contraceptive subsidies, village distribution centers, and clinics. Only the IVFE model has consistently negative signs on all three coefficients. Although the individual coefficients are not significantly different from zero, together they are strongly significant. The F-statistic for the joint significance of the three coefficients is 12.31. Moreover, in specifications not reported here, any two of these three variables are both significantly negative. This suggests the existence of substantial collinearity among the three policy variables, and we do not have large enough sample sizes to differentiate between them. Thus our results suggest that the three family planning program inputs, working together, significantly reduced fertility; but from this evidence alone we cannot evaluate their relative importance.

Using the IVFE estimation method moves the point estimates in the "right" direction. The coefficient on contraceptive subsidies is positive and significantly different from zero in the OLS and fixed-effects models, the fixed-effects model lowers the magnitude of the coefficient by two-thirds, and the IVFE model makes the coefficient negative, albeit not significantly different from zero. The coefficient on the village distribution centers is negative in the OLS model, but triples in size in the IVFE model, suggesting that these significant OLS and fixed-effects estimates could actually underestimate the true effects. The coefficient on clinics is positive and sig-

TABLE 3   Three fertility models: Indonesia, 1985/86 to 1993/94 (Dependent variable = quarterly birth hazards; t-ratios in parentheses)

Independent variable	OLS	Fixed effects	IVFE
Contraceptive subsidies per eligible couple (Rp 000s)	.028 (7.17)	.010 (1.64)	−.005 (0.20)
Village distribution centers per 1,000 eligible couples	−.002 (4.69)	−.001 (0.48)	−.006 (1.37)
Clinics per 1,000 eligible couples	.009 (1.93)	−.001 (0.48)	−.042 (1.16)
Proportion of women by level of education			
No schooling	—	—	—
Some primary school	.008 (0.57)	−.043 (1.28)	−.052 (1.54)
Primary school completed	−.057 (4.64)	.002 (0.05)	.004 (0.12)
Some secondary school	−.030 (1.63)	−.040 (1.02)	−.044 (1.00)
Secondary school completed	−.065 (4.49)	−.104 (3.18)	−.095 (2.84)
Proportion of women by age group			
15–19	—	—	—
20–24	.037 (1.15)	.082 (2.13)	.087 (2.25)
25–29	.036 (1.18)	.032 (0.76)	.029 (0.67)
30–34	−.011 (0.34)	.085 (2.08)	.081 (1.92)
35–39	−.189 (5.16)	−.004 (0.08)	.001 (0.01)
40–44	−.258 (7.32)	−.150 (2.97)	−.147 (2.88)
45–49	−.299 (7.10)	−.227 (3.22)	−.243 (3.39)
Log hourly wage (Rp)			
Male	−.002 (0.31)	.009 (0.98)	.0009 (0.95)
Female	.005 (1.01)	−.006 (0.90)	−.004 (0.71)
Time fixed effects	No	Yes	Yes
District fixed effects	No	Yes	Yes
R-squared	0.06	0.23	

NOTE: Rows containing dashes indicate the reference group.
IVFE = instrumental variables and district and time fixed effects.
Rp = rupiah.
For explanation of models see text.

nificant in the OLS model, essentially zero in the fixed-effects model, and negative but not significantly so in the IVFE model.

The other coefficient estimates are consistent with our expectations. As the age distribution of women grows older, fertility falls and more education is associated with lower fertility. These factors explain much of the fertility decline in Indonesia, where the population is aging and younger cohorts are better educated. These results are consistent with those from our earlier work (Gertler and Molyneaux 1994).

The IVFE fertility model allows the intuitively appealing interpretation that family planning programs matter—the program variables are all negative and jointly significant—but we are concerned that the individual program effects are too imprecisely measured to be of much use. In particular, since roughly 50 percent of the BKKBN's budget is typically allocated to procuring and distributing contraceptives, we would like to be able to estimate how the allocations affect fertility, and how these effects compare with the effects of the other inputs. But the requisite precision is simply lacking. The critical question is whether the coefficients on the policy variables are really zero or are very small but imprecisely measured.

To answer this question we turn to the proximate-determinants model to draw inferences about fertility effects from program effects on contraceptive prevalence. Although the programs affect the other proximate determinants as well, contraception remains the principal factor determining Indonesian fertility. Therefore we examine the effect of these program inputs on contraceptive use, using the same statistical methods. Since there is a higher signal-to-noise ratio in contraceptive use than in fertility, we get more power with the same sample sizes and are able to say much more about the absolute and relative magnitudes of program effects.[2]

The results of the contraceptive-use models are presented in Table 4. As with the fertility models, the OLS and fixed-effects regressions produce results inconsistent with our expectations. However, the coefficient on contraceptive subsidies, which is negative in the OLS and fixed-effects regressions, becomes positive and significant in the IVFE model. The coefficient's point estimate (0.045) implies that the reduction of total contraceptive subsidies by their mean annual level would reduce contraceptive prevalence by 5.6 percent. To infer a potential effect on fertility, we assume that the fertility of contraceptors is zero, and that the fecundity of noncontraceptors is unchanged; that is, it is not influenced by the changes in contraceptive use. Under these conservative (though generally untested) assumptions, the implied effect on fertility is about 6 percent.[3]

This effect is larger but close to the point estimate from the fertility models. The fertility models imply that contraceptive subsidies reduce fertility by about 3 percent. The 95 percent confidence region for the estimate from the contraceptive-use model includes 3 percent. This implies that the

TABLE 4 Contraceptive-use models: Indonesia, 1985/86 to 1993/94
(Dependent variable = district contraceptive prevalence per quarter)

Independent variable	OLS	Fixed effects	IVFE
Contraceptive subsidies per eligible couple (Rp 000s)	−.100 (18.79)	−.017 (4.41)	.045 (2.56)
Village distribution centers per 1,000 eligible couples	.006 (8.46)	.002 (2.35)	.002 (0.71)
Clinics per 1,000 eligible couples	−.045 (7.30)	−.003 (0.29)	.099 (4.05)
Proportion of women by level of education			
No schooling	—	—	—
Some primary school	.217 (10.88)	.070 (3.22)	.086 (3.74)
Primary school completed	.443 (26.71)	.135 (6.68)	.147 (6.86)
Some secondary school	.417 (16.91)	.261 (9.91)	.277 (10.07)
Secondary school completed	.336 (18.75)	.309 (12.42)	.297 (13.18)
Proportion of women by age group			
15–19	—	—	—
20–24	.268 (6.19)	−.115 (4.53)	−.121 (4.60)
25–29	.232 (5.55)	.055 (2.00)	.082 (2.81)
30–34	.617 (14.57)	.215 (7.93)	.232 (8.12)
35–39	.803 (16.21)	.039 (1.17)	.047 (1.37)
40–44	.538 (11.03)	.026 (0.80)	.014 (0.40)
45–49	.601 (10.75)	−.130 (2.81)	−.107 (2.22)
Log hourly wage (Rp)			
Male	−.085 (9.47)	.002 (0.34)	−.002 (0.39)
Female	−.039 (5.78)	.023 (5.74)	.022 (5.09)
Time fixed effects	No	Yes	Yes
District fixed effects	No	Yes	Yes
R-squared	.32	.35	

NOTE: Rows containing dashes indicate the reference group.
IVFE = instrumental variables and district and time fixed effects.
Rp = rupiah.

estimated effect of contraceptive subsidies on fertility, based on the contraceptive-use model, is not significantly different from the point estimate implied by the fertility model. In fact, it suggests that contraceptive subsidies have a small but significantly negative effect on fertility.

Whereas the estimated effect of clinics on contraceptive use is negative and significant in the OLS and fixed-effects models, it is positive and significant in the IVFE model. The order of magnitude suggests that going from zero to mean clinic availability increases contraceptive use by about 21 percent and under conservative assumptions reduces fertility by about 21 percent. This is about half the point estimate of the impact of clinics estimated from the fertility model. However, the 95 percent confidence region for the estimated impact based on the contraceptive-use model includes the point estimate (42 percent) derived from the fertility model. These results suggest that the availability of family planning clinics has a significant effect on reducing fertility.

The estimated impact of village distribution centers on contraceptive use is small and not significantly different from zero in the IVFE model. This finding suggests that the centers did not contribute much to fertility reduction in Indonesia over the study period.

The estimated coefficients of the other variables in the contraceptive-use model are consistent with expectations and with the estimates from the fertility models. Both population aging and expanded educational attainment of women are associated with increased contraceptive use.

Policy implications

The analyses suggest that the effects of government contraceptive procurements on contraceptive use and, by extension, on fertility are only moderate. Given that contraceptive procurements represent Indonesia's single largest family planning expenditure, these results are especially relevant for Indonesian policymakers, since there are probably other, more productive uses for these government resources. Alternative uses include activities to promote greater contraceptive demand and expanding secondary education for women. Indeed, our results suggest that the schooling effects on contraceptive use are much larger than the family planning program effects.

Although contraceptive subsidies might be more effective in a different setting, it may be instructive for policymakers outside Indonesia to understand why the BKKBN's budgets for contraceptive procurement have remained consistently high, despite their minor impact. The BKKBN's rationale for continued subsidies has been to ensure that the poor have access to affordable contraceptives. DHS data from 1991 through 1997, however, indicate that the effectiveness of targeting subsidized contraceptives to poor households has actually diminished in recent years, particularly

FIGURE 3 Contraceptive costs and prevalence trends by contraceptive methods: All eligible couples, and the poorest 40 percent

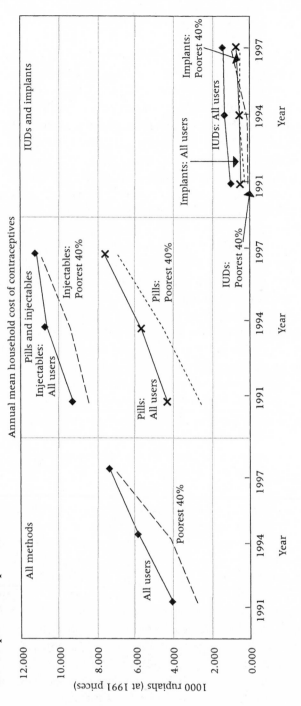

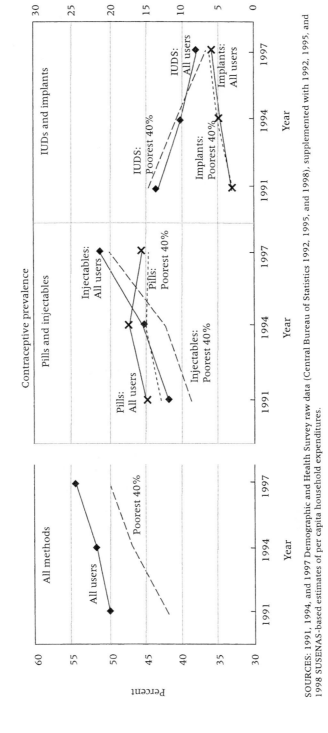

SOURCES: 1991, 1994, and 1997 Demographic and Health Survey raw data (Central Bureau of Statistics 1992, 1995, and 1998), supplemented with 1992, 1995, and 1998 SUSENAS-based estimates of per capita household expenditures.

after the period of this analysis. The upper panel of Figure 3 displays the costs of contraceptive methods (and related services) to households prior to the 1991, 1994, and 1997 DHS; the lower panel shows corresponding prevalence rates by method. Overall, contraceptive costs increased by more than 80 percent over the period; but for the poorest 40 percent of the population, costs increased by nearly 160 percent. This more rapid growth of costs faced by the poor suggests that the effectiveness of contraceptive subsidies in the more recent years is probably even lower than that measured here.

The silver lining for the BKKBN is that despite the more rapid increase in contraceptive costs for the poor, contraceptive prevalence among poor households has continued to converge with that of the nonpoor. This finding suggests that the growth in household demand for contraceptives, particularly among the poor, has more than compensated for the increased costs they face. Perhaps the BKKBN's efforts to promote demand (unmeasured in these analyses) have had their desired effects, or perhaps the broader effects of development have more than compensated for the increased costs. Whatever the cause of the growing prevalence, it is clear that contraceptive subsidies are not a major factor, even though they continue to be the BKKBN's major expenditure.

What are the implications for family planning programs in other countries? We caution against asserting that contraceptive subsidies do not matter elsewhere. In Indonesia in 1996 the annual unsubsidized cost of an injectable contraceptive was about Rp 18,300 (approximately US$8). In the same year, annual household expenditures for a family of four living at the rural poverty line were Rp 1,315,000. Thus even the most expensive privately provided contraceptive method costs less than 1.5 percent of a poor household's total budget. Privately provided pills cost about the same, and privately provided intrauterine devices cost about one-third of that. By contrast, Bulatao (1998) reports that in many African countries, household costs for contraceptive pills constitute 5 percent of *average* household expenditures. For six of those countries they constitute 20 percent. Because of these differences, we do not extrapolate our results to countries where contraceptive costs represent a much higher portion of household expenditures.

Conclusions

In investigating the effects of Indonesia's public family planning programs on fertility while controlling for economic growth and improvements in the status of women, we have overcome one of the major stumbling blocks to such investigations: the fact that family planning programs are not randomly placed. We did so by explicitly modeling the way in which the government allocates family planning resources. We found that the government targets resources to areas of low contraceptive use and dynamically updates those allocations on the basis of program performance. This process implies that the usual method of controlling for the nonrandom placement of programs, a fixed-effects model, produces inconsistent estimates of the effects of family planning programs on fertility. Nevertheless, the model suggested a feasible instrumental-variables procedure for obtaining consistent estimates. Because provincial governments have to allocate resources among districts within an overall budget constraint, an increase in the allocation to one district reduces the amount that can be allocated to other districts. Therefore, variables that shift contraceptive demand in competing districts are valid instruments.

The study has confirmed that both OLS and fixed-effects estimates give biased and misleading results. Only the models using exogenous instruments provided results consistent with theory. The results suggest that contraceptive subsidies in Indonesia lower fertility by about 3 to 6 percent, whereas expanding the distribution network by one standard deviation lowers fertility by about 12 percent. These results have two policy implications. On the one hand, although contraceptive subsidies appear to reduce fertility, the magnitude of the effect is quite small. This calls into question Indonesia's decision to allocate half of its family planning budget to contraceptive subsidies. On the other hand, the expansion of the distribution network in rural areas has had a significant effect on fertility.

Notes

The order of authorship is arbitrary because both of us contributed to this study equally. We are indebted to the Indonesian Central Bureau of Statistics and the BKKBN for making community and program data available, and we gratefully acknowledge financial support from research grants funded by the National Institute of Child Health and Human Development and the Futures Group Policy Project.

1 F-statistics close to 1.0 are a cause for concern that instrumental-variable coefficients are subject to a finite sample bias, even with arbitrarily large sample sizes (Bound, Jaeger, and Baker 1995). But F-statistics as large as these indicate that this is not a problem for our analysis.

2 The "noise" in the birth-hazard equations is due partly to sampling error, but mostly to nonsampling error, particularly to temporal shocks. Based on DHS estimates of sampling errors in the total fertility rate (2 percent of the three-year rate), the sampling standard error is about 7 percent of the quarterly birth hazard (Central Bureau of Statistics 1998.) But as can be seen in Figure 1, the magnitude of annual temporal shocks can be far larger. By contrast, contraceptive prevalence rates appear as almost a straight line in the same figure.

3 In an earlier study (Gertler and Molyneaux 1994) we measured significant program effects on the fertility of unprotected women. Those effects suggested that factors associated with increased contraceptive use also increased the fecundity of noncontracepting women, but not by much.

References

Adioetomo, Sri Moertiningsih, Ayke S. Kitting, and Salman Taufik. 1990. "Fertility transition in Indonesia," in *Population Studies in Sri Lanka and Indonesia Based on the 1987 Sri Lanka Demographic and Health Survey and the 1987 National Indonesia Contraceptive Prevalence Survey*. Demographic and Health Surveys Further Analysis Series, No. 2. New York: Population Council, pp. 43–75.

Ananta, A. et al. 1990. "The dynamics of Indonesian labor markets, 1980–1987," unpublished paper, Demographic Institute, Faculty of Economics, University of Indonesia. Jakarta.

Angeles, G., D. Guilkey, and T. Mroz. 1998. "Targeted program placement and the estimation of the impact of family planning programs on fertility in Peru," paper presented at the Annual Meeting of the Population Association of America, Chicago, IL, March.

BKKBN [Badan Koordinasi Keluarga Berencana Nasional]. 1984. *Our Commitment to the Future*. Jakarta.

Bongaarts, John and Robert G. Potter. 1983. *Fertility, Biology, and Behavior*. New York: Academic Press.

Bound, J., D. Jaeger, and R. Baker. 1995. "Problems with instrumental variables estimation when the correlation between the instruments and the endogenous explanatory variable is weak," *Journal of the American Statistical Association* 90(430): 443–450.

Bulatao, Rodolfo A. 1998. *The Value of Family Planning Programs in Developing Countries*. Santa Monica, CA: The RAND Corporation.

Bulatao, Rodolfo A. and Ronald D. Lee (eds.). 1983. *The Determinants of Fertility in Developing Countries*, 2 vols. New York: Academic Press.

Central Bureau of Statistics. 1989. *1987 National Indonesian Contraceptive Prevalence Survey, Final Report*. Jakarta: Biro Pusat Statistik; Columbia, MD: DHS—Westinghouse-IRD.

———. 1992. *Indonesia Demographic and Health Survey, 1991: Country Report*. Jakarta: Biro Pusat Statistik; Columbia, MD: DHS—IRD/Macro.

———. 1994. *Metode Penyempurnaan Perhitungan Kemiskinan* [Improved methods for calculating poverty]. Jakarta: Biro Pusat Statistik.

———. 1995. *Indonesia Demographic and Health Survey, 1994: Country Report*. Jakarta: Biro Pusat Statistik; Columbia, MD: DHS—IRD/Macro.

———. 1998. *Indonesia Demographic and Health Survey, 1997: Country Report*. Jakarta: Biro Pusat Statistik; Columbia, MD: DHS—IRD/Macro.

Demeny, Paul. 1979. "On the end of the population explosion," *Population and Development Review* 5(1): 141–162.

Freedman, Ronald and Bernard Berelson. 1976. "The record of family planning programs," *Studies in Family Planning*, 7(1): 1–40.

Gertler, Paul J. and John W. Molyneaux. 1994. "How family planning and economic development combined to reduce Indonesian fertility," *Demography* 31(1): 33–63.

Hermalin, A. I. 1975. "Overview," in *Measuring the Effect of Family Planning Programs on Fertility*, eds. C. Chandrasekaran and A. I. Hermalin. Dolhain, Belgium: Ordina, pp. 505–554.

———. 1983. "Fertility regulation and its costs: A critical essay," in *Determinants of Fertility in Developing Countries*, Vol. II, eds. Rodolfo A. Bulatao and Ronald D. Lee. New York: Academic Press, pp. 1–53.

Hull, Terence and Sri Hartati Hatmadji. 1990. "Regional fertility differentials in Indonesia: Causes and trends." Canberra: Australian National University, Research School of Social Sciences, Division of Demography and Sociology, Working Papers in Demography No. 22.

Hull, Terence and Valerie Hull. 1987. "Changing marriage behavior in Java: The role of timing of consummation," *Southeast Asian Journal of Social Science* 15(1): 104–119.

Lembaga Demografi. 1988. *Policy Study of Human Resources in Relation to Development: The Indonesian Case*. Jakarta: Demographic Institute, Faculty of Economics, University of Indonesia.

Lerman, C. et al. 1989. "The correlation between family planning program inputs and contraceptive use in Indonesia," *Studies in Family Planning* 20(1): 26–37.

Mauldin, W. Parker and Bernard Berelson. 1978. "Conditions of fertility decline in developing countries, 1965–1975," *Studies in Family Planning* 9(5): 90–147.

Molyneaux, John W. et al. 1990. "The duration of contraceptive use," in *Secondary Analysis of the 1987 National Indonesia Contraceptive Prevalence Survey:* Vol. 1, *Fertility and Family Planning,* eds. Andrew Kantner and James A. Palmore. Jakarta: Badan Koordinasi Keluarga Berencana Nasional [BKKBN]; Honolulu: East-West Center.

Montgomery, Mark R. and John B. Casterline. 1993. "The diffusion of fertility control in Taiwan: Estimates from pooled cross-section, time-series models," *Population Studies* 47(3): 457–479.

Pitt, Mark M., Mark R. Rosenzweig, and Donna M. Gibbons. 1993. "The determinants and consequences of the placement of government programs in Indonesia," *World Bank Economic Review* 7(3): 319–348.

Rosenzweig, Mark R. and Kenneth I. Wolpin. 1986. "Evaluating the effects of optimally distributed public programs: Child health and family planning interventions," *American Economic Review* 76(3): 470–482.

Schultz, T. Paul. 1973. "Explanation of birth rate changes over space and time: A study of Taiwan," *Journal of Political Economy* 81(2), Part II: S238–S274.

———. 1992. "Assessing family planning cost-effectiveness: Applicability of individual demand-programme supply framework," in *Family Planning Programmes and Fertility,* eds. James F. Phillips and John A. Ross. Oxford: Clarendon Press, pp. 78–105.

Snodgrass, D. 1979. "The family planning program as a model of administrative improvement in Indonesia," Development Discussion Paper No. 58, Institute for International Development, Harvard University, Cambridge, MA.

Tsui, Amy Ong and Donald Bogue. 1978. "Declining world fertility: Trends, causes, and implications," *Population Bulletin* 33(4): 2–56.

Warwick, D. P. 1986. "The Indonesian family planning program: Government influence and client choice," *Population and Development Review* 12(3): 453–490.

Westoff, Charles F., Lorenzo Moreno, and Noreen Goldman. 1989. "The demographic impact of changes in contraceptive practice in Third World populations," *Population and Development Review,* 15(1): 91–106.

Wirakartakusumah, M. Djuhari. 1988. "The impacts of health, education, family planning and electrification programs on fertility, mortality and child schooling in East Java, Indonesia," *Majalah Demografi Indonesia* 15(29): 37–73.

World Bank. 1989. *Indonesia: The Incidence of Poverty.* Washington, DC.

———. 1990. *Indonesia: Family Planning Perspectives in the 90's.* Washington, DC.

PART TWO

INSTITUTIONAL ARRANGEMENTS AND THE ELDERLY

Aging, Wellbeing, and Social Security in Rural Northern China

DWAYNE BENJAMIN
LOREN BRANDT
SCOTT ROZELLE

STEEP DECLINES IN fertility, combined with longer life expectancy, will increase the share of the elderly in the Chinese population. This aging population, with its corresponding increase in the ratio of elderly pension beneficiaries to young contributors, recently has received considerable attention. (For comprehensive discussions of these and related issues, see World Bank 1994 and 1997.) Most of the attention focuses on the present and future pension liabilities of state enterprises and the need for a more modern, financially viable public pension system for workers. Striking by its absence from the discussion, however, is the recognition that the majority of elderly Chinese not covered by formal pensions live in rural areas.[1] The inattention is rationalized on two grounds. First, family values remain strong in rural areas, and Confucian "filial piety" sustains the traditional institution of family care for the elderly. Although it may erode over time, there is already a well-functioning, deeply rooted informal old-age security system in rural areas. Second, any formal public policy response to the needs of the rural elderly may undermine the existing private arrangements. For example, state transfers to the elderly may crowd out existing transfers from younger family members. As the argument goes, it is better to leave well enough alone and focus on the urban elderly and their public pensions.

There is no empirical foundation for this view. Instead, the perceived relative strength of rural social security is based on historical impressions of filial piety and the codification of family responsibility for the elderly in existing laws (see, e.g., World Bank 1994; Fang, Wang, and Song 1992). The Marriage Law of 1950 emphasizes the duty of adult children to care for their elderly parents, and the Constitution of 1954 states that "parents have the duty to rear and educate their minor children, and the children who have come of age have the duty to support and assist their parents." More recently, the Penal Code of 1980 has established that children can be imprisoned for neglecting their parents. We can view these laws either as a reflection of the values and practices of rural society or as a response to unfulfilled social expectations.

Historically, the primary mechanism by which the young cared for the old was through shared living arrangements. Parents would live with their sons, retaining control over family assets until the father's death. Assets would then be divided among the sons, who were expected to care for their mother. But how relevant is this institution now?

The collectivization of agriculture in the early 1950s exerted an equivocal influence on family structure.[2] On the one hand, as suggested by the laws passed in the 1950s, the family institution was enshrined as the principal source of old-age security. As Goode (1963) argues, family law evolved under collectivization much as it had over the previous half-century. Furthermore, restrictions on migration and housing shortages in urban areas tended to keep families together in the same villages. On the other hand, collectivization also undermined the traditional role of the family (Selden 1993). Asset accumulation, notably of land, was curtailed, significantly reducing the bargaining power of the elderly (Davis-Friedmann 1991; Whyte 1995; Yan 1997). Moreover, the village (collective) took more responsibility for transfers to needy households, including the neglected elderly, replacing the role of the family to some degree. Davis-Friedmann (1991) argues that, on balance, the elderly probably came out ahead under collectivization, despite their weakened power within their families.

These authors are less confident of the position of the elderly since the introduction of economic reforms in the late 1970s. Some researchers suggest that the traditional family structure might restore itself in the face of increased commercialization and a diminished role of the collective. Most, however, argue that it will be further weakened (see Whyte 1992), for the following reasons. First, economic growth is usually accompanied by movement toward conjugal, in place of kinship-oriented, families (Goode 1963). With the higher incomes and lower housing prices that accompany economic reform, it is more feasible for the young and old to live separately. Second, restrictions on land ownership constrain individuals from accumulating assets for their old age. Third, village support for the elderly has been reduced to the allocation of land, which may be of little value to an elderly household with few children, a limited ability to work, and imperfectly developed factor markets. If family ties are indeed weakening, then existing transfer mechanisms may be ill-suited to supporting the elderly. Finally, attitudes of the young toward the old may be changing as the economy becomes more oriented toward satisfaction of individual needs. Yan (1997) argues that the increase in the conjugal focus of families serves to divert attention from the care of parents.

Of course, changes in living arrangements need not signal an end to family responsibility for the elderly. Intergenerational transfers can occur across as well as within households. In-kind transfers of goods and labor, remittances, and child-care services can flow across generations. The question is whether these mechanisms fully substitute for the traditional within-household transfers. Davis-Friedmann (1991) expresses concern that weakened family ties, in a situation of market-oriented growth and a decline in government-provided social services, will isolate the elderly. Selden (1993: 147) echoes this concern, noting that "it is difficult to escape the conclusion that in rural China as elsewhere the transition to the nuclear family imposes a heavy price on the rural elderly."

Our objective is to provide an overview of the factual background to these issues. We begin with the current living arrangements of the elderly, since these arrangements underlie many current assumptions about elder care in the countryside. To do so, we draw on a household survey conducted in northern China in 1995. To provide a context for our results, we make two types of comparisons. First, using a historical survey of the same region in the mid-1930s, we compare the present with the past, when extended households are believed to have been a more common form of living arrangement. Second, using data for 1989 obtained from the China Health and Nutrition Survey of 1990, we compare urban and rural households. We then examine the economic circumstances of the elderly, beginning with their ability to work. We consider whether retirement is a meaningful concept in rural China. Most important, we look at the relative economic standing of the elderly as indicated by their income and consumption levels. To anticipate, our results strongly suggest that the current policy emphasis on the urban elderly is misplaced. By almost any criterion, the marginal social value of a yuan transferred to the elderly in rural areas exceeds that of one transferred to the elderly in urban areas. Furthermore, the current level of assets owned by the rural elderly suggests that their economic status may worsen with economic reform. In short, the concerns of Davis-Friedmann and Selden seem well founded.

The data

As just mentioned, we make use of three surveys. The first was conducted by Chinese colleagues and ourselves in 1995. The second, used for historical comparison, was conducted by Japanese investigators in 1936 and covers 1935. The third, containing 1989 data, is the China Health and Nutrition Survey (CHNS), carried out in 1990.

The 1995 survey covered 780 households in six counties and 30 villages in Hebei and Liaoning provinces (north-northeastern China). It provided detailed household-level information on income, expenditure, labor supply, and farm management. The six counties were chosen to correspond to the site of the intensive household-level study carried out by Japanese investigators in 1936. We selected five villages in each of the six counties, one of which had been fully enumerated in the 1930s. The other four villages in each county included one village located in the same township as the administrative capital of the county; another located in the same township as the village surveyed in the 1930s; and two villages drawn from a third township. Altogether, 130 households were surveyed in each county—50 from the village surveyed in the 1930s, and 20 from each of the remaining four villages. Households were chosen by random sampling using the most recent village registry.

The 1936 Japanese survey gathered household data from some of the same villages as those we surveyed in 1995. A detailed description of these data, including a comparison with John Lossing Buck's widely cited survey (Buck 1937), is contained in Benjamin and Brandt (1995). The Japanese survey included 1,095 households in 22 villages of the provinces of Liaoning, Jilin, and Heilongjiang.

Our urban and rural comparisons are made with 1989 data from the CHNS of 1990. A description of these data (as well as the data themselves) can be obtained at the CHNS web site.[3] The CHNS covers eight provinces—Liaoning, Shandong, Jiangsu, Henan, Hubei, Hunan, Guangxi, and Guizhou—only two of which, Liaoning and Shandong, can reasonably be considered as being in northern China. However, to maximize sample size, we use all provinces in this study. We have replicated our results using the northern Chinese provinces only, obtaining virtually identical results.

Living arrangements

Our primary question is whether extended families remain an important means by which the young, primarily the adult sons, care for their elderly parents. One sign of the possible erosion of transfers to the elderly would be a decline in the percentage of the elderly living with adult children.

We begin with a brief description of the age structure of the population. It had significantly fewer children aged 0–10 in 1995 than in 1935 (16.0 percent versus 28.2 percent), more adults in the prime ages of 20–50 (51.5 percent versus 39.3 percent), and slightly more elderly aged 61 and older (8.7 percent versus 6.7 percent). Although the fraction of elderly in 1935 was smaller, the dependency ratio was actually greater because there were proportionately many more children. Moreover, from contemporary data (the CHNS) we find more children living in rural than in urban areas

(20.1 percent versus 14.7 percent), but many more elderly as a share in urban areas: 12.3 percent versus 6.6 percent in rural areas. The basic pattern is also seen in the 1995 census, which recorded 10.6 percent of the urban population as over age 60, as compared with only 5.0 percent of the rural population (State Statistical Bureau 1996). The fraction of the population in the prime ages is approximately the same. This suggests a higher elder dependency ratio in urban areas, but fewer children to support. Seventy percent of elderly Chinese still live in the rural sector.

Using household registries for nineteenth-century Liaoning, Lee and Campbell (1997) provide a useful historical baseline on household structure and living. They use the classification system for household types developed by the Cambridge Group for the History of Population and Social Structure. The key defining feature in the system is the number of conjugal pairs (married couples) in the household. Households are divided into four basic types: fragmentary (no conjugal unit), simple (one conjugal unit), extended (one pair with other co-resident adult kin), and multiple (two or more conjugal units). Lee and Campbell's data show that a majority of individuals lived in multiple-family units. Almost half (47.2 percent) of all households were multiple, and three-quarters of individuals lived in such households.[4] A further 15 percent of households were extended and accounted for 10 percent of the population. The remaining 15 percent of individuals lived in simple or fragmentary households. As for the elderly themselves, a majority (75 percent) lived in extended or multiple households, whereas only 25 percent lived on their own.

The 1995 and 1935 data allow estimates of household size, household type, and living arrangements for the elderly that can be compared directly with the findings of Lee and Campbell. Average household size in rural Hebei and Liaoning in 1995 was only 3.7 persons. By comparison, it was 6.3 in the 1930s, a figure similar to that (6.0) implied by Lee and Campbell's data for the 1800s in Liaoning. However, a decline in household size alone may not tell us much about living arrangements, since fertility also fell sharply over that time period.

Figure 1 compares the percentages of households by type in 1935 and 1995. The 1935 data lack information on the types of relationship between household members. Using the information on the age and sex distribution of members, however, we estimate the number of conjugal pairs in the household, and thus household type. We report two sets of figures for 1995. The first is our "best" estimate of household type, based on extensive information on the relationship of household members to the household head. In the second set (D), we degrade the 1995 data set by ignoring information unavailable in the 1935 survey. This allows us to compare the 1990s and 1930s on a common basis, with the same data restrictions. To minimize detail, we also pool extended and multiple households, distinguishing

FIGURE 1   Distribution of households by type and elderly individuals by household type: Northern China, 1935 and 1995

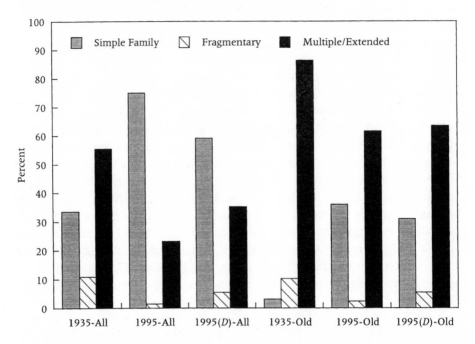

D = Degraded data set. See the text for explanation.

primarily between simple and more broadly defined "extended" households. We can still see whether the elderly are living with relatives other than a spouse.

Figure 1 shows that, by far, most households in 1995 were simple family households. Our "best" estimate identifies 73 percent of all households as simple, with the remainder evenly divided between extended and multiple, which combined represent slightly less than a quarter of all households. The estimates for the 1930s, in contrast, show that one-third of the households were simple, implying a radical shift in household structure. Unfortunately, these two snapshots do not allow us to pinpoint the timing of the decline of the multiple-family household and thus isolate the role of collectivization in shaping family structure. Selden (1993) and others argue that collectivization in the 1950s contributed to the demise of the extended and multiple household. Our own results do not preclude an earlier decline, preceding the establishment of the People's Republic of China and the reorganization of agriculture into collectives. (See Davis and Harrell 1993, Goode 1963, and Whyte 1995 for more discussion of this issue.)

Is the rapidly growing prominence of single-family households paralleled by an equally radical shift in living arrangements among the elderly? Actually not. Both our series for 1995 show that more than 60 percent of the elderly were living in extended or multiple households, while about 30 percent were living on their own (with a spouse). Compared with the rest of the population, the elderly are more likely to live in extended or multiple households. In the 1930s, by contrast, almost none of the elderly lived in simple households, and in comparison with 1995 an even higher share (86 percent) lived in extended or multiple households.

The Cambridge Group's classification is not the only possible way to summarize living arrangements, but it does capture the key features. An alternative would be to look directly at those with whom the elderly live. As it turns out, of the households containing an elderly member, 26 percent are composed of an elderly couple only, and such households comprise three-quarters of the simple-family category. The rest are almost evenly divided between an elderly person living with children but without a spouse (38 percent of elderly households and most of the extended-family category), and an elderly couple living with children (32 percent and most of the multiple-family category). Unfortunately, data limitations do not permit us to show a comparable breakdown for the other data sets.

Our definition of "household" is based on the survey definition, which requires that household members eat together. It may be that some elderly live next door to their children but are not officially part of the same household. In such cases we would understate the economic links between households that came from shared living arrangements. In fact, 77 percent of the elderly who do not live with their children have either a son or daughter living in the same village (75 percent have a son, 31 percent a daughter). The survey, however, was designed to measure interhousehold transfers and should capture these linkages, a point to which we shall return later.

Using the 1989 CHNS data, we find that household size is only slightly larger in rural than in urban areas (4.2 versus 3.8 persons). Part of this difference reflects the earlier and stricter enforcement, in urban areas, of state policy limiting the number of children per household. There is little difference between the urban and rural distributions of household types (Figure 2). In fact, urban areas actually have a slightly higher percentage of extended or multiple households. In both urban and rural areas, almost two-thirds of the elderly live in extended or multiple households, as in the 1995 data. This does not necessarily mean that traditional family values remain as strong in the cities as in the countryside. The price of housing is much higher in the cities, and shared living arrangements may simply reflect an economizing activity of families. As incomes increase, one may expect a rapid shift from shared living arrangements in the city. Neverthe-

FIGURE 2   Distribution of households by type and elderly individuals by household type: Urban versus rural area, northern China, 1989

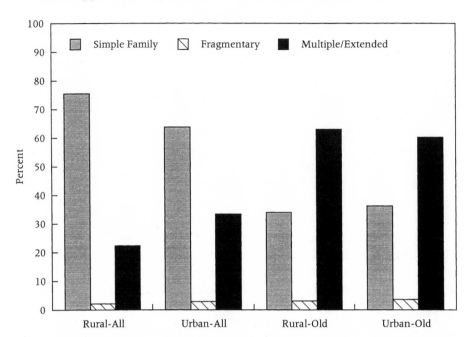

less, these data do not allow us to conclude that there is any observable difference in the living arrangements of the urban and rural elderly. Indeed, the similarity is impressive.

Work and the elderly

The economic welfare of the elderly depends on the resources they command, whether from their own earnings or from transfers from children or the state. Documenting the associations between age and work provides evidence of the elderly's capacity for independence.

We begin by looking at the work patterns of the elderly in 1995, in particular looking for evidence of "retirement." It is withdrawal (voluntary or involuntary) from earning activities that usually explains the loss of income in old age and necessitates some form of provision for the elderly. A simple measure of work activity is an indicator of whether an individual worked during the previous year. Figure 3 shows such a profile of labor force participation for both men and women by age group. The employment indicator refers to work on or off the farm, including family businesses. It excludes housework, however, which may be an important way in which the elderly, especially women, contribute to their families. A fur-

FIGURE 3 Proportion of men and women who worked during the previous year by age: Northern China, 1995

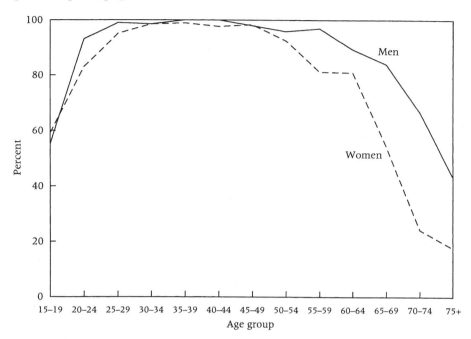

ther word of caution: Although we would like to interpret the differences between age groups as the pure effect of aging, they may be due in part to cohort effects, especially at younger ages. The young, especially girls, are growing up in a different economy from that experienced by their parents at comparable ages. Young women may be more likely to participate in the labor force than their mothers, in which case the age profile would appear to be flatter than it really is.

The most important point is the high labor force participation rate for men and women at all ages, a statistical reflection of the "ceaseless toil" described by Davis-Friedmann (1983: 18). To the extent that withdrawal from employment occurs at all, it begins earlier for women than for men, beginning with the 50–54 age group, versus the 60–64 age group for men. Even so, at ages 60–64 almost 80 percent of men and women are still working. There is no sense in which early retirement occurs in rural China, at least in the ways we think of it in industrialized countries. Women's participation drops off sharply by age 65, whereas men's declines more gradually. If they are still alive, most rural Chinese men can anticipate working into their 70s. A slightly sharper age profile emerges if we consider days worked per year (not shown), instead of the coarser measure of participation reported in Figure 3. If income is proportional to the number of days worked, we would expect that earned income begins to decline at age 45 for men and at age 35 for women.

In urban areas, employees of state enterprises are subject to mandatory retirement at age 55 for women and age 60 for men. By contrast, rural residents have farms from which they need not retire until they are physically incapable of working. Furthermore, most urban workers have state-provided pensions, which reduce the need to work.

Figure 4 shows employment-age profiles based on the 1989 CHNS data. The measure of employment in the CHNS is whether an individual is currently working. We might therefore expect the mean participation rates to be lower in the CHNS than in the 1995 data. The rural pattern for men resembles the 1995 figure, with the steepest age-related drop at ages 60–64 and a large fraction of men working into their 70s. The urban numbers for men reflect the mandatory retirement age at 60, but also show a large drop in participation for those aged 55–59. Urban men are less than half as likely as rural men to work beyond age 60, and urban employment rates are less than 20 percent for men over age 65.

The obviously interesting questions pertain to retirement decisions in the countryside and the city. Do urban men stop working because of mandatory retirement, or do more generous state pensions facilitate earlier retirement in urban areas? In rural areas the main transfer to elderly house-

FIGURE 4 Proportion of men and women currently working, urban versus rural areas: Northern China, 1989

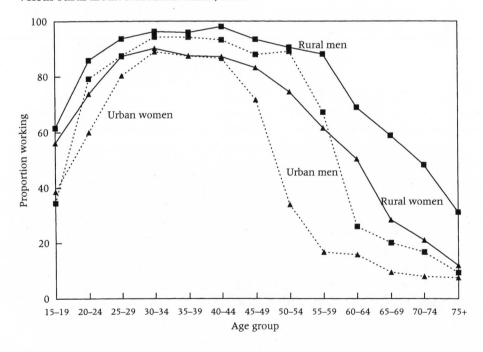

holds is land. Although land remains collectively owned in rural China, households are allocated use rights, usually on the basis of the size of the household or the farm labor force. Transferred land yields income only if it is worked. If land and labor markets are thin, the rural elderly may have a greater need to work than those in the city. Of course, the rural elderly may work more either because the returns to farming are higher than those to participation in state enterprises, or because they have a greater preference for work. Neither explanation seems likely.

As for women, the rural patterns in the CHNS are similar to those in the 1995 data, with gradual withdrawal from employment beginning at age 50. As with the men, the urban-rural comparison reflects the salience of mandatory retirement. Urban women's participation drops sharply beginning at age 50, by which time urban women are less than half as likely as rural women to work.

Have retirement patterns changed since the 1930s? Unfortunately, the data for the 1930s are available only at the household level, so that it is not possible to draw direct comparisons of individual behavior across data sets. We can conduct an indirect exercise, however, comparing aggregate household labor supply in the 1935 and 1995 samples, testing for changes in the correlation between household demographic structure and family labor supply. For example, we can compare the total labor supply of one household with another, one of which differs only by having an elderly male present. If household members do not adjust their labor supply to the presence of other members, then the estimated effect of adding an elderly male to the total household labor supply would be the amount of labor supply he provides. Of course, there are likely to be indirect effects as the labor supply of one household member substitutes or complements others. (See Benjamin and Brandt 1995 for a detailed discussion.)

Our measure of household labor supply is the number of men and women (separately) engaged in farming. The results are presented in Table 1, which shows the effect of adding members to the household. Column 1 suggests an age profile for men in the 1930s. The profile has the expected shape: a young boy adds the equivalent of 0.08 adult males to the farm labor force, a teen adds 0.34 men, a prime-age male adds 0.55, and a man aged 61 or older adds 0.30. The results for 1995 are shown in the next column, and columns 3 and 4 compare the profiles for females. (An asterisk or double asterisk in the 1995 columns indicates coefficients that are significantly different from those for the 1930s.) Overall, for males the 1995 coefficients are larger than those for 1935, except for teens. This could reflect differences in the measure of participation, though such differences should be absorbed by the constant (and 1935 dummy). Alternatively, it could reflect higher participation in agriculture in the 1990s, possibly due to the more even distribution of land. As we would expect, in 1995 younger men were less likely to be working on the farm, and were instead working off the farm or attending school. Nevertheless, we cannot reject the hypothesis that the coefficients in 1995 and 1935 are the same. This is consistent with (though it does not imply) the hypothesis that the relationship between age and participation in agriculture was the same in 1995 as in the 1930s.

TABLE 1   Regression estimates of the effect of the number of household members on male and female labor supply to the family farm: Northern China, 1935 and 1995

Type of labor	Males		Females	
	1935	1995	1935	1995
Children (ages 0–10)				
Males	0.080	0.027	–0.139	0.015**
	(0.033)	(0.037)	(0.038)	(0.035)
Females	0.065	–0.005	–0.024	–0.043
	(0.033)	(0.037)	(0.038)	(0.035)
Teens (ages 11–19)				
Males	0.340	0.313	–0.046	0.036
	(0.040)	(0.039)	(0.045)	(0.037)
Females	–0.002	0.022	0.137	0.310**
	(0.034)	(0.035)	(0.039)	(0.033)
Prime ages (20–50)				
Males	0.552	0.690	–0.072	0.007
	(0.041)	(0.037)	(0.047)	(0.035)
Females	0.088	–0.028	0.509	0.607
	(0.046)	(0.041)	(0.052)	(0.039)
Middle ages (51–60)				
Males	0.595	0.641	–0.264	–0.039*
	(0.069)	(0.060)	(0.079)	(0.056)
Females	0.165	0.078	0.711	0.501
	(0.081)	(0.067)	(0.092)	(0.063)
Elderly (61+)				
Males	0.301	0.449	–0.229	0.172**
	(0.069)	(0.062)	(0.079)	(0.058)
Females	–0.172	0.037*	0.126	0.066
	(0.080)	(0.059)	(0.091)	(0.056)
Intercept	0.286	0.265	0.225	0.311**
	(0.060)	(0.064)	(0.068)	(0.060)

NOTES: The dependent variable is the number of males or females (per household) engaged in agriculture over the previous year. Standard errors are shown in parentheses. Sample size for 1935 is 836; for 1995 it is 734. Each demographic variable is the number of household members in the designated age-sex group.
* Significant at $p = 0.10$.
** Significant at $p = 0.05$.

The corresponding results for women indicate that females in the 1990s were more likely, at any age, to be working on the farm than was the case in the 1930s. The implied age pattern for women is similar to that observed in Figure 3. More interestingly, as with the men, the age profiles are similar in the two samples. The most important differences are that in 1995 teenage females were much more likely to work on the farm than was the case in the 1930s, and the effects of men in the household are different in the two samples. In the 1930s, having additional older men was associated with a decline in the number of women working (all else being equal), whereas this indirect effect is not present in the 1995 data. The 1935 results may reflect the need for care of older men by their wives, or the substitution of older men for older women on the farm. Whatever the case, these data do not provide evidence that work participation of elderly men or women has declined since the 1930s.

Next we consider work patterns and living arrangements. Does the labor supply of the elderly living on their own differ from that of elders living with their children? We can document the interaction between work and family structure, but it is impossible to determine the direction of causality. Perhaps only the "independent" (economically capable) elderly can live on their own, in which case only selected elderly will be able to live apart from their children. Alternatively, the extra resources associated with living in an extended household may permit older individuals to work less, in which case the causality runs from family structure to work. For the remainder of this study we use the terms "extended" and "multiple" households interchangeably when referring to households with more than a single conjugal unit. Essentially, either term is equivalent to "living with children."

Table 2 reports regression estimates of participation and days worked for men and women. In a regression context we can more formally estimate the age profiles, controlling for other individual-level variables, namely measures of education, that might be correlated with the birth-cohort effects we have previously noted. For clarity of presentation we report only the age coefficients for older individuals (ages 50 and over). For each measure of labor supply we show the coefficients for the whole sample, as well as the coefficients interacted with an indicator that the individual lives in an extended or multiple household.

Column 1 confirms the pattern that we have already seen in Figure 3, that participation begins to decline for men over age 60. Column 2 shows that the participation rate for older men in simple family households is much higher (0.94) than for men living in multiple households (0.61). Furthermore, the decline in employment with age occurs only for those men living in multiple households. This result suggests that the elderly who live on their own work as much as they did when they were younger. Again

TABLE 2 Regression estimates of labor participation and days worked per year, by individual age, sex, and household type: Northern China, 1995

	Men				Women			
	Participation		Days per year		Participation		Days per year	
Means and coefficients	(1)	(2)	(3)	(4)	(5)	(6)	(7)	(8)
Means								
All adults	0.91		159.8		0.84		99.01	
Elderly in simple household		0.94		109.4		0.70		43.46
Elderly in multiple household		0.61		60.6		0.34		17.65
Coefficients by age group								
50–54	−.038	−.038	−37.04*	−19.86	0.059	−0.039	−51.21*	−57.05*
	(.025)	(.029)	(16.57)	(19.62)	(0.039)	(0.042)	(13.05)	(15.46)
55–59	−.024	−.026	−58.84*	−61.08*	−0.174*	−0.171*	−61.35*	−64.38*
	(.024)	(.030)	(16.35)	(20.64)	(0.049)	(0.068)	(12.98)	(16.75)
60–64	−.100*	−.070	−75.86*	−69.99*	−0.168*	−0.110	−59.25*	−57.05*
	(.042)	(.048)	(18.35)	(21.94)	(0.065)	(0.079)	(15.34)	(17.24)
65–69	−.146*	.014	−94.40*	−56.89*	−0.431*	−0.281*	−91.70*	−84.19*
	(.067)	(.014)	(18.75)	(25.12)	(0.088)	(0.131)	(12.69)	(16.40)
70–74	−.322*	.016	−112.02*	−53.75*	−0.732*	−0.371*	−105.83*	−91.24*
	(.092)	(.018)	(21.04)	(30.17)	(0.083)	(0.159)	(11.82)	(17.04)
75+	−.553*	−.198	−163.36*	−173.91*	−0.796*	−0.773*	−114.72*	−117.54*
	(.105)	(.177)	(14.55)	(21.68)	(0.070)	(0.183)	(10.80)	(12.77)

Multiple household	.001	9.86	.019	-11.88
	(.006)	(27.67)	(.014)	(22.44)
Multiple household				
x age 50–54	-.004	-60.11	-0.069	22.91
	(.054)	(36.66)	(0.087)	(28.45)
x age 55–59	-.000	-1.10	-0.020	13.88
	(.045)	(36.35)	(0.097)	(27.75)
x age 60–64	-.094	-23.61	-0.138	2.56
	(.096)	(38.87)	(0.124)	(32.17)
x age 65–69	-.265*	-69.36	-0.255	-3.69
	(.102)	(39.26)	(0.169)	(26.52)
x age 70–74	-.484*	-91.50*	-0.568*	-13.88
	(.114)	(42.09)	(0.166)	(25.45)
x age 75+	-.459*	4.46	-0.045	12.50
	(.211)	(33.46)	(0.196)	(22.78)
F-test for multiple family	7.57	2.53	3.77	1.32
	(0.000)	(0.39)	(.005)	(.263)

NOTES: Standard errors are shown in parentheses. The means panel shows sample means for each dependent variable for the whole sample, as well as the separate means for the elderly in simple households (one conjugal unit) and multiple households (more than one conjugal unit). For each dependent variable the coefficients represent the difference of the specified age indicator from individuals aged 35–39. For each dependent variable there are two specifications: without interactions (odd-numbered columns) and with interactions of the age profile with an indicator for multiple households (even-numbered columns). Sample size is 1,072 for men, 1,075 for women. The F-test for differences in age profiles for multiple households is reported in the last row. Regressions also include controls for years of education and technical training.

* Significant at p = 0.05.

we cannot tell whether the elderly living in multiple households are working less because they cannot, or because they do not have to. The elderly living in simple households could be the independent, self-selected elderly who prefer to farm until they die, in which case we cannot conclude that extended households facilitate retirement. However, the numbers do suggest a positive association between living in extended households and the *possibility* of retirement.

The next two columns show the profiles for days worked. The relationship between age and days is stronger than that between age and participation. The average number of days worked for all men is 159.8 per year. Beginning at age 50, men work fewer days. As with employment rates, men in simple households reduce their labor supply less as they age than do those living in multiple households. Older men living alone with their wives work as much as younger men.

The next four columns show the corresponding results for women. Again there are sharp differences in labor force attachment between women living in multiple households and those living on their own. However, despite the overall difference in participation and days worked, the age profiles for employment are similar for women in extended and simple households. This suggests that the economic role of women changes as they age, in a way that is common to the two types of households. It also suggests that need does not drive women in simple households to work any more than those in the multiple households. (See Davis-Friedmann 1991 for a more extensive description of the role of women as they age.)

Living standards of the elderly

How do living standards of the elderly compare with those of the young, and has the relative position of the elderly changed over time? Are living arrangements related to living standards? In addressing these questions we confront several empirical difficulties, particularly because income and consumption are measured at the household, not individual, level. An elderly woman's living standards will depend on both the income of the household in which she lives and the distribution of resources within the household, yet we do not observe her individual share. Instead, we can estimate her access to household resources by attributing to her an equal piece of the household pie—that is, by imputing per capita household income to each household member. Obviously, doing so will be misleading if resources are not shared equally. There is another potential problem. If children require fewer resources than adults, then adults in households with children will actually have higher living standards than adults in households without children and the same per capita income. Essentially, we may overcompensate for household size by counting children and adults as equal.

These issues are discussed in detail by Deaton and Paxson (1992 and 1998). One correction is to calculate the "per adult-equivalent" level of consumption. Following Deaton and Paxson, we assume that children under age 5 are equivalent to 0.25 adults, and that those between ages 5 and 14 are equivalent to 0.45 adults. We have chosen these numbers not because they are necessarily accurate, but because they allow us to explore the sensitivity of our conclusions to the possibility that children need fewer resources.

We begin by assuming that each household member receives an equal share of family resources; that is, we attribute household per capita income to each individual and pretend that it represents the individual's living standard. Table 3 shows estimated age profiles from the 1995 sample (ages 31–50 being the omitted category). The ideal measure of access to resources would be based on consumption, rather than income, especially for the elderly. Column 1 shows that children have lower per capita consumption levels than do prime-age adults, but that per capita consumption is lowest for the elderly. Adults of ages 51–60, however, have consumption levels no different from those of prime-age adults. Column 2 indicates that the age profile for per capita income is virtually identical to that for

TABLE 3   Regression estimates of differences in annual per capita household income and consumption between prime ages (31–50) and other ages: Northern China, 1995

Age category	Per capita consumption	Per capita income (PCY)	Per adult equivalent income	PCY (base: simple household)	PCY (interaction: multiple household)
Children (0–10)	−247.97*	−216.53*	73.99	−209.50	156.99
	(52.03)	(108.63)	(129.15)	(144.21)	(187.37)
Teens (11–19)	−30.17	−82.63	−137.44	−128.32	34.13
	(42.54)	(97.39)	(111.55)	(111.51)	(188.79)
Prime ages 1 (20–30)	−21.23	−120.16	−181.93	177.00	421.55
	(71.41)	(136.44)	(167.66)	(188.51)	(239.61)
Middle ages (51–60)	85.58	−108.89	−459.94*	−188.48	463.32
	(106.17)	(153.00)	(175.09)	(208.07)	(289.67)
Elderly (61+)	−449.50*	−726.22*	−1,038.58*	−927.85*	732.75*
	(79.41)	(171.26)	(189.05)	(336.95)	(351.87)
Multiple-family indicator					−675.53*
					(188.10)
Mean income (yuan)	2,314.45	2,691.13	2,840.06		

NOTES: Coefficients are estimates of individual age indicators from OLS regressions of household per capita income, defined at the head of each column. All specifications include village fixed effects. Standard errors are shown in parentheses. Sample size is 2,881. The omitted category is prime ages 31–50. The F-test for differences between age coefficients in multiple and simple families is 2.73 (p = 0.000). The F-test for whether multiple- and simple-family coefficients for elderly sum to zero is 3.07 (p = 0.082), and the F-test for whether elderly have the same income in multiple and simple households is 0.03 (p = 0.8648). In 1994, 1 RMB (yuan) = US$0.12.
* Significant at p = 0.05.

consumption. (Note that there is virtually no overlap in the measurement of these two variables.) Income does decline more steeply for the elderly than does consumption, a pattern that is consistent with a life cycle model, wherein individuals smooth consumption between their working years and old age. The implied degree of consumption smoothing is quite small, however; income and consumption essentially track each other. As in the employment regressions, it is important to beware of cohort effects when interpreting the age profile. In this case, declines in income and consumption for the current elderly may reflect their permanently poorer economic position in relation to those born more recently. Nevertheless, the interpretation of a purely aging effect is bolstered by the decline between "middle" and "old" age, age spans in which we do not expect the cohort effects to be as strong. Rather than repeat this caution again, we shall treat the estimated age coefficients as age effects throughout the remainder of the discussion. In column 3 we adjust income for adult equivalents. This has the effect of steepening the age profile: the elderly appear much worse off because they tend to live with other adults, rather than with young children. Thus any adjustment in living standards for family composition would probably lead to a downward revision of the relative position of the elderly.

In the last two columns we compare the income levels of individuals in simple and multiple households. As before, the possible endogeneity of household structure contaminates causal interpretations between household structure and income. Our more limited interest is in measuring the differences in living standards between the elderly in the two types of households. In particular we wish to know whether the elderly who live on their own are worse off than those living with their children. If the elderly who live on their own are positively selected (i.e., are the most productive), then we exaggerate their relative position. On the other hand, if living alone reflects neglect and is not a matter of choice, then they may be genuinely worse off.

Column 4 shows the age-income profile for simple households. The profile is slightly steeper than the comparable (pooled) profile in column 2. Column 5 shows the difference in age profiles between persons in extended and simple households, so that the net effect of being in any age group in an extended household is the sum of the relevant coefficient in columns 4 and 5. The elderly in extended households are associated with an age "penalty" that is 732.75 yuan lower than the income of those in simple families. The net effect is that they earn 195.10 (927.85 − 732.75) yuan less than prime-age adults in extended households, although the difference is statistically insignificant. This should not be surprising, since we have assumed that all members of extended households receive the same per capita income; but it also suggests that these households suffer no penalty for having elderly members. Nevertheless, the per capita income of extended households is lower for all ages than that of simple households (by 675.53 yuan).

Given a choice, though, an elderly person would still come out slightly ahead in an extended household, by 57.22 yuan (732.75 − 675.53), though this difference is insignificantly different from zero. If there is any positive selection into simple households, this result suggests that the average elderly person is slightly better off in an extended household, and that the extended household plays some social security role. This implication is even stronger once we recognize that the elderly in simple households also work more.

Table 4 shows comparable results from our other data sets. The first two columns report estimates from the 1935 data. The most striking feature of the 1935 profile, and a key result of this study, is the absence of any effects of old age. The elderly live in as well-off households as the young, unlike the situation observed in 1995. This remains true even when we adjust for adult equivalents. In the last four columns we use the CHNS data to compare the urban and rural age profiles in 1989. The main conclusion here, as we have seen before, is that the profiles are similar. With respect to mean incomes, the elderly fare slightly worse in the rural areas, whereas children fare worse in cities. Mean incomes, however, are significantly higher in urban areas. Furthermore, urban families have access to better public services. If we also take account of the fact that the elderly

TABLE 4   Regression estimates of differences in annual per capita household income between prime ages (31–50) and other ages, three data sets compared: Northern China, 1935 and 1989

Age category	Rural, 1935		Rural, 1989 CHNS		Urban, 1989 CHNS	
	Per capita income	Per adult equivalent income	Per capita income	Per adult equivalent income	Per capita income	Per adult equivalent income
Children (0–10)	−2.50*	−0.33	−33.30	40.96	−110.44*	−59.04
	(1.00)	(1.29)	(19.94)	(24.32)	(35.57)	(39.44)
Teens (11–19)	−1.75	−2.59	−20.85	−65.79*	18.60	−33.01
	(1.11)	(1.42)	(20.72)	(25.27)	(37.64)	(41.72)
Prime ages 1 (20–30)	0.24	−1.10	48.22*	25.11	18.87	−63.64
	(1.14)	(1.46)	(20.92)	(25.52)	(33.71)	(37.37)
Middle ages (51–60)	−0.04	−2.58	80.14*	−20.00	95.89*	−33.25
	(1.54)	(1.98)	(29.24)	(35.67)	(39.69)	(44.00)
Elderly (61+)	0.13	−1.90	−63.04*	−152.42*	−62.85	−171.09*
	(1.56)	(2.00)	(30.13)	(36.74)	(39.77)	(44.09)
Mean income (yuan)	34.72	45.41	703.83	853.51	1,196.60	1,364.73
Sample size	6,719	6,719	10,356	10,356	4,802	4,802

NOTES: Coefficients are estimates of individual age indicators from OLS regressions of household per capita income, defined at the head of each column. All specifications include village fixed effects. Standard errors are in parentheses. The omitted category is prime ages 31–50. In 1935, 1 yuan = US$0.48; in 1989, 1 RMB (yuan) = US$0.27.
* Significant at p = 0.05.

work much harder in rural areas, and if we place a positive weight on nonmarket time, then this further widens the welfare gap in favor of the urban elderly.

We next explore the relative position of the elderly in other parts of the income distribution. (See Chu and Jiang 1997 for a related attempt to explore the links between the age composition of household members and individual-based measures of income distribution—in their case, indicators of income inequality.) We begin by calculating the cumulative distribution functions of per capita income. With these results, one can (for example) choose any poverty line, z, and then compare the proportion of individuals living in households with per capita incomes below z. Figure 5 shows the cumulative distribution functions for the elderly and non-elderly in 1995. As suggested by the regressions, this figure indicates that the elderly have lower mean income than younger household members. However, it also suggests that for whatever poverty line one might choose, the elderly would have a significantly higher cumulative distribution function, or poverty rate, than the non-elderly. For example, at a poverty line of 1,000 yuan, the poverty rate is almost twice as high for the elderly.

Figure 6, based on the 1935 data, provides a striking contrast. Here, the cumulative distribution functions for the two groups are virtually coincident. Thus for any poverty line, the poverty rates of the elderly and the non-elderly are the same. This finding reinforces the case that the elderly were significantly better off in relation to the non-elderly during the 1930s than in the 1990s.

FIGURE 5   Cumulative distribution function of per capita income, elderly versus non-elderly: Northern China, 1995

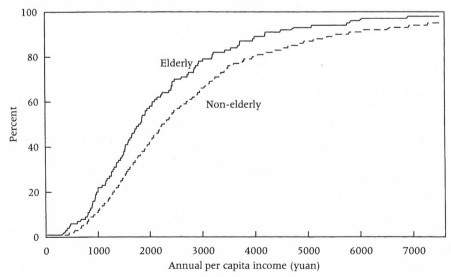

FIGURE 6   Cumulative distribution function of per capita income, elderly versus non-elderly: Northern China, 1935

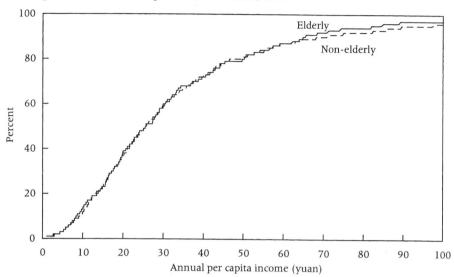

Our final comparison is between the rural and urban CHNS samples. The results (not shown) reinforce the earlier observation that there is no difference between the urban and rural areas besides mean incomes.

As a final exercise, we repackage the individual-level data and examine the overall correlation between household demographic structure and household income. Again we must be careful to avoid placing a causal interpretation on the coefficients. If family structure were exogenous, we could interpret the coefficient on the number of elderly people as the effect on family income of adding an elderly person to the household. But richer households can support more members, and a positive coefficient may only reflect this fact (see Benjamin and Brandt 1995). Nevertheless, the coefficients indicate the level of household resources associated with an increase in the number of individuals of a given type. The results are shown in Table 5. We report results for a logarithmic specification, since it has the advantage of permitting the coefficients to be interpreted (approximately) as percentage increases in household income associated with additional members, and it allows easy comparison among data sets.

Column 1 shows the results for rural households in 1995. Here we see that the elderly are associated with the smallest increases in household income, smaller even than those associated with children. The elderly are the only group with an insignificant coefficient, suggesting that adding an elderly person to a rural household is associated with an increase in household income of only 1 percent, certainly less than enough to cover the cost of caring for an elderly person. These low numbers for the elderly are also

TABLE 5   Regression estimates of log household income and demographic structure: Northern China, 1995, 1989, and 1935

Age category	Rural, 1995	Rural, 1989	Urban, 1989	Rural, 1935
Children (0–10)	0.10*	0.06*	0.02	0.07*
	(0.04)	(0.02)	(0.03)	(0.02)
Teens (11–19)	0.15*	0.13*	0.16*	0.15*
	(0.05)	(0.02)	(0.03)	(0.02)
Prime ages 1 (20–30)	0.27*	0.20*	0.29*	0.20*
	(0.04)	(0.02)	(0.02)	(0.02)
Prime ages 2 (31–50)	0.30*	0.25*	0.37*	0.24*
	(0.04)	(0.03)	(0.03)	(0.03)
Middle ages (51–60)	0.22*	0.23*	0.29*	(0.03)
	(0.05)	(0.03)	0.24*	(0.04)
Elderly (61+)	0.01	0.06	0.16*	0.22*
	(0.04)	(0.03)	(0.03)	(0.04)
Sample size	769	2,448	1,251	1,075

NOTES: Coefficients are estimates of OLS regressions of log household income on the number of people in each age category. All specifications include village fixed effects. Standard errors are shown in parentheses.
* Significant at $p = 0.05$.

reflected in the next column, which presents estimates for the rural CHNS. Here the elderly are also associated with a small (6 percent) and insignificant increase in household income. The urban coefficients (column 3) are slightly different. Here the elderly have lower coefficients than prime-age adults, but the number is higher than for their rural counterparts (16 percent) and significant. The most striking results are for rural households in 1935, shown in the last column. Household income increases as much with the number of elderly as it does with prime-age adults. However it is accomplished, whether by income directly associated with the elderly, or through harder work on the part of the non-elderly, it appears that the elderly lived in more fortunate circumstances in the 1930s (compared with the young) than in the 1990s.

Beyond working, how do the elderly support themselves, especially with the declining prevalence of extended-household living arrangements? Extended *families*, versus households, may yet be important as long as children are supporting their parents through interhousehold transfers. Furthermore, individuals who worked for state-owned enterprises (mostly in urban areas) have state-financed pensions. Finally, local governments may provide direct relief to the poorest elderly.

Tables 6 and 7 document the magnitudes of these types of income transfer: private (family) remittances, pensions, and government transfers. They compare households with and without elderly members, both for simple and extended households. In Table 6 we focus on the 1995 rural

TABLE 6   Mean transfers to households with elderly members, by
household type: Rural northern China, 1995

Indicators of transfer income (per year)	All household types		Only-elderly households	
	Elderly	Non-elderly	Simple family	Multiple family
Mean annual household income (yuan)	10,294.1	11,422.8	3,981.4	13,717.9
Percentage with pensions	7.1	0.1	7.8	6.8
Mean pension income (yuan)	95.4	23.0	75.5	106.3
Percentage with government transfers	8.8	5.0	10.9	7.6
Mean government transfer income (yuan)	25.5	29.8	33.4	21.3
Percentage with remittances	44.0	23.9	70.3	30.0
Mean remittance income (yuan)	516.4	201.9	631.7	453.9
Sample size	182	603	64	118

NOTES: The table shows the percentage of households that received each type of transfer income, as well as the sample average level of that type of income, calculated over all households. Elderly households are defined as those households with members over 60 years of age. In 1994, 1 RMB (yuan) = US$0.12.

sample. To begin, very few rural elderly households have pension income, and it represents a tiny fraction of their income. Similarly, government transfers are irrelevant to elderly and non-elderly households alike. This finding reflects the limits of village financial resources and indicates that access to land is the primary form of social relief. Private transfers (remittances), however, are very important. Forty-four percent of elderly households, versus 24 percent of non-elderly households, receive remittances. Moreover, the level of remittance income is also more than twice as high in the elderly households (accounting for about 5 percent of total income) as in non-elderly households. Remittance activity appears to be highly age-motivated. In the last two columns we compare transfers to simple and extended elderly households. The most striking feature is that 70 percent of simple families receive remittances, compared with 30 percent of extended households. In levels, the elderly in simple households receive slightly higher remittances. Although remittances are more important to those elderly living outside extended families (remittances accounting for almost one-sixth of their household income), remittances are still large for the elderly in extended households. On the basis of these levels, it is difficult to argue that the elderly living on their own receive enough remittances to offset the implicit intrahousehold transfers they would receive in an extended household.

Table 7 draws an urban-rural comparison. Two features stand out. First, the elderly in urban areas have significantly higher pension income than do the rural elderly. More surprisingly, they are also more likely to receive remittances, though this receipt is less age-related than in rural

TABLE 7   Mean transfers to households with elderly members, by household type: Rural and urban northern China, 1989

Indicators of transfer income (per year)	Rural		Urban	
	Elderly	Non-elderly	Simple family	Multiple family
Mean annual household income (yuan)	3,044.6	2,929.2	4,517.1	4,616.9
Percentage with pensions	11.9	1.7	49.3	14.1
Mean pension income (yuan)	120.9	14.2	670.4	14.1
Percentage with gov. transfers	3.3	0.1	1.6	1.1
Mean gov. transfer income (yuan)	5.0	1.8	4.1	2.2
Percentage with remittances	31.0	20.3	36.5	29.1
Mean remittance income (yuan)	100.4	41.5	122.1	91.9
Sample size	521	1,943	436	818

NOTES: The table shows the percentage of households that received each type of transfer income, as well as the sample average level of that type of income, calculated over all households. Elderly households are defined as those households with members over 60 years of age. In 1989, 1 RMB (yuan) = US$0.27.

areas. In their broader implications for social security, these results, combined with the evidence on living arrangements, suggest that there is little difference between urban and rural areas with respect to private support for the elderly. Families are as important in urban as in rural areas, but they have the bonus of state-financed pensions. An interesting question at this point is how much the state pensions crowd out some of the private urban transfers. If there is any crowding out, it is nevertheless the urban, not the rural, elderly who have the more developed private social security system. (See Case and Deaton 1998 for a discussion of the difficulties in addressing this question, and Jensen 1998 for an attempt to answer the question in a South African context.)

A common theme in the study of Chinese families is that the elderly have lost control over resources as the balance of power has shifted away from them, especially with collectivization (Davis-Friedmann 1991; Goode 1963; Selden 1993; Whyte 1995; Yan 1997). This helps explain the worsening economic standing of the elderly both inside and outside extended households. Prior to collectivization the elderly did not need to rely on the goodwill of their children, since "the heart of the family compact was the exchange of the care of aged parents by male offspring and the eventual transfer of land" (Selden 1993: 148). Parents could disinherit negligent sons. The elderly also embodied considerable human capital. As Goode (1963) notes, there was a high return to the accumulated farming experience. Neither of these advantages of age is present now. According to Whyte (1995: 1012), "the elimination for a generation of meaningful family property, combined with the rising education of the young and other trends, significantly softened the power of the senior generation in Chinese families."

Compounding the loss of bargaining power, the inability to accumulate land reduces the ability of the elderly to save, and their relative decline in human capital reduces their current earning power. Thin land and labor markets may further constrain the ability of the elderly to convert even their allocated land into income. This shows how a seemingly egalitarian institution, such as a property rights regime that prohibits land ownership, can have unintended adverse consequences on income distribution, and it provides another example of the need to evaluate the distribution of land in the context of the development of factor markets. (See Benjamin and Brandt 1997 for a more extensive discussion of these issues, focusing on the 1930s.) As emphasized by Davis-Friedmann (1991), the reduction in the bargaining position of the elderly was not a problem when the state was committed to care for the elderly; but with the demise of social programs the elderly have been left to fend for themselves, and the current elderly are particularly at a disadvantage.

This decline in asset holdings of the elderly is apparent in our data. In Table 8 we show estimates of household per capita land and its relationship to household demographic structure. In the 1990s land was distributed on an egalitarian, essentially per capita, basis. Not surprisingly, then, column 1 shows that household per capita land is virtually orthogonal to

TABLE 8   Regression estimates of per capita controlled land and household demographic structure: Northern China, 1995 and 1935

Age category	Additional household land per capita (in *mu*)	
	1995	1935
Children (ages 0–10)	−0.31	−0.24
	(0.17)	(0.33)
Teens (11–19)	−0.17	−0.18
	(0.19)	(0.35)
Primes ages 1 (20–30)	−0.11	−0.28
	(0.14)	(0.36)
Prime ages 2 (31–50)	0.24	2.13*
	(0.17)	(0.45)
Middle ages (51–60)	−0.01	2.39*
	(0.19)	(0.62)
Elderly (61+)	−0.11	2.41*
	(0.17)	(0.66)
Sample size	787	1,095

NOTES: Coefficients are estimates from OLS regressions of household-controlled land per capita (owned in 1935 and allocated in 1995) on the number of household members in each age category. All specifications include village fixed effects. 1 *mu* = 0.067 hectares.
* Significant at p = 0.05.

household age structure: the old command no more land than the young. In the 1930s, in contrast, the age of household members was highly correlated with per capita land. Column 2 reveals that those households with the most elderly had the most per capita owned land, reflecting the accumulation of land over the lives of the elderly. These two regressions show the most striking difference in the relative economic position of the elderly in rural China before and after collectivization. There is no way to confirm this view, but we doubt that it is pure coincidence that the elderly controlled more land and enjoyed relatively higher living standards before collectivization.

Finally, in the 1995 survey we find large differences in educational attainment by birth cohort, on the order of one year's education for each ten years of age (not shown). The gap between young and old is especially pronounced for women. Given the increased value of education, especially in gaining off-farm income, the elderly will continue to be at a disadvantage for decades to come. (See Benjamin et al. 2000 for more discussion of this point.)

Conclusion

The living conditions of the Chinese rural elderly documented here indicate that an urban bias, reflected in other aspects of public policy, extends to the provision of social security. There is no foundation for the notion that the rural elderly are well taken care of, at least in comparison with the urban elderly. Most evidence instead points to a relative deterioration of the economic position of the elderly in rural areas, and a weakening of the family as a social security institution. It is difficult to build a case that urban elderly are at a particular disadvantage and merit additional pension resources. To design alternative social security schemes will undoubtedly be complicated, but the evidence reviewed here suggests that the rural elderly warrant more attention than they have received.

Notes

We appreciate the comments of seminar participants at the University of Melbourne, Australian National University, and the University of New South Wales. Benjamin and Brandt thank the Social Sciences and Humanities Research Council of Canada for financial support.

1 One telling sign of this inattention is that the World Bank's (1997) volume in the China 2020 series devotes only a one-page sidebar to the rural elderly, essentially suggesting that old-age security in rural areas is not a matter of concern.

2 Excellent discussions of the evolution of families under collectivization, and the implied position of the elderly, can be found in Davis and Harrell (1993), Davis-Friedmann (1983 and 1991), Goode (1963), Selden (1993), and Whyte (1992 and 1995).

3 http://www.cpc.unc.edu/china/home.html.

4 A referee correctly points out that care must be taken in drawing inferences from the Liaoning data because they are drawn from a regimented population administered directly

by central authorities (the banner system). Under the banner system, households were organized into groups called *zu* that were modeled after organizational units (*mukun*) originating in the Manchu Dynasty. *Zu* were not lineage groups based on descent from a common male ancestor; rather, they functioned as basic units of state civil, fiscal, judicial, and military administration. A group typically consisted of two or three households. Leaders of each group, who occupied the lowest rung in the banner system's formal organizational hierarchy, were charged with carrying out the administrative work associated with the official functions of the group. They had other duties as well, including authorizing marriages, ruling on inheritance disputes, and ratifying family divisions. Lee and Campbell (1997) argue that the impediments to household division under the banner system may have contributed to the high percentage of nonsimple households. Despite these caveats, their data, along with those of Wolf (1984 and 1985) for Taiwan, suggest that a majority of individuals lived in multiple or extended households, as do our data for the 1930s.

References

Benjamin, Dwayne and Loren Brandt. 1995. "Markets, discrimination, and the economic contribution of women in China: Historical evidence," *Economic Development and Cultural Change* 44(1): 63–104.

———. 1997. "Land, factor markets, and inequality in rural China: Historical evidence," *Explorations in Economic History* 34(4): 460–494.

Benjamin, Dwayne et al. 2000. "Markets, human capital, and inequality: Evidence from rural China." W. Davidson Institute Working Paper No. 298 (March), University of Toronto.

Buck, John Lossing. 1937. *Land Utilization in China*. New York: Paragon Press.

Case, Anne and Angus Deaton. 1998. "Large cash transfers to the elderly in South Africa," *Economic Journal* 108(450): 1330–1361.

Chu, C. Y. Cyrus and Lily Jiang. 1997. "Demographic transition, family structure, and income inequality," *Review of Economics and Statistics* 79(4): 665–669.

Davis, Deborah and Stevan Harrell (eds.). 1993. *Chinese Families in the Post-Mao Era*. Berkeley: University of California Press.

Davis-Friedmann, Deborah. 1983. *Long Lives: Chinese Elderly and the Communist Revolution*. Cambridge, MA: Harvard University Press.

———. 1991. *Long Lives: Chinese Elderly and the Communist Revolution*. Expanded ed. Stanford, CA: Stanford University Press.

Deaton, Angus and Christina Paxson. 1992. "Patterns of aging in Thailand and Côte d'Ivoire," in *Topics in the Economics of Aging*, ed. David A. Wise. Chicago: University of Chicago Press, pp. 163–202.

———. 1998. "Measuring poverty among the elderly," in *Inquiries in the Economics of Aging*, ed. David A. Wise. Chicago: University of Chicago Press, pp. 169–200.

Fang, Yuan, Wang Chuanbin, and Song Yuhua. 1992. "Support of the elderly in China," in *Family Support for the Elderly: The International Experience*, eds. Hal L. Kendig, Akiko Hashimoto, and Larry C. Coppard. New York: Oxford University Press, pp. 250–259.

Goode, William J. 1963. *World Revolution and Family Patterns*. London: Free Press of Glencoe.

Jensen, Robert. 1998. "Public transfers, private transfers, and the 'crowding out' hypothesis: Evidence from South Africa." Unpublished manuscript, John F. Kennedy School of Government, Harvard University, Cambridge, MA.

Lee, James Z. and Cameron D. Campbell. 1997. *Fate and Fortune in Rural China: Social Organization and Population Behavior in Liaoning, 1774–1873*. Cambridge: Cambridge University Press.

Selden, Mark. 1993. "Family strategies and structures in rural North China," in *Chinese Families in the Post-Mao Era*, eds. Deborah Davis and Stevan Harrell. Berkeley: University of California Press, pp. 139–164.

State Statistical Bureau. 1996. *Quanguo 1% Renkou Chouyang Tiaocha Ziliao* [1995 1% National Sample Population Survey]. Beijing.

———. Various years. *Provincial Statistical Yearbook.* Beijing.

———. Various years. *Zhongguo Tongji Nianjian* [Statistical Yearbook of China]. Beijing.

Tuan, Chi-hsien. 1992. "The process of population ageing and the status of old people in China," in *The Elderly Population in Developed and Developing World*, eds. P. Krishnan and K. Mahadevan. Delhi: B. R. Publishing Corporation, pp. 218–260.

Whyte, Martin King. 1992. "Introduction: Rural economic reforms and Chinese family patterns," *China Quarterly*, No. 130: 317–322.

———. 1995. "The social roots of China's economic development," *China Quarterly*, No. 144: 999–1019.

Wolf, Arthur. 1984. "Family and the life cycle in rural China," in *Households: Comparative and Historical Studies of the Domestic Group*, eds. Robert McC. Netting, Richard Wilk, and Eric Arnould. Berkeley: University of California Press, pp. 279–298.

———. 1985. "Chinese family size: A myth revitalized," in *The Chinese Family and Its Ritual Behavior*, eds. Hsieh Jih-chang and Chuang Yinghang. Taipei: Institute of Ethnology, Academia Sinica, pp. 30–49.

World Bank. 1994. *Averting the Old Age Crisis*. New York: Oxford University Press for the World Bank.

———. 1997. *Old Age Security: Pension Reform in China*. China 2020 Series. Washington, DC: World Bank.

Yan, Yunxiang. 1997. "The triumph of conjugality: Structural transformation of family relations in a Chinese village," *Ethnology* 36(3): 191–212.

Demographic Transition and Social Security in Taiwan

Sheng-Cheng Hu

Kuo-Mei Chen

Lii-Tarn Chen

THE POPULATION OF Taiwan is aging at a more rapid rate than is the case in Western industrialized countries. The share of the population aged 65 and older, which was 7.8 percent in 1996, is projected by the Council for Economic Planning and Development to increase to 9.9 percent by 2010 and to 21.0 percent by 2035 (Council for Economic Planning and Development 1999: Table 3). The share of the population aged 80 and older is projected to rise from 1.5 percent in 1996 to 2.3 percent by 2010 and to 4.9 percent by 2035. Figure 1 illustrates projected changes in Taiwan's age structure between 2000 and 2035.

The elderly dependency ratio, defined here as the ratio of the population aged 65 and older to the population aged 25–64, is projected to rise from 15.3 percent in 1996 to 17.4 percent in 2010, then jump to 42.0 percent in 2035. By that time, every 2.3 workers will have to support one elderly person (Council for Economic Planning and Development 1996: 83).

Taiwan's extremely rapid population aging is the result of a fall in both the birth rate and the death rate. The crude birth rate, which was 15.5 per thousand population in 1995, is projected to fall to 14.5 by 2010, and further to 11.7 in 2035. The crude death rate, at 5.6 per thousand in 1995, is projected to rise to 7.0 in 2010 and to 10.5 by 2035 (Council for Economic Planning and Development 1999: Table 1-2).

In a traditional society the family is responsible for taking care of its elderly members. This practice worked well in Taiwan when agriculture dominated the economy and the elderly population was small. However, the resources that the elderly can count on for support will decline as the population ages. Lin (1987: Table 1) projects that the number of children per elderly person aged 75–79 will fall from 5.8 in 1985 to 3.6 in 2010 and

FIGURE 1 Projected population of Taiwan, ages 25–79, by single-year age groups, both sexes, as percent of the population aged 25 and older, 2000, 2010, and 2035

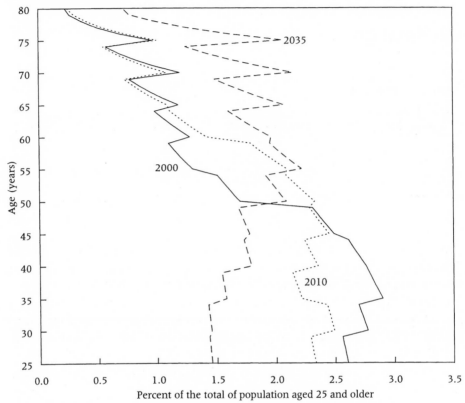

SOURCE: Council for Economic Planning and Development (1999).

to 1.6 in 2035. Likewise, Lin (1987: Table 2) projects that the number of employed children per person aged 75–79 will decline from 4.0 in 1985 to 2.4 by 2010 and to 1.0 in 2035. The sharp rise in the number of dual-career couples further aggravates the problems the country faces in caring for its elderly. According to a survey conducted by the Executive Yuan's Directorate General of Budget, Accounting and Statistics (1997: Table 44), 65.8 percent of Taiwan's elderly (those 65 and older) were supported by their children in 1986; but the figure fell to 52.3 percent by 1993 and to 48 percent by 1996.

Population aging per se does not necessarily pose a problem for the economy if working-age people prepare for a longer life span by increasing their saving or postponing retirement, or if the rate of productivity rises, creating additional output for the retired population. Cutler et al. (1990) argue that the anticipated population aging in the United States will improve that country's standard of living in the near future but lower it slightly over the very long run. Hu (1999) shows that within the framework of an endogenous growth model, an extension of the average length of life may increase the long-run growth of an economy because it promotes human-capital accumulation by lengthening the period in which the investment in human capital can be rewarded. Human capital is the main engine of economic growth, according to Lucas (1988).

It is ironic that just when the population is aging and life expectancy is lengthening, both labor force participation and saving rates have been declining in Taiwan. The overall labor force participation rate fell from a peak of 60.4 percent in 1986 to 58.0 percent in 1998. The household saving rate also fell, from 29.3 percent in 1986 to 18.4 percent in 1993 and again to 17.0 percent in 1998 (Figure 2). Several explanations have been suggested for the decline in the propensity to save. First, the financial liberalization that the country has undertaken since the early 1980s has led to a relaxation of credit constraints on consumption. Second, a sharp rise in housing prices in 1988–89 provided homeowners with windfall profits for increased consumption.[1] Finally, the rise in welfare expenditures and the establishment of the National Health Program in 1994 have reduced

FIGURE 2 Household saving rate (from household disposable income): Taiwan, 1968–98

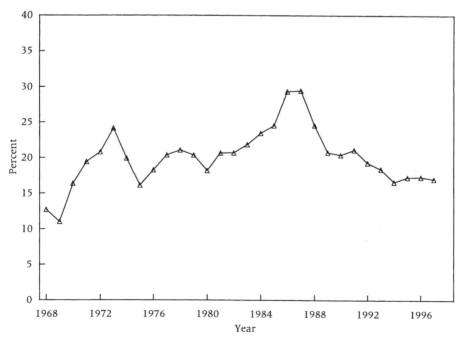

SOURCE: Council for Economic Planning and Development (1998b).

the need for precautionary saving. Whatever the reasons are, the declining propensity to save implies that a segment of the population may not be inclined to save for their retirement and that many elderly will have few financial resources available for retirement consumption.

To prepare the economy for an aging population and a changing family structure, the Taiwan government decided to establish an economy-wide social security system by 2001. The objectives of the system are to ensure old-age income security and relieve the burden on the working-age population of caring for elderly parents. The objectives are to be achieved partly through forced saving and partly through intergenerational transfers. In other words, the government adopted a partially funded system rather than a pure pay-as-you-go system of funding social security (Council for Economic Planning and Development 1995).

Just as Taiwan is launching the National Pension Program, social security programs in the United States and other developed countries are encountering difficulties. The main reason is that their programs are financed mostly by a pay-as-you-go system, achieving old-age income security through intergenerational transfers. Such a system works well in an economy where the population growth rate is high and the ratio of the elderly to the total population is low. When the population ages, however, the system imposes a heavy burden on the working population and thereby distorts decisions about saving and labor force participation. Some countries have recently enacted social security reforms to extend the normal retirement age, reduce retirement benefits, or increase the payroll tax rate, whereas others have attempted to partially or fully fund their social security programs in an effort to maintain the financial soundness of those programs (Holzmann 1997).

In Taiwan there is likewise concern about whether the National Pension Program will adversely affect aggregate savings and thereby dampen economic performance. As we have mentioned, although Taiwan's saving rate is still high, it is declining. Too much saving is not necessarily a good thing (Aaron 1966). However, Krugman (1994) and Lau (1998) argue that economic growth in East Asia's newly industrialized economies is due primarily to increases in inputs rather than to technical progress. Acceptance of this argument implies that Taiwan needs a high saving rate to continue economic growth.

Another reason for Taiwan to have a high saving rate is that it needs a large foreign-exchange reserve because it faces the possibility of a military conflict with mainland China, is politically isolated from the international community, and is excluded from such international organizations as the International Monetary Fund and the World Bank. Taiwan has no "contingent credit lines" to draw upon in an emergency. At the end of 1998 it had foreign-exchange reserves totaling US$90.3 billion, or 10.5

months' worth of imports, more than three times the amount recommended by the International Monetary Fund. Its huge foreign-exchange reserves and the prevalence of resilient small and medium-size firms in the economy are the main reasons Taiwan has been able to cope with the recent Asian financial crisis, suffering minimal harm.

This chapter examines how the proposed National Pension Program will interact with projected demographic changes to affect aggregate savings. The analytical framework employed here is the life cycle or permanent-income model, but it allows for the possibility that a segment of the population may be myopic in the sense that its behavior is better described by Keynes's current-income hypothesis than by the life cycle or permanent-income hypothesis of consumption (Hu 1996). In the following section we describe Taiwan's pre-existing social security programs and the new program. Next we discuss the effect of social security on aggregate savings, then follow the discussion with simulations. The final section summarizes our findings and their policy implications. The Appendix provides the technical details of the simulations.

Pre-existing old-age insurance programs and the National Pension Program

Taiwan's National Pension Program will not start from scratch. Two-thirds of the population have been covered by one of two public insurance programs that provide retirement benefits. The Public Employees Insurance Program covers government employees, and the Labor Insurance Program covers other workers. In March 1995 the National Health Insurance Program became effective.

The Public Employees Insurance Program, established in 1958, provides retirement, survivors, and disability insurance to regular government employees, who in 1994 accounted for about 5.1 percent of the population aged 25 and older. An insured person is eligible for retirement benefits if he or she has worked for 25 years or has reached age 60 and has worked for at least five years. Each eligible government retiree is paid a lump-sum retirement benefit up to 36 times the last working month's salary. The premium (contribution) is currently 9 percent of covered payroll, of which 35 percent is paid by the employee and 65 percent by the government.

The Labor Insurance Program, established in 1960, also provides retirement, survivors, and disability insurance to insured persons. It covers workers in enterprises that employ at least five persons, professionals, and temporary government workers, accounting for 59.3 percent of Taiwanese aged 25 and older in 1994. An insured person is eligible for retirement benefits upon reaching age 60 (55 if female), or upon reaching age 55 (50 if female) if the worker has been insured for at least ten years. The insured person is paid additional benefits equal to one month's salary per additional year of coverage. The maximum amount of benefits is 45 times the last working month's salary. The premium is 6.5 percent of covered wage income, of which 20 percent is borne by the worker, 70 percent by the employer, and 10 percent by the government.

Initially, health insurance was included in both the Public Employees and the Labor Insurance programs. In March 1995 the National Health Insurance Program took over this part of insurance and expanded it to cover all persons who had resided in the country for at least four months, including aliens with residence permits. The program's coverage reached 96.3 percent of the population by the end of 1997. Under this program, medical care (including preventive and prenatal care, inpatient and outpatient hospital treatment, surgery, and prescription drugs) is provided directly by public and private clinics and hospitals under contract with the National Health Insurance Bureau. The co-insurance rates are 20 percent for scheduled fees; 30–50 percent for hospital visits; from 10 percent for the first 30 days of inpatient care for short-term illness to 30 percent for the 61st day and thereafter; and from 5 percent for the first 30 days of inpatient care for long-term illness to 30 percent for the 181st day and thereafter. The premium is 4.25 percent of the covered payroll, of which 30 percent is borne by the employee, 60 percent by the employer, and 10 percent by the government.

Both the Public Employees Insurance Program and the Labor Insurance Program are financed on a pay-as-you-go basis, partly by premiums and partly by general revenue through government subsidies. They have accumulated large implicit debts. For example, in 1997 the Public Employees Insurance Program had an annual deficit of NT$6.9 billion (US$211 million at the exchange rate of US$1 = NT$32.7 in April 1999), or 42 percent of receipts. Its implicit debt ranges from about NT$80 billion to NT$100 billion. The Labor Insurance Program had a surplus of NT$22.0 billion, or 16.3 percent of revenue, and about NT$287 billion of assets in 1997 (Council for Economic Planning and Development 1998b: Table 16.9). But it also had an implicit debt three times as large as its assets.

In contrast, social security systems in other Asian countries are either partially or fully funded. For example, Singapore fully funds its old-age pensions through individual saving accounts managed by its Provident Fund. Every worker who earns a monthly wage of more than S$200 (US$117.6 at the exchange rate of US$1 = S$1.7 in April 1999) and his or her employer are each required to contribute 20 percent of the worker's earnings to the Provident Fund. Upon reaching age 65, the worker is paid a lump sum equal to the total employer and employee contributions, plus at least 2.5 percent compound interest, less an amount (S$15,000, or US$8,824) that is set aside for medical emergencies (US Social Security Administration 1997).

Governments in such countries as Japan and South Korea partially fund their social security systems. Japan has a two-tier system. The first tier is the National Pension Program, which provides mandatory coverage to all citizens aged 20–59 and voluntary coverage to citizens aged 60–64. The second tier is the earning-related Employees Pension Insurance, which covers employees in industry and commerce. (Employees in other private industries, public employees, and teachers are covered by other special insurance programs.) Workers' contributions to the National Pension Program are included in their contributions to Employees Pension Insurance, which amount to 8.675 percent of earnings. Other workers pay a flat amount each month of 12,800 yen (approximately US$100 at the exchange rate of US$1.00 = 119 yen in April 1999). If fully insured—that is, after having made contributions for 480 months—an insured person is entitled to a flat annual benefit of 785,500 yen, equivalent to US$6,600 (US Social Security Administration 1997: 194). In contrast, the Korean system is based entirely on earnings. It covers workers in firms employing at least five persons and farmers, fishermen, and rural self-employed persons aged 18–59. The premium is 3 percent of payroll for employed persons and 6 percent for their employers. The monthly benefits are 2.4 times the sum of average monthly earnings of all insured persons for the preceding year and average monthly earnings of retired persons over their entire contribution period (US Social Security Administration 1997: 207–208).

If Taiwanese workers were all paid salaries or wages, the Labor Insurance Program would be an economy-wide social security program. However, Taiwan's economy is dominated by small and medium-size enterprises. In 1999, 51.0 percent of workers were employed by enterprises having fewer than ten persons, while only 4.0 percent of workers were employed by enterprises having more than 500 employees (Directorate-General of Budget, Accounting and Statistics 1999: Table 15). Many workers in small enterprises are self-employed, and their earnings are difficult to determine. The Labor Insurance Program, which covers workers in enterprises employing at least five workers, thus excludes a large number of workers from insurance. As a result nearly one-third of the population is not covered by either the Labor Insurance Program or the Public Employees Program. The need to provide this segment of the population with some form of old-age income security has become an important political issue in recent elections.

An easy way to establish a new social security system is of course to extend the coverage of the two existing programs. Their implicit debts must first be settled, however. Moreover, those who are not currently covered by one of the two programs, most of whom are self-employed workers, workers in small businesses, farmers, and housewives, either do not have reported earnings or their earnings contain some elements of capital income and therefore are not entirely wage earnings. As a result the proposed social security system retains and revises the existing Public Employees and Labor Pension programs while creating a National Pension Program to cover those who are not yet insured by either of the existing programs. Each of the three programs will be managed by its own governing board. In other words, the proposed program will be essentially a two-tier system similar to Japan's system. The main difference between the two countries is that in Taiwan all new entrants into the labor market in both private and public sectors will be required to join the new pension program instead of the existing ones. Thus the two pre-existing programs will be eventually phased out, although it may take 40 years or longer to complete the process.

The new program has the following features (Council for Economic Planning and Development 1998a). First, it is a defined-benefit program. All individuals will receive an identical flat monthly benefit that provides only basic living expenses. Specifically, the full benefit level at program inception (in 2000) is set equal to 65 percent of the average consumption expenditures in the preceding two years, or around NT$9,100 ($278) per month. The minimum guaranteed benefit level is NT$2000 ($61) per month. The benefits are indexed for subsequent years on the basis of consumer prices and labor productivity (real wages). All insured persons pay a flat monthly premium equal to 10 percent of the basic benefits level, or NT$910 ($27.80).

Second, upon reaching age 65, insured persons who are aged 25–39 at program inception will receive a benefit equal to the full benefit, divided by the number of years between 65 and their age at program inception, for each year in which they have paid premiums, provided that they have paid premiums for at least ten years. Thus they will be eligible to receive full benefits when reaching age 65 if they have paid premiums during all their working years. Those who are 40 and older at program inception will be entitled to one-twenty-fifth of full benefits for each year in which they have paid premiums if they have paid premiums for at least ten years or for $65 - A$ years (where A is their age at program inception), whichever is smaller.

Third, all those who are 65 and older at program inception are eligible for the retirement subsidy of NT$2,000 per month mentioned above without having to pay any premium.

Fourth, the benefits provided by the Public Employees and Labor Insurance programs will be divided into a basic and a supplemental part. The basic benefits are unified across the board and set equal to the full benefit level of the National Pension Program. The supplemental benefits, that is, the portions of benefits provided by the two existing programs that are in excess of the basic level, can vary between the two programs.

To be true to its stated purpose of being a forced saving program, the National Pension Program should be fully funded. However, the premium for a fully funded program would be too high, and there is a political need to maintain a premium not too different from the premiums paid to the other two programs. Therefore the premium has been set equal to 10 percent of the full-benefit level so as to gradually fund the system. It will result in an accumulation of reserves to the level that maintains financial soundness of the program for at least 25 years. In other words, Taiwan's new system is in reality a partially funded system, with the funding ratio increasing over time.

Figure 3, which projects the net lifetime benefits, or social security wealth, that each age cohort will receive from the National Pension Program, shows that the program will have differential effects. (See the Appendix for an explanation and derivation of social security wealth.) Persons aged 45 at program inception among the working population and retirees aged 65 are the biggest winners under the proposed program.

FIGURE 3 Projected social security wealth per capita (present value of benefits less present value of premiums) from the National Pension Program at inception, by age: Taiwan

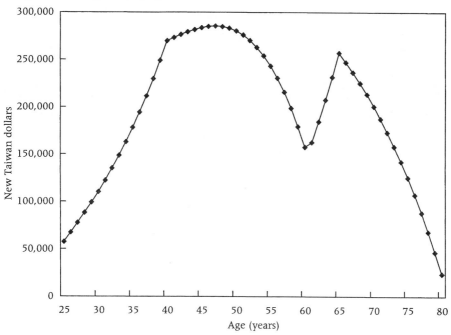

SOURCE: Calculations by the authors.

The estimated saving effect of the National Pension Program

We now focus on how the National Pension Program interacts with projected demographic changes to affect aggregate saving. The literature has shown that the saving effect of social security depends critically on the method by which it is funded, whether as a fully funded system or as a pay-as-you-go system.

In a fully funded system the government collects social security contributions from workers and invests their contributions in securities to earn interest. When a worker retires, the government returns the principal plus compound interest to him in the form of a lump-sum payment or an annuity. A rational person who saves for his retirement will simply reduce his private saving by the amount of social security contributions, leaving his consumption unchanged. But because the social security account is maintained fully funded, the sum of his private and social security savings will remain unchanged. The fully funded social security system does not affect aggregate saving regardless of changes in the population's age structure and longevity due to demographic transition. Of course, as life expectancy is extended and the length of retirement increases, people must save more for retirement. Likewise, if the retirement benefit per annum remains unchanged, the premium paid under the fully funded system must increase, as must social security assets.

A pay-as-you-go system, on the other hand, is an intergenerational-transfer system. The government directly transfers the contributions from workers to retirees in the form of benefits rather than depositing the contributions in the workers' retirement accounts. Thus the social security account for each worker is actually unfunded. The effect of a pay-as-you-go system is to crowd out aggregate savings, at least in part, unless retirees save their entire pension benefits for bequest purposes (Barro 1974).

The pay-as-you-go system also distorts saving decisions because the rate of return depends greatly on the demographic structure of the economy and is not necessarily equal to the market rate of return. The average premium paid by workers per dollar of benefit is determined by the dependency ratio (the ratio of the elderly population to the working population). The premium rises and the rate of return on social security falls when the dependency ratio rises. For example, the number of working-age persons aged 25–64 supporting each elderly person in Taiwan was 6.5 in 1996, but will fall to 5.7 by 2010 and to 2.4 by 2035 (Council for Economic Planning and Development 1999: Table 3). By then the premium required by a pay-as-you-go system will be three times as high as it was at program inception.

The empirical evidence concerning the effect of social security can be found in Feldstein (1974 and 1996) and in Bailliu and Relsten (1997).

Feldstein (1974) studied the US time-series data for the period from 1930 to 1972. He concluded that the US pay-as-you-go system resulted in a decline in personal savings of 50 percent. His study has been challenged, especially by Leimer and Lesnoy (1982), who found that social security had only an insignificant effect on US aggregate savings. Recently Feldstein (1996) replicated his 1974 study with additional data from the 1973–92 period. His findings indicate that unfunded social security in the United States has resulted in an even greater fall in personal saving, by nearly 60 percent. Bailliu and Relsten (1997), studying panel data from 11 countries for the period from 1982 to 1993, found that the pension reserve per worker contributed to an increase in aggregate saving. This result was stronger in developing countries than in industrialized countries.

One way to quantify the saving effect of Taiwan's new social security system is to perform a regression analysis of the effects of the two pre-existing programs on aggregate savings and from that infer the effect of the new program. This approach, however, is subject to the criticism that a policy change affects economic behavior and causes structural changes in the economy. We have therefore decided to provide a simulation analysis of the saving effect of social security using the structural parameters of the economy.

The structural model for our analysis is the augmented permanent-income or life cycle hypothesis. We first assume that individuals are rational or foresighted in the sense that they save for retirement, and therefore their behavior can be described by the hypothesis. Their consumption each year depends on their lifetime resources. Thus a social security system affects their consumption by causing a change in their lifetime resources. Following Feldstein (1974), we define the change in lifetime resources of an individual aged a that is brought about by social security as "social security wealth," denoted by $W(a)$ and illustrated in Figure 3. This is simply the present value of benefits minus the present value of premiums paid by the insured. It represents the net transfers from future generations and is denoted by Barro (1974) as national debt, although it is a component of individual wealth. The change in consumption of an individual aged a induced by social security equals the individual's social security wealth multiplied by $\Gamma(a)$, where $\Gamma(a)$ is the marginal propensity to consume out of wealth. As shown in the Appendix, $\Gamma(a)$ depends on the interest rate, the rate of time preference, and the degree (coefficient) of aversion to relative risk.

There are some individuals, however, who display myopic behavior because they either do not have information to plan their futures, or find such information too expensive, or are unable to commit to their lifetime planning. We assume that the behavior of myopic individuals can be described by Keynes's current-income hypothesis (see Hu 1996). For these individuals, social security contributions decrease their consumption by reducing their current disposable income, whereas social security benefits increase their consumption by augmenting it. The total consumption effect of social security on the myopic population equals $\gamma \Delta Y_d$, where ΔY_d is the change in total current disposable income. ΔY_d can be explicitly written as

$$\Delta Y_d = \sum_{a=R}^{T} N(a)b(a) - \sum_{a=A}^{R-1} N(a)x(a) , \tag{1}$$

where $b(a)$ represents the retirement benefits receivable at age a ($a = R...T$), $x(a)$ is the contribution paid at age a ($a = A...R-1$), $N(a)$ is the size of the age cohort a, and γ is the marginal propensity to consume (out of current income).

To summarize, the change in aggregate savings due to social security is as follows:

$$\Delta S = -m \left[(1-\phi) \sum_{a=A}^{T} N(a)\Gamma(a)W(a) + \phi\gamma\Delta Y_d \right] , \tag{2}$$

where ϕ is the fraction (income weighted) of the population aged a that is myopic and m is the fraction of the population that is covered by the National Pension Program. The first term inside the brackets is the change in consumption of the rational population, whereas the second term is the change in the total consumption of the myopic population.

A study by Deaton and Paxson (1994) of the Taiwan Household Expenditure Survey data suggests that, on average, young people are foresighted and do know how to prepare for the likelihood that they will have few children to provide for their retirement consumption. Even so, the life cycle or permanent-income hypothesis is not the perfect, although it is the best, model to describe Taiwanese consumer behavior. A study by Chan and Hu (1997) suggests that it describes the behavior of 70 percent of the population, and the current-income hypothesis explains the remaining 30 percent (ϕ).

Simulation results

The first step in our simulation analysis is to calculate social security wealth for each age cohort on the basis of the government's plan (Council for Economic Planning and Development 1998a), described in the preceding section. As we have already mentioned, the full benefit level is equal to 65 percent of individual consumption expenditures for the previous two years, which amounts to NT$9,100 per month, or NT$109,200 in the first year of National Pension Program. The benefit, however, is indexed to consumer prices and labor productivity (the real wage rate). Consumer prices are assumed to rise at an annual rate of 1.5 percent. The growth rates of gross domestic product (GDP) per capita and labor productivity (the real wage rate) are both assumed to be 3 percent per annum. Partial benefits are then calculated according to the stipulations explained earlier. The projected premium is set equal to 10 percent of the full benefit level, or NT$910 per month in the first year of the program. We find (see Figure 3) that the social security wealth so calculated is positive for all age cohorts. In the first year it is the largest for the cohort of age 47, NT$285,251 ($8,723) per capita, and is only relatively insignificant, at NT$57,473 ($1,756) per capita, for the cohort of age 25. Thus the new program is both a forced-saving and an intergenerational-transfer program. When it matures, however, the forced-saving component will dominate the transfer component.

The population of each age cohort a, $N(a)$, is based on the demographic tables constructed by the Council for Economic Planning and Development (1999) for 1995–2035. The council provides three population projections based on different assumptions about birth rates. Our simulations are based on the medium series, although in Tables 1, 3, and 5, panels 4 and 5, we also provide simulated results based on the high and low series.

As mentioned earlier, the Public Employees and Labor Insurance programs cover 73 percent of the population. Thus the National Pension Program will affect only 27 percent of the population (income-weighted). This ratio (m) is taken to be unchanged throughout our simulations. Following Chan and Hu (1997), we assume that the myopic population accounts for $\phi = 30$ percent of the total population in the benchmark case. The relative risk-aversion coefficient is 1 (see the Appendix) for foresighted individuals, and the marginal propensity to consume is $\gamma = 1$ for myopic individuals. (Chan and Hu 1997 are able to show only that $\phi = 0.3$.)[2]

Tables 1 through 6 show the simulated effects of the National Pension Program on aggregate savings on the basis of the stipulations described above. The values within parentheses indicate the change in savings as a percentage of GDP (on the assumption that GDP grows at the rate of 3 percent per annum). Tables 1 and 2 assume that the fraction of the myopic population is $\phi = 30$ percent. Tables 3 and 4 assume that the insurance benefits are as stipulated in Tables 1 and 2 but that the premium levels are set so that the system is maintained at a fully funded level and is actuarially fair. Tables 5 and 6 assume that there is no myopic population, so that the economy can be described entirely by the life cycle or permanent-income hypothesis. The difference between Tables 1, 3, and 5 on the one hand and 2, 4, and 6 on the other is that the first group assumes that the demographic transition is as projected by the Council for Economic Planning and Development (1996), whereas the second group assumes that the age distribution of the population from 2000 through 2035 remains the same as in 2000. In each table we perform sensitivity analysis by allowing the risk-aversion coefficient to change from $\rho = 1$ to $\rho = 0.6$ (second row of panels 1 and 2), the real interest rate to change from $r = 6$

percent to r = 8 percent (third panel) and, for Tables 1, 3, and 5 only, the demographic scenario to change from the medium estimates to high estimates (fourth row) or low estimates (fifth row).

We see from the first row of Table 1 that the government's proposed plan for partially funding the National Pension Program would result in a fall in aggregate savings by NT$25 billion in the first year, or 0.25 percentage points in the saving rate. The decline in the saving rate would increase to 0.69 percentage points by 2010 and further to 3.04 percentage points by 2035. That the program lowers aggregate savings indicates that it is both a forced-saving and an intergenerational-transfer program. Whereas it forces myopic individuals to save, its transfers component actually encourages consumption by foresighted individuals that exceeds forced saving. The fall in aggregate savings is not as small as it appears to be. The reason is that the program affects only 27 percent of the population. A full-scale program would result in a fall in the saving rate by 11.26 percentage points, or equivalently more than 60 percent in aggregate savings, by 2035. This result is consistent with the findings of Feldstein (1996). Although Feldstein does not explicitly consider whether part of the population is myopic, the coefficients of disposable income in his regression equations implicitly take myopia into account.

TABLE 1   Simulated effects of the National Pension Program on aggregate savings in millions of constant NT dollars and as percentage of real GDP: Taiwan, 2000, 2010, and 2035

Assumptions	2000	2010	2035
No. 1			
r = 6%	−24,958	−90,580	−837,632
ρ = 1	(−0.25%)	(−0.69%)	(−3.04%)
No. 2			
r = 6%	−13,561	−69,232	−792,618
ρ = 0.6	(−0.14%)	(−0.53%)	(−2.87%)
No. 3			
r = 8%	−12,890	−64,220	−614,926
ρ = 1	(−0.13%)	(−0.49%)	(−2.23%)
No. 4			
r = 6%	−24,965	−90,747	−843,390
ρ = 1	(−0.25%)	(−0.69%)	(−3.06%)
No. 5			
r = 6%	−24,958	−90,580	−835,607
ρ = 1	(−0.25%)	(−0.69%)	(−3.03%)

NOTES: In panels 1–3, birth rates are assumed to equal medium rates projected by the Council for Economic Planning and Development (1999). In panels 4 and 5, they are assumed to equal projected high and low rates, respectively.
r = real interest rate.
ρ = risk-aversion coefficient.

Table 2 demonstrates what would happen if there were no demographic changes. The first panel shows that the decline in aggregate savings due to the National Pension Program would be 0.25 percentage points of GDP for 2000, 0.47 percentage points for 2010, and 0.94 percentage points for 2035. A comparison of the first panel of Tables 1 and 2 shows that population aging aggravates the adverse saving effect of national pensions only slightly for the first ten years but to an increasingly large extent afterward. By 2035 it exacerbates the adverse saving effect by as much as threefold (3.04 versus 0.94 percentage points). The main reason is that between 2000 and 2010 the demographic transition will affect primarily the age distribution of the working population but will not substantially increase the ratio of the retired population to the working population. This is seen in Figure 1 by the fact that the upper parts of the age distributions for 2000 and 2010 almost coincide.

Tables 3 and 4 show that if fully funded (and actuarially fair), the National Pension Program itself does not cause any significant change in saving, regardless of whether there are demographic changes. The reason is that although demographic changes affect the amount of savings needed for retirement and the premiums that must be paid per dollar of retirement benefits, they do not affect social security wealth (equal to zero) and therefore leave unchanged the saving effect of fully funded social security. With a segment of the population being myopic, the program initially will have a positive effect on aggregate saving because it forces those myopic workers to save more than they would in the absence of the program. But when those myopic workers retire, they will have more income than otherwise to consume, and thus the effect of social security on aggregate sav-

TABLE 2 Simulated effects of the National Pension Program on aggregate saving in millions of constant NT dollars and as percentage of real GDP in the absence of demographic changes: Taiwan, 2000, 2010, and 2035

Assumptions	2000	2010	2035
No. 1			
$r = 6\%$	−24,958	−61,933	−258,645
$\rho = 1$	(−0.25%)	(−0.47%)	(−0.94%)
No. 2			
$r = 6\%$	−13,561	−46,863	−228,642
$\rho = 0.6$	(−0.14%)	(−0.36%)	(−0.83%)
No. 3			
$r = 8\%$	−12,890	−40,333	−143,675
$\rho = 1$	(−0.13%)	(−0.31%)	(−0.52%)

NOTES: Birth rates are assumed to equal medium rates projected by the Council for Economic Planning and Development (1999).
r = real interest rate.
ρ = risk-aversion coefficient.

TABLE 3   Simulated effects of fully funded national pensions on aggregate savings in millions of constant NT dollars and as percentage of real GDP: Taiwan, 2000, 2010, 2035

Assumptions	2000	2010	2035
No. 1			
r = 6%	14,402	18,267	−24,012
ρ = 1	(0.15%)	(0.14%)	(−0.09%)
No. 2			
r = 6%	14,402	18,267	−24,012
ρ = 0.6	(0.15%)	(0.14%)	(−0.09%)
No. 3			
r = 8%	14,402	18,014	−53,795
ρ = 1	(0.15%)	(0.14%)	(−0.19%)
No. 4			
r = 6%	14,406	18,337	−23,593
ρ = 1	(0.15%)	(0.14%)	(−0.09%)
No. 5			
r = 6%	14,402	18,267	−25,687
ρ = 1	(0.15%)	(0.14%)	(−0.09%)

NOTES: In panels 1–3, birth rates are assumed to equal medium rates projected by the Council for Economic Planning and Development (1999). In panels 4 and 5, they are assumed to equal projected high and low rates, respectively.
r = real interest rate.
ρ = risk-aversion coefficient.

TABLE 4   Simulated effects of fully funded national pensions on aggregate savings in the absence of demographic changes in millions of constant NT dollars and as percentage of real GDP: Taiwan, 2000, 2010, 2035

Assumptions	2000	2010	2035
No. 1			
r = 6%	14,402	15,704	5,361
ρ = 1	(0.15%)	(0.12%)	(0.02%)
No. 2			
r = 6%	14,402	15,704	5,361
ρ = 0.6	(0.15%)	(0.12%)	(0.02%)
No. 3			
r = 8%	14,402	15,471	−6,132
ρ = 1	(0.15%)	(0.12%)	(−0.02%)

NOTES: Birth rates are assumed to equal medium rates projected by the Council for Economic Planning and Development (1999).
r = real interest rate.
ρ = risk-aversion coefficient.

ing could become negative. Positive or negative, however, the saving effect of fully funded national pensions is small.

Our calculations in Tables 1 and 2 assume that individuals do not have bequest motives. Barro (1974) argues that individuals have bequest motives and take into account the tax burden of social security on their heirs. Should they do so, social security wealth would be equal to zero. Thus Tables 3 and 4 also represent the saving effect of social security under the assumption that foresighted individuals have full bequest motives. In this case the consumption of foresighted individuals is not affected, but myopic individuals are forced to save. The negative saving effect of social security is minimal in this case.

Tables 5 and 6 assume that there is no myopic population. We see that the negative saving effect of partially funded social security is greater than when part of the population is myopic (as in Tables 1 and 2). In the presence of population aging especially, the decline in aggregate saving due to national pensions increases from 0.46 percentage points of GDP in 2000 to 4.05 percentage points by 2035. Thus, according to the standard literature, if social security were entirely pay-as-you-go, the negative saving effect would be larger. The case for increased funding for social security is stronger and is further enhanced by population aging.

TABLE 5   Simulated effects of the National Pension Program on aggregate savings in millions of constant NT dollars and as percentage of real GDP in the absence of myopia: Taiwan, 2000, 2010, and 2035

Assumptions	2000	2010	2035
No. 1			
$r = 6\%$	−45,119	−141,244	−1,116,126
$\rho = 1$	(−0.46%)	(−1.07%)	(−4.05%)
No. 2			
$r = 6\%$	−28,838	−114,117	−1,051,821
$\rho = 0.6$	(−0.29%)	(−0.87%)	(−3.81%)
No. 3			
$r = 6\%$	−27,879	−106,957	−797,974
$\rho = 1$	(−0.28%)	(−0.81%)	(−2.89%)
No. 4			
$r = 6\%$	−45,132	−141,539	−1,124,443
$\rho = 1$	(−0.46%)	(−1.07%)	(−4.08%)
No. 5			
$r = 6\%$	−45,120	−141,244	−1,111,597
$\rho = 1$	(−0.46%)	(−1.07%)	(−4.03%)

NOTES: In panels 1–3, birth rates are assumed to equal medium rates projected by the Council for Economic Planning and Development (1999). In panels 4 and 5, they are assumed to equal projected high and low rates, respectively.
r = real interest rate.
ρ = risk-aversion coefficient.

TABLE 6   Simulated effects of the National Pension
Program on aggregate savings in millions of constant NT
dollars and as percentage of real GDP in the absence of
myopia and demographic changes: Taiwan, 2000, 2010,
and 2035

Assumptions	2000	2010	2035
No. 1			
r = 6%	−45,119	−98,951	−353,874
ρ = 1	(−0.46%)	(−0.75%)	(−1.28%)
No. 2			
r = 6%	−28,838	−77,422	−311,216
ρ = 0.6	(−0.29%)	(−0.59%)	(−1.13%)
No. 3			
r = 8%	−27,879	−68,092	−188,897
ρ = 1	(−0.28%)	(−0.52%)	(−0.68%)

NOTES: Birth rates are assumed to equal medium rates projected by the Council for
Economic Planning and Development (1999).
r = real interest rate.
ρ = risk-aversion coefficient.

We have also conducted sensitivity analysis and shown that the results are robust with respect to parameter specification. In general the higher
the interest rate, or the higher the intertemporal elasticity of substitution,
the smaller is the saving effect of the National Pension Program. The use of
the high series or the low series of demographic projections does not significantly change the saving effect of the program.

Conclusion

As Taiwan embarks on its new National Pension Program, it must choose
between a pay-as-you-go and a fully funded system. A pay-as-you-go system is not viable in the long run because of the rapid aging of the population. A fully funded system will avoid a negative effect on aggregate saving
but result in the accumulation of huge social security assets. If the government controls all those assets, it will become a socialist-style financial mo-
nopoly. The Taiwan government has chosen the middle ground by adopting a partially funded system. This chapter has shown that given Taiwan's
rapid population aging, the partially funded program will have a negative
effect on aggregate saving. This finding suggests that the funding ratio is
on the low side.

The negative saving effect of the program will be relatively small in
the first ten years but will increase afterward. To ensure that economic
growth and living standards are sustained as the population ages, a possible solution is to gradually increase the funding ratio so as to achieve the

forced-saving effect. This is essentially what Japan did in its 1994 reform of social security. It raised the retirement age gradually from 60 to 65, slowed the rate at which pension benefits were indexed, and increased the pension contribution rate. Adopting these steps in Taiwan will avoid the negative impact of population aging under the pay-as-you-go system and protect the long-term financial soundness of the social security system.

As we have noted, however, the Public Employees and Labor Insurance programs are seriously underfunded and have accumulated large implicit debts. If the National Pension Program forces the other two programs to clear their implicit debts or to increase their funding ratios, its negative saving effect may be alleviated.

We have concentrated on the saving effect of the National Pension Program, but there are other components of the program that may also affect the economy. First, the literature has shown that social security affects both labor force participation and saving decisions. Since the National Pension System does not impose a retirement test, however, its effect on labor force participation is likely to be small and can even be positive. The Public Employees and Labor Insurance programs provide full retirement benefits at age 55. If workers have to reach age 65 before they are allowed to receive pension benefits, early retirement might become less common.

Appendix

This Appendix derives analytic formulas for the marginal propensity to consume out of wealth and for the change in consumption of each cohort due to social security. We assume that the instantaneous utility function displays constant relative risk aversion (ρ). We use the discrete time version of the Blanchard (1985) model. The lifetime optimization problem faced by an individual aged a is

$$\text{Max} \sum_{t=a}^{T}\left(\frac{1}{1+\delta}\right)^{t-a}\frac{1}{1-\rho}c_t^{1-\rho}, \tag{A1}$$

subject to

$$w_{t+1} = (1+r)[w_t + y_t - c_t], \ t = a, \ a+1 ..., T , \tag{A2}$$

where T is the maximum life span, δ is the rate of time preference plus the mortality rate, c_t and y_t are respectively consumption and labor income, w_t is real assets, and r is the real rate of interest plus the mortality rate. The Euler equation is given by

$$c_t^{-\rho} = \left(\frac{1+\delta}{1+r}\right)c_{t-1}^{-\rho}, \ \text{ or } \ c_t = \left(\frac{1+r}{1+\delta}\right)^{\frac{1}{\rho}}c_{t-1} . \tag{A3}$$

Substituting the above equation in equation (A2) yields consumption at age a:

$$c(a) = \Gamma(a)\left(w_a + \sum \frac{y_t}{(1+r)^{t-a}} \right),$$
(A4)

where $\Gamma(a)$ is the marginal propensity to consume (social security) wealth and is given by

$$\Gamma(a) = \frac{(1-\theta)}{(1-\theta^{T-a+1})}, \quad \theta = \frac{(1+r)^{\frac{1}{\rho}-1}}{(1+\delta)^{\frac{1}{\rho}}}.$$
(A5)

We now consider how social security affects the lifetime resources, the terms inside the parentheses in (A4). Assume that the individual's current age is a, lifespan is $T = 80$ years, normal retirement age is $R = 65$, the age at which the individual is required to join the National Pension Program is 25. We assume that the real interest rate is r. The individual's social security wealth is

$$W(a) = \sum_{t=R-a}^{T-a} \frac{b(t)}{(1+r)^{t-a}} - \sum_{t=a}^{R-a-1} \frac{x(t)}{(1+r)^{t-a}},$$
(A6)

where $x(t)$ is the premium and $b(t)$ is benefits received at age t. If social security is pay-as-you-go, then the benefit level is determined by

$$x = \frac{\sum_{a=R}^{T} N(a)}{\sum_{a=A}^{R-1} N(a)} b,$$

where the denominator is the total population of age between A and R–1, and the numerator is the total population aged 65 and above. $N(a)$ is the population of age cohort a.

If the system is fully funded and actuarially fair, then the relationship between benefits and premiums is

$$\sum_{t=R-a}^{T-a} \frac{b(t)}{(1+r)^{t-a}} = \sum_{t=a}^{R-a-1} \frac{x(t)}{(1+r)^{t-a}}.$$

Combining the above equation with equation (A1), we find that the social security wealth is equal to zero.

The social security wealth for the entire population is

$$W = \sum_{A=a}^{T} N(a)W(a).$$
(A7)

According to the life cycle or permanent-income hypothesis, the change in consumption brought about by social security is

$$\Delta C_f = (1 - \phi) \sum_{a=A}^{T} \Gamma(a) N(a) W(a) .$$ (A8)

The current disposable income brought about by the National Pension Program is

$$\Delta Y_d = \left[\sum_{a=R}^{T} N(a) \right] b - \left[\sum_{a=A}^{R-1} N(a) \right] x .$$ (A9)

Assume that myopic individuals' marginal propensity to consume with respect to income is γ. The change in consumption due to national pensions is then

$$\Delta C_k = \phi \gamma \Delta Y_d .$$ (A10)

If the fraction of the total population not covered by social security is m, the change in aggregate saving due to the introduction of the National Pension Program is

$$\Delta S = -m \left(\Delta C_f + \Delta C_k \right) .$$ (A11)

This is equation (2) in the main text, which is used in the simulations.

Notes

We thank Ling Wang of the Council for Economic Planning and Development, the Executive Yuan, for providing the updated demographic projection on Taiwan.

1 The average price of housing per square meter after adjustment for inflation rose by nearly 50 percent between 1987 and 1989 (Lin, Chang, and Peng 1994).

2 Although studies of the US data suggest that the degree (coefficient) of relative risk aversion is between 2 and 4, the study by Chan and Hu (1997) seems to suggest that the relative risk-aversion coefficient is much lower. We cannot exclude the possibility that the coefficient may approach 0.

References

Aaron, Henry. 1966. "The social insurance paradox," *Canadian Journal of Economics and Political Economy* 32(3): 371–374.
Bailliu, Jeanine and Helmet Relsten. 1997. *Do Funded Pensions Contribute to Higher Aggregate Savings? A Cross-Country Analysis.* Technical Papers, No. 130. Paris: Development Centre, Organization for Economic Co-operation and Development (OECD).

Barro, Robert. 1974. "Are government bonds net wealth?" *Journal of Political Economy* 82(6): 1095–1117.

Blanchard, Olivier J. 1985. "Debt, deficits and finite horizons," *Journal of Political Economy* 93(2): 223–247.

Chan, Vei-Lin and Sheng-Cheng Hu. 1997. "Financial liberalization and aggregate consumption: The evidence from Taiwan," *Applied Economics* 29(11): 1525–1535.

Council for Economic Planning and Development, Executive Yuan. 1995. *National Pensions Consolidation Planning Report*. Taipei. (In Chinese.)

———. 1996. *The Projected Population for the Taiwan Area, Republic of China*. Taipei. (In Chinese.)

———. 1998a. *A Brief Report on the Preliminary Planning of the National Pensions by the National Pension System Planning and Research Committee*. Taipei. (In Chinese.)

———. 1998b. *Taiwan Statistical Data Book*. Taipei.

———. 1999. *The Projected Population for the Taiwan Area, Republic of China*. Taipei. (In Chinese.)

Cutler, David et al. 1990. "An aging society: Opportunity or challenge?" *Brookings Papers on Economic Activity* 1: 1–56, 71–73.

Deaton, Angus and Christina Paxson. 1994. "Saving, growth, and aging in Taiwan," in *Studies in the Economics of Aging*, ed. David A. Wise. Chicago: Chicago University Press for the National Bureau of Economic Research, pp. 331–357.

Directorate-General of Budget, Accounting and Statistics, Executive Yuan. 1997. *Report on the Elderly's Status Survey, Taiwan Area, Republic of China*. Taipei.

———. 1999. *Yearbook of Manpower Survey Statistics, Taiwan Area, Republic of China*. Taipei.

———. 2000. *Statistical Abstract of National Income in Taiwan Area, Republic of China, 1951–2000*. Taipei.

Feldstein, Martin S. 1974. "Social security, induced retirement and aggregate capital accumulation," *Journal of Political Economy* 82(5): 905–926.

———. 1996. "Social security and saving: New time-series evidence," *National Tax Journal* 49(2): 151–164.

Holzmann, Robert. 1997. *Fiscal Alternatives on Moving from Unfunded to Funded Pensions*. Technical Paper No. 12. Paris: Development Centre, Organization for Economic Co-operation and Development (OECD).

Hu, Sheng-Cheng. 1996. "Myopia and social security financing," *Public Finance Quarterly* 24(3): 319–338.

———. 1999. "Economic growth in the perpetual youth model: Implications of the annuity market and demographics," *Journal of Macroeconomics* 21(1): 107–124.

Krugman, Paul. 1994. "The myth of Asia's miracle," *Foreign Affairs* 73(6): 62–68.

Lau, Lawrence. 1998. "The sources of Asian economic growth," in *The Political Economy of Development in Taiwan*, eds. Gustav Ranis, Sheng-Cheng Hu, and Yunn-Peng Chu. Cheltenham, United Kingdom: Edward Elgar.

Leimer, Dean and Selig Lesnoy. 1982. "Social security and private saving: New time-series evidence," *Journal of Political Economy* 90(3): 606–629.

Lin Chung-Cheng. 1987. "Demographic transition in Taiwan and the care for the elderly," *Demographic Review* 10: 1–15. (In Chinese.)

Lin, Chu-Chia, Ching Oh Chang, and Chien Wen Peng. 1994. "An equilibrium analysis of vacancy rate and housing price: A case of Taiwan," paper presented at the Allied Social Science Association Meetings, Washington, DC, 3–5 January.

Lucas, Robert E. 1988. "On the mechanics of economic development," *Journal of Monetary Economics* 22(1): 3–42.

US Social Security Administration. 1997. *Social Security Programs throughout the World—1997*. Washington, DC.

PART THREE

DEMOGRAPHIC CHANGE, SAVING, AND CAPITAL ACCUMULATION

Growth, Demographic Structure, and National Saving in Taiwan

ANGUS DEATON

CHRISTINA PAXSON

THIS CHAPTER IS concerned with the effects that changes in demographic structure have had on Taiwan's national saving rate, and how coming changes in its age structure—notably population aging—will affect the future saving rate. We examine this topic within the framework of the life cycle hypothesis. Life cycle theory is a natural starting place, because it implies that changes in demographic structure can exert potentially large effects on national saving. According to the theory, increases in the number of people who save (presumably those in middle age) relative to those who save little or dissave (the very young and the elderly) will increase the aggregate saving rate. A related implication of the life cycle hypothesis is that changes in the rate of growth of per capita income affect saving. Higher rates of economic growth increase the lifetime wealth of the young relative to the old, and the effects of higher growth on saving are much the same as the effects of increasing the numbers of young relative to the old. The life cycle hypothesis also delivers a rich set of predictions about interactions between economic growth and the age structure. As is emphasized in the variable-rate-of-growth models of Fry and Mason (1982) and Mason (1987 and 1988), the effects of changes in age structure on the saving rate will depend on the lifetime wealth of individuals in different age groups, something that is determined by economic growth. These interactions are important for understanding how the Taiwanese saving rate has evolved over time and how it may change in the future.

A large empirical literature examines the relationships between demographic structure, economic growth, and saving. Early international comparisons of saving rates by Leff (1969) and Modigliani (1970) provided empirical support both for a positive association between growth and saving rates and for a negative effect of dependency rates—the ratio of young and old to the working ages—on aggregate saving. Subsequent empirical analysis has been less positive. The demographic effects were shown not to be robust to improvements in data and econometric technique (see, e.g., the review in Gersovitz 1988: 415–417). Although the correlation between per capita growth and saving rates remains robust in the aggregate data, there is strong and accumulating evidence from the analysis of microeconomic data in individual countries that life cycle saving is not the cause (Carroll and Summers 1991; Deaton and Paxson 1997; Paxson 1996).

An older literature implicates dependency rates, not only in decreasing saving rates, but also in hindering growth. Under the presumption that saving drives growth, not the other way round, Coale and Hoover (1958) argued that with high population growth the burden of children would decrease workers' ability to save and so limit growth. More recently Higgins and Williamson (1997), using pooled cross-sectional and time-series data from a number of Asian countries, have found strong negative effects of the dependency rate on saving and concluded that "Coale and Hoover were right." Indeed Bloom and Williamson (1998) and the Asian Development Bank (1997) attribute about a third of East Asia's recent growth performance to the increases in saving and labor supply, relative to population, provided by the "demographic gift" of low fractions of children and the elderly associated with the postwar baby boom and the rapid subsequent drops in fertility. Since the "gift" will have to be repaid as the baby boomers age, once again there are concerns for the future, not only for saving rates, but also for growth.

Taiwan's saving, growth, and demographic structure conform to the broad patterns of East Asia. High rates of economic growth have accompanied an increase in private saving rates from 5 percent of disposable income in 1950 to around 25 percent in the early 1990s. A sharp drop in fertility succeeded the postwar baby boom, so that the dependency ratios became low when the baby boomers entered the labor force around 1970; and they will remain low until the boomers leave around 2010. In 1950, 52 percent of the population were under age 20 and 43 percent were between ages 20 and 60; by 1995 the corresponding fractions were 33 percent and 56 percent (Table 1). The results of Bloom and Williamson (1998) as well as Coale and Hoover (1958) imply that Taiwan's future may look quite different from its recent experience. Lee, Mason, and Miller (in this volume) have simulation results for Taiwan that point in the same direction.

Our own recent work has been on the determinants of saving in Taiwan, in Asia, and elsewhere, with a primary focus on the effects of economic growth on saving and a good deal less attention to the effects of demographic structure on saving. Working with repeated cross-sectional surveys, our approach has been to estimate age and cohort effects in income and consumption in order to derive the age profiles of saving that are the fundamental determinants of the relationship between growth and

TABLE 1 Percentage distribution of the population by 10-year age groups: Taiwan, selected years, 1950–95

Age group	1950	1965	1980	1995
0–9	29.08	30.95	21.34	14.94
10–19	23.26	23.42	21.99	18.23
20–29	17.44	13.24	20.49	17.14
30–39	12.36	12.61	11.66	17.87
40–49	8.56	9.13	9.54	13.07
50–59	5.11	6.15	8.16	7.77
60–69	2.99	3.07	4.51	6.46
70+	1.19	1.42	2.31	4.53

NOTE: Before 1969, professional servicemen, conscripts, and prison inmates were not included in the population numbers.
SOURCES: Data for 1950, 1965, and 1980 were obtained on diskette from the Directorate General of Budget, Accounting and Statistics. Data for 1995 are from Ministry of Interior (1996: Table 1).

aggregate saving in the life cycle hypothesis. If saving rates are negatively correlated with age—as in the simplest model of saving for retirement—higher growth redistributes resources toward high savers and increases saving. In Paxson (1996) and Deaton and Paxson (1997 and 2000) we find that age-saving profiles for Taiwan, Thailand, Indonesia, the United States, and Britain show little negative correlation with age, which implies little effect of growth on aggregate household saving. These results also have implications for the relationship between demographic structure and saving. Because our estimated age profiles of saving are uncorrelated with age, changes in the rate of population growth have little or no effect on aggregate saving, at least for comparisons between demographic equilibria. The absence of such equilibrium effects for Taiwan and other countries is documented in Deaton and Paxson (1997). However, the changes in demographic structure that take place during a demographic transition are quite distinct from differences in structure across demographic equilibria with different fertility rates, so that the absence of an effect of population growth rates on aggregate savings does not imply that there will be no effects of demographic structure on saving during a transition. In consequence, our earlier results are not necessarily inconsistent with either those of Higgins and Williamson (from macroeconomic cross-country evidence) or those of Lee, Mason, and Miller (from simulations.)

In this chapter we use improved techniques and updated data from Taiwan to see if, after all, it is possible to tell a story in which demographic change has large effects on saving. We do this not because we have any reason to revise our previous empirical results—indeed they are replicated on the most recent data—but because our previous work paid too little explicit attention to demographic factors, and because our results looked only at demographic structures in equilibrium, rather than at the actual transition. Furthermore, our previous work relied on information about *households*, and on how saving rates vary over the household life cycle, where the latter is defined by the age of the household head. This approach, which is dictated by the data, poses problems when we try to translate demographic change, which makes predictions about people, into predictions about households, whose saving is what we know about from the data. It is far from obvious how changes in the age structure of population translate into changes in the age structure of household heads, and whether the age profiles of saving by heads' ages can be expected to be invariant to changes in demographic structure. In consequence, results about growth and saving are determined as much by assumptions about household structure as by our measurements of the age profiles of saving.

Following our more recent approach (Deaton and Paxson 2000), we construct life cycle saving profiles for *individuals*, not households. This new approach, like the household approach, makes its own assumptions and requires its own suspensions of disbelief. But the assumptions and suspensions are different, and it turns out that the new approach gives different results. Specifically, our estimated life cycle saving profile for Taiwan has a pronounced "hump" that is consistent with the hypothesis that greater old-age and youth dependency rates depress saving. These negative effects of children and the elderly on saving are masked when one is working at the household level, since few elderly and virtually no children live in independent households.

Given the hump-shaped age-saving profile we estimate, the life cycle hypothesis implies that increases in the rate of population growth can either increase or reduce the aggregate saving rate. At higher rates of population growth there will be fewer elderly dissavers relative to middle-aged savers, and this will cause the saving rate to rise. Children, however, will make up a greater fraction of the population, and this will depress the saving rate. Which effect dominates depends on the rate of economic growth. At very high rates of per capita income growth—in excess of 6 percent per annum—the lifetime wealth of the elderly is small relative to that of younger persons, and their dissaving contributes little to the aggregate saving rate. In this case the depressing effect on saving of relatively more children predominates, and increases in the rate of population growth are predicted to reduce the aggregate saving rate. Conversely, at slow rates of economic growth—in the range of 0 to 3 percent per annum—the lifetime wealth of the elderly is relatively large, as is their (negative) contribution to aggregate saving. Increases in the rate of population growth that reduce the elderly fraction of the population increase the aggregate saving rate.

Although these positive or negative effects of population growth on saving are possible at high or low rates of economic growth, the growth rates that have characterized recent Taiwanese history fall between these two extremes. We show that at growth rates in the range of 5 or 6 percent per annum, increases in the rate of population growth produce almost no change in the aggregate saving rate. The effects of having relatively fewer elderly are almost exactly offset by the effects of having relatively more children. The same is true for the Taiwanese demographic transition: given Taiwan's economic performance, actual changes in demographic structure account for a very small fraction of the increase in the private saving ratio since 1950. Likewise, the aging of the baby-boom generation will not adversely affect saving rates provided that growth rates of income are maintained. However, if growth rates were to fall, the aging of Taiwan could indeed drive saving rates back to their levels in 1950.

The following section begins with a summary of the life cycle model and its estimation using the "household" method. We lay out the basic implications of the life cycle hypothesis for the relationship between age structure and saving, then provide an explanation of the general methodology for parsing consumption and income into age and cohort effects, and for estimating the age profiles of saving. The presentation is verbal and brief; mathematical statements are given in the Appendix. The next section moves to an approach in which the family is seen "as a veil concealing purely individualistic behavior" (Gersovitz 1988: 401). This "individual" life cycle model allows a reinterpretation of the household data, permits a much cleaner link between population structure and aggregate saving, and shows much clearer demographic effects on age profiles of saving. We then use the individual results to construct counterfactuals for the past, running Taiwan's demographic transition through the estimated age profiles to assess the contribution of demographic trends to the rise in the saving rate. We also estimate the likely future effects on saving of the aging of Taiwan's baby-boom generation. In the final section we summarize our conclusions and discuss some of the more important and controversial assumptions on which the work is based.

Life cycle and aggregate saving by households

The life cycle hypothesis of consumption asserts that consumption over the life cycle follows an age profile, the shape of which is determined by preferences (or needs, or incentives to postpone consumption), and whose level—but not shape—is set by lifetime resources. The age profile of earnings or of income has no effect on the shape of the age profile of consumption, but serves only to determine its level. The budget must balance over the lifetime; but in any given period, borrowing and lending make up the difference between consumption and income. The life cycle hypothesis rests on the questionable assumption that capital markets are sufficiently developed to allow people to borrow against future earnings. Despite its short-comings and the mixed empirical evidence on its validity, the model nevertheless provides a coherent framework for the analysis of life cycle saving patterns. (See Deaton 1992 for a thorough discussion and assessment of the life cycle hypothesis.)

In a growing economy like Taiwan's, successive birth cohorts are each richer over their lifetimes than were their predecessors, so that, according to the hypothesis, the age profiles of consumption, earnings, and income are higher for later-born cohorts. Although the levels of these profiles differ across cohorts, their shapes remain the same, provided there are no changes in tastes or in incentives to postpone consumption, and provided also that earnings profiles retain a characteristic age profile that does not change shape across cohorts. Given these assumptions (which are not trivial and will be discussed further below), the ratio of consumption to income or equivalently its complement, the ratio of saving to income, can be described by an age profile that has the same shape for all cohorts. A final assumption, that bequests are either zero or an unchanging fraction of lifetime wealth, implies that the level of the age profile of the saving ratio will be the same for all cohorts.

The shape of the age profile of saving determines how the aggregate saving rate responds to changes in economic growth and demographic structure. In what Modigliani (1970) calls the "stripped-down" model, income is constant until retirement, and consumption is constant throughout life, so that there is positive saving until retirement, and negative saving (dissaving) from retirement until death. This negative association between age and the rate of saving implies that the aggregate saving rate will be larger the larger is the rate of per capita economic growth. That is so because the young, who are saving, have higher lifetime resources than the old, who are dissaving. The aggregate saving rate will also be larger the larger is the ratio of young to old (by exactly the same scale effect.) Faster economic growth drives higher aggregate saving rates, as does faster population growth. According to this argument, saving in Taiwan is threatened by the "graying" of the population, as it would be by a reduction in the rate of per capita income growth.

The stripped-down model needs to be modified to recognize the existence of children and their likely effects on the age profiles of consumption, earnings, and saving. While there is no lack of theoretical models, it is unclear from theory alone how these effects will work. The most popular view is that children act as a substitute for retirement saving. Children are costly to rear and to educate, and they require parental time and attention that lowers family earnings. The saving of families with children will therefore be lower, at least while the children are in the household. But children help care for their elderly parents, and their support reduces the need for parents to save when their children are young and lowers dissaving in retirement. There are other possibilities, however. If bequests are an important motive for saving, the presence of children may raise their parents' saving throughout the life cycle, for example to provide housing or small businesses for their children and grandchildren. Or, if parents have strategic bequest motives, they may accumulate assets so as to ensure their children's attention and good behavior.

Whatever the effects, it is clear that the presence and age structure of children are potentially important "taste and need" factors that shape the age profile of family saving. In the aggregate, changes in the ratio of children to adults in the population will also affect the aggregate saving ratio. Further, as Fry and Mason (1982) emphasize, these effects of demographic structure can be expected to interact with the effects of economic growth in determining national savings. For example, suppose that children lower saving for young families enough to cause dissaving at the beginning of the family life cycle, but that saving occurs in the household's middle age and perhaps some dissaving takes place in its old age. An increase in the number of children relative to middle-aged adults (with the fraction of elderly held fixed) will depress the saving rate. This is the familiar "youth dependency" effect. In addition, at higher rates of economic growth, young families will have greater lifetime resources than middle-aged families, the scale of their dissaving will be larger, and the depressing effects of additional children on the saving rate will be bigger. This is the interaction effect.

A similar story, which is more relevant to Taiwan's future, can be told about the effects of population aging. Shifts in the population from middle-aged savers to older dissavers will depress saving. The slower the rate of economic growth, the greater is the lifetime wealth of the older dissavers relative to middle-aged savers and the larger is the decline in the saving rate.

Taiwan is well-endowed with the kind of data required to investigate life cycle saving behavior. The Survey of Family Income and Expenditure (sometimes referred to as the Survey of Personal Income Distribution), collected by the Directorate-General of Budget, Accounting and Statistics, has gathered annual data on income and consumption since 1976 on approximately 14,000 households (fewer in the first two years), and this time series of cross-sectional surveys can be used to track birth cohorts of Taiwanese over time. At the time of writing, we have data through 1995, so that we can track the cohort of individuals born in 1945, for example, through their randomly sampled representatives in 20 surveys, from age 31 to age 50. Although we do not have enough years to track any one cohort through its whole life course, we can take the 20-year segments for many overlapping birth cohorts and infer from them both the cohort effects—the position of the segment for each birth cohort—and the age profiles, which are taken to be common across cohorts.

The techniques, which are straightforward, are described in full detail in our earlier work (Deaton and Paxson 1994a, 1994b, 1997, and 2000; Paxson 1996). The main equations are summarized in the Appendix, equations (A1) through (A6). Since consumption for each household is an age profile scaled by a lifetime wealth effect, the logarithm of consumption is the sum of a logarithmic age profile and a logarithmic wealth effect. For a birth cohort observed in a specific year, say the cohort of 1945 observed at age 40 in 1985, the average of the logarithm of consumption is therefore the sum of an age effect (that for age 40) and a cohort effect (that for persons born in 1945). To estimate these effects, we go through each survey, calculate the average of the logarithm of consumption for each cohort in that year, and then pool the data across the 20 survey years. Because the data are for households rather than individuals, we must define age and cohort in terms of a characteristic of the household. We take the age of the household head as that characteristic, a decision that we discuss at some length in the next section. For each survey we include only observations in which the head is between the ages of 25 and 75; there are too few heads outside this range to allow useful inference. These calculations give us averaged data on 70 cohorts, born between 1901 and 1970, who are observed as household heads for up to 20 years each. These averages of the logarithm of consumption are the observations on our dependent variable, which is regressed on a set of age and cohort dummy variables, thus allowing the shape of the age and cohort profiles to be determined by the data. There is no need to assume any particular parametric form. We then repeat the procedure for the logarithms of income, to obtain age and cohort effects for log income. The difference between the logarithm of income and the logarithm of consumption is approximately the saving ratio, which can also be decomposed into age and cohort effects.

The results are shown in Figure 1, which is an updated version of Figure 9.9 in Deaton and Paxson (1994a). Cohort effects in log consumption, income, and the saving ratio are shown in the two left panels, and the corresponding age effects in the two right panels. Because cohorts are defined here by age in 1995, we move from later-born to earlier-born cohorts as we move from left to right; and because earlier-born cohorts are poorer over their lifetime, the cohort effects decline from left to right. The age profiles of income and consumption do not have the hump shape that is often used to illustrate life cycle models. Instead, both consumption and income appear to increase steadily throughout the life course.

Of greatest interest here are the associated age and cohort profiles of saving, neither of which conforms very well to the standard expectations of life cycle theory. In particular, the estimated income and consumption cohort effects do not cancel out (i.e., they are not proportional in levels), and the lower left panel shows higher *lifetime* saving rates out of *lifetime*

FIGURE 1   Cohort and age effects in log consumption, log income, and the saving ratio: Taiwan, household model

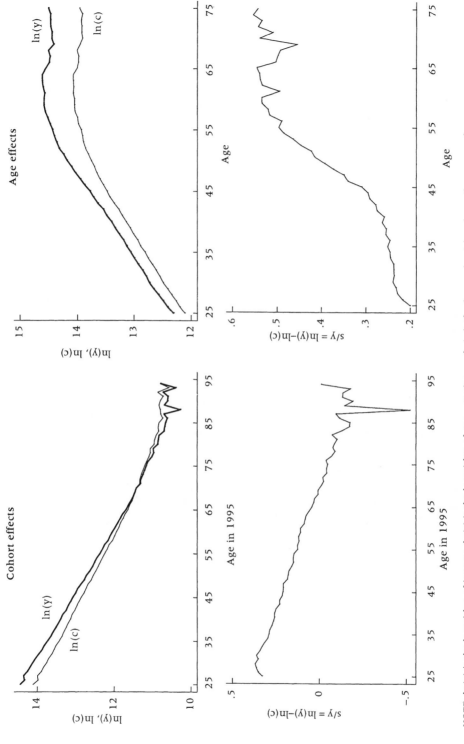

NOTE: ln(y) is the logarithm of income, ln(c) is the logarithm of consumption, and s/y is the (approximate) saving ratio, measured as ln(y)−ln(c). Age refers to the age of the head of the household.

resources for younger Taiwanese households. Taken at face value, this finding implies that bequest motives are becoming more and more important over time, with later-born households leaving larger fractions of their lifetime wealth to their descendants. The age effects are even more contrary to standard theory. Instead of saving rates being negatively correlated with age, with saving characterizing young households and dissaving characterizing the elderly, saving rates simply rise with age. Households with the oldest heads are saving about 30 percentage points more of their incomes than households with the youngest heads.

How can we explain these patterns? The life cycle explanation remains possible, but we would have to assign a great deal of importance to bequests, and we must accept quite unconventional age patterns of saving. When we first began this work, that was the explanation we adopted. However, when these methods were applied to the United States and Britain in Paxson (1996), the difficulties of interpretation were even more extreme, and it became necessary to think of other explanations. Suppose that for reasons we do not understand, everyone in Taiwan decides that it is more important to save, so that all cohorts, at all ages, slowly raise their saving ratios over time. (In the United States the supposition runs the other way, with everyone deciding to decrease their saving ratios over time.) We do not know what causes this change, except that, by assumption, it has nothing to do with the life cycle hypothesis. Suppose, then, we look for a life cycle interpretation, and fit cohort and age effects to these data. For any given cohort, we can fit the facts by choosing a rising age profile for saving; as people move through time, they will save more because the age profile is rising with age. But to match the assumption, we also want the 40-year-olds today to be saving more than the 40-year-olds did yesterday; and to make this happen, we need to choose cohort effects that are higher for later-born cohorts or, equivalently, are falling with cohort age in the base year. Offsetting time trends in age and cohort effects are just a complicated way of matching a time trend in the data, and this is what we see in Figure 1. See also Appendix equations (A9) through (A11). When the same calculations are done for the United States, we find the same phenomenon in reverse, with saving showing falling age and rising cohort effects, thus matching the secular fall in the saving ratio. For both Taiwan and the United States the changes in saving ratios have taken place for all households and are synchronized in calendar time.

These results tell us something of great importance: over the periods of our data the rise in the aggregate saving rate in Taiwan (and the decline in the aggregate saving rate in the United States) cannot be explained by the life cycle hypothesis, which attributes the trend to changing relative lifetime incomes and sizes of different age groups, each with a different saving rate. Instead, individual households at all ages and from all birth cohorts have been saving more in Taiwan, just as they have been saving less in the United States.

That the life cycle hypothesis cannot explain the trends does not mean that life cycle motives are not operative, nor that changes in demographic structure and economic growth would not affect aggregate saving rates. We can find out how much they might do so by conceding the time trend to "forces unknown," and then examining the cohort and age effects that remain. One way to do this is to force the cohort effects in the consumption and income regressions to be identical, so that there are no cohort effects in the estimated saving ratios, or, equivalently, to regress the average saving ratios for each cohort at each age on age dummies, without including cohort effects. More generally, this last regression can be estimated by allowing year effects (a dummy variable for each year) in addition to the age effects. Although the year effects are significant, their inclusion or exclusion has little effect on the estimated age effects, which are shown (from the regressions with year effects excluded) in Figure 2.

The age profile of saving in Figure 2 makes a good deal more sense than that in Figure 1, though it is still very far from the hump shape of

FIGURE 2   Age effects in saving with restricted cohort effects and time trends: Taiwan, household model

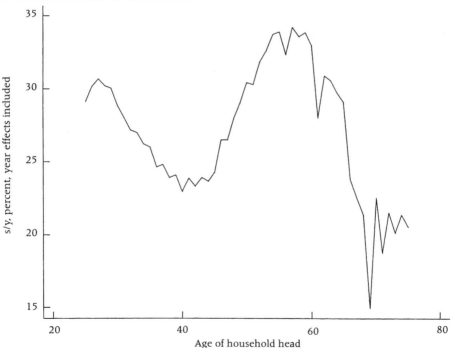

NOTE: s/y is the approximate saving ratio, measured as $\ln(y)-\ln(c)$, multiplied by 100 to convert to a percent. The age effects that are graphed come from a regression that excluded year effects.

standard life cycle theory. Saving rates are high for young households, when their heads are in their mid-20s. The saving rate then declines with age, until families with heads in their early 40s are saving 7 percentage points less than those in their mid-20s. Saving rates then rise until late middle age, declining once again thereafter. That saving should be lower for heads in their 60s and 70s is consistent with life cycle theory, although their saving positive amounts is not what one would expect from dissaving in retirement. The obvious candidate for explaining the low saving trough earlier in the life cycle is the presence in the household of children, and possibly of elderly adults.

Figure 3 shows age and cohort effects in the average number of children (left panel) and the average number of persons aged 60 and over (right panel), by the age of the head. The cohort effects in the number of children (left panel) show the decline in fertility: households with more recently born heads contain fewer children. Those in the right panel indicate that households with more recently born heads contain more elderly members. This reflects the increasing fraction of the elderly in the population, which more than offsets the increasing tendency of the elderly to live alone. Both sets of age effects peak at around age 40, which coincides with the trough in the age profile of saving in Figure 2, giving some support to the idea that children and dependent elderly depress saving.

The "twin trough" pattern of lifetime saving in Figure 2 implies that, in general, aggregate saving will respond to changes in both demographic structure and the distribution of lifetime income across birth cohorts. Even so, we have shown elsewhere (Deaton and Paxson 2000: Table 1; Paxson 1996: Table 3) that the effects are small. Indeed, at a rate of population

FIGURE 3   Age and cohort effects in number of children and number of elderly in the household: Taiwan

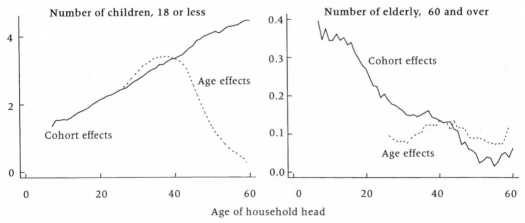

Age of household head

growth of 2 percent, the results in Figure 2 imply a small *negative* effect on aggregate saving of increases in the rate of per capita income growth. With steady-state income growth at 2 percent per annum, the predicted saving rate is 20.3 percent. This falls to 20.1 percent at 4 percent growth and to 20.0 percent at 6 percent growth. These are quite different from the large positive effects predicted by stripped-down models, in which a rise in the growth rate of a percentage point increases the saving rate by about two percentage points. The reason for the small effects is clear from the figure; changes in the rate of growth smoothly redistribute lifetime resources across age groups, so that the effect of growth on saving depends on the correlation over the life cycle of saving and age. Because of the twin troughs in the age profile of saving, this correlation is close to zero, indicating that changes in the equilibrium rate of income growth have little effect on aggregate saving. Of course these conclusions concern changes in the equilibrium rate of growth; patterns of growth that enrich particular cohorts at the expense of others could exert large temporary effects on the aggregate saving rates as those cohorts moved through the relevant age ranges. We shall return to this issue later in the chapter.

The effects of changes in demographic structure on aggregate savings are a good deal harder to deal with than those of income growth. It is straightforward to redistribute population mass across the ages in Figure 2, which would be the effect of changes in the equilibrium rate of population growth, and to calculate the effects on aggregate saving. And for the same reason as before—the low correlation between saving rates and age over the life cycle—the effects are small. However, changes in the rate of population growth not only change the weights of the age profile in aggregate saving, they must also change the age profile itself. Recall that the age profile relates to households, not individuals, and that the ages are the ages of household heads, not of individuals. When fertility falls, there are fewer children per adult and fewer children per household head at each age, so that if the first trough in Figure 2 is associated with children, we might reasonably expect it to flatten out. Similarly, there are now relatively more elderly people, only some of whom live by themselves. Others live with their children, and the higher ratio of elderly to adults in each household is likely to reduce household saving in the age group of the household head.

In our previous work, particularly Deaton and Paxson (1997), we made allowance for these effects as best we could. Two steps are required in making the adjustment. First, the age profiles need to be explicitly linked to the demographic composition of the household, which is done by adding variables for average household composition to the age dummies in the consumption, income, and saving regressions. Second, in making projections with different rates of population growth, it is necessary to "repackage" the numbers of people at different ages into numbers and compositions of households by the age of the head. Neither step is straightforward. The estimation of demographic effects on saving, unlike the age and cohort effects, is done parametrically, and an inappropriate functional form or unfortunate selection of age groups could compromise the results. But the second step is the more difficult. We use headship probabilities by age from recent surveys to turn population predictions into household predictions, but we have little confidence in these essentially mechanical projections. In consequence, when we find that changes in the rate of population growth have little effect on aggregate savings, it is possible that our results are driven as much by our auxiliary assumptions to get from people to households, as by the age profile in Figure 2, about which we are relatively confident.

Figure 2 suggests that different results might be possible under different assumptions. If the first trough in the age profile were to be raised by lower fertility, the negative correlation between saving and age would be increased, so that aggregate saving would become more responsive to changes in the rate of economic growth. This is exactly the sort of effect emphasized by the "variable rate of growth" model.

Life cycle and aggregate saving by individuals

It is difficult to move from population projections to their consequences for saving because the projections are about the numbers of *individuals* at different ages, whereas our theory and our data about saving relate to *households* indexed by the age of the household head. In our work to date we have solved this disjunction in favor of the households, transforming population projections into household projections. In this section we discuss the alternative, which is to turn the life cycle theory and its empirical implementation into a theory of individual behavior and to use estimates of age profiles for individuals, not households. The idea is to think of each person as following his or her own life cycle trajectory from birth, each being endowed with an age-specific consumption and income profile, and each satisfying a lifetime budget constraint tying lifetime income to lifetime consumption. Using Gersovitz's (1988) term, we regard households as veils for the individuals within, behind which individual consumption, income, and saving take place unobserved, with only the household totals revealed to the investigator. As Gersovitz emphasizes, such households permit individuals to consume more or less than their income without the household necessarily having to save or dissave, and by removing credit constraints, may allow household members to conform more closely to the theory than would be the case on their own. Young children and many of the elderly have no earnings, and their consumption can be supported from the earnings of other family members without the transfer of assets or liabilities. It would be possible to extend this model to allow household consumption to be different from the aggregate of the consumption of each of its members, thus recognizing joint consumption, public goods in the household, and economies of scale. But in the current analysis, which can be thought of as a first cut, we adopt the simplest version—that household income, consumption, and income are the sums of income, consumption, and saving of each household member.

There are other good reasons for moving away from households, and they have to do with being forced to define a household by the age of its head. When we track cohorts of households from one survey to another, the 40-year-olds in one survey followed by the 41-year-olds in the next, any changes in headship from one year to another will mean that we are not truly observing the same cohort through time. In Taiwan the head is defined as the main earner in the household. For example, in a household consisting of a working couple, children, and the husband's father, the older man will be head as long as he earns more than his son. But if, from one year to the next, the son's earnings overtake those of his father, the "age" of the household head will drop by perhaps 25 years, even though household composition has not changed. Equally problematic is the treatment of the elderly. Because many elderly people in Taiwan live with their children, where they may not be recorded as household heads, households headed by people in their 60s and 70s are a selected sample that is likely to become less and less representative with age. When we look at the saving behavior of those households, and how it changes with age, we have no way of separating out the changes that come from behavior and those that come from selection.

That selection is important can be demonstrated in a number of ways. For example, the education of male heads relative to the education level of all males of the same age increases with age from age 40 (Deaton and Paxson 2000). The heads who survive as such are more highly educated than those who do not. Figure 4 illustrates the selection more directly. It shows for each age (on the horizontal axis) the average age of the heads of households (on the vertical axis) to which individuals of that age belong. (For example, the figure indicates that 30-year-old Taiwanese individuals live in households in which the average age of the household head is approximately 35.) If it were true that once a household head, always a household head, the lines on the graph would coincide with the 45-degree line, at least after the age at which individuals become heads. Instead, the graphed lines fall at first, because many people in their 20s live in their parents' homes. Once we are beyond the age at which people have set up independent households, the head's age rises more or less one for one with age; this is the area of the graph where there is no selection. But after about age 50, the head's age ceases to rise with the individual's age, either be-

FIGURE 4   Age of head of household by individual's age: Taiwan, selected years 1976–95

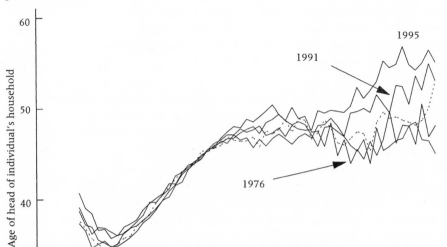

cause the earnings of a younger person in the household exceed that of the previous head, so that the household becomes "younger," or because a previous head moves in with his or her children or relatives. (The increase in the slope in the last few years indicates that more elderly Taiwanese are living alone.) But the deviation of these lines from the 45-degree line shows that it is dangerous to base a research strategy on the assumption that heads remain heads until they die. If instead of following households, we follow cohorts of individuals, we avoid most of these problems. Emigration, immigration, and death apart, the cohort of 41-year-old individuals is the same as the cohort of 40-year-old individuals a year before.

Our empirical procedures are explained in detail in Deaton and Paxson (2000), and the main equations are given in the Appendix, equations (A7) and (A8). Here we present a nontechnical summary. As before, our starting point is the set of 20 cross-sectional surveys on household income, consumption, and saving. For each cross-section in turn, we regress household consumption on the numbers of people of each age in the household, with age running from 0 to 99. Each regression, which is estimated without a constant, thus has 100 right-hand side variables (most of which are zero for any given household). Suppose we write the coefficient on age a from the survey in year t as $\beta(t, a)$. This quantity is the average consumption in year t of people of age a, which, according to the theory, is the product of an age effect (preferences) and a cohort wealth effect (the lifetime budget constraint). We can therefore treat each $\beta(t, a)$ in exactly the same way as we treated the household consumption data in the household approach in the previous section. That is, taking logarithms, we regress on a set of age and cohort dummies. The resulting coefficients are the estimated age and cohort effects for individual consumption, not household consumption. As before, the procedure is replicated for income and for the saving ratio, or at least its approximation, the difference between the logarithm of income and the logarithm of consumption.

There are two main differences between this approach and that outlined in the previous section. First, allowing for all ages separately allows needs to vary with age in a flexible way; this is something like including general controls for household demographic structure in the household regressions. Second, we are tracking individuals, not households, through the successive cross-sections, thus avoiding the problem of selection into and out of household headship.

Where there are only a few observations for an age group, particularly among the elderly, the estimates of the β's are imprecise and occasionally are negative. We deal with these by smoothing the estimates over adjacent age groups, essentially by taking moving averages. We impose a priori the restriction that incomes are zero for those aged 16 or less. Because these numbers are small in any case, and occasionally negative if children take a parent out of the labor force, we would risk obtaining many negative numbers by attempting to estimate these effects. We also impose the restriction that income is zero for those aged 80 and older. An alternative procedure for estimating age and cohort effects, one that does not require taking logarithms and so can accommodate zero or negative values, is described by us in Deaton and Paxson (2000). That method yields results very similar to those shown here.

Figure 5 (top row) shows the resulting age profiles for the logarithms of income and consumption for both the individual (left panel) and household (right panel) approaches, together with the saving profiles for both approaches (bottom row). (The bottom right panel reproduces Figure 2.) The issue of time trends in saving rates is the same for the household and individual approaches so that, as before, we restrict the cohort effects in income and consumption to be identical in the top row. The saving profiles in the bottom row are obtained simply by regressing the "saving rate," defined as the difference between the average logarithm of income and the average logarithm of consumption, on a set of age dummies. No cohort effects are included because these are restricted to be equal in income and consumption. A set of year effects can be included (but are not in these results); their inclusion makes little difference to the age profile of saving.

FIGURE 5 Cohort and age effects, log income, log consumption, and the saving rate: Taiwan, individual and household models

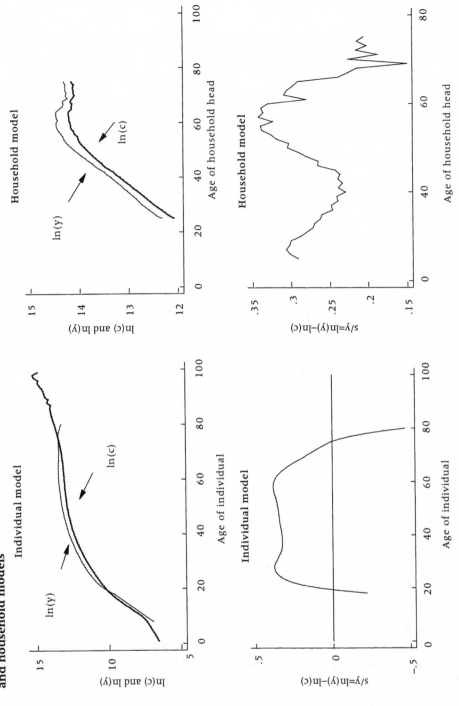

NOTE: ln(y) is the logarithm of income, ln(c) is the logarithm of consumption, and s/y is the (approximate) saving ratio, measured as ln(y)−ln(c).

In the household approach we must restrict age to the range in which there are household heads, here 25–75. In the individual approach we cover the full age range, 0–99 for consumption and 17–79 for income. We graph the saving rate for the age range 17–79, for which income is positive. Note that we are not assuming that saving is zero for individuals either older than 79 or younger than 17. Since income is assumed to be zero for these groups, and consumption positive, saving is negative and the saving rate is not defined.

The two graphs in the top row are reassuringly similar; after all, we are looking at the same data. Over the common age range, the two pairs of age profiles are quite similar, with log income lying above log consumption. The main difference lies in the range of ages not covered by the household approach. Partly by construction and partly by measurement, consumption exceeds income at low and high ages. As a result the two saving-rate profiles in the bottom row look much more different from each other than do the two profiles for either consumption or income (but note the different scales). In the individual model, saving rates are negative at the beginning and end of the life cycle. At intermediate ages, saving rates are similar to those based on the household data—indeed there is still a trough around age 40—but higher, as must be the case to compensate for the dissaving of children and the elderly.

It is straightforward to use the age profiles of consumption and income shown in Figure 5 to examine the effects of population growth on the national saving rate. The consumption and income levels of a cohort of individuals at each age are simply the product of lifetime wealth, which is assumed to grow at a constant rate across cohorts, and the exponents of the age effects of the logarithm of income and of consumption shown in Figure 5. Different rates of population growth imply different distributions of the population across ages. For any rate of population growth, the aggregate saving rate can be calculated as the ratio of the population-weighted sum of saving (income minus consumption) to the population-weighted sum of income, as shown in Appendix equation (A12). This aggregate rate can be calculated by using either the "household" or "individual" results in Figure 5, although when working with households it is necessary to make assumptions about the fractions of each age group that are household heads (Deaton and Paxson 1997). Another difference is that, when working with households, we compute the sums only over the age range 25–75, for which we have estimates; for individuals we use the full age range, 0–99.

Figure 6 shows aggregate saving rates as a function of the rate of population growth, with each panel calculated at a different rate of economic growth across cohorts. We show results using both the "individual" and "household" methods. Using either method, the results confirm our calcu-

FIGURE 6   Aggregate saving rates and rates of population growth for four rates of per capita economic growth: Taiwan

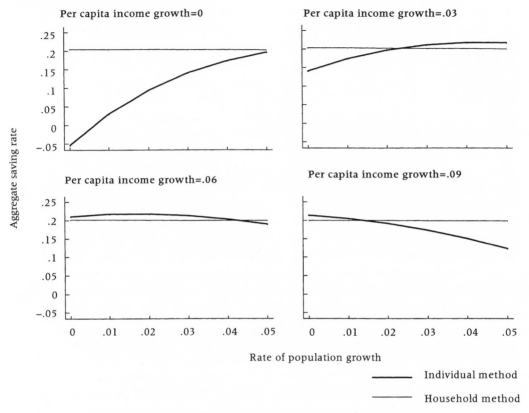

lations in Deaton and Paxson (1997) that at the high growth rates of per capita income that Taiwan has enjoyed for much of the last quarter-century, changes in the rate of population growth have little effect on national saving (see the bottom left panel). Higher population growth increases the numbers of middle-aged savers in relation to elderly dissavers; but it also increases, by even more, the numbers of the young who are dissaving, and the net effect is small. The results using the individual method are different, however, at lower and higher rates of income growth. In the top left panel we have assumed a per capita growth rate of zero, so that lifetime wealth is identical across cohorts. Because the youngest dissavers are not wealthy relative to middle-aged savers, the dominant effect of a decline in equilibrium population growth is through the increase in the numbers of the elderly relative to the middle aged—the young have insufficient resources to count for much—and the aggregate saving rate falls. Fertility decline can have strong negative effects on aggregate saving in Taiwan, but only when per capita incomes are growing slowly. The bottom right panel shows the other extreme, in which the growth rate of per capita income is very high, illustrated here at 9 percent per annum. Because young people are now so much richer than the old—at 9 percent growth a 5-year-old is 8.6 times richer than her 30-year-old father, 74 times richer than her 55-year-old grandfather, and 641 times richer than her 80-year-old great-grandfather—the dissaving associated with children is large enough to become the dominant effect when the young are more plentiful. At high enough growth rates of per capita income, saving declines with increases in the rate of growth of the population. The "household" method does not deliver these predicted effects of population growth on the saving rate, because (using this method) saving rates are similar across age groups.

Demographic structure and the past and future of saving

The calculations in Figure 6 are of saving rates when demographic and economic growth are in equilibrium, and when the growth rates of income and population have been the same for an indefinite period of time. Because these equilibria take so long to be established—we have to wait for the whole population to be replaced before the new patterns of age groups and lifetime wealth effects are established—it is possible that they are not relevant or useful for interpreting history over a few decades, or for projecting future saving, except in the very distant future. Indeed, as Higgins and Williamson (1997) argue, the effects that arise from a baby-boom generation working through the population are unlikely to be captured by a model that can handle only equilibrium demographic structures. Figure 7 and Table 1 show the actual structure of the Taiwanese population at 15-year intervals from 1950 through 1995, and the progress of the postwar baby boom is clearly visible. (The "missing" 20-year-olds in the 1965 data were in the military, who were not included in the population data until 1969. The massive age heaping at age 70 in the 1950 distribution reflects the fact that, in that year, the highest age category was "70 or older.")

It is straightforward to calculate the effects of the actual demographic structure on saving using the results that we have already obtained. The procedure is essentially the same as that which produced the results in Figure 6, except instead of using the steady-state age distribution of the population implied by different rates of population growth, we use the actual age distribution of the Taiwanese population from 1947 to the present. As before, consumption and income at each age for each cohort is the product of the lifetime wealth of cohort members and the exponents of the age effects in Figure 5 (with income set to zero for the youngest and oldest individuals). The cohort-specific lifetime wealth terms can be obtained up

FIGURE 7   Age structure of the population: Taiwan, 1950–95

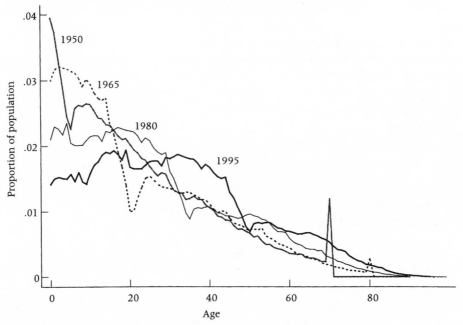

SOURCES: See Table 1.

to scale—and the scale factor cancels in the aggregate saving rate—in one of two ways: either by using the actual estimated cohort effects from the regressions shown in Figure 5, or by assuming that cohort effects grow from year to year at a constant rate equal to the average growth in our estimated cohort effects. The latter approach, which yields a growth rate of lifetime wealth across cohorts of 6.08 percent per year, has the attraction of allowing us to project backward as far as we like, while the former, although more realistic, confines us to cohorts alive during our data period of 1976 through 1995. (Since the estimated cohort effects grow fairly steadily, the difference is not large, as we shall see.) These calculations are not intended to capture year-to-year fluctuations in saving rates, for example those associated with oil shocks or other unanticipated events. But they should give us a good guide to trends and an indication of the contribution of demographic changes to those trends.

Figure 8 and Table 2 present the results graphically and numerically. It is important to start by establishing that the data from the surveys on which our analysis rests are consistent with the aggregate data. The first three columns of Table 2, the first two of which are illustrated in Figure 8, show the aggregate private saving from the national accounts, the private saving rate from the survey documentation, and the private saving rate as calculated by us from the survey data. The first two series differ somewhat,

FIGURE 8   Actual and counterfactual saving rates: Annual figures, Taiwan 1950–95

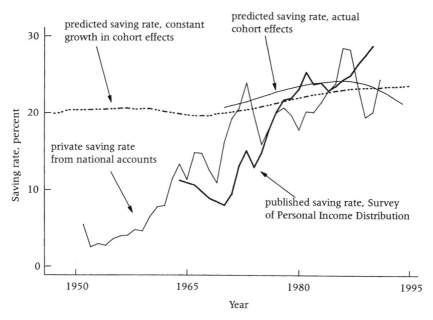

NOTE: The lines in this figure correspond to columns 1, 2, 4, and 5 in Table 2.

which is not surprising given that the former is private saving (including that by not-for-profit institutions) and the latter is household saving out of disposable income. However, both series follow similar trends. Our own calculations are a point or two lower than the published survey tables, again because of the precise definitions of consumption and income (we include transfers made to others in consumption, whereas the survey tables report net transfers out of income), not because our calculations differ from those of the government statisticians. The microdata are consistent with the aggregate behavior in the national accounts.

Table 2 and Figure 8 also show the two hypothetical saving figures that come from applying the actual age structure of the population to our estimates of age effects. Neither set of counterfactuals explains more than a very small fraction of the growth in the aggregate saving rate, and none at all before the 1970s. None of this should be surprising in the light of the results presented in the earlier sections of the chapter. From the first household estimates it was clear that, in order to fit the data, it was necessary to supplement the age profile of saving with a set of year dummies to capture the secular rise in the saving rate. As we saw then, and as reappears now, the life cycle hypothesis cannot explain the rising saving rate in Taiwan. That rise comes from a secular trend in saving rates among all cohorts at

TABLE 2   Actual and projected saving rates (percent): Taiwan, alternate years, 1952–94

Year	Private saving rate from national accounts (1)	Published saving rate, Survey of Personal Income Distribution (2)	Calculated saving rate, Survey of Personal Income Distribution (3)	Predicted saving rate, actual cohort effects (4)	Predicted saving rate, constant growth in cohort effects (5)
1952	2.55				20.41
1954	2.75				20.47
1956	3.95				20.59
1958	4.79				20.46
1960	6.52				20.56
1962	7.93				20.18
1964	13.34	11.23			19.88
1966	14.84	10.61			19.63
1968	12.55	8.87			19.63
1970	16.27	8.00		20.73	20.01
1972	20.62	13.12		21.26	20.30
1974	19.65	12.96		21.82	20.64
1976	18.03	17.92	16.53	22.47	21.09
1978	20.73	21.73	20.06	23.05	21.56
1980	17.86	23.17	21.43	23.54	22.03
1982	20.13	23.76	21.62	23.91	22.44
1984	22.90	22.96	20.38	24.14	22.75
1986	28.53	24.36	22.16	24.25	23.06
1988	23.57	26.38	23.80	24.07	23.25
1990	20.17	28.80	25.75	23.48	23.37
1992			26.43	22.55	23.48
1994			25.07	21.35	23.54

NOTES: The private saving rate from national accounts is calculated as the saving of households and private nonprofit institutions, divided by saving plus final private consumption expenditure. Columns 4 and 5 are predicted saving rates that are based on actual population figures and our estimates of expenditure and income by age, and estimates of cohort-specific lifetime wealth.
SOURCES: Column 1 is based on data from Directorate General of Budget, Accounting and Statistics (1991a: Tables 16 and 18). Column 2 is from Directorate General of Budget, Accounting and Statistics (1991b: Table 9). The calculations in column 3 are based on the series of cross-sectional household surveys described in the text.

all ages; it cannot be attributed to changes in the age distribution of the population or to changes in the distribution of spending power over an unchanging but age-varying profile of saving.

What, then, of the future? The baby-boom generation is aging, and according to our estimates the elderly save less. Does this mean that aggregate saving rates will fall? The answers, given in Figures 9 and 10, are based on population projections taken from Bos et al. (1994). The differences in the three graphs are due to differences in assumptions about the rate of per capita income growth, and to differences in the way we handle the cohort effects.

In both parts of Figure 9, cohort effects are set according to their equilibrium pattern for the relevant rate of economic growth. In the left panel the rate of growth is set at 6 percent, close to its historical value, and is held constant as the population ages; this can be taken as our central projection. The growth in saving rates still has some way to go, but will become negative after 2010. Even so, the effects are modest, and the aggregate household saving rate in 2030 will be only a percentage point or two lower than it is now. The right panel repeats the calculation, but with the cohort wealth effects growing at 3 percent and 9 percent in addition to the original 6 percent, which is shown for comparison (note the change in scale from left to right panel.) In the case in which the assumed growth rate of income is halved, from 6 to 3 percent, the fall in saving rates is large, and by 2035 the saving rate is below 11 percent.

These last calculations can be criticized on the grounds that, although we are using actual demographic data and the best available demographic projections, the cohort wealth effects are set at their equilibrium values so that, when income growth is 3 percent, we assume not only that it will be 3 percent in the future, but also that it was 3 percent in the past. We correct this problem in Figure 10. There we assume that growth changes from 6.08 percent to its stipulated new value in 1998 and calculate new wealth figures for each cohort, assuming that everyone knows immediately that the change will be permanent. For persons beyond age 65, we assume that lifetime resources are set and are unaffected by the change in income growth. For those who are in the middle of their working careers, their lifetime wealth is adjusted downward according to age, with the youngest suffering the largest change because they have the largest number of years to work at the new, lower growth rate.

FIGURE 9 Projections of aggregate saving rates under alternative assumptions about the annual rate of economic growth: Taiwan, 1947–2035

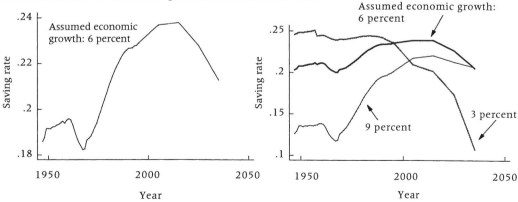

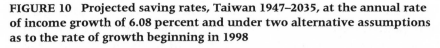

FIGURE 10   Projected saving rates, Taiwan 1947–2035, at the annual rate of income growth of 6.08 percent and under two alternative assumptions as to the rate of growth beginning in 1998

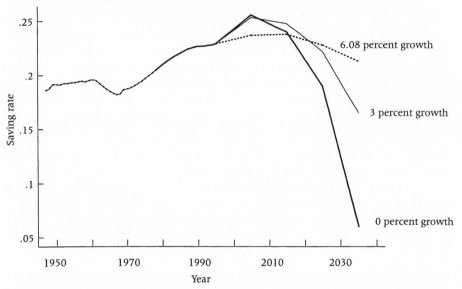

With these modifications, the drop in saving rates with lower growth is less severe than previously: compare the 3 percent line in Figure 10 with the 3 percent line in the right panel of Figure 9. Nevertheless, the same general effect is present. If Taiwan's economic growth rate falters, the combination of lower growth and the aging of the baby-boom generation is capable of sharply reducing the rate of saving. If economic performance is maintained, likely changes are small enough to be of little concern, and in that circumstance there is no reason to see the graying of Taiwan as a threat to its rate of saving.

Summary and conclusions

The life cycle hypothesis of saving supposes that the profile of consumption over the life cycle is set by preferences, including demographic choices and outcomes, whereas the position of the profile is set by lifetime resources. As a result the average consumption, income, and saving of a birth cohort in any given year can be decomposed into the product of an age effect, which is the same for all cohorts, and a cohort effect that summarizes the average lifetime resources of the cohort. In this chapter we have used time series of cross-sectional household surveys from Taiwan to estimate these age profiles for consumption, income, and saving; and we have used the results to investigate the extent to which demographic change and economic growth can account for the increase in Taiwan's saving rate within a life cycle story of saving. The methodological advance of the study, apart from an updated and extended data base, consists in the use of an "individual" version of the life cycle model in which we apply the life cycle hypothesis to the complete life cycle of individuals and trace cohorts of individuals through the various surveys, rather than use the more conventional approach of treating households as the unit of analysis and tracking them by the age of the household head. The new approach allows us to recognize that people regroup from one household to another over time, for example as the elderly move in with their children, and it requires no arbitrary assumptions about how changes in population structure affect household formation and structure.

Several important results emerge from the analysis. First, as in previous work, we find that the increase in Taiwan's saving rate, like the decline in the saving rate in the United States, cannot be explained by the life cycle mechanism, which attributes changes in aggregate saving to changes in relative population and relative resource weights over an unchanging age profile of saving. As in our own and others' previous work, we find that the upward trend in saving is not an aggregation effect, but an individual effect. Young Taiwanese now save a larger fraction of their resources than did their parents at the same age.

Once this is admitted, and the main part of the change in saving is attributed to unexplained time trends, more modest effects can be attributed to the changing structure of the population and changing patterns of lifetime resources. In particular, we find an age profile of saving with "two troughs," one associated with children, the other associated with old age. There is no overall correlation between age and saving rates, so that there are no large differences in aggregate saving rates across populations in demographic equilibrium at different population growth rates. Nevertheless, because of the two-trough pattern, changes in population structure through a demographic transition can have temporary effects on saving rates, where "temporary" is understood to be relative to demographic equilibrium. We use the model to assess the historical evidence in Taiwan, and to see how much of the actual increase in saving can be attributed to its actual demography and economic growth. Between 1970 and 1990, Taiwan's household saving rate rose from around 10 percent to around 30 percent. Of this 20 percentage point increase, only about 4 percentage points can be attributed to life cycle effects generated by economic growth and population change. Nor does the demographic future of Taiwan, and in particular its rapid aging, threaten its saving rate, at least if economic growth is maintained. It is only in the most pessimistic scenarios, in which very much slower income growth interacts with aging, that saving rates are predicted to fall sharply.

Our results are rather different from those in the two related chapters in this volume, by Lee, Mason, and Miller, who attribute a substantial share of the increase in Taiwan's saving rate to demographic change over the transition, and by Tsai, Chu, and Chung, who find that the higher saving rates of successive cohorts of Taiwanese can be tied to their own rising life expectancy and to the enhanced probabilities of survival for their children. Perhaps the most fundamental difference between our work and that of the others is the lesser extent to which we believe that the life cycle hypothesis provides an adequate account of household saving in Taiwan, or indeed elsewhere. In our earlier work (Deaton and Paxson 1994b), which is the platform on which Tsai, Chu, and Chung build, we assume that the life cycle hypothesis is valid and estimate parameters conditional on its truth. In our subsequent work, particularly Paxson (1996) and Deaton and Paxson (1997 and 2000), and the current study, the anomalies that seemed minor in our first study reappeared in much more serious forms, not only for Taiwan, but for other countries as well, including the United States. In consequence we were forced to conclude that time trends in saving ratios—upward in Taiwan and downward in the United States—could not be well explained within the life cycle framework, a conclusion that other researchers have also reached and is increasingly accepted in much of the recent consumption literature (e.g., Bosworth, Burtless, and Sabelhaus 1991; Poterba 1994). If this conclusion is denied and an attempt is made to fit the life cycle hypothesis to the Taiwanese data, the result is an upward trend of saving rates with age in the age profile and an offsetting upward trend with date of birth in the cohort profile. This latter result can be linked to other trending variables, such as the declining force of mortality, as discussed in Tsai, Chu, and Chung. The question then arises whether other trending variables might not do the same job as well or better, or indeed whether cohort effects are not simply a label for the time trend in Taiwanese saving for which we have no explanation. Lee, Mason, and Miller's simulations, like our own earlier work, take the truth of the life cycle model for granted. As we know, such a model can be used to make demographic trends affect saving rates, but the validity of the simulations depends on denying the central empirical anomaly that is revealed by our work and by other research in the literature.

Like all analyses and forecasts, our results rest on a number of assumptions, and we conclude by noting the most important and most controversial. In particular, we assume the constancy of various age profiles over time. As in most of the work on life cycle saving, and following Modigliani's (1970) original lead, we assume that the age profile of earnings is not changed by economic growth, so that economic growth affects earnings only across cohorts and not the age pattern of earnings for any given cohort. That this assumption may not be true has been pointed out many times in the past, as has the fact that the prediction that economic growth increases saving depends on it. Unfortunately, an examination of how growth changes age profiles requires more than the 20 years of data that are currently available, and we have maintained the standard (Modigliani) assumption on the grounds that it gives the growth-to-saving link the best chance of accounting for the data. Similar considerations prevent us from examining the effects of changes in female labor force participation on the age profiles of earnings. Our attempts to allow for it were frustrated by the brevity of the time series, at least for this purpose. We are also conscious of the absence of any treatment of decreases in the force of mortality. In a world where retirement ages are legislated and fixed, lengthening of the retirement span can be expected to increase the rate of individual saving if retirement saving is important. In an economy as flexible as Taiwan's, and without state-mandated retirement, we would expect an increase in life expectancy to increase the work span as well as the retirement span, with no obvious predictions for the rate of saving. If this were to be the case, the age profile of earnings would change in response to decreases in mortality rates, and for the same reasons as before we have made no attempt to take this into account.

Appendix

In the life cycle hypothesis with perfect certainty, consumption at any age is proportional to lifetime resources. Hence for individual i (household or person) born at date b and observed at age a (i.e., at date $b + a$), consumption c_{iab} is given by

$$c_{iab} = f_i(a)W_{ib} \ , \tag{A1}$$

where $f_i(a)$ is the age profile of consumption and W_{ib} is a measure of lifetime resources. Note that whereas the age profile is indexed on i, and so varies over individuals, it is independent of birth date b, so that the distribution of age profiles over individuals within each cohort is the same for all cohorts. The measure of resources W_{ib}, however, is invariant with respect to age. Taking logarithms of (A1) and averaging over all members of the same cohort at the same age, we obtain

$$\overline{\ln c_{ab}} = \overline{\ln f(a)} + \overline{\ln W_b} \ , \tag{A2}$$

where the lines over the variables denote means. Equation (A2) can be estimated by regressing the average of the logarithm of consumption for those born in b and observed in $b + a$ on a set of age and cohort dummies—that is, from the regression

$$\overline{\ln c} = D^a \beta_c + D^c \gamma_c + u_c \ , \tag{A3}$$

where $\overline{\ln c}$ is a stacked vector of log consumption with elements corresponding to each cohort in each year, D^a is a matrix of age dummies, and D^c is a matrix of cohort dummies. The coefficients β_c and γ_c are the age effects and cohort effects in consumption (c subscripts stand for consumption, c superscripts for cohorts), and u_c is the sampling (or, equivalently, measurement) error that comes from the fact that $\overline{\ln c_{ab}}$ is a sample estimate of the average log consumption of all individuals born at b and observed at $b + a$.

Earnings, like consumption, are assumed to follow an invariant age profile over the life cycle, but to shift up with growth. Income is earnings plus the interest income on accumulated wealth. Given that (log) consumption and (log) earnings can both be decomposed into cohort and age effects, so can income y_{iab}. Thus we can write, corresponding to (A3),

$$\overline{\ln y} = D^a \beta_y + D^c \gamma_y + u_y \; , \tag{A4}$$

where β_y and γ_y are the age and cohort effects in income. The difference between (A3) and (A4), if consumption is close to income, is approximately the saving ratio, so that

$$s/y \approx \overline{\ln y} - \overline{\ln c} = D^a(\beta_y - \beta_c) + D^c(\gamma_y - \gamma_c) + (u_y - u_c) \; . \tag{A5}$$

The age and cohort effects in Figure 1 are from estimates of equations (A3), (A4), and (A5), where averages of the logarithm of income and consumption are computed over household heads of the same age in the same year.

Under the usual assumptions that there are no bequests and that lifetime consumption exhausts lifetime resources, the cohort effects in income and consumption will be the same, so that (A5) will have only age effects. It can therefore be rewritten as

$$s/y \approx D^a(\beta_y - \beta_c) + (u_y - u_c) \; . \tag{A6}$$

Figure 2 graphs the age effects from this equation.

In the "household" version of the model, the subscript i in the foregoing is interpreted to refer to a household, whose age is given by the age of the household head. In the "individual" version, i is taken to be an individual, and (A1) is modified to read

$$c_{iab} = c_{ab} + \varepsilon_{iab} = f(a)W_b + \varepsilon_{iab} \; , \tag{A7}$$

where ε_{iab} is a mean zero error. We are now decomposing the mean cohort consumption into an age effect $f(a)$, and a cohort effect, W_b, interpretable as cohort average lifetime resources. For a household, h, included in the survey at time t, we observe household consumption, c_{ht}, which is the sum of individual consumption, so that

$$c_{ht} = \sum_{a=1}^{N} n_{aht} f(a) W_{t-a} + \sum_{i \in h} \varepsilon_{iat-a} \; , \tag{A8}$$

where n_{aht} is the number of people aged a in household h at time t, where N is the maximum age in the population, and where we have used the fact that someone aged a and observed in t was born in $t - a$. In the main text we refer to coefficients $\beta(t,a)$, which are defined as the product $f(a)W_{t-a}$ in (A8). These coefficients are calculated from (A8), which we estimated from regressions, one per survey year, of household consumption on the numbers of people of each age in the household. The estimated $\beta(t,a)$ are then "smoothed" as described in Deaton and Paxson (2000). We then treat them as estimates of individual consumption that we further decompose into age and cohort effects by taking logs and regressing on age and cohort dummies as in the household version of the model. These age effects are shown in Figure 5.

In Deaton and Paxson (2000) we describe an alternative procedure for estimating age and cohort effects that does not require taking logarithms and so avoids having to "smooth" out nonpositive values. This procedure involves stacking the coefficients $\beta(t,a)$ into a BxA matrix, where B is the number of birth cohorts and A is the number of ages. This matrix can be expressed as the product of a Bx1 vector of cohort effects and a 1xA vector of age effects. We estimate these vectors using an iterative principal components technique. This chapter reports results based on the log-linear decomposition, but results using the alternative technique are similar.

The fact that time trends in saving rates show up as offsetting cohort and age effects can be demonstrated as follows. Suppose that the saving rate for age a at time t is σ_{at} and that, for "reasons unknown," these rates are increasing over time at rate θ; that is,

$$\sigma_{at} = a_a + \theta t . \tag{A9}$$

Cohort c is measured as age in a base year, for example in 1976, so that year of birth b is $1976 - c$ and we have the identity

$$t = 1976 - c + a . \tag{A10}$$

Substituting (A10) into (A9) gives

$$\sigma_{at} = (a_a + 1976\theta) + \theta a - \theta c , \tag{A11}$$

so that the time trend appears as offsetting age and cohort effects in the saving ratio. When there are "genuine" age and cohort effects, the time trend will be added to one and subtracted from the other.

The aggregate saving ratios in any given year are calculated from formulas of the form

$$\left(\frac{S}{Y}\right)_t = \frac{\sum\limits_{a=1}^{A} \eta_{at} \gamma_{t-a} \left[\exp(\beta_{ay}) - \exp(\beta_{ac})\right]}{\sum\limits_{a=1}^{A} \eta_{at} \gamma_{t-a} \exp(\beta_{ay})} , \tag{A12}$$

where S and Y are aggregate saving and aggregate income, η_{at} is the number of people aged a at time t, γ_{t-a} is the cohort wealth level for people born in $t-a$ and β_{ay} and β_{ac} are respectively the age effects in the logarithmic income and consumption profiles. These β's are estimated as described above, as are the γ's in the case where the estimated profiles are used. Otherwise, when we assume that cohort effects are generated by an equilibrium economic growth path along which per capita income is growing at rate g, γ's are set to be $(1+g)^{t-a}$. Similarly the η's are either the actual numbers of people, or in equilibrium population growth are taken to be $(1+n)^{t-a}p_a$, where n is the rate of population growth and p_a is the probability of living to age a. In the household model, p_a must be replaced by p_a^h, the probability of surviving to age a and being a household head at that age.

Note

We are grateful to seminar participants at Princeton and Yale for helpful discussions and suggestions. We acknowledge financial support from the National Institute on Aging through the National Bureau of Economic Research.

References

Asian Development Bank. 1997. *Emerging Asia: Changes and Challenges*. Manila.

Bloom, David E. and Jeffrey G. Williamson. 1998. "Demographic transitions and economic miracles in emerging Asia," *World Bank Economic Review* 12(3): 419–455.

Bos, Eduard et al. 1994. *World Population Projections*. Baltimore: Johns Hopkins University Press for the World Bank.

Bosworth, Barry, Gary Burtless, and John Sabelhaus. 1991. "The decline in saving: Some microeconomic evidence," *Brookings Papers on Economic Activity* 1: 183–241.

Carroll, Christopher D. and Lawrence H. Summers. 1991. "Consumption growth parallels income growth: Some new evidence," in *National Saving and Economic Performance*, ed. B. Douglas Bernheim. Chicago: University of Chicago Press for the National Bureau of Economic Research, pp. 305–343.

Coale, Ansley J. and Edgar M. Hoover. 1958. *Population Growth and Economic Development in Low-Income Countries*. Princeton, NJ: Princeton University Press.

Deaton, Angus. 1992. *Understanding Consumption*. Oxford: Oxford University Press.

Deaton, Angus and Christina H. Paxson. 1994a. "Intertemporal choice and inequality," *Journal of Political Economy* 102(3): 437–467.

———. 1994b. "Saving, growth, and aging in Taiwan," in *Studies in the Economics of Aging*, ed. David A. Wise. Chicago: Chicago University Press for the National Bureau of Economic Research, pp. 331–357.

———. 1997. "The effects of economic and population growth on national saving and inequality," *Demography* 34 (1): 97–114.

———. 2000. "Saving and growth among individuals and households," *Review of Economics and Statistics* 82(2): 212–225.

Directorate General of Budget, Accounting and Statistics, Executive Yuan. 1991a. *National Income in Taiwan Area of the Republic of China: 1991*. Taipei.

———. 1991b. *Report on the Survey of Personal Income Distribution in Taiwan Area of the Republic of China: 1991*. Taipei.

Fry, Maxwell J. and Andrew Mason. 1982. "The variable rate-of-growth effect in the life-cycle saving model," *Economic Inquiry* 20(3): 426–442.

Gersovitz, Mark. 1988. "Saving and development," Chapter 10 in *Handbook of Development Economics*, Vol. 1, eds. Hollis Chenery and T. N. Srinivasan. Amsterdam: Elsevier North-Holland, pp. 381–424.

Higgins, Matthew and Jeffrey G. Williamson. 1997. "Age structure dynamics in Asia and dependence on foreign capital," *Population and Development Review* 23(2): 261–293.

Leff, Nathaniel.1969. "Dependency rates and saving rates," *American Economic Review* 59(5): 886–896.

Mason, Andrew. 1987. "National saving rates and population growth: A new model and new evidence," in *Population Growth and Economic Development: Issues and Evidence*, eds. D. Gale Johnson and Ronald D. Lee. Madison: University of Wisconsin Press, pp. 523–560.

———. 1988. "Saving, economic growth, and demographic change," *Population and Development Review* 14(1): 113–144.

Ministry of the Interior. 1996. *1995 Taiwan-Fukien Demographic Factbook*. Taipei.

Modigliani, Franco. 1970. "The life-cycle hypothesis of saving and intercountry differences in the saving ratio," in *Induction, Growth, and Trade*, eds. W. A. Eltis, M. F. G. Scott, and J. N. Wolfe. Oxford: Oxford University Press.

Paxson, Christina H. 1996. "Saving and growth: Evidence from micro data," *European Economic Review* 40(2): 255–288.

Poterba, James, ed. 1994. *International Comparisons of Household Saving*. Chicago: Chicago University Press for the National Bureau of Economic Research.

Demographic Transition and Household Saving in Taiwan

I-Ju Tsai
C. Y. Cyrus Chu
Ching-Fan Chung

Since the 1960s, economic development in Taiwan has been characterized by high growth rates in per capita income and high saving rates. In contrast to the saving rates in Western developed countries, which ranged between 18 and 24 percent during the years 1974 to 1987 (International Monetary Fund, various years; Organization for Economic Co-operation and Development, various years), the saving rate was above 30 percent in Taiwan. Taiwan has also experienced a fast pace of demographic transition. Life expectancy has been increasing since 1900, and fertility has fallen sharply since 1950, dropping to the levels of developed countries around 1995 (Department of Budget, Accounting and Statistics 1946; Department of Statistics, Ministry of Interior, various years; Directorate-General of Budget, Accounting and Statistics, various years). Lee, Mason, and Miller illustrate these demographic changes and corresponding changes in the saving rate in their chapter in this volume. It is well known that the decline in fertility among the developed countries started during the nineteenth century (World Bank 1980 and 1994), which means that it took Taiwan a comparatively short period to complete its fertility transition. This unusual experience of rapid demographic transition provides us with a perfect setting for investigating its effects on economic behavior.

Using household survey data, Deaton and Paxson (1994 and 1997) and Paxson (1996) have studied the link between income growth and saving rates in Taiwan. According to Paxson, two theories can be offered to describe the causal mechanism linking high growth rates to high saving rates. The first is the life cycle theory, which states that higher growth rates increase lifetime wealth of younger savers relative to older dissavers, thereby increasing the aggregate saving rates. The second theory focuses on habit formation and argues that unexpected income generally does not affect consumption, so that growth in unexpected income can induce high saving rates, at least over the short run. Paxson's (1996) empirical evidence, however, does not provide strong support for these two theories. It indicates that given a 1 percent increase in the economic growth rate, only small increases in the saving rate, of between 0.15 and 0.25 percent, are attributable to the life cycle theory, whereas an increase of between 0.16 and 0.34 percent is associated with the habit-formation theory. In contrast, Deaton and Paxson (1994) provide fairly convincing evidence for the view that behavioral differences across generations, known as the cohort effect, can explain quite well the changing patterns of saving rates in Taiwan. They contend that what causes the cohort effect are longer life expectancy and declining fertility. Recently Paxson (1996) and Deaton and Paxson (1997) have suggested another possibility, that cohort effects may reflect a spurious time trend that essentially is an unexplained upward trend. In their chapter in this volume they imply that increased child survival should reduce savings, but they argue against the possibility that longer life might account for higher savings of more recent cohorts.

The argument that the cohort effect is due to longer life expectancy and reduced fertility is not derived from rigorous economic theory and therefore leaves room for further investigation. We note that both saving and childrearing are major family decisions that are necessarily closely related. The impact of population growth on the saving rates has been examined by Fry and Mason (1982), Kelley and Schmidt (1996), Leff (1969), and Mason (1981 and 1987), using extensions of the life cycle theory framework. But the assumption in this literature that population growth is exogenous to saving rates is questionable because it ignores joint decisionmaking.

This chapter studies Taiwanese household saving behavior in a broad framework that not only is compatible with economic theory but also allows for the effects of demographic factors. We first take a closer look at Deaton and Paxson's (1994) analysis, from which we hope to obtain some basic ideas about how the model should be specified. In an attempt to test the life cycle theory for consumption in Taiwan, Deaton and Paxson suggest that long-term household saving decisions are exposed to three types of influences: (1) the cohort effect, which indicates that household heads who were born in different years would have different saving behavior; (2) the age effect, which reflects the life cycle pattern of household saving; and (3) the year effect, which summarizes the effects of macroeconomic shocks on household saving decisions.[1] Moreover, they argue that only from an empirical investigation of the age effect can one ascertain whether the life cycle theory holds or not. More specifically, if the life cycle theory does hold, then older persons should have lower saving rates than younger persons, since there is less need to save as one ages. But Deaton and Paxson could not find clear evidence of such an age effect in their empirical investigations based on Taiwanese data. They did find significant cohort effects that could be rationalized, as mentioned before, by Taiwan's longer life expectancy and falling fertility. Although the cohort-effect argument is intuitively appealing, it would be of greater use for more in-depth analysis if it were supported by an integral economic theory. It is to this end that we turn to Ehrlich and Lui's (1991) dynamic model of the joint decisions about household saving, fertility, and investments in children's education. Their model also permits us to consider the effects of prolonged life expectancy and children's higher survival rates on household decisions.

To examine empirically the dynamic effects of demographic changes on household saving, it is desirable to employ panel data. But no relevant panel data are available for Taiwan. What we have are data from separate surveys over a 20-year period between 1976 and 1995. The econometric methodology we adopt to deal with this data problem is to construct pseudo panel data from those surveys. Our main empirical findings are that household saving rates are indeed negatively related to children's rising survival rates and positively related to prolonged life expectancy. We also assess the life cycle patterns of household saving. We find that temporary increases in household income cause higher saving, whereas the presence of old parents and more children in the family, along with higher expenditures on children's education, results in lower household saving. However, our attempt to estimate the separate effects of different demographic factors on the desired number of children and on educational investment in each child is not particularly successful, perhaps because these two household decisions about children take a long time to respond to demographic changes. Lee, Mason, and Miller (in this volume) find substantial effects of increased longevity on saving and a negative effect of increased child survival. But they do not take into account the tradeoffs between fertility, saving, and investment in the education of children, nor do they consider the effect of survival on the rate of return to investment in children.

In the following section we briefly review Ehrlich and Lui's model. Next we introduce the data and propose the specification of the empirical model. We then present and analyze the estimation results. Finally, we summarize the main findings.

The theory

Many possible motives for parents to rear children have been suggested in the literature. One of them is the altruism motive, which holds that parents simply enjoy having children and derive utility directly from them. Another is the transaction motive, which posits that parents expect financial support from children in the future. Becker and Barro (1988), Becker and Murphy (1989), Becker, Murphy, and Tamura (1990), Kohlberg (1976), and Riboud (1988) focus on the role of altruism in parents' investment in children's human capital. Ehrlich and Lui (1991) argue that the transaction motive better explains the changes in both human-capital investment and fertility. Here we present a brief review of Ehrlich and Lui's theory, stressing those comparative statics results that serve as guidelines for our later empirical analysis. A more detailed analysis is given in the Appendix.

In Ehrlich and Lui's model, the lifetime of an individual is divided into three overlapping generations—those of a child, a young parent, and an old parent. The model assumes that children depend completely on young parents for support whereas old parents depend on both their own savings and the support of young parents. It is young parents who make decisions on the saving rate, the rate of human-capital investment in each child, and the number of children to have. The model implicity assumes that young parents cannot vary the length of their working life, which is exogenously fixed to coincide with the next generation. This assumption is similar to the treatment of working life in Lee, Mason, and Miller's chapter, which holds age profile of earning fixed while mortality declines. Deaton and Paxson, however, argue in this volume that people work longer rather than save more as their life expectancy rises.

Ehrlich and Lui postulate that each young parent during childhood receives from his or her parents human-capital investment, H_1, which is then added to his or her own fixed endowment. The accumulated human capital represents the total resource available to young parents, from which a specific portion, s, is saved while the portion h is devoted to human-capital investment in each of the n children they decide to have. Moreover, upon receiving the human capital (H_1), young parents are expected by their older parents to return the favor. This is what we refer to as the transaction motive on the part of older parents. But not all older parents survive to enjoy this returned favor, and their survival probability is assumed to be π_2. By combining all these considerations, we can define the expected resource available for young parents' current consumption.

In Ehrlich and Lui's framework, young parents' future utility consists of three parts. First, its basic amount of consumption is generated from human-capital accumulation as well as savings. Second, the transaction motive dictates that when young parents provide for their children, they expect to retrieve a portion of the human capital received by each of their children, while they also know that not all their children may live to their adulthood and that the children's survival probability is π_1. And third, besides the consumption due to the transaction motive, the altruistic motive dictates that older parents may derive utility directly from the companionship of their children, which is a function of the expected number of children as well as the quality of each child implied by the human capital each child receives.

Young parents' utility is assumed to be an intertemporally separable function of current consumption and future consumption. Young parents choose the optimal levels of saving rate *(s)*, the number of children *(n)*, and the rate of human-capital investment *(h)* in each child to maximize utility. Since the analytical solution to such utility maximization is too complicated to solve, Ehrlich and Lui simulate the dynamic effects of young persons' survival probability (π_1) and old persons' survival probability (π_2) on the solutions to *s*, *n*, and *h*. Here we concentrate on the comparative statics and examine the effects of π_1, π_2, and H_1 on the choices of *s*, *n*, and *h*. To make the analysis manageable, we divide the utility-maximizing process into two cases: the transaction case, in which there is no altruism motive, and the altruism case, in which parents do not expect support from children. The mathematical derivation of comparative statics is included in the Appendix, and the results are presented in Table 1.

From Table 1 we note that irrespective of the type of motive, the saving rate *(s)* is negatively related to young persons' survival probability (π_1) and positively related to old persons' survival probability (π_2). These results can be explained as follows: When young persons' survival probability rises, the expected returns to both the human-capital investment in children and the number of children tend to go up and therefore reduce the importance of saving. But when old persons' survival probability increases, then saving becomes more important simply because a longer life is expected. How the amount of human-capital investment that the young parents received affects their saving is less clear, particularly under the transaction motive. This is understandable because H_1 appears in both current consumption and future consumption, so that its effects on utility cannot be determined without additional assumptions. Nevertheless, if only the

TABLE 1   Comparative statics for transaction and altruism models

	Choice variables					
	Saving rate *(s)*		Human-capital investment *(h)*		Number of children *(n)*	
Parameters	Transaction	Altruism	Transaction	Altruism	Transaction	Altruism
π_1	−	−	+	0	−	+
π_2	+	+	?	0	0	+
H_1	?	+	?	0	0	−

NOTE: A plus sign (+) means a positive relationship; a minus sign (−) means a negative relationship; a zero means no relationship; and a question mark (?) means that the relationship is unclear.
π_1 = children's survival probability.
π_2 = older parents' survival probability.
H_1 = the amount of human-capital investment the young parents received.

altruism motive is present, then H_1 is positively related to the returns to saving and therefore to the level of the saving rate *(s)*.

It is also noteworthy that in the altruism case the optimal rate of human-capital investment *(h)* in each child can be shown to be independent of π_1, π_2, and H_1, as indicated in the fourth column of Table 1. Because the desired number of children in the transaction case is simply $n = 1/\pi_1$, n is inversely related to π_1 and is unrelated to the other two factors. As for the positive relationship between h and π_1 in the transaction case, the intuition is that the rate of return with respect to investment in children's education will increase when their survival probability rises. The effects of the demographic factors on the desired number of children *(n)* under the altruism motive can also be explained as follows: the increases in π_1 and π_2 raise the utility of children to young parents so that n will increase. But if the amount of human-capital investment (H_1) the young parents have received becomes larger, then the time cost of rearing children increases and therefore n will fall.

Because our findings in Table 1 are derived for the two separate cases of altruism and transaction motives, it goes without saying that the empirically relevant comparative statics will be something in between if both motives are believed to be present. Angus Deaton has pointed out to us that since altruism is a luxury good, the relative importance of the transaction and altruism motives may vary with lifetime income.

The data

The data we use come from the Survey of Personal Income Distribution conducted by the Directorate-General of Budget, Accounting and Statistics of the Executive Yuan in Taiwan. This survey, conducted each year, covers between 13,000 and 16,000 households (between 7,000 and 9,000 households in 1976 and 1977). We use these cross-sectional data for the 20 years between 1976 and 1995. For any given year we partition the sampled households into cells based on the values of five variables: cohort (i.e., the birth year of the household head), education level, residence location, the presence of older parents, and the number of working members. Each cohort consists of those households whose heads were born in the same five years, 1916–20, …, 1961–65, so that we have ten cohorts. The reason for considering five-year cohorts, instead of the usual single-year cohorts, is to match the definition of cohorts with the definitions of the survival rates π_1, π_2, which we will discuss shortly.

Cells based on the same definitions across different years are identified and matched. Such a cell-based data set is the so-called pseudo panel data in which the basic sample unit in each year is not an individual household but a cell. The values of all the variables are cell averages. Because our study is concerned mainly with the decisions of working adults, we discard those households whose heads are below age 30 and above age 60. The total number of cells is 5,944. Basic information about the construction of these pseudo panel data are presented in Table 2.

The main variables in our analysis are the saving rate (s), the human-capital investment in each child (h), and the number of children (n). Here we briefly explain how these variables are defined. Given that saving is defined as the difference between household disposable income and consumption, the saving rate is simply the ratio of saving to household disposable income. The human-capital investment in each child is the most difficult to obtain from the source data. Here we use the expenditure on education, culture and information, and related expenses as a proxy. These expenses include spending on books, stationery, magazines, and newspapers; they are expressed as a percentage of household disposable income. As for the number of children, it is defined to be the number of household members who are younger than 20. Here the definition of n is the same as that used in Deaton and Paxson (1994 and 1997) and Paxson (1996). In Table 3 we present the cohort averages for s, h, and n.

The data we use to define the number of children (n) are the number of children in the household. But what we are concerned with in this chapter is planned fertility, the number of children that a couple decide to have. Since children tend to move away from their parents' home as they age, older parents are likely to have fewer children living with them even if their fertility was higher than that of younger parents. And because the earlier-born cohorts are observed at older ages and the later-born at younger ages, the data will erroneously indicate lower fertility for the older cohorts. This is what we see in Table 3, where the cohorts born at the earlier dates

TABLE 2   The basic structure of the pseudo panel data: Taiwan, 1976–95

Birth year of household head	Sample years	Ages of household heads in sample year	Sample sizes of birth cohorts
1916–20	1976–78	58–60	459–790
1921–25	1976–83	53–60	669–1,283
1926–30	1976–88	48–60	1,034–1,767
1931–35	1976–93	43–60	1,010–1,770
1936–40	1976–95	38–57	967–1,725
1941–45	1976–95	33–52	935–1,727
1946–50	1978–95	30–47	1,370–1,988
1951–55	1983–95	30–42	1,800–2,382
1956–60	1988–95	30–37	1,636–2,031
1961–65	1993–95	30–32	1,136–1,358

TABLE 3 Cohort averages of the main variables: Taiwan, 1976–95

Birth year	Saving (s) (%)	Human-capital investment (h) (%)	Number of children (n)	h x n (%)	π_1	π_2
1916–20	19	1.0	1.9	2.0	0.78	0.33
1921–25	21	1.4	1.7	3.0	0.86	0.40
1926–30	22	1.5	1.8	3.3	0.88	0.42
1931–35	23	1.8	1.8	3.9	0.91	0.46
1936–40	22	2.0	2.1	4.7	0.93	0.48
1941–45	20	2.2	2.4	5.1	0.95	0.53
1946–50	20	2.1	2.4	5.0	0.95	0.59
1951–55	20	2.1	2.3	4.7	0.96	0.59
1956–60	22	2.0	2.0	4.2	0.96	0.62
1961–65	22	1.6	1.6	3.4	0.97	0.64

NOTE: For definition of variables see discussion in the text.

have lower values of n. The data for the human-capital investment run into similar problems. We discuss these problems further in the next section, where we explain how we deal with them in our empirical model.

The data on survival rates are drawn from the *Taiwan-Fukien Abridged Life Tables*, published by the Department of Statistics, Ministry of Interior. We construct the values of π_1, which we define as the probability of survival from age 0 to age 29, and π_2, the probability of survival from age 60 to age 74, for the ten five-year spans between 1950 and 1995. The results, presented in the last two columns of Table 3, show that both survival rates have been rising, although π_1 has gradually stabilized.[2] To understand how the data of π_1 and π_2 are matched to cohorts, let us consider, for instance, the cohort born during 1936–40. The corresponding π_1 and π_2 (which from Table 3 are 0.93 and 0.48, respectively) are those from the five-year span of 1966–70, during which the cohort was, on average, 30 years old.

The empirical model

In our empirical model we assume that the saving rate (s), the number of children (n), and the human-capital investment in each child (h) are determined by a representative individual at age 30. The reduced form for each of these three variables is specified as in the following general expression:

$$y_{i(t),t} = f_{i(t)} + x'_{i(t),t}\beta + \varepsilon_{i(t),t} , \tag{1}$$

for $i(t) = 1, ..., N_t$ and $t = 1, ..., T$, where the subscript $i(t)$ refers to cells and the number of cells (N_t) is different for each year t. The total number of years (T) in our data is 20. In this regression equation the dependent variable $y_{i(t),t}$ can be either the saving rate (s), the number of children (n), or the human-capital investment in each child (h). On the right-hand side, besides the usual vector of explanatory variables, $x_{i(t),t}$, and the disturbance term, $\varepsilon_{i(t),t}$, we have the time-invariant individual effect, $f_{i(t)}$, which characterizes the pseudo panel data.

In an earlier version of this study we tried to interpret our empirical setting as a simultaneous equation system. But as an anonymous referee indicated, the estimation of such a simultaneous equation system suffers from the identification problem because it is difficult to find instrumental variables that can be reasonably thought to enter into one equation but not the other two. We eventually gave up on that attempt and now focus on the estimation of the reduced form. But estimating the particularly interesting structural effect of h and n on the saving rate s is possible only in the simultaneous system. Given the reduced form of equation (1), our focus is necessarily narrowed to the estimation of the exogenous cohort effects, as will become clear shortly.

The time-invariant individual effect, $f_{i(t)}$, can be broadly decomposed as $f_{i(t)} = C_{i(t)} + H_{i(t)}$, where $C_{i(t)}$ is the cohort effect and $H_{i(t)}$ represents the human-capital stock. The most important assumption with respect to our model specification is that, following Deaton and Paxson's (1994) suggestion, we assume that the cohort effect can be characterized by the two survival rates of $\pi_{1,i(t)}$ and $\pi_{2,i(t)}$ that are faced by an individual when he or she is 30 years of age. More specifically, we assume that the cohort effect is a linear combination of $\pi_{1,i(t)}$ and $\pi_{2,i(t)}$:

$$C_{i(t)} = \delta_1 \pi_{1,i(t)} + \delta_2 \pi_{2,i(t)} , \qquad (2)$$

where δ_1 and δ_2 are parameters.

As for the specification of the time-invariant human capital stock, $H_{i(t)}$, we assume that it is a linear function of an individual's education level and residence location at the age of 30. The education level can be viewed as a proxy for H_1, the amount of human-capital investment that young parents received, and therefore reflects an approximation of the lifetime income. (If changes in permanent income affect consumption, they will also affect savings, which are the difference between disposable income and consumption.) In our data the education level is represented by two dummy variables for the high school and college levels of education, while the base is the elementary level. The residence location is also represented by two dummies, one for metropolitan areas and the other for township or village areas; the base is the rural area.

The particular time-variant explanatory variables contained in the vector $x_{i(t),t}$ are different in the three equations for s, h, and n. Although we regard the regression model for the saving rate as the main subject of our study, we first specify the vector $x_{i(t),t}$ in the two equations for the human-capital investment and the number of children. The vector $x_{i(t),t}$ in both equations includes two dummies for the presence of aged parents and for whether there is more than one working family member. Furthermore, since changing physical conditions and socioeconomic situations of individuals, such as the patterns of female labor force participation and birth timing, over different cohorts and periods of time obviously affect decisions about human-capital investment and the number of children, we add age, the interaction of age and the cohort effect, and a yearly dummy into $x_{i(t),t}$. We also include the interaction of squared age and the cohort effect in the equation for h.[3]

The main reason for designing such complicated age and year effects and their interactions with the cohort effects is the aforementioned problem with h and n, that older parents tend to have fewer children living with them and make less human-capital investment than do younger parents. We believe that our specification of the age and year effects captures the dynamic pattern that describes how children move away from their parents' home. The implicit assumption here is that such a pattern is fairly stable across cohorts. If the age pattern of h and n in the data is controlled by our specification of the age and year effects, then the cohort effects on h and n can be consistently estimated by the $f_{i(t)}$ term in equation (1), which is the main objective of this study.

We now turn to $x_{i(t),t}$ in the equation for the saving rate. Just as in the previous two regression equations, this one includes two dummies for the presence of aged parents and for whether there is more than one working family member. To specify more fully the age and year effects, we add three adjusted variables into $x_{i(t),t}$: the adjusted household disposable income, the adjusted human-capital investment, and the adjusted number of children. Our reason for not adopting the specifications of the age and year effects as in the previous two equations for h and n is that the data on saving rates do not suffer from the age-bias problem, as explained in the discussion of Table 3. Before explaining how the three adjusted variables are defined, we should emphasize that only through the use of pseudo panel data is it possible for us to separate the cohort effect (which is a part of the fixed effects) from the age and year effects. The cohort effect would be inseparable from the age and year effects if we used survey data for only one year. This is because for any given year the data on the cohorts (i.e., π_1 and π_2) will be exactly collinear with the corresponding ages and years.

The household disposable income needs to be adjusted before it is introduced into the saving rate equation, for the following reason. Like Deaton and Paxson (1994) in their analysis of saving, we contend that income is also subject to three influences—the cohort effect, the age (life cycle) effect, and the year (cyclical) effect, whereas life cycle and yearly changes in household disposable income, $y_{i(t),t}$, affect the saving rate. The cross-cohort changes in income are irrelevant for determining the saving rate and should be subtracted from $y_{i(t),t}$. The argument for this is based on our earlier assumption that the cohort effect on the saving rate follows the specification in equation (2), where only $\pi_{1,i(t)}$ and $\pi_{2,i(t)}$ are pertinent. The cross-cohort differences in income mainly affect the cross-cohort differences in living standards, which are reflected not only by the current consumption level but also the future consumption level (i.e., savings). As a result the cross-cohort changes in income tend to affect consumption and saving in approximately equal proportions so that the saving rate should be fairly independent of the cross-cohort changes in income. The specific procedure we adopt to adjust household disposable income begins with the following linear regression model:

$$\log(\text{income})_{i(t),t} = C_{i(t)} + A_{i(t),t} + Y_{i(t),t} + u_{i(t),t} \ , \tag{3}$$

where $u_{i(t),t}$ is a disturbance term whereas the cohort effect $C_{i(t)}$, the age effect $A_{i(t),t}$, and the year effect $y_{i(t),t}$ are respectively specified as linear combinations of dummies for cohorts, two-year ages, and years.[4] We adjust the disposable income by eliminating the component of the cohort effect. That is, given the fitted values $\hat{C}_{i(t)}$ of the cohort effect, we define the adjusted household disposable income as income$_{i(t),t}$/exp$[\hat{C}_{i(t)}]$. Finally, we should point out that what the adjusted disposable income reflects may well be the short-term unexpected variations in income, which can be contrasted to the long-term cohort effects.

To allow for more flexibility, we further divide the ten cohorts into five groups: (1) cohorts 1, 2, and 3; (2) cohorts 3, 4, and 5; (3) cohorts 5, 6, and 7; (4) cohorts 7, 8, and 9; and (5) cohorts 9 and 10. We let $A_{i(t)}$ and $Y_{i(t),t}$ have different regression coefficients across these five groups. More specifically, we run the regression separately for these five groups. The overlapping cohort in each two adjacent groups permits us to use it as a base and estimate the differences between other cohorts and such a base. It is then possible to construct a set of comparable cohort effects using any particular group as the base. In our computation the third group is set as the base.

The construction of the adjusted human-capital investment and the adjusted number of children is similar to that of the adjusted household disposable income: we subtract the estimated cohort effects from the predicted values (or fitted values) that are obtained from our earlier estimation of the reduced forms for human-capital investment *(h)* and number of children *(n)*. As we have made explicit earlier, the resulting adjusted variables consist mainly of the flexibly structured age and year effects in *h* and *n*. Using the predicted values of *h* and *n* here in defining the adjusted *h* and the adjusted *n* certainly helps to avoid the potential endogeneity problem of h and n in the saving-rate equation. Moreover, it is easily shown that if the cohort effects are already included in the saving-rate equation, whether or not we subtract the cohort effects from the predicted values of h and n in defining the adjusted h and the adjusted n will not affect their respective regression coefficients in the saving-rate equation. We conclude our discussion of the three adjusted variables by noting that, on the one hand, the introduction of age and year effects into the saving-rate equation through income is motivated by the observation that a close relationship exists between life-time savings and income; on the other hand, the introduction of age and year effects into the saving-rate equation through the number of children is motivated by the theory of human-capital investment.

Estimation results

The estimation results are presented in Table 4. The most interesting finding is that the estimated effects of π_1 (young persons' survival probability) and π_2 (old persons' survival probability) on the saving rate are statistically significant and consistent with the theoretical prediction, irrespective of the type of motive, given in Table 1. More specifically, we find that a 1 percent increase in the survival probability to age 30 (π_1) will cause the saving rate to decline by about 0.37 percentage points; that is, a 0.01 increase in π_1 causes the value of s to be reduced by 0.0037. The intuition for this result is, as explained before, that increasing young persons' survival probability helps raise the expected returns to both the human-capital investment in children and the number of children so that the need for saving becomes less important. In contrast, when the survival probability from age 60 to age 75 (π_2) increases by 1 percent, a 30-year-old individual is expected to increase his saving rate by 0.69 percentage points to prepare for a longer life; that is, a 0.01 increase in π_2 causes the value of s to be increased by 0.0069.

It is possible to use the subsample in which the ages of household heads are all above 45 to consider specifically the effects of changing π_2 alone. It is quite conceivable that the fertility decision in these households with older heads has been largely settled. As a result, π_1 is unlikely to affect the saving decision in these households so that, on the basis of these households, we can re-estimate the saving-rate equation without the π_1 term. Such re-estimation yields a positive estimate of 46.41 for the coefficient of π_2 with a highly significant t-ratio of 7.28. The other coefficient estimates are all very similar to those reported in Table 4. This finding further confirms the positive relationship between saving rates and the survival probability π_2 to the age of 75.

The estimated coefficients of the two education dummies are significantly positive and are also consistent with the prediction of the altruism model (Table 1), given that education dummies can be regarded as a proxy

TABLE 4   Estimation results of interactions between s, h, and n: Taiwan

Variable	Saving rate (s)		Human-capital investment (h)		Number of children (n)	
	Estimate	t-ratio	Estimate	t-ratio	Estimate	t-ratio
Constant	24.75	3.08	3.62	0.33	127.98	4.81
π_1	−36.94	−2.84	−10.60	−0.72	−87.95	−2.49
π_2	68.94	7.89	15.50	2.77	−45.39	−3.17
College	6.47	14.71	0.68	15.01	−4.51	−19.51
High school	1.78	4.87	0.50	11.73	−1.55	−7.19
Metropolitan	−3.28	−8.73	0.38	8.72	−2.27	−10.11
Township or village	−0.41	−1.14	0.22	4.94	−0.12	−0.53
Old parents	−2.96	−10.26	−0.15	−4.13	−0.45	−2.45
Two or more workers	13.10	38.80	−0.36	−9.70	3.29	17.08
Adjusted income x 10^{-5}	1.17	8.01				
Adjusted h	−130.66	−5.56				
Adjusted n	−3.44	−10.37				
F-statistics						
Age effect			8.42	(15)	28.06	(15)
Cohort x age			3.37	(10)	10.52	(10)
Cohort x age^2			5.05	(10)		
Year effect			7.01	(18)	1.46	(18)
R^2	0.35		0.29		0.55	

NOTES: The coefficient estimates in the columns for s and h are multiplied by 100, and those for n are multiplied by 10. The sample size is 5,944 for the estimation of the s and n equations, but is 5,671 for the h equation because the data from 1976 are excluded. The definition of h in 1976 is not consistent with that of other years in the original data. The variables of college, high school, metropolitan, township or village, old parents, and two or more workers are all dummies. Under our definitions of dummy variables, the base household is the one with only one worker in the family, without old parents, living in a rural area, and the head's education being at the elementary school level. To the right of each F-statistic, in parentheses, is the number of parameters. A blank cell indicates that the variable is not applicable.

for H_1. As for the age (life cycle) effect and the year (cyclical) effect on the saving rate, which are carried by the adjusted disposable income, we estimate a significantly positive effect. This result indicates a positive short-run relationship between the saving rate and unexpected income changes, which may be viewed as empirical support for the habit-formation theory (i.e., that consumption is not sensitive to unexpected income changes but saving is). Noteworthy are the negative effects of adjusted n and adjusted h on the saving rate, which reflect some substitutability between saving and childrearing.

Turning now to the estimation result for the equation showing the human-capital investment in each child, we find that the estimated coefficient of π_1 is negative but insignificant, whereas that of π_2 is significantly positive. The estimates of the coefficients for the two education dummies are positive and highly significant. These results cannot provide us with much evidence for the theoretical prediction given in Table 1, which itself is admittedly not clear-cut. It seems that our findings, both theoretical and empirical, regarding human-capital investment in children are not particularly fruitful. Recall that it is the education-related expenses that are used as a proxy for human-capital investment. The effectiveness of such a proxy is thus thrown in doubt.[5] The individual coefficient estimates for the age, year, and their interaction effects are not presented in Table 4. Instead, their joint F-test statistics are shown and are significant. To illustrate these estimation results in an alternative format, in Figure 1 we show the (centered) predicted values of human-capital investment in each child at different ages while keeping all other effects fixed. The life cycle of human-capital investment peaks at the parental age of 50.

The estimation result of the equation for the number of children (n) shows that the effects of π_1, π_2, and the education dummies on n are all significantly negative. On the one hand, the finding about young persons' survival rate, π_1, supports the theory based on the transaction motive. On the other hand, the result of the education dummies supports the altruism model. Moreover, the result on old persons' survival rate, π_2, seems to be inconsistent with either theory. From this disappointing result regarding π_2, as well as the earlier finding about the significantly positive effect of π_2

FIGURE 1 Parental age profile of the predicted human-capital investment rate in each child: Taiwan

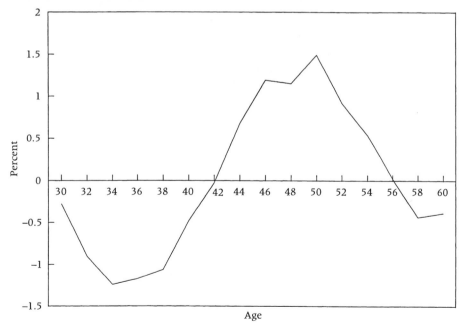

Age

FIGURE 2   Parental age profile of the predicted number of children in the household: Taiwan

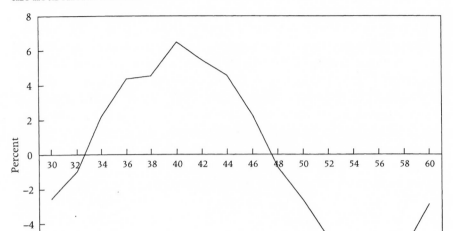

on human-capital investment, we can only conclude that the reaction to longer life expectancy in Taiwan is to reduce the number of children while increasing the investment in each of these fewer children.

Finally, in Figure 2 we show the (centered) predicted values of the number of children at different parental ages based on the estimation results. The life cycle of the number of children in a typical Taiwanese household reaches its peak when its head is 40 years old.

Conclusion

Our dynamic model, based on that of Ehrlich and Lui (1991), has allowed us to examine the two motives for rearing children, transaction and altruism, and to analyze the effects on savings of such demographic changes as prolonged life expectancy and children's higher survival rates. Our theoretical analysis has shown that when children's survival rates increase, so that the probability for aged parents to obtain their adult children's support becomes greater, parents having a transaction motive are inclined to reduce the number of children they have while raising their educational investment in each child to substitute for their own savings. They do this because the rate of return on the educational investment in children rises in relation to the returns on saving. For parents with an altruism motive, the theory suggests that they will rear more children at the expense of their own saving. Furthermore, when life expectancy increases, parents with either motive will raise saving to prepare for a longer life, whereas parents motivated by altruism will further try to increase the number of children. In addition to these inferences, which in Deaton and Paxson's (1994) terms can be referred to as an analysis of the cohort effect, our framework allows for the effects of parents' own education and time-variant variables, such as the number of children, on the life cycle of household saving. These further theoretical results can be contrasted to those of Deaton and Paxson's (1994) study, in which the life cycle pattern of household saving is simply attributed to an all-embracing (household heads') age effect.

By using pseudo panel data based on 20 years' cross-sectional observations, we have been able to separate the cohort effects on saving of prolonged life expectancy and higher children's survival rates from the life cycle (age) and cyclical (year) effects. The way we included the last two effects in the saving-rate equation was through the construction of adjusted disposable income, adjusted human-capital investment, and an adjusted number of children. Our empirical results support the theoretical prediction that prolonged life expectancy helps raise the saving rate, whereas children's improved survival rates reduce it. We also have found a positive relationship between the saving rate and adjusted disposable income, which in turn supports the habit-formation theory. We believe that our estimation of the saving-rate equation is quite successful and provides many useful insights into household saving behavior in Taiwan.

Our theory suggests two more equations, for human-capital investment in children and for the number of children. The estimation of the two equations proves to be less satisfactory, however. We cannot quite identify effects of changing survival rates on human-capital investment and the number of children that are compatible with the theory. It seems that the yearly data on individual households that we have used may not be suitable for an investigation of long-run simultaneous relationships among saving, fertility, and human-capital investment, especially an investigation of the effects of saving on the other two variables. We thus leave this issue for future studies.

Appendix

In Ehrlich and Lui's model, each child is assumed to receive from his or her parents' human-capital investment, H_1, which is then added to the fixed endowment, H_0. As a result the accumulation of human capital, $H_0 + H_1$, from childhood represents the total resources of young parents, of which the portion s is saved, the portion v is used to rear children, and the portion h is devoted to human-capital investment in each child. Consequently, the amount left for consumption is simply

$$\tilde{c}_1 = (H_0 + H_1)(1 - s - nv - nh) , \tag{A1}$$

where n is the number of children. Moreover, upon receiving human capital H_1 in childhood, young parents are expected by their parents to return the favor by transferring to them a proportion of H_1, w_1. This is what we refer to as the transaction motive on the part of older parents. Nevertheless, not all old parents survive, and therefore the survival probability is assumed to be π_2. Given all these assumptions, the expected resource available for young parents' current consumption is

$$c_1 = \tilde{c}_1 - \pi_2 w_1 H_1 . \tag{A2}$$

The resources available for young parents' future consumption are generated mainly from human-capital accumulation, $H_0 + H_1$, and savings, $s(H_0 + H_1)$, through a Cobb-Douglas type of process,

$$\tilde{c}_2 = D \cdot (H_0 + H_1)^{1-m} [s(H_0 + H_1)]^m , \tag{A3}$$

for some parameters, D and m, such that $D > 0$ and $0 < m < 1$. Moreover, given the transaction motive, when young parents provide for their children, they expect to retrieve a portion, w_2, of the human capital, H_2, received by each of their children. We further assume that the amount of H_2 that each child receives is proportional to the investment made earlier, with the proportionality (technology) factor $A > 0$. Specifically, $H_2 = Ah(H_0 + H_1)$. Moreover, not all children live to their adulthood, and we assume that their survival probability is π_1. Given all these assumptions, the expected resource available for young parents' future consumption can be expressed as

$$c_2 = \tilde{c}_2 + n\pi_1 w_2 Ah(H_0 + H_1) . \tag{A4}$$

Finally, besides the consumption originating from the transaction motive, that is, the second term on the right-hand side of (A4), the altruistic motive means that old parents may derive utility directly from the companionship of their children. We assume that such utility is a Cobb-Douglas function of the expected number of children as well as the quality of each child implied by the amount of human capital H_2:

$$c_3 = \left[Ah(H_0 + H_1) \right]^\alpha (n\pi_1)^\beta , \tag{A5}$$

for some parameters, α and β, such that $0 \leq \alpha \leq 1$ and $\alpha < \beta$.

Young parents' utility is assumed to be an additively separable function of c_1, c_2, and c_3, each having constant elasticity of intertemporal substitution:

$$u = \frac{1}{1-\sigma} \left(c_1^{1-\sigma} - 1 \right) + \delta \cdot \pi_2 \left[\frac{1}{1-\sigma} \left(c_2^{1-\sigma} - 1 \right) + \frac{1}{1-\sigma} \left(c_3^{1-\sigma} - 1 \right) \right] , \tag{A6}$$

where σ (< 1) is the reciprocal of the elasticity of substitution and $\delta = 1/(1+\rho)$, while ρ is the time-preference rate. Young parents choose the optimal levels of the savings rate, s, the rate of human-capital investment, h, in each child, and the number of children, n, to maximize utility.

To make the analysis manageable, we divide the utility-maximizing process into two cases. First we have the transaction case, in which there is no altruistic motive, $c_3 = 0$. In this case the utility function (A6) reduces to

$$u = \frac{1}{1-\sigma} \left(c_1^{1-\sigma} - 1 \right) + \delta \cdot \pi_2 \frac{1}{1-\sigma} \left(c_2^{1-\sigma} - 1 \right) . \tag{A7}$$

Second, the altruism case is also possible in which parents do not expect support from children ($w_1 = w_2 = 0$), so that the current consumption of the young parents is $\tilde{c}_1$ and their future consumption is $\tilde{c}_2$. In this case the utility function (A6) reduces to

$$u = \frac{1}{1-\sigma} \left(\tilde{c}_1^{1-\sigma} - 1 \right) + \delta \cdot \pi_2 \left[\frac{1}{1-\sigma} \left(\tilde{c}_2^{1-\sigma} - 1 \right) + \frac{1}{1-\sigma} \left(c_3^{1-\sigma} - 1 \right) \right] . \tag{A8}$$

We first derive the first-order conditions with respect to the utility function (A7) for the case of a transaction motive. It turns out that the expected number of children, $\pi_1 n$, must be the lowest possible positive integer, which is 1. Consequently we have $n = 1/\pi_1$. The various partial derivatives of the solutions to s, n, and h with respect to π_1, π_2, and H_1 can be derived from standard comparative statics. The determination of the signs of the partial derivatives depends crucially on these two assumptions, which indicate how π_1 and π_2 affect the level of w_2 (the support that young parents expect to receive from each of their children after retirement). In Ehrlich and Lui's analysis, w_2 is determined by young parents as they try to maximize their children's future utility. Consequently π_1 and π_2 can affect the value of w_2, which in turn affects young parents' decisions, particularly regarding the optimal human-capital investment rate, h, in each child. The first assumption is that $\partial w_2/\partial \pi_1 \approx 0$, and the second assumption is that $\partial w_2/\partial \pi_2 < 0$, meaning that a higher survival rate π_2 implies longer and heavier burdens for their adult children and therefore a lower yearly rate of w_2. In their analysis of the transaction motive, Ehrlich and Lui also make these assumptions.

The first-order conditions for utility maximization with respect to the utility function (A8) for the case with altruistic parents can also be derived. For such a case we can show that $h = \alpha v/(\beta - \alpha)$ and note that the second-order conditions for utility maximization will hold if $1 - \beta + \beta\sigma > 0$ and $1 - \alpha + \alpha\sigma > 0$, which will be assumed. Standard comparative statics lead to the signs given in Table 1. Details are available from us upon request.

Notes

We are grateful to David Bloom, Ronald Lee, Andrew Mason, and especially Angus Deaton for their valuable suggestions.

1 Attanasio and Browning (1995) suggest that five factors affect household consumption: (1) the cohort effect; (2) the life cycle effect, which includes the age effect; (3) the cyclical effect, which is similar to the year effect; (4) the lifetime income effect; and (5) heterogeneity.

2 The construction of π_1 is as follows: From the *Abridged Life Tables* we have the five-year average death rates $p_1, p_2, ..., p_7$ for the seven age groups (0, 1–4, 5–9, 10–14, 15–19, 20–24, and 25–29), respectively. π_1 is defined as

$$\prod_{j=1}^{7}(1-p_j) \ .$$

We compute π_2 in a similar fashion. These definitions of π_1 and π_2 are the same as in Ehrlich and Lui (1991).

3 Since the sum of birth year and age is necessarily equal to year (plus a constant), the three sets of dummies for cohorts, ages, and years are perfectly collinear, so that the ordinary least squares estimation for the regression model in the equation would not work. One way to solve this perfect-multicollinearity problem is to impose linear constraints on the corresponding regression coefficients. Here we restrict the sum of the coefficients for the age effects to zero, the sum of the coefficients for the year effects to zero, and the weighted sum of the coefficients for the year effects to zero with the time trend $t = 1, 2, ..., 20$ as weights. Such constraints imply that the coefficients for the age effects represent the differences from the mean age effect, and the coefficients for the year effects represent the differences from the mean and trend in the year effect. Similar procedures have been suggested by Moffitt (1993).

4 For two-year ages we specify 15 two-year age dummies for ages 30–31, 32–33, ..., 58–59 and a single-year dummy for 60 years of age. Since the sum of birth year and age is necessarily equal to year (plus a constant), the three sets of dummies for cohorts, ages, and years are perfectly collinear, as mentioned in note 3. We therefore impose the same linear restrictions as in note 3 on the regression coefficients for the age and year effects.

5 Ehrlich and Lui (1991) use the growth rate of per capita gross national product as a proxy for human-capital investment in their empirical investigation of the effects of π_1 and π_2. Using cross-country aggregated data, they find that the estimated coefficient of π_1 is significantly positive whereas that of π_2 is not significant.

References

Attanasio, O. P. and M. Browning. 1995. "Consumption over the life cycle and over the business cycle," *American Economic Review* 85(5): 1118–1137.

Becker, G. S. and R. J. Barro. 1988. "A reformulation of the economic theory of fertility," *Quarterly Journal of Economics* 103(1): 1–25.

Becker, G. S. and K. M. Murphy. 1989. "Economic growth, human capital, and population growth," in *The Problem of Development: Proceedings of the Institute's First International Conference, May 27–29, 1988*, eds. I. Ehrlich, G. Hariharan, and R. Lutter. Buffalo: Institute for the Study of Free Enterprise Systems, State University of New York.

Becker, G. S., K. M. Murphy, and R. Tamura. 1990. "Human capital, fertility, and economic growth," *Journal of Political Economy* 98(5, Pt. 2): S12–S37.

Deaton, Angus and Christina H. Paxson. 1994. "Saving, growth and aging in Taiwan," in *Studies in the Economics of Aging*, ed. D. A. Wise. Chicago: Chicago University Press, pp. 331–364.

————. 1997. "The effects of economic and population growth on national saving and inequality," *Demography* 34(1): 97–114.

Department of Budget, Accounting and Statistics. 1946. *Statistical Abstract of Taiwan for 51 Years*. Nantou: Taiwan Provincial Government.

Department of Statistics, Ministry of Interior. Various years. *Taiwan-Fukien Abridged Life Tables*. Taipei.

Directorate-General of Budget, Accounting and Statistics, Executive Yuan. Various years. *The Survey of Personal Income Distribution*. Taipei.

Ehrlich, I. and F. T. Lui. 1991. "Intergenerational trade, longevity, and economic growth," *Journal of Political Economy* 99(5): 1237–1261.

Fry, Maxwell J. and Andrew Mason. 1982. "The variable rate of growth effect in the life-cycle saving model," *Economic Inquiry* 20(3): 426–442.

International Monetary Fund. Various years. *International Financial Statistics*. Washington, DC.

Kelley, Allen C. and Robert M. Schmidt. 1996. "Saving, dependency and development," *Journal of Population Economics* 9(4): 365–386.

Kohlberg, E. 1976. "A model of economic growth with altruism between generations," *Journal of Economic Theory* 13(1): 1–13.

Leff, N. H. 1969. "Dependency rates and savings rates," *American Economic Review* 59(5): 886–896.

Mason, Andrew. 1981. "An extension of the life-cycle model and its application to population growth and aggregate saving," *East-West Population Institute Working Papers*, No. 4. Honolulu: East-West Center.

————. 1987. "National saving rates and population growth: A new model and new evidence," in *Population Growth and Economic Development: Issues and Evidence*, eds. D. G. Johnson and R. D. Lee. Madison: University of Wisconsin Press.

Moffitt, R. 1993. "Identification and estimation of dynamic models with a time series of repeated cross-sections," *Journal of Econometrics* 59(1/2): 99–123.

Organization for Economic Co-operation and Development. Various years. *Quarterly National Accounts*. Paris.

Paxson, Christina. 1996. "Saving and growth: Evidence from micro data," *European Economic Review* 40(2): 255–288.

Riboud, M. 1988. "Altruisme au sein de la famille, croissance économique et démographie," *Revue Economique* 39(1): 127–154.

World Bank. 1980 and 1994. *World Economic Development*. Washington, DC.

Life Cycle Saving and the Demographic Transition: The Case of Taiwan

RONALD LEE
ANDREW MASON
TIMOTHY MILLER

MIGHT THE DEMOGRAPHIC transition from high fertility and mortality to low fertility and mortality cause an increase in saving rates and a rise in capital per worker? A large literature addresses this important question; and after a period of neglect, new but contradictory research has focused on the topic. Here we return to this issue, extending our earlier work and attempting to reconcile it with findings from household-level data.

We argue that demographic change over the transition leads to a substantial increase in the demand for life cycle wealth—that is, a desire for claims on future output to support consumption in old age—held in the form of either capital or transfer wealth. This increase comes in part from the expectation of longer life, in part from fewer children, and in part from an older population age distribution. Before the transition, old-age support is provided largely by families, and the expectation of such support is a form of transfer wealth. The elderly are also supported in part from their holdings of property (capital), and savings flows will be partly an attempt to acquire such holdings of capital. A full account of demographic influences on saving behavior would have to take explicit account of the system of family transfers and its changes over time. Here, however, we give a partial account, for a hypothetical situation in which there are no transfers to the elderly.

We simulate the effect of the demographic transition on saving rates and the demand for capital, assuming that all savings are for the purpose of spreading consumption smoothly over the life cycle, and that there are no transfers for this purpose other than to children. We assume further that individuals correctly foresee all demographic changes, but that they base their expectations about future rates of interest and productivity growth on recent experience, using an ad hoc procedure, and that those expectations are typically incorrect. We treat actual interest rates and productivity growth as exogenous variables that are unaffected by saving behavior or demographic change. Future work will determine these within the model. We find that under the assumption of pure life cycle saving, aggregate saving rates would decline modestly during early stages of the demographic transition, then rise quite substantially during a long middle period, and then decline again as the population aged rapidly in the last stage of the transition. Our simulated age patterns of income, consumption, and saving rates for Taiwan agree in some respects, but not all, with aggregate savings data and with survey data from Taiwan. Comparisons with other approaches show general qualitative agreement that the demographic transition should boost saving rates for a number of decades, but disagreement about the magnitude of this effect. We believe that our results are of general relevance for countries passing through the demographic transition, provided that life cycle saving, and the financial institutions necessary to sustain it, are present at least in the later stages of the transition.

Research on population and saving

Fisher (1930), among many others, recognized that life cycle variation in individual productivity would lead individuals to vary their saving over their life time in order to smooth their consumption. Changes in a population's age structure weight differently the various stages of the life cycle and thus affect aggregate saving. If pension motives dominate life cycle saving, slower population growth leads to reduced saving (Modigliani and Ando 1957). If, however, childrearing costs dominate life cycle saving, slower population growth leads to increased saving (Coale and Hoover 1958).

Most theoretical analyses of aggregate saving based on the life cycle model have used comparative statics, examining the impact of different steady-state population age structures. Mason (1981 and 1987) and Fry and Mason (1982) consider the impact of demography on the age schedules of consumption and earning, as well as on the age structure of the population, but within a comparative-static framework. Higgins (1994) uses a simple overlapping-generations model to examine the impact of changes in the number of children on saving during the transition between steady states.

Several recent empirical studies based on international time series of cross-sections have found a close link between demographic change and saving (Fry and Mason 1982; Kelley and Schmidt 1996; Mason 1981, 1987, and 1988; Higgins and Williamson 1997). Analyses at the microlevel are less supportive. Although household saving rates do vary with the demographic characteristics of the household, the age variation is sufficiently small that changes in age structure have only modest effects on aggregate saving or no effect at all (Deaton and Paxson 1997; Mason, Woramontri, and Kleinbaum 1993). Deaton and Paxson find a substantial impact of demographic change on household saving over the transition in their microlevel analysis in this volume, but the impact is much smaller than that found by Kelley and Schmidt (1996) or Higgins and Williamson (1997) from cross-national analyses.

A consensus about the importance of demographic factors requires a reconciliation of these micro and macro approaches. Our microdata-based macrosimulations in this chapter offer a first step toward such a reconciliation.

Demographic change and the demand for wealth over the life cycle

During childhood and old age, people on average consume more than they produce through their labor. During their middle years they produce in excess of their consumption. Consumption in childhood is generally supported by transfers from parents, with whom a child co-resides. Children, being financially dependent, can be treated as part of their parents' planning problem. Support in old age, however, is another matter. Working-age people must develop claims on future output beyond their own expected future production; without such claims, they could not consume once they ceased working. Such claims are called "wealth" or sometimes "life cycle wealth." This wealth can be held in the form of expected future net transfers or in the form of property (capital).

Figure 1 illustrates the accumulation of wealth by households in a stylized manner. Adults enter the work force and begin to accumulate wealth. They continue do so until they retire. During retirement they draw down their wealth to support themselves in the absence of labor income. (Wealth need not actually begin to decline until some years after retirement.) Life cycle models frequently assume that wealth is accumulated only to support consumption during retirement and declines to zero at death. There are many reasons why this may not be the case, however. Uncertainty about time of death may lead people to overaccumulate wealth. People may hold additional wealth as a buffer against uncertain income streams or consumption needs, and they may save to provide bequests for their children. The need to provide for old-age consumption is only one of a number of factors that motivate accumulation. Irrespective of the motivation, wealth profiles typically increase with age. The extent to which wealth declines among the elderly is an empirical issue about which there is considerable debate (Hurd 1997).

In Taiwan, as in many countries, "retirement," conceived as an abrupt cessation of labor that takes place at some conventional age, such as 65, is

FIGURE 1 Schematic wealth profiles

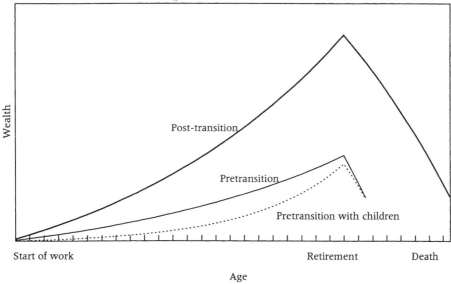

rare. Instead, there is a gradual diminution of labor after age 50, but substantial proportions of people still work at age 70. Nonetheless, in discussing the problem of providing for old age, it is convenient to use some conventional marker for retirement age, which here we take to be 65.

The retirement motive for wealth accumulation is a relatively weak force in a pretransition population because, as a result of high mortality, the expected number of years spent in old age are few. For the pretransition mortality rates used here to characterize Taiwan, a typical individual could expect to live only 0.078 years after age 65 for every year lived between ages 20 and 64. As illustrated in Figure 1, a modest level of wealth is sufficient to finance average retirement needs in such a population. In a post-transition population, the number of years lived after age 65 for every year lived during working ages is greater by a factor of 4 or 5. To provide the same measure of economic support in old age, saving rates and average wealth also must be substantially greater.

The age-wealth profile also should be influenced by the number of children in a family. If children are costly, an increase in the number of children reduces consumption by their parents. If parents smooth consumption over their life cycle, then an increase in the number of children leads to an increase in consumption, by less than the cost of children, during years in which children are being reared. Consumption during years in which the parents incur no childrearing costs, including their retirement years, is lower. Thus the wealth profile is more bowed and peaks at a lower level. The impact of the number of children is attenuated because there are substantial economies of scale to childrearing and parents may reduce spending on individual children. Parents may also limit their fertility because they choose to spend more on each child. Changes in the number of children may influence other saving motives, such as bequests or uncertainty, affecting the wealth profile in ways that cannot be determined a priori.

Nondemographic factors also influence the wealth profile. If people desire to leave larger bequests, the demand for wealth shifts upward. A higher rate of interest may lead people to postpone consumption, thereby increasing their holdings of wealth. With higher interest rates, however, the wealth necessary to support a given level of consumption in old age is reduced. Interest rates consequently have an ambiguous effect on wealth profiles. Productivity growth also has an ambiguous effect on wealth profiles. A higher rate of productivity growth means that younger households will have higher lifetime earnings than older households and will consequently accumulate more wealth. But a higher rate of productivity growth means that households earn a smaller share of lifetime earnings at young ages. This will lead them to accumulate less wealth when they are young and their earnings are low, and more wealth when they are older and their earnings are high. Earnings that are sufficiently low at young ages may lead individuals to go into debt if that is institutionally possible. The net impact on the wealth profile cannot be determined a priori.

Total wealth is determined by the wealth profile and the number of adults at each age. If pre- and post-transition populations were stationary and everyone died at the same age, wealth per person would be given by the area under the life cycle wealth profile, divided by the number of years of life. From inspection of Figure 1, we can conclude that because life expectancy is greater in a post-transition population, wealth per adult will be greater (provided that increases in the age at retirement do not offset increases in years lived), and that because post-transition families have fewer children, wealth per adult will be greater (provided that greater expenditures per child do not completely compensate for the decline in the number of children).

The age composition of a population reinforces these life cycle effects, given that a pretransition population has a large proportion of its population concentrated at younger ages, in which the demand for wealth is relatively low. Table 1, based on the experience of Taiwan, illustrates the sharp difference between pre- and post-transition demography. The ratio of expected number of years lived at old ages to the number of years lived during working ages is much greater in a post-transition population. The average number of children reared is smaller, and the proportion of the population concentrated at older ages is greater. Individually these demographic factors push the demand for wealth higher, and together they do so significantly.

TABLE 1 Characteristics of a population before and after demographic transition

Characteristic	Pre-transition	Post-transition	Ratio (post/pre)
Population growth rate (per year)	1.1%	0.0%	
Life expectancy at birth (years)	28.3	78.8	2.8
Total fertility rate (TFR), births per woman	6.0	2.0	0.3
Number of children surviving to age 20 (= TFR x l_{20})	3.1	2.0	0.7
Retirement years/working years	.078	.361	4.6
Proportion of population under age 20	.49	.26	0.5
Proportion of adult population over age 50	.21	.50	2.4
Wealth/income per year	1.6	5.4	3.5
Savings/income (per year)	4.0%	8.3%	2.1

The hypotheses advanced above and those derived from most life cycle saving models apply to comparatively steady states. Demographic conditions prevailing before and after a demographic transition may be approximated as steady states, but conditions prevailing in transitional populations cannot. During a typical transition the number of surviving children per family first increases substantially and population growth rates rise as mortality declines, and then drop after fertility decline sets in some decades later. The population age distribution initially grows younger early in the transition, and the total dependency ratio rises, depressing the demand for wealth. Then growth slows and the dependency burden declines over a long period of 50 or 60 years, before population aging sets in. This is the period of the so-called demographic gift, when demographic conditions may be particularly favorable to the economy. A further complexity is that during the transition, different cohorts experience different rates of fertility and mortality. This is particularly the case in East Asia, where demographic change has been very rapid. Thus no simple generalizations about the relationship between population, wealth, and saving during transition can be made.

Nonetheless, once we realize that under conditions of life cycle savings, equilibrium wealth holdings per capita must be greater after the transition than before and that aggregate saving rates will be low both before and after the transition, then there are two implications. First, saving rates must temporarily rise during the transition to generate the increased wealth. That is so unless population growth rates are reduced below their pretransition levels, which ordinarily occurs only late in the transition if it occurs at all. Second, the level to which saving rates rise during the transition will depend on the speed of the transition. Populations that reach their post-transition wealth level quickly can do so only if saving rates are higher during the transition. (We explore the effects of the pace of transition on saving rates in Lee, Mason, and Miller 1998.) Of course the effects of changes in transfer behavior will be superimposed on these effects, or interact with them. We shall see below that patterns may be quite complex, and that saving rates may both decline and rise at different times during the transition.

Despite the complexities of the life cycle model applied to the transition, if the increased demand for wealth per capita were not satisfied, then old people would experience sharp discontinuities in consumption when they no longer worked; they might even starve. In fact we do not observe that elders in societies nearing the end of the demographic transition consume at or below subsistence levels. In Taiwan, cross-sectional age profiles of consumption for recent years do not show such discontinuities; rather, household consumption per capita is flat across ages of individuals (Mason and Miller 1998). It follows that per capita wealth holdings must have increased substantially over the course of the transition. In one way or another the elderly have acquired claims on resources that permit them to consume increasing amounts per year during increasingly long periods of retirement.

Life cycle wealth as transfer wealth or capital

Wealth as we have defined it is quite general, consisting at the societal level of both transfer wealth and capital. Either form of wealth can be used by the elderly to sustain their consumption. However, transfer wealth has no direct impact on economic production or total income, although transfer systems alter incentives and thereby may generate indirect effects. The accumulation of capital, in contrast, is central to modern economic growth.

In traditional societies the elderly are supported primarily by transfers within the extended family, either through co-residence with adult children or through transfers between households. Life cycle wealth is largely transfer wealth, taking the form of expected net transfers in the future, not of holdings of productive property (although livestock, structures, and land are also common forms of wealth). If family transfers continued to dominate throughout the demographic transition, the transition would have little impact on capital accumulation, but the anticipation of an obligation to make transfers to elderly parents might affect saving by their children.

Economic development typically, perhaps always, erodes the system of family transfers. If the system is replaced by a pay-as-you-go public pension system with transfer income from those who are currently working to those who are currently retired, one form of transfer wealth (public) is simply substituted for another form (private). Under these circumstances the demographic transition increases transfer wealth (or the size of the public pension system) and may have a fiscal impact (raising taxes on earnings), but has no direct impact on capital formation. It simply leads to a heavier support burden on the working-age population.

If, however, the family transfer system is replaced by a prefunded system, in which real wealth supports retirement, then the demographic transition leads to increased holdings of capital, fueling economic growth. Institutional forms of prefunded systems vary from country to country. Farmers and owners of small businesses may save by investing directly in productive enterprises. Workers may save directly through a variety of financial instruments or by participating in funded company-sponsored pension programs. Fully funded public pensions would have the same effect. Some countries—Singapore and Malaysia, for example—have institutionalized such individual "life cycle saving" through large, mandatory saving and retirement programs.

The transition from a transfer system to a prefunded system for supporting the elderly must create a transitory increase in aggregate savings that will be superimposed on, and reinforce, the demographically induced temporary increase in savings. These dynamic effects of the movement from a family support system to a system of individual responsibility or funded pensions are not reflected in the simulations we report below, which assume that life cycle saving (individual responsibility) has prevailed throughout.

There is ample evidence of a shift away from family support in East Asia, although family transfers are still considerably more common there than in the West. The proportion of Japanese elderly living with their children declined from about 70 percent to about 50 percent between 1970 and 1990 (Feeney and Mason 1998: 17). In 1973 more than 80 percent of Taiwan's elderly lived with their children (Weinstein et al. 1994: Table 12.6), but by 1993 only 60 percent of elderly men and 70 percent of elderly women were living with their children (calculated from the Family Income and Expenditure Survey; see Taiwan, Directorate-General of Budget, Accounting and Statistics 1993).

The planned accumulation of wealth should depend more on expectations about support by those who are currently working than on the current arrangements of those who have already retired, and these expectations are changing rapidly. In 1950, 65 percent of Japanese women of childbearing age expected to rely on their children in old age. By 1990, only 18 percent expected to turn to their children for support in the future (Ogawa and Retherford 1993: 590, Table 2).

The following matrix illustrates how the demographic transition and institutional arrangements for old-age support interact to determine saving behavior and capital holdings. The biggest effect on saving rates and capital formation occurs when the demographic transition is combined with a transition to individual responsibility for old-age support.

Demographic stage	Private or public transfers	Prefunded system (individual responsibility)
Pretransition	Initial situation	Small increase in savings and capital
Post-transition	Small increase in savings and capital	Large increase in savings and capital

Here we analyze the effect of the demographic transition on savings and capital accumulation under the assumption that the system of individual responsibility has existed throughout the demographic transition. This assumption will exaggerate the effect on savings and capital of the movement down the left-hand column from pre- to post-transition, while maintaining the system of transfers. It will understate the effect of the movement diagonally from the upper left to the lower right of the matrix. We believe that this diagonal movement is the most appropriate representation of the changes taking place in East Asia and eventually in industrializing countries elsewhere. In a number of countries of Latin America that are currently switching to mandatory private saving for retirement, the movement to the lower right cell has already taken place or is in process.

The dynamic simulation model

Our simulation model shows how aggregate saving rates and wealth change during the demographic transition if life cycle considerations (individual responsibility) before, during, and after the transition entirely determine saving by members of the population. The model takes the approach of Tobin (1967) and is similar to the one we used in Lee, Mason, and Miller (1997), wherein further details about it can be found.

The population composition in our 1997 study reflected actual census data, but here we generate the population from the historical and projected trajectories of mortality and fertility. (See the Appendix for details.) Consequently the population composition does not reflect the massive immigration from mainland China that occurred around 1950. We refer to the resulting transition as "pseudo-Taiwan." A comparison with the results in our previous study indicates that this treatment of immigration does not alter the conclusions reached here in any important respect. The trajectories for life expectancy at birth and the total fertility rate for Taiwan, as well as the implied population growth rates, are shown in Figure 2. The total fertility rate is assumed to move slowly up to replacement level in future decades, and life expectancy at birth is assumed to rise to about 80 years by 2050.

On the basis of actual household headship rates, we set the age of an individual's economic independence at 25, a change from our previous

FIGURE 2 Actual and projected total fertility rate and life expectancy at birth: Taiwan, 1900–2050

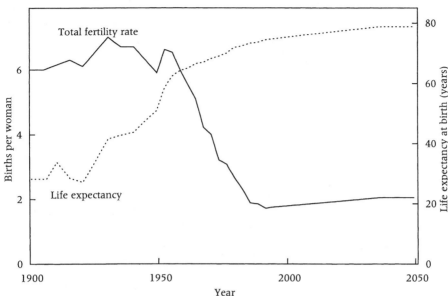

study, in which it was 21. We assume that until this age, children remain in the parental home, pooling their income with that of their parents, although some marry and begin childbearing at an earlier age. Until then their income is treated as the income of their parents, and its disposition is governed by the parents' life cycle budget constraint and consumption plan. In fact, in 1980 only about a quarter of Taiwanese males aged 25–29 were household heads, and so the actual age at which males leave home is typically later than 25. However, we assume (with no direct evidence) that adult children have increasing control over their earnings as they grow older, whether or not they continue to reside with their parents. Once they leave home and set up their own households, we assume they remain in their own households for the remainder of their lives. In reality many elderly currently reside with their adult children, but we anticipate that this arrangement will become less common as time passes. We do not know the extent to which the co-resident elderly are financially dependent on their children.

Consumption behavior within the household is governed by a utility-maximization model. In each period, adults decide how much of their income to consume and how much to save on the basis of their current wealth, family size, and expectations about future childbearing, mortality conditions, interest rates, and earnings. We make no allowance for intergenerational transfers: parents make no bequests to their children, and adult children provide no support to their parents. (In our earlier study we analyzed the impact of transfers in steady states.) While children are present in the home, they are supported by their parents, who give them half of their own weight, on average, in setting household consumption levels. The mechanics of this calculation are such that each child in a two-child family is allocated 70 percent more resources than in a six-child family if household income is the same. Thus our model does entail some tradeoff between the number of children and their "quality."

Each householder calculates the present value of expected lifetime earnings, including the earnings of co-resident children. The present value of expected consumption over the household's lifetime is constrained to equal this amount. Couples distribute their household consumption over time so as to maximize their lifetime utility. Given the lifetime utility function employed, household consumption per equivalent adult consumer is planned to rise at a rate equal to $(r - \rho)(1/\gamma)$, where r is the real rate of interest, ρ is the rate of subjective time preference, and $(1/\gamma)$ is the intertemporal elasticity of substitution. In our simulations we take r to be 0. For $(1/\gamma)$ we use an estimate of 0.6 for Taiwan calculated by Ogaki, Ostry, and Reinhart (1996). Because cohort wealth is never negative in the simulations presented here, we have not imposed a nonnegative wealth constraint in our model. We assume that the weight of children in consumption calculations by their parents rises as the children age, averaging 0.5. Additional elements of the simulation model are described in the Appendix and in greater detail in Lee, Mason, and Miller (1997).

For life cycle planning it is the anticipated future values of the demographic and economic variables that matter. We assume that couples correctly anticipate their fertility and the survival probabilities of all family members. Mortality expectations take the form of proportions or probabilities, but we assume that all the uncertainty around these average rates is absorbed by institutions, whose exact nature we do not consider. Householders formulate their plans on the basis of their expected years of life at each future date. Those who die bequeath their wealth to all other householders of the same age, and likewise the orphans created by death are shared out among all surviving householders of the same age.

Earnings in each year are determined by changes in the general wage level, the productivity growth rate, and a fixed cross-sectional profile of age earnings. The profile is equal to the average shape over the years from 1976 to 1990 in Taiwan, calculated from the annual Family Income and Expenditure Survey. The level of this profile shifts according to the assumed time path of productivity growth. We depart here from the standard implementation of the life cycle model, which assumes that the longitudinal earnings profile has a fixed shape. We believe our specification to be preferable on both theoretical and empirical grounds as discussed in Lee, Mason, and Miller (1999).

For the interest rate and productivity growth rate, we do not assume perfect foresight. Instead we make the ad hoc assumption that people base their expectations on the average experience of the past five years. Then, rather than assuming that this rate continues for the rest of their lives, we assume that they expect the rate to tend exponentially toward a long-term target rate, which is their long-term future expectation. These rates we have taken in our baseline simulation to be an interest rate of 0.03 and a productivity growth rate of 0.015. Our rationale is that long-term interest rates will converge to international levels as global capital markets are increasingly integrated and that productivity growth will depend only on technological advance, which will occur at a rate similar to the rates experienced in mature economies once the economy reaches equilibrium. Given that r has averaged 7.4 percent since 1950, and productivity growth has averaged 5.5 percent, we assume that people have been constantly surprised by continuing high rates. Our analysis is inconsistent, however, because although people are repeatedly surprised by economic outcomes, they continue to believe that they know the future with certainty. It would be preferable to develop a model incorporating both uncertainty and demographic factors (see Attanasio et al. 1997), but that is beyond the scope of this chapter.

We start the simulations in 1800 to permit convergence to the steady state before the transition begins. Our results are presented either for 1900–2050 or, in some cases, for 1950–2050. We have not tried to take into account the loss of capital during World War II or, as mentioned earlier, the massive immigration to Taiwan of the 1950s. For our baseline scenario the productivity growth rate conforms to our best guess at historical and future trends. Thus it rises from a pretransition level of 1.0 percent per year, peaks at 5.5 percent over the period 1950–99, and then declines to a long-run average of 1.5 percent. The real interest rate is set at 1.5 percentage points above the productivity growth rate. People's expectations about eventual long-term values remain unchanged at 3.0 percent for the interest rate and 1.5 percent for the productivity growth rate. We assume a zero rate of time preference throughout.

Results of the simulations

Figures 3 and 4 chart the trend in saving and wealth from 1950 to 2050 for the baseline simulation and several alternatives. The most prominent feature of the baseline simulation is the substantial swing in saving that begins about 1973 (Figure 3). The saving rate increases by almost 14 percentage points, doubling the 1973 rate by the time it peaks in 2007. This is followed by an even greater decline in the saving rate. The large swing in saving is a phenomenon that comparative-static analyses miss entirely but

FIGURE 3   Simulated saving rate: Pseudo-Taiwan, two scenarios 1950–2050

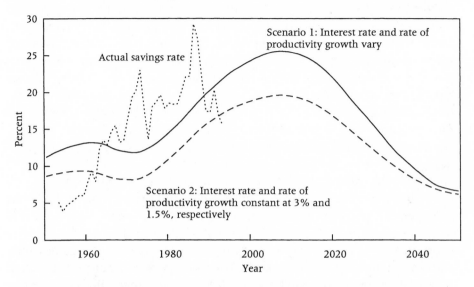

NOTES: In Scenario 1 (the baseline scenario) the interest rate equals the productivity growth rate plus 1.5 percent, whereas the productivity growth rate equals 1 percent (pre-1950), 5.5 percent (1950–99), 4.5 percent (2000–19), 2.5 percent (2020–29), and 1.5 percent (2030–50). In Scenario 2 the interest rate equals 3.0 percent and the productivity growth rate equals 1.5 percent. Long-run expectations are the same as in Scenario 2.

FIGURE 4   Simulated wealth-to-output ratio: Pseudo-Taiwan, two scenarios 1950–2050

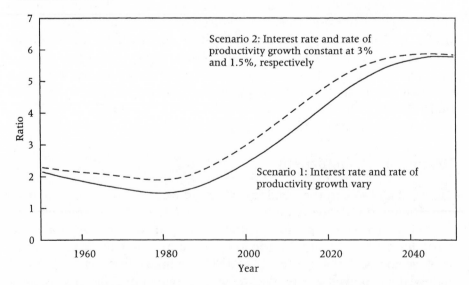

NOTE: Interest rates and productivity rates for the two scenarios and long-run expectations are as described in the Note to Figure 3.

which we noted above as an outcome of rapid demographic transition under life cycle savings. The swing in saving rates is accompanied by a rapid increase in W/Y, the wealth-to-output ratio (Figure 4). A second important feature of the saving simulation is the dip that occurs in the 1960s and early 1970s. This dip in saving is related in complex ways to the changing numbers of surviving children in households.

In the baseline simulation, demography, interest rates, and productivity growth rates are all changing and influencing the outcome. The direct impact of demography is isolated by an additional simulation that holds the interest rate and productivity growth rate constant at 3.0 and 1.5 percent, respectively, throughout the simulation (Scenario 2). If only demographic factors change, the saving rate reaches a higher peak and declines more modestly than in the baseline. Note, however, the artificial nature of assuming a constant rate of interest (return to capital) and a constant productivity growth rate in light of the large increase in capital. In a more complete model of the economy, which we are currently developing, interest rates and productivity growth would be determined in large part by the changes in capital induced by demographic factors. As W/Y approached its equilibrium level, productivity growth would decline to a lower long-term growth governed solely by technological innovation.

Figure 3 also plots the time path of the actual net national saving rate for the available years. There are significant dissimilarities between it and the simulated rates. The short-term fluctuations need not concern us; persistent differences are more relevant. As compared with the life cycle simulation, Taiwan was saving too little during the 1950s and early 1960s, too much between 1964 and 1988, and too little during the most recent years. There was no obvious medium-term downturn in the saving rate prior to 1975. The recent decline in saving occurred several decades before the simulated decline and seems not to be associated with demographic factors. On the positive side, the dynamic life cycle model does predict a large increase in saving rates (about 14 percentage points), and the level of the simulated saving rate is fairly consistent with actual saving rates.

At least two difficult aspects of the life cycle model require more careful attention and could account for some differences between the simulated and actual saving rates observed. The first is the formation of expectations. Our treatment of economic expectations is problematic because we assume that people repeatedly underestimate the future productivity growth rate and interest rate. The second issue is the erosion of the family support system. Low saving rates are sufficient to satisfy life cycle needs when the elderly rely heavily on their children for economic support. Hence the rapid increase in saving is consistent with a shift from a transfer-based system to a system of self-reliance combined with purely demographic changes. As discussed earlier, during such a shift, saving rates could easily rise above their normal life cycle level. In a similar vein, the development of public transfer systems in Taiwan in recent years may account for the downturn in national saving.

Sensitivity tests

The baseline simulation is based on Taiwan's experience (to the extent that it is documented), with the exception of the massive immigration and disruption of the war years. To assess the robustness of our results we have investigated different parameter values, different economic-input time series, and different formations of expectations. Given the many parameters of the model, it would be possible to tailor our assumptions to improve the fit to the observed results. For example, raising the long-run expected interest rate from 0.03 to 0.04 makes the simulations fit the survey data considerably better by raising saving rates at younger ages. We have avoided doing this, however, preferring to see whether our best guesses at parameter values would produce a rise in saving during the transition.

For parameter values, we set the elasticity of substitution at 0.3 and at 1.0, in contrast to 0.6 in the baseline. The resulting level of the saving rate is much lower for 0.3 and higher for 1.0; but the shape, timing, and magnitudes of the resulting swings in the saving rate remain very similar to the baseline case. We obtain similar results when we vary the Equivalent Adult Consumer weights. For the assumptions about productivity growth and interest rates, we have sometimes held these constant and sometimes varied them independently of one another. Other things being equal, a higher interest rate raises saving rates, and higher rates of productivity growth reduce savings, but the impact of demography on the saving rate remains qualitatively similar.[1] For expectations, the results are largely unchanged if, instead of having perfect foresight about future mortality, householders expect that each period's age-specific mortality will persist. We conclude that the effects of demographic change on aggregate saving rates are quite robust to these kinds of variations in the details of the model.

Simulated saving at the household level

The simulation model also provides detailed age data that can be used to construct cross-sectional or longitudinal profiles of income, consumption, and saving by age of household head. Comparing these profiles with household data provides another check on the realism of the simulations, once we take into account some issues of noncomparability. First, household surveys provide a narrow measure of saving and wealth, excluding, for example, employers' contributions to employee pension funds. Second, household headship is highly selective at younger and older ages, when only a small fraction of the population consists of heads or spouses of heads. The age at which young adults establish a separate household may be influenced by unobserved factors that also influence the accumulation of wealth. Likewise the age at which older adults become members of households headed by their offspring may be influenced by conditions that also bear on wealth. Under these circumstances the saving and wealth of younger and older household heads may differ substantially from the saving and wealth of the average individuals at those ages.

Figure 5 compares household saving, by age of household head, from survey data for 1976–90 with the simulated age-saving profile for the same period. The actual and simulated profiles both have a distinctive M shape. The dip in the middle ages corresponds to a rise in dependency relative to household income at those same ages (Mason and Miller 1998). Saving rates in the survey are higher than in the simulation among young households, and first lower, then higher, among older households. The apparent failure of the elderly to dissave during retirement is a common point of criticism of the life cycle model. However, the selectivity of headship and of survival makes it difficult to interpret survey data on the age patterns of saving at both the younger and older ages. Thus the high rate of saving among households with young and old household heads does not provide clear evidence about the applicability of the life cycle model to Taiwan. (See Hurd 1997 for a recent review of these issues.)

Results presented in Figure 6 address a recent criticism of the life cycle saving model. Empirical studies show that consumption tracks income quite closely (Carroll and Summers 1991; Paxson 1996), whereas the standard

FIGURE 5   Household age-specific saving rates: Baseline simulation and actual survey results for Taiwan

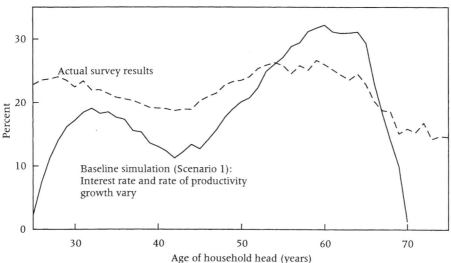

**FIGURE 6   Household consumption and earnings by age of head:
Our simulations for Taiwan and Deaton and Paxson's estimates
from survey data**

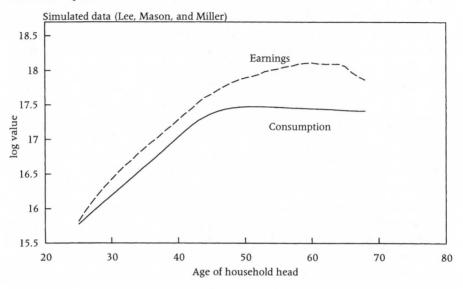

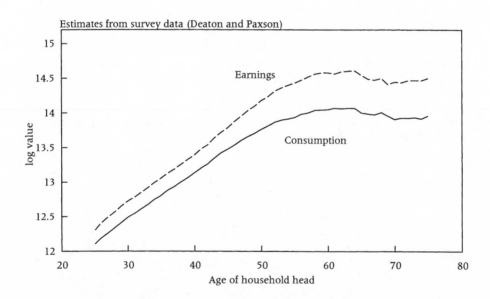

life cycle model implies that the path of consumption should depend only
on total lifetime income and be independent of current income. Attanasio
et al. (1997) consider this issue in their research and show that demographic
factors and uncertainty can also lead to tracking. We examine the issue
with respect to our simulation model by duplicating the upper right portion of Figure 1 from Deaton and Paxson's chapter in this volume, except

more, people faced with longer life would choose to postpone retirement, in which case the mortality decline would have less, if any, effect on saving. But at this point in the history of industrial populations, the trend in retirement age has been strongly downward even as longevity has increased.

It is striking that the simulated effects of demographic transition on saving rates for Taiwan are similar in timing and direction when based on several completely different methods: microanalysis of survey data, macroanalysis of cross-national data, and our macrosimulation based on microdata. However, the simulation based on analysis of survey data shows swings of much smaller magnitude than the other approaches.

We have shown that the demographic transition, operating through the life cycle saving motive, is capable of accounting for a substantial rise in saving rates, and for very high levels of saving rates, in Taiwan. Our simulations do not fit the timing of changes particularly well, and they predict a modest early decline in saving rates in the 1950s and 1960s that was not observed. The levels and expected changes in family transfers must surely play an important role in the explanation of saving behavior in Taiwan, and we have not yet examined this possibility systematically. Other influences on saving, such as buffering against the uncertainty of income streams, preparing for intended bequests, or slowly changing consumption habits, must also play a role. We do believe, however, that life cycle saving is an important part of this picture, and that through it the massive demographic changes over the course of the demographic transition have influenced saving behavior and wealth accumulation, and will continue to do so in the future.

Appendix

For the demographic components of our model, we specify time paths of life expectancy at birth (e_0) and the total fertility rate (TFR). We then derive age-specific rates from these summary measures by assuming that rates for age x and time t are described by $m_{x,t} = a_x + b_x k_t$, where a and b are age-specific parameters that do not change over time, and k is an index of the level of mortality or fertility (see Lee 1993; Lee and Carter 1992). In the case of mortality, $m_{x,t}$ is the log of the age-specific death rate for age x at time t, and in the case of fertility it is the age-specific birth rate. The trajectory of k then determines the trajectory of mortality or fertility, and the time path of k can be chosen to match the time path of e_0 or TFR. The vectors a and b are chosen (for each of fertility and mortality) to provide a good fit to Taiwan's historical experience, but the same vectors can also fit the experience of other populations reasonably well. This setup makes it easy to experiment with alternative demographic scenarios. Here, unlike elsewhere, we assume that the population is closed to migration. This means that we ignore the demographic effects of immigration from the Chinese mainland to Taiwan, which is an unfortunate implication of the greater generality of our current approach. We refer to the resulting transition as "pseudo-Taiwan."

Details of our model of economic behavior can be found in the appendixes to Lee, Mason, and Miller (1997). Here we begin by describing a few elements of the model for the static case. When a household is formed, the heads seek to maximize lifetime utility, V:

$$V = \int_z^\omega e^{-\rho x} u\big[C(x), H(x)\big] dx \ ,$$

where z is the head's age at forming a household, ω is oldest age with nonzero survival probability, $C(x)$ is total household consumption at age x, $H(x)$ is the expected (survival-weighted) total household size measured in Equivalent Adult Consumer (EAC) units, and ρ is the discount rate.

The instantaneous household-utility function in V is specified as

$$u\big[H(x), C(x)\big] = H(x)\left(\left(\left[\frac{C(x)}{H(x)}\right]^{1-\gamma} - 1\right)\Big/(1-\gamma)\right) \ ,$$

where γ is the inverse of the intertemporal elasticity of substitution.

In this specification, household utility is proportional to the number of Equivalent Adult Consumers (EACs) in the household, denoted as $H(x)$, times a standard constant-relative-risk-aversion utility function, with consumption per EAC as its argument. If $H(x)$ were instead replaced by the simple number of household members, giving children the same unitary weight as adults, then optimization would lead parents to squeeze higher consumption per EAC into years in which children were present, since children become super-efficient producers of household utility, contrary to empirical reality.

Life cycle utility is maximized but subject to the constraint that the present value of expected future lifetime earnings of householders, and their children while co-resident *[PV(Y$_t$)]*, evaluated when the heads are age z, equals the present value of expected future household consumption. Both expectations are survival-weighted. The maximization yields the following planned age-time path for household consumption:

$$C(x) = \frac{H(x) PV[Y_1] e^{(r-\rho)x/\gamma}}{\int_z^\omega e^{-ra} H(a) e^{(r-\rho)u/\gamma} da} \ .$$

It follows that the life cycle trajectory of consumption per EAC rises at the rate $(r-\rho)/\gamma$, where γ is the inverse of the intertemporal elasticity of substitution. Bearing in mind that $C(x)/H(x)$ is consumption per surviving EAC, we readily show this to be consistent with the well-known analysis by Yaari (1965: Case C) for consumption paths under uncertain lifetimes, given the availability of fair annuities.

The extension to a context of economic and demographic change is based on rules for formulating expectations as circumstances change, and then on reoptimization at each age, taking as given the situation that has resulted from earlier decisions. We assume that actors make every decision as if they were completely certain about the future (except that survival is a probability, albeit a fully ensured one). We make this assumption despite the fact that householders are repeatedly surprised as the future unfolds, which is an inconsistency in our model.

In our main implementation of the dynamic model, actors have full and correct knowledge of future fertility and mortality probabilities, so that the only uncertainty concerns future economic change as reflected in productivity rates and interest rates. Actors form their life cycle plans on the basis of their expectations of future productivity rates and interest rates, which turn out to be incorrect. Each year they must form new life cycle plans because their current circumstances are different from what they foresaw earlier.

The dynamic version of the age-time path of consumption is given below. It differs from the static version in that optimization occurs at all ages $x \geq z$ rather than solely at age $x = z$, and that these optimizations are based on expectations about future interest rates [$r^*(t)$] and productivity growth rates (which are reflected in Y^*_t); these expectations are described in the text. Consumption is optimized at age x, looking forward a years ($a \geq 0$) into the future when the household head will be aged $x+a$ in year $t+a$. In the dynamic equation the value of future lifetime wealth must include both expected future earnings (as in the static model) and current wealth that reflects the accumulation of past savings. Wealth [$W(x,t)$] is defined so that cohort wealth is maintained. That is, there are lateral, not vertical, bequests: wealth saved by last year's households aged $x{-}1$ is shared among this year's surviving heads aged x.

$$C(x,a,t) = \frac{H(x,a,t)\left[W(x,t) + PV\left[Y_1^*(x,a,t)\right]\right]e^{(r^*(t)-\rho)a/\gamma}}{\int_0^{\omega-x} e^{-r^*(t)g}H(x,g,t)e^{(r^*(t)-\rho)g/\gamma}dg} \ .$$

Notes

We acknowledge with thanks the assistance of Jeff Brown and Noreen Tanouye at the East-West Center and Bryan Lincoln at the Center for Economics and Demography of Aging, University of California, Berkeley. Lee and Miller's research for this chapter was funded by National Institute on Aging grant AG11761. Mason received support for this study from the US Agency for International Development, the Rockefeller Foundation, the William and Flora Hewlett Foundation, and the Ministry of Foreign Affairs of Japan.

1 The reason that higher productivity growth rates reduce savings is that, in our model, productivity growth occurs in all age groups in a given year, rather than only in the cohort entering the labor force in that year. Therefore profiles of life cycle earnings rise more rapidly in our simulations when productivity growth is more rapid, contrary to the usual formulation.

References

Attanasio, Orazio P. et al. 1997. "Humps and bumps in lifetime consumption," unpublished paper, Institute for Fiscal Studies, University College, London, and the National Bureau of Economic Research, Cambridge, MA.

Carroll, Christopher D. and Lawrence H. Summers. 1991. "Consumption growth parallels income growth: Some new evidence," in *National Saving and Economic Performance: A National Bureau of Economic Research Project Report*, eds. B. Douglas Bernheim and John B. Shoven. Chicago: The University of Chicago Press, pp. 305–343.

Coale, Ansley J. and Edgar M. Hoover. 1958. *Population Growth and Economic Development in Low-income Countries: A Case Study of India's Prospects*. Princeton, NJ: Princeton University Press.

Deaton, Angus S. and Christina H. Paxson. 1997. "The effects of economic and population growth on national saving and inequality," *Demography* 34(1): 97–114.

Directorate-General of Budget, Accounting and Statistics. 1993. *Report on the Survey of Personal Income Distribution in Taiwan Area, Republic of China*. Taipei.

Feeney, Griffith and Andrew Mason. 1998. "Population in East Asia," East-West Center Working Papers: Population Series, No. 88-2. Honolulu: East-West Center.

Fisher, Irving. 1930. *The Theory of Interest As Determined by Impatience to Spend Income and Opportunity to Invest It*. New York: Macmillan.

Fry, Maxwell J. and Andrew Mason. 1982. "The variable rate of growth effect in the life cycle saving model," *Economic Inquiry* 20(3): 426–442.

Higgins, Matthew D. 1994. "The demographic determinants of savings, investment and international capital flows," Ph.D. dissertation, Department of Economics, Harvard University, Cambridge, MA.

Higgins, Matthew and Jeffrey G. Williamson. 1997. "Age structure dynamics in Asia and dependence on foreign capital," *Population and Development Review* 23(2): 261–293.

Hurd, Michael D. 1997. "The economics of individual aging," in *Handbook of Population and Family Economics*, eds. Mark R. Rosenzweig and Oded Stark. Amsterdam: Elsevier, pp. 892–966.

Kelley, Allen C. and Robert M. Schmidt. 1996. "Saving, dependency and development," *Journal of Population Economics* 9(4): 365–386.

Lee, Ronald D. 1993. "Modeling and forecasting the time series of U.S. fertility," *International Journal of Forecasting* 9(2): 187–202.

Lee, Ronald D. and Lawrence R. Carter. 1992. "Modeling and forecasting U.S. mortality," *Journal of the American Statistical Association* 87(419): 659–671.

Lee, Ronald, Andrew Mason, and Timothy Miller. 1997. "Saving, wealth, and the demographic transition in East Asia," *East-West Center Working Papers: Population Series*, No. 88-7. Honolulu: East-West Center.

———. 1998. "Saving, wealth, and population," paper presented at the Symposium on Population Change and Economic Development, Bellagio Center, Como, Italy, 2–6 November.

———. 1999. "Reply," in *Population Economics, Demographic Transition, and Development: Research and Policy Implications*, eds. Andrew Mason, Tom Merrick, and Paul Shaw. [Unnumbered] World Bank Institute Working Paper. Washington, DC: World Bank.

Mason, Andrew. 1981. "An extension of the life-cycle model and its application to population growth and aggregate saving," *East-West Population Institute Working Papers*, No. 4. Honolulu: East-West Center.

———. 1987. "National saving rates and population growth: A new model and new evidence," in *Population Growth and Economic Development: Issues and Evidence*, eds. D. Gale Johnson and Ronald D. Lee. Madison: University of Wisconsin Press, pp. 523–560.

———. 1988. "Saving, economic growth, and demographic change," *Population and Development Review* 14(1): 113–144.

Mason, Andrew and Tim Miller. 1998. "Family and intergenerational income transfers in Taiwan," in *The Changing Family in Comparative Perspective: Asia and the United States*, eds. Karen O. Mason, Noriko O. Tsuya, and Minja Kim Choe. Honolulu: East-West Center, pp. 215–236.

Mason, Andrew, Varai Woramontri, and Robert M. Kleinbaum. 1993. "Domestic resource mobilization: Analysis of survey data," in *The Economic Impact of Demographic Change in Thailand, 1980–2015*, eds. Burnham O. Campbell, Andrew Mason, and Ernesto M. Pernia. Honolulu: East-West Center, pp. 115–143.

Modigliani, Franco and Albert Ando. 1957. "Test of the life cycle hypothesis of saving," *Bulletin of the Oxford University Institute of Statistics* 19 (May): 99–124.

Ogaki, Masao, Jonathan Ostry, and Carmen Reinhart. 1996. "Saving behavior in low- and middle-income developing countries: A comparison," *International Monetary Fund Staff Papers*, No. 43. Washington, DC: International Monetary Fund.

Ogawa, Naohiro and Robert D. Retherford. 1993. "Care of the elderly in Japan: Changing norms and expectations," *Journal of Marriage and the Family* 55(3): 585–597.

Paxson, Christina. 1996. "Saving and growth: Evidence from micro data," *European Economic Review* 40(2): 255–288.

Tobin, James. 1967. "Life cycle saving and balanced economic growth," in *Ten Economic Studies in the Tradition of Irving Fisher*, ed. William Fellner. New York: Wiley Press, pp. 231–256.

Weinstein, W. et al. 1994. "Co-residence and other ties linking couples and their parents," in *Social Change and the Family in Taiwan*, eds. Arland Thornton and Hui-Li Sheng Lin. Chicago: The University of Chicago Press, pp. 305–334.

Yaari, Menahem. 1965. "Uncertain lifetime, life insurance, and the theory of the consumer," *The Review of Economic Studies* 32(2): 137–150.

PART FOUR

POPULATION AND DEVELOPMENT

The Quantity–Quality Transition in Asia

MARK R. MONTGOMERY
MARY ARENDS-KUENNING
CEM METE

ONE CAN HARDLY imagine macroeconomic development being sustained without support from a quantity–quality transition, during which families decrease their fertility and increase their human-capital investments in children. The reductions in fertility are expressed, after a lag, in slower rates of growth in the population of labor force age. Greater schooling investments per child likewise translate into higher levels of human capital per worker. In this way the substitution of quality for quantity in family strategies helps to guide the macroeconomy toward higher income per worker.

Yet quantity–quality transitions are neither automatic nor self-propelling. Their progress depends on a host of contending forces acting at the family and the macroeconomic levels; the balance can easily tip against further transition. Consider family decisions about schooling, which are motivated mainly by its private economic returns. These returns are determined in labor markets, and here the logic of supply and demand applies. When families decide to invest more intensively in their children, they will collectively increase the supply of educated young labor. If other things are held fixed, the rate of return to schooling should then fall, and this, in turn, should dampen parental enthusiasm for further educational investments. Reductions in the rate of return should also weaken the case for continued reductions in fertility. Unless they are counterbalanced by other forces, such negative feedbacks would tend to bring a quantity–quality transition to a halt.

In the well-documented case of South Korea (Kim and Topel 1995), economic returns to tertiary schooling fell considerably during the 1980s, evidently in response to such supply shifts. Similar changes have been detected for Taiwan in the late 1980s (Huang 1998). What is the record elsewhere? Are high returns generally maintained in spite of shifts in the supply of skills? If so, is this due to the spillover benefits of trade, technological change that sustains the demand for skilled labor, or capital accumulation that complements skills?

The aim of this chapter is to explore both the negative and positive feedbacks that have affected the quantity–quality transition in Asia. We assemble the leading hypotheses and evidence on the macroeconomic forces, both domestic and international, that could influence returns to schooling. We also examine family factors, giving particular attention to the intergenerational linkages that seem to have maintained the momentum of the Asian transition.

The chapter is organized as follows. In the next section we outline the microeconomic perspective on fertility and schooling that motivates the study. In the third section we briefly review the record of fertility decline and rising school enrollments in the countries of East and Southeast Asia and in a set of comparison countries in South and South-Central Asia. In the fourth section, which constitutes the major portion of the chapter, we present evidence on the key variables that link the macroeconomic forces to family-level decisions: rates of return to primary, secondary, and tertiary schooling. Rate-of-return calculations from Psacharopoulos (1985 and 1994) are examined, together with supplementary evidence drawn from other sources. We discuss the macroeconomic factors that are thought to influence those rates of return and test several of the leading hypotheses with country-level data. In the fifth section we turn to family-level evidence, presenting a set of estimates of fertility and children's schooling from Pakistan, Bangladesh, Indonesia, Malaysia, the Philippines, Thailand, and Taiwan. The issue of interest in this section is whether, even with the aggregate returns to schooling held constant, powerful family-level forces continue to promote quantity–quality transitions. We find strong evidence of such positive feedbacks at the family level. The implications of these findings are discussed in the concluding section.

A microeconomic perspective

It is appropriate to begin by considering families and their decisionmaking, recognizing that families are set in environments whose parameters are established by markets and governments. The macroeconomic and policy climates are exogenous to families, but, as we have noted, aggregated family-level decisions can shift such exogenous parameters.

Consider a newly married couple just embarking on a reproductive career. Over the course of that career the couple will make decisions about the number of children to have and the educational resources to be invested in each child. The time horizon for reproduction is limited by the reproductive span of the woman, but educational decisions will continue to be made after reproduction has ceased. The parents will periodically consult their evolving information set, which summarizes their current knowledge of the macroeconomy and, in particular, perceptions and expectations of the economic returns to schooling. These economic rates of return affect decisions because parents may anticipate some benefits for themselves from schooling, in the form of transfers from grown children, and are also altruistically concerned with their children's wellbeing. In addition the information set will contain accumulated family-specific information on the educational abilities of each child, which may be combined with the aggregate returns to form child-specific forecasts.

At each decision point, having had a certain number of children and having equipped them with given amounts of schooling, the parents will choose whether to have another child (provided the woman is still capable of doing so) and whether to further the education of all, none, or a selected few of their children. Policy constraints may come into play with respect to education, such as when one child has scored too poorly on a primary school leaving exam to proceed to academic secondary training.

This chapter is not the place to discuss a fully dynamic model incorporating such features, but several points deserve emphasis. (Further discussion of the issues can be found in Montgomery and Lloyd 1997 and Montgomery et al. 1998; Mete 1999 develops a dynamic programming model of schooling decisions.) First, parents desiring to deepen their human-capital investments are unlikely to be able to finance those investments by borrowing against future income. They can restrict fertility in order to invest, but an alternative is to finance the investments from reductions in their own consumption. Another possibility is to reduce both fertility and consumption. Alternatively the parents can solicit transfers from grown children and the wider family to help meet the school costs. Our point is that although fertility reduction is a plausible consequence of the desire to capture educational returns, it is not the only possible outcome.

The required degree of reduction will depend, in part, on the direct costs of schooling. These costs are sometimes dismissed as trivial, but they can be important in low-income, rural settings when considered in relation to the scarcity of cash. In addition to the direct costs of schooling, parents may confront time costs in childrearing that are associated with schooling. Parents who themselves have had little or no schooling may not depart much from traditional modes of child care, but second-generation parents—those who have been further in school—may see a need to prepare their own children quite differently. We suspect that associated with the quantity–quality transition is a fundamental change in the nature of child care (LeVine et al. 1991), which may have reinforcing effects over the generations.

In the early stages of a quantity–quality transition, inequalities in investments among children are to be expected (Parish and Willis 1993), whether as the result of ability-based differences in the returns to schooling or of sex preferences on the part of parents (Behrman 1988). Where such inequalities are tolerated, parents may feel little compulsion to divide educational resources equally among their children. A strategy of differential investment may let some parents escape the need to severely restrict fertility (or some other dimension of consumption) in order to finance schooling.

This discussion has presumed that the economic returns to schooling are known to parents, but the sources of such knowledge deserve comment. It is far from obvious that parental perceptions about educational returns are firmly grounded in empirical realities. It is more likely that knowledge of these returns is based on impressions gleaned variously from social networks, peers, and the media. Very little research has considered the sources of these perceptions and their linkage, or the lack of it, to the relevant macroeconomic data. (See Dominitz and Manski 1994 and 1997 and Manski 1992 for an application to US labor markets. See also Montgomery 1998 and 1999 for a discussion of the role of social learning in demographic dimensions.)

Fertility and schooling: The macrolevel record

Armed with this microlevel perspective, we briefly examine the Asian record on fertility and schooling, contrasting the experiences of the rapidly growing economies of East and Southeast Asia with those of the slower-growing economies of South-Central Asia. As will become evident, these subregions present some sharp contrasts, but similarities can also be found. The lessons that can be derived from the successful experiences of East and Southeast Asian countries cannot be thoroughly understood without reference to the wider regional context.

Figure 1 traces the record of fertility decline in Asia, the top panel depicting the country-by-country data series in East and Southeast Asia, and the bottom panel doing so for South-Central Asian countries. In the East Asian context, the Philippines, Malaysia, and Indonesia now form a comparatively high-fertility group, with total fertility rates above 2.5 births per woman. The remaining countries of the subregion have reached or fallen below replacement-level fertility, with the declines in Singapore and Hong Kong preceding those of similar magnitude in South Korea, Thailand, and China. As can be seen, Japanese fertility rates have long been near replacement. The South-Central Asian countries (bottom panel) have exhibited slower, shallower, or more delayed fertility declines, with the fertility fall in Bangladesh being a notable development of the 1980s. However, the differentials that once separated South from Southeast Asia are no longer

FIGURE 1 Total fertility rates in selected Asian countries, by subregion: 1950–95

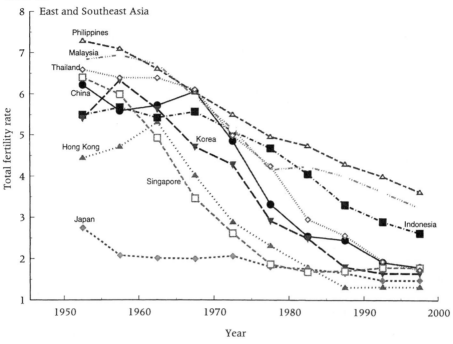

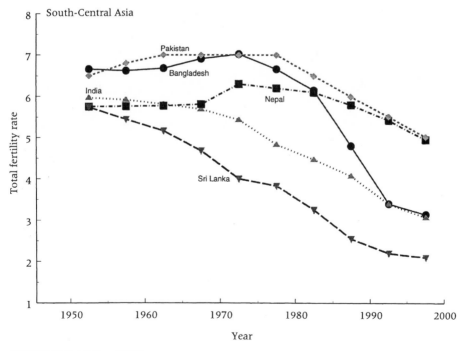

SOURCE: United Nations (1996).

so clearly evident. Indian fertility levels approach those of Indonesia, and Sri Lanka more closely resembles its East Asian than its South Asian counterparts.

Accompanying fertility decline in the region has been an expansion of school enrollments at all levels. We rely on enrollment data from the World Bank (1997), which are based primarily on data from the United Nations Educational, Scientific and Cultural Organization (UNESCO). (See Behrman and Rosenzweig 1994 for a discussion of data quality.) In East and Southeast Asia (data not shown), gross primary enrollment ratios were very high throughout the period under consideration (1970–90); but elsewhere in Asia, countries such as Sri Lanka, Nepal, and Bangladesh recorded significant gains at the primary level. Pakistan is notable for its relative lack of progress at the primary level.

At the secondary level (Figure 2), several East Asian countries have made rapid advances, South Korea being the clearest example. Apart from Thailand, where gains at the secondary level have been modest at best, steady improvement has been the regional norm. In South-Central Asia, by contrast, progress has been slower, with Sri Lanka again being the exception and surprising gains apparent in Nepal in spite of its poverty. Indeed, by the end of the period, Nepal had nearly attained Thailand's level of secondary enrollments.

Perhaps the single most important difference between the experiences of the East and Southeast Asian countries and those of the other Asian countries is the earlier achievement of nearly universal primary schooling in the former group. With the exception of Pakistan, the other Asian countries have gone on to make rapid progress in primary enrollments, but the initial advantages of the East Asian countries (often called the Asian "tigers") may well have been the decisive factor.

According to Mingat (1998) and Mundle (1998), these successful countries realized and acted early on the need to expand primary and lower-secondary education. Government subsidies clearly favored these levels of the education system. The governments also encouraged the private sector's involvement in education, for the most part in tertiary schooling, although in Indonesia in primary schooling as well. Moreover, highly selective admission and promotion policies (such as those practiced in Latin America and Africa) were abolished, and the successful East Asian countries moved toward a system of automatic grade progression at the primary and lower secondary levels. (See Birdsall and Sabot 1994 and Birdsall, Ross, and Sabot 1995 for insightful comparisons of Latin American and East Asian schooling policies.) They also rapidly increased the number of schools in rural areas. Perhaps such government investments are made more easily where the growth rate of the school-age population is lower (Mason 1993; Mason and Campbell 1993).

FIGURE 2 Secondary school gross enrollment ratios in selected Asian countries, by subregion: 1970–90

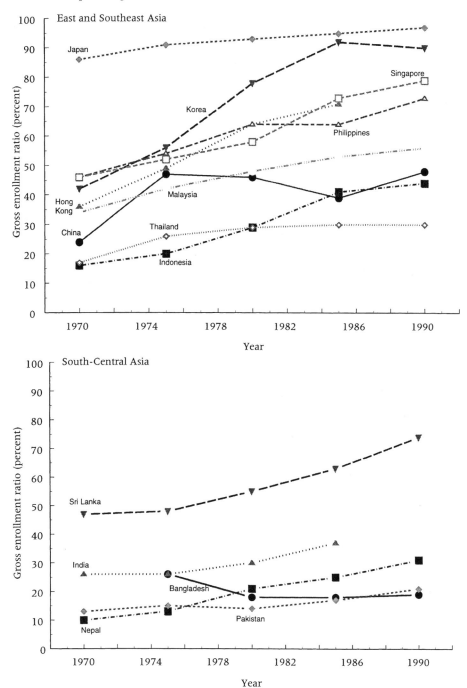

NOTE: The gross enrollment ratio for a given level of schooling is calculated as the ratio of the number of children enrolled at that level to the number of children in the population whose age falls in the range appropriate to the level of schooling. The definition of an appropriate age range is country-specific.
SOURCE: World Bank (1997).

Returns to schooling

Rates of return to schooling are the fundamental building blocks of human-capital theory (Willis 1986).[1] They play the dominant role in determining demands for schooling and thus can potentially affect decisions about fertility as well. The returns to schooling are not fixed or exogenous quantities; rather, they are akin to prices and therefore would be expected to vary with supply and demand conditions, a country's stage of development, and its exposure to world market forces (Stokey 1996). We emphasized at the outset the possibility of negative feedbacks, by which growth in the supply of educated labor could bring about a decline in rates of return. The scale of such supply shifts was indicated just above. Here we must also consider the potential for positive feedbacks and other external influences.

For developed countries, numerous studies have documented the rates of return to schooling and explored their determinants, most often through cross-sectional studies but also, on occasion, using time series of cross-sections to examine temporal change. The possibilities for exploring time trends are more limited in developing countries, where differences in data collection and methodology make intertemporal comparisons difficult.

One important source of data for developing countries has yet to be fully exploited. In a series of publications, Psacharopoulos has assembled estimates of internal rates of return to schooling, the most recent of these being Psacharopoulos (1985 and 1994). The data sources vary, but in most cases these estimates are based on earnings regressions from cross-sectional labor force surveys. The estimates compiled by Psacharopoulos include some from his own research, but most are derived from studies by others. In screening such studies, Psacharopoulos has consistently excluded regressions with inappropriate controls (e.g., those including occupational dummies or other clearly endogenous variables) and studies that assign forgone earnings to young children.

The estimates that meet these criteria can be criticized on other grounds. The internal rate-of-return method favored by Psacharopoulos requires assumptions about the number of years needed to progress from one level of schooling to the next. In many countries the time taken to complete a given educational level is greatly affected by grade repetition, dropout, and reenrollment. With data lacking, applications of the method have also had to assume that the direct costs of schooling can be ignored.[2] Despite the impressive effort to preserve their consistency, the labor force data and regressions vary in many aspects, including the nature of sampling, the inclusion or exclusion of women and those who do not work for wages, the treatment of unemployment, the use of questionable explanatory variables, and adjustments for urban–rural differentials in the cost of living. Furthermore, the reliance on cross-sectional data need not accord with the concept of expected returns over the longer run and does not permit cohort-specific technical change to be disentangled from other factors. Finally, labor force surveys do not allow either the quality of schooling or individual ability to be taken into account.

Nevertheless, few alternatives to the Psacharopoulos estimates present themselves. Some Asian countries (e.g., South Korea and Taiwan) are now in a position to supply repeated cross-sectional labor force surveys, and as the number of these countries expands, such surveys will provide a firmer foundation for the study of trends and differentials in rates of return. But for the moment there are too few countries with such data to allow macroeconomic factors to be investigated. Although we recognize the limits of the Psacharopolous estimates, for present purposes these data will suffice.

The empirical record

Figures 3 to 5 provide the full set of Psacharopoulos estimates of returns to primary, secondary, and tertiary schooling for Asia. Where estimates are available for two or more points in time for a given country, we have linked the country observations with dotted lines to aid in the detection of trends. Few

FIGURE 3 Private rates of return to primary schooling, selected Asian countries, 1965–89

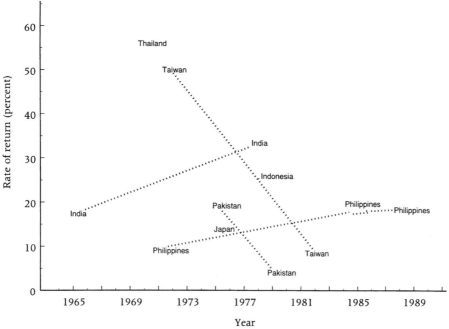

SOURCE: Estimates compiled by Psacharopoulos (1985, 1994).

FIGURE 4 Private rates of return to secondary schooling, selected Asian countries, 1965–89

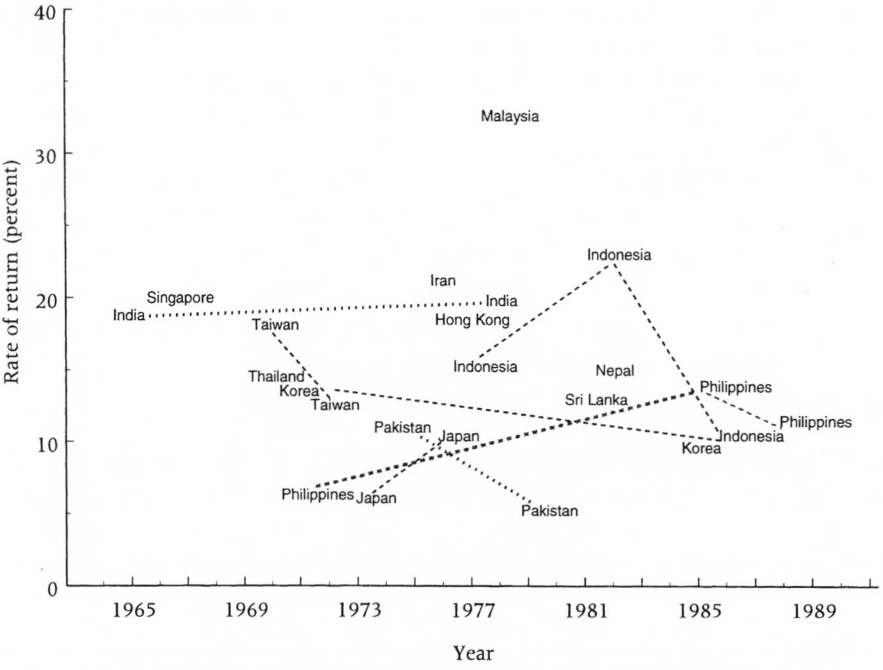

SOURCES: Estimates compiled by Psacharopoulos (1985, 1994).

estimates are available for the rate of return to primary schooling, but there are a number of estimates to examine at the secondary and tertiary levels.

These figures exhibit three main features. The first, and perhaps most important, is that the rate of return to schooling is quite high in absolute terms, almost irrespective of the level of schooling considered. The second noteworthy feature is the considerable variation in returns by country and time period. Interestingly, the East and Southeast Asian countries display neither consistently higher nor consistently lower rates of return. (Single-year estimates for Hong Kong and Singapore are high, as are the single-year estimates for Malaysia.) Third, time trends in the returns to schooling in Asia are difficult to discern. In the case of primary schooling (Figure 3), the few observations available permit no conclusion. At the secondary level (Figure 4) the picture is not much clearer. India exhibits little change in the rate of return; South Korea presents evidence of a slight decline; estimates for Taiwan suggest (implausibly) a sharp drop in a two-year period around 1970; Indonesian returns rise and then fall from the mid-1970s to the mid-1980s; and similar behavior is evident for the Philippines. Estimates at the tertiary level (Figure 5) are also mixed and inconclusive in regard to trend.

FIGURE 5   Private rates of return to tertiary schooling, selected Asian countries, 1965–89

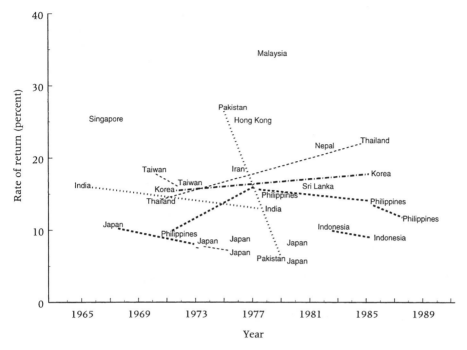

SOURCES: Estimates compiled by Psacharopoulos (1985, 1994).

For two countries with richer data series, South Korea and Taiwan, additional evidence is available on wage ratios by level of education. (Wage ratios—calculated as the ratio of the average wages of workers with a given level of education to those with another level—are not equivalent to internal rates of return, but one would expect similar trends in these alternative measures.) In the Korean case (Kim and Topel 1995), wages for university graduates rose in relation to those for high school graduates until the mid-1970s and then fell through the late 1980s. This pattern is also seen in studies of South Korea by S. J. Davis (1992) and Park, Ross, and Sabot (1996). In the case of Taiwan, Gindling, Goldfarb, and Chang (1995) summarize the situation as one of relative stability from 1982 to 1991 in the returns to schooling. Yet, by the 1987–94 period, evidence was emerging of declining wage ratios among those with junior college or higher education relative to those with lower schooling. The decline was due to supply shifts, although it seems to have been masked by demand-side factors that had an opposite influence (Huang 1997 and 1998). (Topel 1998 cites supporting evidence, referring to a Ph.D. dissertation by H. C. Lu that found falling returns to human capital in Taiwan in response to increasing supplies of educated labor.)

One reading of the Asian record, then, is that with the exception of South Korea and, more recently, Taiwan, high economic returns to schooling have persisted. If macroeconomic forces have affected these returns, they have not so strongly affected them as to produce uniform or easily identifiable trends. Looking at the broadest features of the empirical record, one could even say that the returns to schooling have been remarkably stable, with the inevitable year-to-year and country-to-country variation dominated by the high mean level of returns. If stability in this sense is the correct characterization, then it is a striking feature of the Asian experience. Surely, in all Asian labor markets, the economic returns to schooling must reflect changes on the supply side (Fields 1994; Funkhouser 1998; Mazumdar 1993). How can the returns have remained largely unaffected?

Shifts in demand

To produce relative stability in returns to schooling, the supply shifts described above must have been counterbalanced by shifts in the demand for educated, skilled labor. Demand shifts are subtler and more difficult to detect than supply shifts, and there is considerable controversy about which demand-side influences may have been dominant in Asia. Here we consider several leading hypotheses. (A fuller discussion can be found in Montgomery, Arends-Kuenning, and Mete 1999.)

Capital accumulation. One possibility is that the accumulation of physical capital in Asia has encouraged a disproportionate shift in the demand for better-educated labor. If capital and skilled labor are strong complements, such accumulation would tend to sustain the returns to schooling. As is well known, some Asian countries have compiled an impressive record of capital accumulation. Data on nonresidential capital-to-worker ratios (Summers and Heston 1991) reveal remarkable increases in Taiwan and South Korea, although the series for Hong Kong, Thailand, and the Philippines exhibit somewhat lesser increases.

But increases in physical capital, however remarkable in some cases, need not disproportionately stimulate the demand for skilled labor. On the key question of whether physical capital is complementary to skilled labor, there is little Asian research to cite. Hamermesh (1986) summarized much of the literature in an early and still influential review, which unfortunately included no developing countries. Although there was more variation in the estimates than might have been supposed, the tentative conclusion from his review was that capital and skilled labor were likely to be more complementary than were capital and unskilled labor.[3]

To our knowledge, no econometric research focusing on Asia has estimated the elasticities of substitution between physical capital, skilled labor, and unskilled labor. Trends in the composition of manufacturing from

1973 to 1988 suggest that capital–skill complementarities could have sustained the returns to skills (World Bank 1993). In East Asian manufacturing, three subsectors are believed to have strong complementarities between capital and skilled labor—metal products, electronics, and machinery. These subsectors grew rapidly during 1973–88 in their shares of total manufacturing value added. Taken together, their shares doubled in Japan and Singapore, nearly tripled in Indonesia and South Korea, and quadrupled in Malaysia. To the degree that this growth was fueled by capital investment and produced shifts in the demand for skilled labor, these subsectors may well have supported the returns to education. The textile and garment sectors, however, not usually viewed as having strong complementarities between capital and skills, continued to account for an important share of manufacturing value added.

The evidence favoring the existence of complementarities between capital and skills in Asia is therefore weak and indirect. Nevertheless, in view of the region's impressive record of capital accumulation, this remains a persuasive hypothesis.

Technological change. An alternative explanation stresses the role of skill-biased technological change in enhancing the returns to schooling. Much evidence for developed countries suggests that technology and skilled labor are complementary (Montgomery, Arends-Kuenning, and Mete 1999). How relevant are such findings to Asia?

In a study of educational wage differentials in South Korea, Choi (1993) found that workers were paid more in industries characterized by rapid technological change than in other industries, technological change being measured by total factor productivity (TFP) growth rates. The spread of technology evidently benefited all workers in these industries. For men the interaction between the TFP growth rate and schooling suggested that faster technological change raised the returns to education, particularly in relation to low levels of schooling. Yet, somewhat contrary to expectations, Choi found that for women the interaction between the TFP growth rate and high school education had a greater effect on wages than did the interaction with college education.

Choi also examined the effects of research and development (R&D) spending within industries, focusing on R&D as a determinant of wages. Increases in R&D intensity in an industry (intensity being the ratio of R&D expenditures to sales) were associated with higher wages for both men and women in that industry, but only for women did greater intensity bring about an increase in the educational wage differential at the secondary and tertiary levels. The interaction between R&D intensity and college schooling was positive and significant for women, suggesting that although increases in intensity raised all women's wages, female college graduates benefited especially. Results such as these suggest a complex web of relationships linking technological change, returns to schooling, and gender. Unfortunately, we have not found similar studies for other Asian countries.

Does trade affect returns? Did the outward trade orientation of the East and Southeast Asian economies affect their returns to schooling? Observers of East Asia's economic growth have often emphasized the region's adoption of export-promoting development policies. Export sectors in this region tend to be more labor-intensive than import-competing sectors, raising the possibility that export promotion will increase employment and encourage a more equal distribution of income. (See Birdsall, Ross, and Sabot 1997; Birdsall and Sabot 1994; A. O. Krueger 1990.) The link to educational differentials in earnings, however, has been left unclear.

The theory on this question is inconclusive because competing models of trade give different answers about how trade liberalization affects wage differentials. According to the standard Heckscher–Ohlin and Stolper–Samuelson theories, when a labor-abundant country opens trade with a capital-abundant country, wages will rise and returns to capital will fall in the labor-abundant country. If East Asian countries are more labor-abundant than the rest of the world, then wages should rise in these countries with increased trade. Alternatively, one can abstract from capital and other factors, and focus on a world in which the two factors are skilled and unskilled labor (Katz and Murphy 1992; Lawrence and Slaughter 1993; Robbins 1996; Wood 1995). In this way of thinking, if unskilled labor is the relatively abundant factor in Asia, trade liberalization will cause the wages of unskilled labor to rise in relation to the wages of skilled labor, and the returns to schooling will then fall. As D. R. Davis (1996) and Leamer (1998) point out, however, the appropriate points of comparison for factor abundance may not be the world but rather the country's regional trading partners. Taiwan may have been abundant in unskilled labor relative to the world economy, but in comparison with the Philippines or Thailand it would have been well-endowed with skilled labor. Opening of trade with such regional partners could have increased the returns to skilled labor in Taiwan.

Apart from effects attributable to comparative advantage and factor prices, trade may play an important indirect role in affecting returns to schooling by spurring capital accumulation. A country's success in exporting may encourage foreign direct investment by multinational corporations because export orientation signals that the macroeconomy is being well managed. If capital accumulation is faster as a result of foreign direct investment, and if capital is complementary with schooling, then the returns to schooling could rise with trade.

In an article that concisely summarizes these theories and links them to family decisions, Stokey (1996) has traced out their dynamic implications. Her simulation model incorporates three factors—capital, unskilled labor, and skilled labor. Skilled labor and capital are assumed to be complements. In the context of this model, trade liberalization encourages the inflow of capital. The increase in capital raises the returns to skilled labor over the medium term. Households, noting the increase in these returns, respond by increasing their investments in human capital. Over the long term the ensuing supply shift then bids down the returns to skilled labor. The return to skill thus increases with the opening of trade but subsequently decreases as educational levels rise.

The trade–technology link. Trade may also function as a conduit for technological change. If trade is associated with technology transfer, and if technology and skills are complementary, then this too could be a mechanism that supports the returns to schooling.

According to Pack and Page (1994), by exporting, countries can obtain recent, "best practice" technology. For example, Taiwan's substantial export earnings have allowed it to import the latest equipment. In addition, exporting can encourage direct technology transfer from developed-country buyers to their suppliers as the former strive to ensure quality control. As Keller (1997) notes, trade also allows countries to obtain R&D cheaply through another route: the practical implications of R&D are evident in blueprints, for example, which can be reverse-engineered.

Although the means of technology transfer may be difficult to pin down, a growing empirical literature examines whether countries benefit from the R&D investments made by their trading partners. Much of the evidence is from developed countries,[4] but a few studies have examined developing countries. Choi (1993) investigated the spillover benefits for South Korea of changing R&D intensity within the member countries of the OECD. The R&D intensities of those developed countries had a positive effect on Korean workers' wages, although only for Korean women did the educational wage differential increase. Indeed, for men this mechanism seems to have compressed wage differentials. Once again the empirical evidence suggests a more complicated picture than would be indicated by the theory.

Cross-country evidence

To summarize this wide-ranging discussion, we present in Table 1 a set of descriptive, cross-country regression models in which the dependent variables are the rates of return to schooling at the primary, secondary, and tertiary levels. The regression models are estimated separately by level of education. Very few observations are available on primary rates of return, and therefore these findings can only be taken as suggestive.

The explanatory factors entering these models include the value of nonresidential capital per worker (data from Summers and Heston 1991),

TABLE 1 Regression estimates of private rates of return to education by educational level: Recent decades

Explanatory variables (|z|-statistic in parentheses)	Completed primary			Completed secondary			Any tertiary		
	I	II	III	I	II	III	I	II	III
Constant	19.920	24.686	1.113	15.192	12.206	12.232	13.506	19.960	17.046
	(1.69)	(1.43)	(0.05)	(7.26)	(3.96)	(3.46)	(8.43)	(6.07)	(4.42)
Africa	23.136	16.483	-1.209	14.622	25.848	28.113	17.406	11.710	11.726
	(1.98)	(0.84)	(0.06)	(5.26)	(5.85)	(5.68)	(7.28)	(2.92)	(2.54)
Latin America	9.035	3.287	-3.911	5.126	2.387	5.334	8.514	4.848	6.164
	(0.81)	(0.20)	(0.21)	(2.19)	(0.82)	(1.51)	(4.23)	(1.87)	(1.84)
East and Southeast Asia	7.713	4.356	-7.141	4.206	-.426	.092	3.992	-1.491	-1.422
	(0.64)	(0.29)	(0.44)	(1.57)	(0.13)	(0.03)	(1.92)	(0.60)	(0.52)
Other Asia	.430	1.290	9.741	3.677	3.904	5.130	6.079	-.332	.806
	(0.03)	(0.06)	(0.44)	(1.07)	(0.93)	(1.22)	(1.97)	(0.08)	(0.19)
Adult education ratio		-1.623	-6.341		2.390	6.483		-3.759	-2.740
		(0.13)	(0.53)		(0.39)	(1.03)		(1.53)	(1.00)
Nonresidential capital per worker (1985 international dollars, in thousands)		-.434	-.311		-.052	-.034		-.255	-.231
		(0.50)	(0.37)		(0.36)	(0.25)		(2.24)	(1.89)
Trade openness			.364			.063			.046
			(2.11)			(1.81)			(1.32)
1970–79	-2.233		22.227	-5.013		-5.007	-2.426		.428
	(0.23)		(1.11)	(2.12)		(1.72)	(1.29)		(0.16)
1980 and later	-3.700		11.265	-4.769		-7.781	-4.197		-1.838
	(0.43)		(0.52)	(1.91)		(2.16)	(2.05)		(0.55)
R^2	.124	.092	.273	.247	.453	.510	.353	.353	.331
Number of observations	54	33	33	109	71	71	115	77	77

NOTES: Adult education ratio: for primary education the ratio is of those with completed primary education to those with less or no schooling above age 25; for secondary education the ratio is of adults with completed secondary education to those with incomplete secondary education; for tertiary education the ratio is of those with any tertiary education to those with completed secondary education. Omitted region: developed countries. No data are included from the Middle East or developing-country Oceania. Japan is grouped with East and Southeast Asia. For specifications of models I, II, and III, see text.
SOURCES: See text.

the ratio of adults over age 25 having the specified level of education to those with the next lower level of educational attainment (data from Barro and Lee 1996), a measure of openness to trade (from Summers and Heston 1991), regional dummy variables, and dummy variables for each time period. The specification we employ is loosely modeled on that of the constant-elasticity-of-substitution production function often used in the labor economics literature (e.g., Freeman 1979).

We would expect the capital-per-worker variable to have a positive influence on returns to both secondary and tertiary education. The ratio of adults by educational level should have a negative effect because it is a measure of the relative supply of skills in the labor market. According to the discussion above, openness to trade should be associated with the transfer of skill-intensive technology, among other things, and may have a positive effect on the returns to schooling at the secondary or tertiary level.

In Table 1 we first present results from models containing only the regional dummy variables and time-period dummies (see columns headed by "I" for completed primary, completed secondary, and any tertiary schooling). The omitted regional category is "developed countries," although Japan is grouped with East and Southeast Asia. Two features of these benchmark regressions are noteworthy. First, there is little here to suggest that East and Southeast Asian returns to schooling are very different from those of developed countries, whereas rates of return in Africa and Latin America (at least at the secondary and tertiary levels) are clearly higher. Second, only weak evidence emerges of time trends in returns at the primary or tertiary levels, although evidence of downward trends is somewhat stronger at the secondary level.

In the second specification (columns headed by "II"), we include measures of nonresidential capital per worker and the ratio of adults by educational level. The third specification (denoted by "III") adds a trade-openness measure, defined as the ratio of imports plus exports to gross domestic product. Contrary to expectations, neither capital per worker nor the adult education ratio makes much of a difference. Capital per worker is negatively associated with educational returns at all levels of schooling, although significant only at the tertiary level. More consistent with theory is the negative sign of the education ratio coefficients for primary and tertiary returns—as would be expected from shifts in the relative supplies of labor—but these estimates are also insignificant. The lack of significance is surprising, given the Korean results (Kim and Topel 1995) and similar findings from other countries with cross-sectional, time-series data. Commenting on the growth literature, economists A. B. Krueger and Lindahl (1998) and Topel (1998) caution that the international data on the educational levels of workers are prone to measurement error, a potential weakness of the Barro and Lee data that we employ.

In the full specification, only the trade-openness measure is positively associated with returns to schooling. It is a (weakly) significant influence on both primary and secondary returns, although insignificant in the tertiary-returns regression. Finally, the time-period dummy variables, which in the full specification can be viewed as proxies for skill-related technological progress, are significant only in the secondary schooling regression. As in the benchmark regressions, in the full model they suggest a downward trend in the returns to secondary schooling.

A number of additional specifications, the results of which are not reported here, have been explored. We have examined various specifications for adult educational attainment ratios and capital per worker, and we have investigated whether measures of school quality (Barro and Lee 1996) made an appreciable difference. Although the alternative regressions differ from those of Table 1 in the details, we uncovered no important substantive differences.

Our results provide weak support for the proposition that trade affects the returns to schooling, to judge from the coefficients in the regressions for primary and secondary returns. Perhaps the coefficients reveal the aspect of trade associated with comparative advantage and tendencies toward factor-price equalization. Had trade been an important conduit for new technology, then one would have expected the openness-to-trade measures to be more clearly associated with the returns to tertiary schooling. The industry-level findings of Choi (1993) for South Korea, however, seem to suggest that technological progress could have a greater effect on returns to secondary schooling than on tertiary returns.

Our regression estimates should be interpreted cautiously because cross-national data do not provide a firm foundation for understanding the complementarity of capital and skills or the precise roles of trade and technology. Country fixed effects undoubtedly have a major role in determining the returns to schooling, as do specific aspects of labor market policies and schooling policies that influence, respectively, wage levels and degrees of access to secondary and higher levels of schooling. Even in the absence of country-level panel data, however, we anticipated clearer evidence in the cross-country data of the influence of skills accumulation, growth of capital per worker, and technological change, which must be among the fundamental forces shaping the returns to schooling.

Quantity and quality decisions at the family level

From an Asian family's perspective, the workings of the surrounding macroeconomy may be hidden from view or only dimly perceived. As we argued at the outset, little is known about how families themselves gauge the returns to schooling, and it is possible that local rather than national labor markets exert a disproportionate influence on their thinking. Even if the national labor markets are salient, family perceptions of returns could significantly differ from, or lag well behind, the national-level empirical realities. Socially pertinent information about economic change would tend to filter slowly through a family's networks of peers and relatives; and although the media would transmit information more rapidly, it is not clear that their inevitable focus on novelty and crisis would supply families with information bearing on longer-run concerns.

Given the limited and fragmentary information that families possess, it is sensible to conceive of their schooling and fertility decisions as being based only on the broadest features of the returns to schooling. The dominant empirical regularity identified above is that returns to schooling in Asia are high—even very high—in absolute terms. Perhaps it is sufficient that Asian families appreciate this central fact; perhaps, in most circumstances, variations in returns about the high mean are of second-order importance.

If they take the high returns to schooling as a given, families are then likely to be more concerned with the direct costs of schooling, the time costs entailed in properly preparing their children for schooling, and the examination-based and other policy barriers that may prevent them from securing access to these high returns. In following this line of thinking, we are led to consider evidence of quantity–quality tradeoffs in family decisionmaking.

Here we explore a range of microlevel data sets that contain information on fertility and child-by-child schooling investments. We examine data from Pakistan (1991), Bangladesh (1993), Indonesia (1993), Malaysia (1988), the Philippines (1993), Thailand (1987), and Taiwan (1989).[5] The aim is to estimate reduced-form models of fertility and children's schooling that may elucidate the factors that can produce a quantity–quality tradeoff. We adopt specifications that, although not identical across countries, are sufficiently similar to permit a comparison of effects.

The data sets form a diverse group. For Pakistan we employ the 1991 Living Standards Measurement Survey (LSMS), a nationally representative data set containing a substantial amount of information on both fertility and children's schooling. For Bangladesh we use data from the rural population that has been under demographic surveillance since 1982 by the Extension Project (EP), a study similar in design to the better-known Matlab Project. The data for Indonesia and Malaysia are drawn from the Family Life Surveys (FLS) conducted by RAND and its country collaborators. Demographic and Health Surveys (DHS) data are available for the Philippines and Thailand; and for Taiwan we use the Taiwan Women and Family Survey (TWFS) described in Parish and Willis (1993).

To the degree possible we have assembled data on the fertility of the respondent (the woman) in each household and on the education of all her own children. Our fertility measure is the number of children ever born, which is available in all the data sources we use. A key concern across the surveys, however, is the measurement of children's education. Typically, less is known about the education of children who no longer reside in the household than about the schooling of those who are still resident. For example, surveys do not usually ascertain current school attendance for nonresident children, and often they summarize levels of schooling attained by nonresident children in broader groupings than for resident children.

In our data sets the designs of the Pakistan LSMS, the Malaysian and Indonesian FLS, the Thailand DHS, and the Taiwan TWFS all permit useful information on schooling to be retrieved for nonresident children. The Philippines DHS data on schooling are limited to resident children, as are the Bangladesh EP data. Elsewhere we have studied the likely selection bias for the Philippines (Montgomery et al. 1998) and have concluded that as long as children aged 18 and younger (but not older age groups) are considered, the biases are likely to be small. In the case of Bangladesh, levels of schooling are low enough that serious bias is also unlikely.

Model specification

In modeling fertility and children's school attainment, we use ordered-probit methods for each. This is a sufficiently flexible approach to capture the main features of the relationship between fertility and educational attainment. Since many of the women interviewed were in the midst of their reproductive careers, and likewise many of the children had not completed their schooling, we must employ controls for the woman's age and her children's ages. Another approach would be to use an ordered-probit model with a right-censoring correction for children still enrolled. We have used this approach extensively in other research, including studies of some of the countries in the present sample, but have found that it had little effect on the coefficients of interest here.

To understand the specification from the perspective of the quantity–quality tradeoff, recall that the models being estimated are reduced-form in nature. A tradeoff is therefore evident if a given exogenous variable has the effect of reducing fertility *and* raising children's educational attainment. This *sign pattern* does not in itself reveal the mechanism producing the tradeoff, but rather signals the existence of such a tradeoff.

Our discussion focuses on a small set of such explanatory covariates. The woman's own educational attainment enters each model, as does the education of her spouse (if she is unmarried the spouse's variables are set to zero). Urban residence is included, although this is current residence. A collection of indicators of the household's economic status is also included. These heterogeneous measures range from indexes of household possessions (in Pakistan, Bangladesh, Malaysia, the Philippines, and Thailand) to indicators of the occupation of the spouse (in Taiwan). As discussed elsewhere (Montgomery et al. 2000), such indexes are likely to be weak but nonetheless useful proxies for the preferred measures of permanent or longer-term income.

For three countries—Pakistan, Indonesia, and Malaysia—we can introduce time-specific controls for the presence of schools in the community. We use the dates on which the schools were established to construct measures of access to schools as of the year in which the woman in question reached age 17. The idea is to characterize this aspect of the decision environment as it existed around the time of the woman's marriage. In Pakistan, data on schools were not available for urban areas, and therefore we set these variables to zero in estimating our models. This procedure confounds the effect of urbanness as such with that of (missing) school availability.

Given the data available, it is difficult to identify general time trends. We include measures of the birth cohort of the mother, recognizing that such measures must be associated with the mother's age and thus with the degree to which her fertility career is complete (and, less directly, with the completeness of her children's education). For Taiwan we have access to information on fertility and education in the previous generation, as measured by the number of respondent's siblings and their education. Like Parish and Willis (1993), we use these data to shed light on earlier regimes of fertility and educational decisionmaking.

Results

We do not dwell here on the country-by-country details of the estimates, but rather seek to identify common features of the results, focusing on woman's education, spouse's schooling, urban residence, economic status, and cohort effects. Fuller results are reported in the Appendix Tables.

A striking result is that better-educated women have lower lifetime fertility and equip their children with more education than do less-educated women. This finding is consistent across countries and data sets, with the curious exception of Indonesia, where fertility is not significantly reduced except by senior secondary schooling or higher. The effects of the woman's education on her fertility range from modest to powerful (results not shown), and the effects on the level or years of children's education are also substantial. As we seek to understand the quantity–quality tradeoff at the family level, therefore, this variable merits prime consideration.

The schooling of the spouse tends to reduce fertility, although it is generally of less importance than the woman's schooling. Taiwan and the Philippines present exceptions to the rule; there the spouse's schooling has a positive influence on fertility. This may be evidence of an income effect not captured by other controls. Where children's education is concerned, the spouse's schooling usually exerts a significant positive influence, although the magnitude of the effect again tends to be smaller than for the woman's schooling. (See Behrman 1997 for an extensive review.) In general, however, increases in the schooling of men tend to induce a quantity–quality tradeoff.

In view of the easier access to family planning services and schools in urban areas, and the profound changes underway in the distribution of population between rural and urban areas of Asia (Chen, Valente, and Zlotnik 1998), the role of urban residence in promoting a tradeoff is of considerable interest. The results indicate that urban residence is an important positive influence on children's educational attainment except in the Philippines and, depending on the country, exerts a modest negative influence on fertility.

Because the data sets have heterogeneous measures of economic status, we do not draw detailed conclusions from these coefficients. The effects of economic status on fertility are variable, with positive influences apparent in Pakistan and Malaysia but negative effects evidenced in the Philippines and Thailand. In Taiwan the clearest contrast is between households with spouses who work in agriculture, which have higher fertility, and all other households. With respect to children's educational attainment, we see uniformly positive effects of higher economic status. If attention were restricted to the Philippines and Thailand, improvements in economic status would have the potential to induce a quantity–quality tradeoff. In other settings (e.g., Pakistan), we can identify no such potential.

The clearest evidence of cohort effects is seen in the sibling analysis for Taiwan, which identifies time trends associated with the birth cohort of the respondent's mother that act to reduce fertility and increase children's educational investments. We also included a dummy variable distinguishing children born after 1956 from those born earlier, to see whether the 1968 increase in the mandatory level of schooling in Taiwan had any effect. This variable did not prove to be significant (results not shown).

Summary

Although our results are drawn from a varied collection of Asian countries, they display an impressive consistency. In distilling conclusions from these results, we are intrigued by the central role played by women's education. Much attention has been given to the effect of women's education on fertility; but with a few important exceptions (Behrman 1997; Lam and Duryea 1999; Lillard and Willis 1994; Schultz 1998), less consideration has been given to its influence on the education of children.

Human-capital theory can offer a general characterization of the relationship between the education of the mother and that of her children, but it is less revealing on the specifics. Usually the relationship is described simply as exemplifying the greater efficiencies that educated women achieve in home production. This abstract description fails to illuminate the mechanisms clearly.

One could view the connection as reflecting income effects in settings in which better-educated women tend to be engaged in the labor market and are thus better positioned to help meet the monetary costs of schooling. Lam and Duryea (1999), however, find little direct support for this proposition in Brazil. A related proposition is that better-educated women possess greater bargaining power in the household, and may thus be able to secure a greater share of household resources for their children. Reviewing the literature, Behrman (1997) and Schultz (1998) find a good deal of evidence favoring this view.

Another possibility is that better-educated women are linked to social networks that contain other better-educated members. Through such network ties, women may develop a keener appreciation of the economic benefits of schooling, as well as its non-economic benefits as manifested in health care and related areas. The information available to educated women may reduce the variance of their perceptions and lessen their aversion to risk in making human-capital investments. Such network-related information may well be expressed in the regression coefficient of mother's education. Behrman (1997) outlines a similar argument in stressing the informational advantages of educated women and their abilities to cope with change and economic disequilibrium.

An alternative explanation also merits consideration. Women who have been to school themselves are likely, we think, to take a new view of the nature of child care. They may come to believe that their own time must be devoted to such care if their children are to be properly prepared for schooling and supported during the school years. LeVine et al. (1991) report that educated women in Mexico tend to engage in a form of interaction with their children that is different from that of uneducated women, more often employing highly verbal and other time-intensive modes of communication. If this is so in general, then the changed nature of child care would raise the cost of large numbers of children, with consequent negative effects on fertility. Perhaps the new norms about proper child care are transmitted to the younger generation of children, who act on them when they enter their own childbearing years. Behrman (1997) suggests that better-educated mothers may provide more vivid role models for their children, and research by Lillard and Willis (1994), among others, shows that such intergenerational mechanisms can be empirically important. In all of these areas the education of the spouse has, it seems, a supportive influence, as does urban residence.

However plausible the proposition about child care may be, for the moment it must remain speculative. One may expect to find some confir-

mation of the mother's schooling effect in data on maternal time use. Yet
the comprehensive review by Behrman (1997) lists only two studies of
mothers' schooling and home time use. Both of these lend support to the
hypothesis, but more research is clearly required.

Conclusions

The question posed at the outset was how the quantity–quality transition
in Asia could have continued as it did, given the negative feedback effects
that are inevitably associated with shifts in the supply of educated labor.
Had other things remained constant, these supply shifts should have reduced the returns to schooling and weakened the motivation for deeper
investments in human capital and for the fertility reductions that facilitate
such investments. Although its workings are not always evident in the macroeconomic data, this theory appears unassailable.

But in Asia, other things did not remain constant, and the outcome
was that returns to schooling continued to be high, apart from some recent declines documented for Taiwan and, earlier, for South Korea. The
macroeconomic forces sustaining these returns include capital accumulation, technological change, and a set of effects associated with trade. None
of these influences is well understood, and the descriptive regressions that
we presented could only suggest that the link to trade deserves closer attention.

The Asian transition was also propelled by powerful intergenerational
forces operating at the level of families. These positive feedbacks, by which
the level of schooling invested in one generation encourages deeper schooling investments in the next, also remain poorly understood. They are linked,
we believe, to evolving standards of child care that came to require a more
intensive use of parental time, and that may have increased the time costs
of childrearing. Interestingly, these effects are as clearly visible in the poorest
South Asian countries of our sample (Pakistan and Bangladesh) as they
are in the richest Southeast Asian countries (Taiwan and Thailand). In this
respect, at least, there is more commonality among Asian countries than
the literature's preoccupation with Asian "tigers" would suggest.

Since the downturn of the East Asian economies, the phrase "Asian
tigers" has been used ironically, and one wonders whether the region's
current economic and financial turmoil will so shake Asian parents as to
put in doubt the future of the quantity–quality transition. The opportunity
cost of their children's time in school has surely risen as the income of
parents has fallen, and this may bring about a temporary lull in human-
capital investment. Whether the crisis will permanently alter perceptions
of the returns to schooling is another matter. We predict that the returns
will be perceived to be diminished but still superior to what can be pro-

vided by alternative investments or uses of time. Such predictions are hazardous because little is known about parents' perceptions of returns, the role of local labor conditions as against national conditions, and other factors that affect parental views of schooling. These issues are among the high-priority areas for research.

APPENDIX TABLE 1   Children ever born and level of education: Pakistan, 1991

Background variables (|z|-statistic in parentheses)	Children ever born (N = 3,296)	Children's level of education (N = 9,177)
Child's sex: Female		.589
		(24.25)
Woman's education		
Primary	−.302	.421
	(4.54)	(9.58)
Middle school or higher	−.656	.493
	(9.66)	(10.57)
Spouse's education		
Primary	−.024	.219
	(0.49)	(6.65)
Middle school	−.079	.584
	(1.61)	(18.49)
Secondary or higher	−.300	.803
	(4.03)	(15.97)
Household possessions		
Index	.104	.217
	(2.11)	(2.69)
Index, squared	−.012	−.010
	(1.55)	(0.08)
Residence: Urban	.117	.527
	(1.80)	(11.01)
Woman's year of birth		
Before 1950	.667	.010
	(5.05)	(0.16)
1950–55	.322	−.014
	(3.77)	(0.30)

NOTES: Children's education levels are none, primary, middle, secondary, and college and higher. Coefficients not shown are woman's age and powers of age, child's age and powers of age, school availability, and ordered-probit cut points.
SOURCE: Pakistan Living Standards Measurement Survey, 1991.

APPENDIX TABLE 2 Children ever born and level of education: Bangladesh, 1993

Background variables (|z|-statistic in parentheses)	Children ever born (N = 9,782)	Children's level of education (N = 19,779)
Child's sex: Female		−.225
		(12.87)
Woman's education		
Incomplete primary	−.058	.399
	(1.96)	(17.12)
Complete primary or higher	−.191	.594
	(5.70)	(21.26)
Spouse's education		
Incomplete primary	.028	.213
	(0.98)	(9.20)
Complete primary or higher	−.117	.590
	(3.91)	(25.52)
Household possessions		
Radio	−.105	.186
	(4.41)	(9.87)
Electricity	−.040	.272
	(1.28)	(11.76)
Medium house size	.031	.243
	(1.27)	(12.17)
Large house size	.090	.417
	(2.53)	(15.56)
Woman's year of birth		
Before 1950	.200	.117
	(2.23)	(2.58)
1950–55	.198	.029
	(3.72)	(0.92)

NOTE: Coefficients not shown are woman's age and powers of age, child's age and powers of age, regional dummies, and ordered-probit cut points.
SOURCE: Bangladesh Extension Project, 1993.

APPENDIX TABLE 3 Children ever born and level of education: Indonesia, 1993

Background variables (|z|-statistic in parentheses)	Children ever born (N = 3,678)	Children's level of education (N = 8,602)
Child's sex: Female		−.075
		(2.90)
Woman's education		
Primary	.215	.562
	(0.99)	(7.07)
Junior secondary	−.013	1.148
	(0.04)	(8.58)
Senior secondary or higher	−.647	1.425
	(2.03)	(7.16)
Spouse's education		
Primary	−.308	.101
	(1.39)	(1.34)
Junior secondary	−.339	.134
	(1.14)	(0.99)
Senior secondary or higher	−.101	.019
	(0.31)	(0.10)
Residence: urban	−.044	.349
	(1.20)	(12.52)
Woman's year of birth		
Before 1950	.119	−.035
	(0.72)	(0.50)
1950–55	.004	−.104
	(0.05)	(2.20)

NOTES: Children's education levels are none, primary, junior secondary, senior secondary, and college and higher. Coefficients not shown are woman's age and powers of age, marital status, child's age and powers of age, religion, school availability, and ordered-probit cut points.
SOURCE: Indonesian Family Life Survey, 1993.

APPENDIX TABLE 4   Children ever born and level of education: Malaysia, 1988

Background variables (|z|-statistic in parentheses)	Children ever born (N = 858)	Children's level of education (N = 4,222)
Child's sex: Female		−.204
		(5.55)
Woman's education		
Primary	−.294	.354
	(3.55)	(8.42)
Secondary or higher	−.637	.470
	(4.30)	(5.34)
Spouse's education		
Primary	.108	.098
	(1.09)	(1.92)
Secondary or higher	−.244	.338
	(1.72)	(4.18)
Household possessions		
Index	.200	.234
	(2.35)	(4.89)
Index, squared	−.014	−.008
	(1.81)	(1.83)
Residence: Urban	−.056	.119
	(0.64)	(2.95)
Woman's year of birth		
Before 1950	−.346	−.041
	(0.90)	(0.33)
1950–55	−.294	−.088
	(1.03)	(0.75)

NOTES: Children's education levels are none, any primary, any secondary, and any tertiary. Coefficients not shown are woman's age and powers of age, marital status, child's age and powers of age, ethnicity, school availability, and ordered-probit cut points.
SOURCE: Malaysian Family Life Survey, 1988.

APPENDIX TABLE 5   Children ever born and level of education: Philippines, 1993

Background variables (|z|-statistic in parentheses)	Children ever born (N = 15,029)	Children s level of education (N = 14,290)
Child's sex: Female		.263
		(15.11)
Woman's education		
Secondary	−.363	.273
	(14.08)	(12.11)
Higher	−.829	.291
	(25.11)	(9.10)
Spouse's education		
Secondary	.198	.216
	(7.64)	(9.51)
Higher	.243	.243
	(7.47)	(7.88)
Household possessions		
Index	−.079	.292
	(4.17)	(17.93)
Index, squared	−.002	−.014
	(0.83)	(9.62)
Residence		
Town	−.009	.010
	(0.28)	(0.37)
Small city	−.041	−.014
	(1.60)	(0.63)
Manila	−.190	.009
	(5.23)	(0.25)
Woman's year of birth		
Before 1950	.094	.059
	(1.02)	(1.12)
1950–55	.083	−.008
	(1.75)	(0.26)

NOTE: Coefficients not shown are woman's age and powers of age, marital status, child's age and powers of age, and ordered-probit cut points.
SOURCE: Philippines Demographic and Health Survey, 1993.

APPENDIX TABLE 6   Children ever born and level of education: Thailand, 1987

Background variables (|z|-statistic in parentheses)	Children ever born (N = 6,760)	Children's level of education (N = 8,196)
Child's sex: Female		−.012
		(0.52)
Woman's education		
Primary	−.270	.457
	(5.91)	(12.06)
Secondary	−.515	.680
	(7.96)	(10.73)
Higher	−.981	.707
	(11.58)	(7.72)
Spouse's education		
Secondary	−.250	.310
	(6.60)	(7.97)
Higher	−.317	.211
	(4.78)	(2.86)
Household possessions		
Index	−.228	.129
	(7.59)	(4.55)
Index, squared	.019	.002
	(5.75)	(0.55)
Residence		
Bangkok	−.239	.271
	(6.64)	(7.67)
Other urban	−.173	.169
	(4.56)	(4.50)
Woman's year of birth		
Before 1950	.135	.169
	(1.23)	(2.45)
1950–55	.008	.065
	(0.12)	(1.46)

NOTE: Coefficients not shown are woman's age and powers of age, marital status, child's age and powers of age, and ordered-probit cut points.
SOURCE: Thailand Demographic and Health Survey, 1987.

APPENDIX TABLE 7   Children ever born and level of education: Taiwan, 1989

Background variables (|z|-statistic in parentheses)	Children ever born (N = 3,803)	Children's level of education(N = 9,512)
Child's sex: Female		−.114
		(4.77)
Woman's education		
Completed primary	−.207	.274
	(3.88)	(8.80)
Some secondary	−.522	.305
	(7.23)	(5.88)
Completed secondary or higher	−.972	.088
	(13.21)	(1.61)
Spouse's education		
Completed primary	.169	.311
	(2.67)	(8.77)
Some secondary	.079	.483
	(6.60)	(10.14)
Completed secondary or higher	−.091	.677
	(1.20)	(13.58)
Own home	.120	.042
	(3.17)	(1.54)
Spouse's occupation		
Professional/technical/teacher	−.217	.084
	(2.35)	(1.17)
Administrator/manager	−.144	.008
	(1.63)	(0.12)
Clerical	−.148	−.022
	(1.79)	(0.35)
Sales	−.121	.078
	(1.65)	(1.41)
Service	−.137	−.162
	(1.48)	(2.42)
Production/transport worker	−.217	−.117
	(3.50)	(2.33)
Soldier/other	−.261	−.241
	(3.00)	(4.59)
Residence: urban	−.159	.141
	(4.03)	(5.20)
Woman's year of birth: before 1950	−.051	−.023
	(0.68)	(0.42)

NOTES: Children's education levels are none, some primary, completed primary, some secondary, completed secondary, and university. Omitted category for spouse's occupation is agriculture. Coefficients not shown are woman's age and powers of age, marital status, child's age and powers of age, dummies for missing husband's education and occupation, and ordered-probit cut points.
SOURCE: Taiwan Women and Family Survey, 1989.

APPENDIX TABLE 8 Number of siblings and their level of education: Taiwan, 1989

Background variables (|z|-statistic in parentheses)	Children ever born to respondent's mother (N = 3,796)	Siblings' and respondent's level of education (N = 21,304)
Child's sex: Female		−.534
		(34.37)
Mother's education		
Completed primary	−.108	.374
	(2.17)	(16.41)
Any secondary or higher	−.292	.709
	(3.35)	(16.43)
Father's education		
Completed primary	.052	.531
	(1.16)	(26.66)
Any secondary or higher	.028	.798
	(0.40)	(25.20)
Father's occupation		
Professional/technical/teacher	−.098	.551
	(0.93)	(11.09)
Administrator/manager	−.053	.734
	(0.60)	(17.84)
Clerical	−.001	.551
	(0.02)	(17.13)
Sales	−.098	.356
	(1.68)	(13.59)
Service	−.066	.252
	(0.71)	(5.97)
Production/transport worker	−.108	.127
	(2.09)	(5.50)
Soldier/other	−.512	.848
	(4.90)	(15.89)
Residence at age 15: urban	−.163	.248
	(4.51)	(15.14)
Subjective adequacy of income		
Adequate	−.052	.271
	(1.33)	(15.59)
Well-off	−.045	.485
	(0.60)	(14.14)
Mother's year of birth		
1910–14	.063	.233
	(0.75)	(6.35)
1915–19	−.031	.455
	(0.41)	(13.39)
1920–24	−.091	.580
	(1.20)	(17.26)
1925–29	−.379	.713
	(5.09)	(21.18)
1930–34	−.533	.764
	(6.84)	(21.51)
1935–39	−.756	.770
	(8.71)	(18.87)
1940–44	−.840	.683
	(6.02)	(9.93)

NOTES: Respondent's and siblings' education levels are none, completed primary, any secondary, and higher. Omitted category for father's occupation is agriculture; omitted category for mother's year of birth is before 1910. Coefficients not shown are dummies for father's missing education and occupation, mother's missing age and education, missing income adequacy, and ordered-probit cut points.
SOURCE: Taiwan Women and Family Survey, 1989.

Notes

We thank Cynthia Lloyd and T. Paul Schultz for helpful comments. The research reported here was supported by the Rockefeller Foundation through its "Investing in Children: New Research Frontiers" grant to the Population Council.

1 Capital investments, such as an investment in an additional year or level of schooling, may entail costs borne over several years in the future and likewise are expected to generate a stream of future benefits. An internal rate of return on a discrete capital investment is the discount factor that, when applied to current and future costs and benefits, causes them to be equal in expected present value terms. In the context of a schooling investment, the benefits of the investment are expressed in the increment it makes to future earnings; the costs include both the direct costs of the additional schooling year or level, and the opportunity costs of income forgone while the additional schooling is being acquired. Private rate-of-return calculations define benefits as net of any taxes paid on earnings; costs are defined as the full costs facing the investor and are net of government subsidies and transfers.

2 As the supply of educated labor increases, the costs of investing in schooling and other forms of human capital may decrease, at least to the extent that costs are dominated by teacher and administrator salaries (Topel 1998). Most studies of returns to schooling assume that the main costs of education are forgone earnings, and will therefore miss the impact on returns due to reduced costs on the supply side of schooling.

3 This conclusion has been incorporated in much subsequent work, such as the model of Krusell et al. (1997), who specify a production function for the United States with a much higher elasticity of substitution between unskilled labor and capital equipment than between skilled labor and capital. Their model generates estimates that replicate closely the variation in skilled–unskilled wage differentials over the period 1963 to 1991.

4 Using data from eight OECD countries, Keller (1997) finds evidence that the benefit derived from foreign R&D in an industry is 50 to 95 percent of the productivity effect of domestic R&D. Coe and Helpman (1993), in a much-cited study of 22 developed-country economies, found that R&D investment by trading partners had a large effect on total factor productivity. Perhaps the most interesting finding for present purposes is that foreign R&D capital stocks appear to have had particularly large effects on the smaller countries in the Coe–Helpman sample. See Eaton and Kortum (1994 and 1995) for additional work in this vein.

5 These data are drawn from several sources. The Pakistan data are documented in World Bank (2000); Haaga and Maru (1996) describe the Bangladesh data set; the surveys for Indonesia and Malaysia are described in RAND (2000); for the Philippines, see National Statistics Office and Macro International (1994); for Thailand, see Chayovan, Kamnuansilpa, and Knodel (1988); and for Taiwan, see Parish and Willis (1993).

References

Barro, Robert J. and Jong-Wha Lee. 1996. "International measures of schooling years and schooling quality," *American Economic Review* 86(2): 218–223.

Behrman, Jere R. 1988. "Intra-household allocation of nutrients in rural India: Are boys favored? Do parents exhibit inequality aversion?" *Oxford Economic Papers* 40(1): 32–54.

———. 1997. "Mother's schooling and child education: A survey," unpublished paper, Department of Economics, University of Pennsylvania, Philadelphia.

Behrman, Jere R. and Mark R. Rosenzweig. 1994. "Caveat emptor: Cross-country data on education and the labor force," *Journal of Development Economics* 44(1): 147–172.

Birdsall, Nancy, David Ross, and Richard Sabot. 1995. "Inequality as a constraint on growth in Latin America," in *Social Tensions, Job Creation and Economic Policy in Latin America,* eds. David Turnham, Colm Foy, and Guillermo Larrain. Paris: Organization for Economic Co-operation and Development (OECD), pp. 175–207.

———. 1997. "Education, growth and inequality," in *The Pathways to Growth: Comparing East Asia and Latin America*, eds. Nancy Birdsall and Frederick Jaspersen. Washington, DC: Inter-American Development Bank, pp. 93–130.

Birdsall, Nancy and Richard Sabot. 1994. "Inequality, exports, and human capital in East Asia: Lessons for Latin America," in *Redefining the State in Latin America*, ed. Colin I. Bradford. Paris: Organization for Economic Co-operation and Development (OECD), pp. 153–171.

Chayovan, Napaporn, Peerasit Kamnuansilpa, and John Knodel. 1988. *Thailand Demographic and Health Survey 1987*. Columbia, MD: Institute for Resource Development/Westinghouse.

Chen, Nancy, Paolo Valente, and Hania Zlotnik. 1998. "What do we know about recent trends in urbanization?" in *Migration, Urbanization, and Development: New Directions and Issues*, ed. Richard E. Bilsborrow. New York: United Nations Children's Fund and Kluwer Academic Publishers, pp. 59–88.

Choi, Kang-Shik. 1993. "Technological change and educational wage differentials in Korea," Discussion Paper No. 698, Economic Growth Center. New Haven, CT: Yale University.

Coe, David T. and Elhanan Helpman. 1993. "International R&D spillovers," NBER Working Paper No. 4444. Cambridge, MA: National Bureau of Economic Research.

Davis, Donald R. 1996. "Trade liberalization and income distribution," NBER Working Paper No. 5693. Cambridge, MA: National Bureau of Economic Research.

Davis, Steven J. 1992. "Cross-country patterns of change in relative wages," NBER Working Paper No. 4085. Cambridge, MA: National Bureau of Economic Research.

Dominitz, Jeff and Charles F. Manski. 1994. "Eliciting student expectations of the returns to schooling," unpublished paper, Institute for Social Research, The University of Michigan, Ann Arbor.

———. 1997. "Using expectations data to study subjective income expectations," *Journal of the American Statistical Association* 92(439): 855–867.

Eaton, Jonathan and Samuel Kortum. 1994. "International patenting and technology diffusion," NBER Working Paper No. 4931. Cambridge, MA: National Bureau of Economic Research.

———. 1995. "Engines of growth: Domestic and foreign sources of innovation," NBER Working Paper No. 5207. Cambridge, MA: National Bureau of Economic Research.

Fields, Gary S. 1994. "Changing labor market conditions and economic development in Hong Kong, the Republic of Korea, Singapore, and Taiwan, China," *The World Bank Economic Review* 8(3): 395–414.

Freeman, Richard B. 1979. "The effect of demographic factors on age-earnings profiles," *Journal of Human Resources* 14(3): 290–318.

Funkhouser, Edward. 1998. "Changes in the returns to education in Costa Rica," *Journal of Development Economics* 57: 289–317.

Gindling, T. H., Marsha Goldfarb, and Chun-Chig Chang. 1995. "Changing returns to education in Taiwan: 1978–91," *World Development* 23(2): 343–356.

Haaga, John G. and Rushikesh M. Maru. 1996. "The effect of operations research on program changes in Bangladesh," *Studies in Family Planning* 27(2): 76–87.

Hamermesh, Daniel. 1986. "The demand for labor in the long run," in *Handbook of Labor Economics*, Vol. 1, ed. Orley Ashenfelter. Amsterdam: Elsevier Science, pp. 429–471.

Huang, Fung-Mey. 1997. "Education, earning and fertility in Taiwan," paper presented at the Conference on Population and the Asian Economic Miracle, Program on Population, East-West Center, Honolulu.

———. 1998. "The effect of demographic factors and labor demand on the structure of wages in Taiwan: 1978–1997," paper presented at the Conference on Economic Aspects of Demographic Transition: The Experience of Asian-Pacific Countries in Asia, Institute of Economics, Academia Sinica, Taipei, Taiwan, June.

Katz, Lawrence F. and Kevin M. Murphy. 1992. "Changes in relative wages, 1963–1987: Supply and demand factors," *Quarterly Journal of Economics* 107(1): 35–78.

Keller, Wolfgang. 1997. "Trade and the transmission of technology," NBER Working Paper No. 6113. Cambridge, MA: National Bureau of Economic Research.

Kim, Dae-Il and Robert H. Topel. 1995. "Labor markets and economic growth: Lessons from Korea's industrialization, 1970–1990," in *Differences and Changes in Wage Structures*, eds. Richard B. Freeman and Lawrence F. Katz. Chicago: University of Chicago Press, pp. 227–264.

Krueger, Alan B. and Mikael Lindahl. 1998. "Education for growth: Why and for whom?" unpublished paper, Department of Economics, Princeton University, Princeton, NJ.

Krueger, Anne O. 1990. "The relationship between trade, employment, and development," in *The State of Development Economics: Progress and Perspectives*, eds. T. Paul Schultz and Gustav Ranis. Cambridge, MA: Basil Blackwell.

Krusell, Per et al. 1997. "Capital-skill complementarity and inequality: A macroeconomic analysis," Research Department Staff Report No. 239. Minneapolis, MN: Federal Reserve Bank of Minneapolis.

Lam, David and Suzanne Duryea. 1999. "Effects of schooling on fertility, labor supply, and investments in children," *Journal of Human Resources* 34(1): 160–192.

Lawrence, Robert and Matthew Slaughter. 1993. "International trade and American wages in the 1980s: Giant sucking sound or small hiccup?" in *Brookings Papers on Economic Activity: Microeconomics*, Vol. 2. Washington, DC: Brookings Institution Press, pp. 161–225.

Leamer, Edward E. 1998. "In search of Stolper-Samuelson linkages between international trade and lower wages," in *Imports, Exports, and the American Worker*, ed. Susan M. Collins. Washington, DC: Brookings Institution Press, pp. 141–214.

LeVine, Robert A. et al. 1991. "Women's schooling and child care in the demographic transition: A Mexican case study," *Population and Development Review* 17(3): 459–496.

Lillard, Lee A. and Robert J. Willis. 1994. "Intergenerational educational mobility: Effects of family and state in Malaysia," *The Journal of Human Resources* 29(4): 1126–1166.

Manski, Charles F. 1992. "Adolescent econometricians: How do youth infer the returns to schooling?" in *Studies in Supply and Demand of Higher Education*, eds. Charles Clotfelter and Michael Rothschild. Chicago: University of Chicago Press, pp. 43–57.

Mason, Andrew. 1993. "Demographic change, household resources, and schooling decisions," in *Human Resources in Development along the Asia-Pacific Rim*, eds. Naohiro Ogawa, Gavin Jones, and Jeffrey Williamson. Singapore: Oxford University Press, pp. 259–282.

Mason, Andrew and Burnham O. Campbell. 1993. "Demographic change and the Thai economy: An overview," in *The Economic Impact of Demographic Change in Thailand, 1980–2015*, eds. Burnham O. Campbell, Andrew Mason, and Ernesto M. Pernia. Honolulu: University of Hawaii Press, pp. 1–52.

Mazumdar, Dipak. 1993. "Labor markets and adjustment in open Asian economies: The Republic of Korea and Malaysia," *The World Bank Economic Review* 7(3): 349–380.

Mete, Cem. 1999. "Three essays on the economics of education," Ph.D. dissertation, Department of Economics, State University of New York at Stony Brook.

Mingat, Alain. 1998. "The strategy used by high-performing Asian economies in education: Some lessons for developing countries," *World Development* 26(4): 695–715.

Montgomery, Mark R. 1998. "Learning and lags in mortality perceptions," in *From Death to Birth: Mortality Decline and Reproductive Change*, eds. Mark R. Montgomery and Barney Cohen. Washington, DC: National Academy Press, pp. 112–137.

———. 1999. "Mortality decline and the demographic response: Toward a new agenda," Policy Research Division Working Paper No. 122. New York: Population Council.

Montgomery, Mark R., Mary Arends-Kuenning, and Cem Mete. 1999. "The quantity–quality transition in Asia," Policy Research Division Working Paper No. 123. New York: Population Council.

Montgomery, Mark R. and Cynthia B. Lloyd. 1997. "Excess fertility, unintended births, and children's schooling," Policy Research Division Working Paper No. 100. New York: Population Council.

Montgomery, Mark R. et al. 1998. *The Consequences of Imperfect Fertility Control for Children's Survival, Health, and Schooling.* Demographic and Health Surveys Analytical Reports, No. 7. Calverton, MD: Macro International.

———. 2000. "Measuring living standards with proxy variables," *Demography* 37(2): 155–174.

Mundle, Sudpito. 1998. "Financing human development: Some lessons from advanced Asian countries," *World Development* 26(4): 659–672.

National Statistics Office, Philippines, and Macro International. 1994. *National Demographic Survey 1993.* Calverton, MD.

Pack, Howard and John Page. 1994. "Accumulation, exports, and growth in the high-performing Asian economies," *Carnegie-Rochester Conference Series on Public Policy* 40: 199–236.

Parish, William and Robert Willis. 1993. "Daughters, education, and family budgets," *The Journal of Human Resources* 28(4): 863–898.

Park, Young-Bum, David Ross, and Richard Sabot. 1996. "Educational expansion and the inequality of pay in Brazil and Korea," in *Opportunity Foregone: Education in Brazil*, eds. Nancy Birdsall and Richard Sabot. Washington, DC: Inter-American Development Bank, pp. 267–288.

Psacharopoulos, George. 1985. "Returns to education: A further international update and implications," *The Journal of Human Resources* 20(4): 583–611.

———. 1994. "Returns to investment in education: A global update," *World Development* 22(9): 1325–1343.

RAND. 2000. Family Life Surveys. On-line documentation at http://www.rand.org/FLS.

Robbins, Donald J. 1996. "HOS hits facts: Facts win: Evidence on trade and wages in the developing world," Development Discussion Paper No. 557. Cambridge, MA: Harvard Institute for International Development, Harvard University.

Schultz, T. Paul. 1998. "Why governments should invest more in educating girls than boys," unpublished paper, Economic Growth Center, Yale University, New Haven, CT.

Stokey, Nancy. 1996. "Free trade, factor returns, and factor accumulation," *Journal of Economic Growth* 1: 421–447.

Summers, Robert and Alan Heston. 1991. "The Penn World Tables, Mark 5: An expanded set of international comparisons, 1950–1988," *Quarterly Journal of Economics* 106(2): 327–368.

Topel, Robert H. 1998. "Labor markets and economic growth," unpublished paper, Department of Economics, University of Chicago.

United Nations Population Division. 1996. *World Population Prospects: The 1996 Revision, Annex 1, Demographic Indicators.* Department for Economic and Social Information and Policy Analysis. New York: United Nations.

Willis, Robert J. 1986. "Wage determinants: A survey and reinterpretation of human-capital earnings functions," in *Handbook of Labor Economics*, eds. Orley C. Ashenfelter and Richard Layard. Amsterdam: Elsevier Science, pp. 525–602.

Wood, Adrian. 1995. "How trade hurt unskilled workers," *Journal of Economic Perspectives* 9(3): 57–80.

World Bank. 1993. *The East Asian Miracle: Economic Growth and Public Policy.* Washington, DC: Oxford University Press for the World Bank.

———. 1997. *World Development Indicators, 1997.* Washington, DC.

———. 2000. Living Standards Measurement Study of the World Bank. On-line documentation at http://www.worldbank.org/html/prdph/lsms/lsmshome.html.

Population Dynamics
and Economic Growth
in Asia

DAVID E. BLOOM

DAVID CANNING

PIA N. MALANEY

EAST ASIA'S NEAR-TRIPLING of real income per capita between 1965 and 1990 is one of the most extraordinary economic phenomena of the twentieth century. Never before has income per capita grown so rapidly in such a large group of countries for such a prolonged period. Several economies in the subregion that began this period as low- or middle-income developing countries are now industrial leaders.

Numerous studies have sought to explain East Asia's economic "miracle." The literature highlights a wide range of possible explanations, including trade and industrial policies, technological progress, savings and capital accumulation, governance, education and health spending, geography and culture, and initial income levels (Asian Development Bank 1997; Krugman 1994; Landes 1998; Rodrik 1994 and 1998; Sachs and Warner 1995; World Bank 1993; Young 1994 and 1995). These studies rely on a variety of conceptual frameworks, statistical methods, and data sources. Although they stress different causal factors, they reach the common conclusion that economic growth in general, and East Asia's unrivaled growth performance in particular, has various causes. Many factors affect economic growth, and their cumulative influence can account for much of East Asia's superior performance in relation to that of the world economy as a whole during 1965–90, as well as for the relatively poor performance of South Asia and sub-Saharan Africa. However, even accounting for these influences on economic growth, the literature still finds significant unexplained differences in regional economic performance. East Asia performs better than its measured characteristics would otherwise suggest, whereas South Asia and Africa perform worse.

One striking feature of the literature is the generally superficial attention it pays to the influence of demographic factors on economic growth.

By including the rate of population growth among the list of variables used to explain cross-country differences in income growth, the standard approach acknowledges the possibility that rapid population growth may impede economic growth. More often than not, however, population growth does not emerge as being significantly associated with the pace of economic growth, thereby supporting the conclusion of population neutralism (Bloom and Freeman 1986) that has held sway for nearly two decades (Kelley and Schmidt 1995).

In recent years investigators have revisited the connection between population and economic growth, emphasizing the demographic transition as the process underlying population growth in most developing countries (Bloom and Canning 1999; Bloom and Freeman 1988; Bloom and Sachs 1998; Higgins and Williamson 1997; Bloom and Williamson 1997; Bloom et al. 1998). The demographic transition is a change from a situation of high fertility and high mortality to one of low fertility and low mortality. The research indicates that high rates of population growth are temporary consequences of the decline in mortality preceding the decline in fertility. Less widely recognized, though perhaps more important, it also suggests sizable changes in the age distribution of the population. These changes occur for two main reasons. First, the initial mortality decline is concentrated among infants and young children, thereby concentrating its effects at the lower end of the age distribution. Second, the subsequent fertility decline has an effect on the age distribution that is, naturally, entirely concentrated at age zero. The combination of these two forces introduces a bulge into the population pyramid. Its leading edge is created by the decline in infant and child mortality and its trailing edge by the decline in fertility. Over time the bulge ages and moves from being concentrated among young people to being concentrated at the prime ages for working, saving, and reproduction, and eventually to being concentrated at the years of old age. The eventual increase in the numbers of the old is also due to the fact that mortality rates among the old decline substantially in the later stages of the demographic transition.

The young and the old tend to consume more output than they generate, unlike working-age individuals, whose contribution to output and to savings tends to be more than commensurate with their consumption (Higgins 1998; Higgins and Williamson 1997; Kelley and Schmidt 1996; Lee, Mason, and Miller 2000; Leff 1969; Mason 1988; Webb and Zia 1990). As a result the value of output per capita—the most widely used indicator of economic performance—tends to be boosted when the population of working-age individuals is relatively large, and it tends to be depressed when a relatively large part of the population consists of young and elderly dependents. In addition, a fall in the youth dependency ratio permits schooling per child to rise, adding further to future economic growth. Numerous studies report microeconomic evidence that smaller family size leads to increased school enrollment rates or educational attainment (Hanushek 1992; Knodel, Havanon, and Sittitrai 1990; Knodel and Wongsith 1991; Rosenzweig 1990).

As the population age distribution changes over the course of a demographic transition and beyond, levels of income per capita will change correspondingly, revealing patterns of economic growth that have proven to be robustly evident in cross-national data. Indeed, changes in age structure appear to account for a remarkably high share of cross-country differences in rates of income growth. For example, demographic change accounts for as much as a third to a half of the sustained high rates of income growth that came to be known as the East Asian "miracle." During 1965–90 the working-age population of East Asia grew nearly ten times faster than the dependent population. Age structure is not the only influence on economic growth, but it certainly emerges as one of the most potent influences.

Changes in the age distribution of a population can have important economic effects. These effects reflect the influence of changes in the number of working-age individuals per capita (which we term the "accounting effect") and of shifts in behavior—for example, increased savings and greater investment in schooling per child as both desired and completed fertility fall. These effects are not automatic consequences of fertility decline, however. They depend on many policies, institutions, and conditions that determine an economy's capacity to equip its people with human and physical capital and to absorb them into productive employment.

These recent findings indicate that when it comes to economic growth and development, population matters. This conclusion gains significance in light of existing knowledge regarding policy interventions aimed at accelerating the pace of fertility decline, such as investments in child survival; in basic and secondary education, especially for girls; in family planning and reproductive health; and in improved labor market opportunities for women. Because the need for improved access to schooling and health care, as well as unmet needs for family planning supplies and services, are concentrated among the poor and those living in rural areas, social spending on these initiatives can improve not just income per capita, but also social equity.

The recent studies of the effects of population change on economic growth have two key features in common with another study that was published more than 40 years ago: Coale and Hoover's seminal *Population Growth and Economic Development in Low-Income Countries* (1958). All these works highlight and exploit the fundamental insight that reducing the current rate of population growth does not lead to a corresponding reduction in the current rate of labor force growth.

These studies also share some potentially significant limitations. An important limitation is that the imposition of a structure in which causality runs only from population growth to income growth is at odds with well-established microeconomic theory and a large body of supporting empirical evidence, which suggest that income levels influence the growth and structure of population. For example, people with high incomes naturally tend to place a high implicit value on their time. Given that childrearing is time-intensive, it is not surprising that they also tend to have fewer children than other people. This suggests that income growth tends to promote fertility decline.[1]

Reverse causality potentially undermines the accuracy of recent estimates of the effects of population change on economic growth because those estimates presume unidirectional causality. Policies based on those estimates therefore may be seriously misguided. Bloom and Williamson (1998) make an attempt to address this matter, but their estimates are very imprecise, making it difficult to draw decisive conclusions. In this chapter we apply a combination of economic reasoning and appropriate statistical methods to address the issue of reverse causality. We find strong evidence that population change affects income growth and that changes in income affect population growth, mainly through their effect on fertility. Our results confirm the importance of rapid and pronounced demographic change in East Asia for the region's economic success. They also suggest that the decline in fertility rates in the region was itself spurred by rapid economic growth. By contrast, South Asia's demographic transition was impeded by relatively stagnant and low income, which in turn slowed the decline of fertility.

In both the landmark study by Coale and Hoover and the recent literature, attention to population age structure is the key innovation. However, population growth and changes in age structure are only two of several plausible demographic influences on economic growth. An important feature of the modern literature on the effects of demography on economic growth is the consideration of a broader range of demographic variables than simply the population growth rate (Barlow 1994; Bloom and Freeman 1988; Bloom and Sachs 1998; Bloom and Williamson 1998; Brander and Dowrick 1994; Coale 1986; Kelley and Schmidt 1995). In this chapter we consider two demographic variables in addition to the growth rate and age structure that may have effects on income per capita: life expectancy and population density.

A robust finding from the recent literature on economic development concerns the positive effect of good health status, as measured by life expectancy, on economic growth (Bloom and Canning 2000b). Presumably this finding reflects the greater incentives that long-lived people have to save for old age (Lee, Mason, and Miller 2000), increased returns to investments in human capital associated with having longer time horizons over which to recoup those returns (Meltzer 1995), higher productivity, and lower rates of absenteeism.

Another potential influence on the pace of economic growth is population density. If natural resources, such as agricultural land, are fixed, increases in population density are likely to depress income per capita (Ehrlich 1968; Malthus 1798 [1986]). By contrast, opportunities for specialization and scale economies can cause increased population density to promote higher income per capita (Boserup 1981; Kuznets 1967; Simon 1981). Like Bloom and Sachs (1998) and Gallup, Sachs, and Mellinger (1999), who argue that coastal regions can enjoy greater benefits of specialization through trade, we examine population density in coastal regions separately from population density in inland regions.

Our main objective in this chapter is to examine the linkages between population change and economic growth within a framework that permits bi-directional causality. We begin by examining the effect of demographic variables on the pace of economic growth, taking into account other influences on growth that are standard in the economics literature. We do this using statistical tools that account for the possibility of a feedback effect of income growth on the demographic variables. These tools permit us, in principle, to decompose the correlation between demographic change and income growth into two parts, one that reflects the effect of demographic change on income growth and another that reflects the reverse effect of income growth on demographic change.

Our examination is based on data for 70 countries from all regions of the world (all those for which the requisite data are available) and covers the period from 1965 to 1990. We examine data for the entire period, as well as within the five five-year intervals it spans. Our results indicate that sizable portions of both East Asia's economic success and South Asia's economic failure are attributable to demographic influences—namely, differences in health status, dependency burdens, and the spatial distribution and concentration of people. We also find strong evidence of a negative effect of higher income on fertility rates, together with a sharp downward trend in fertility between 1965 and 1990. Finally, we show that life expectancy increased substantially during that period, apparently independently of changes in average country income, notwithstanding the fact that rich countries had higher life expectancies than poor countries.

In the following section we present and analyze key facts about the growth and structure of Asia's population since 1970 and its economic performance. We then examine the influence of various aspects of population change on the growth of income per capita in Asia and its subregions, emphasizing the contributions of population change that are independent of other influences on economic growth and any confounding feedback effects from income to population. This is followed by a look at the effects of income on the two most important components of population change: fertility and mortality. Here too we seek to isolate the effects of income from those associated with feedback effects running in the other direction. We conclude by offering some thoughts on the implications of our findings for population policy and for the prospects for economic growth and development elsewhere in Asia and the world.

The contribution of demographic factors to Asia's economic growth

We use cross-country regression analysis to estimate the contribution of demographic factors to economic growth in Asia. The appendix in an earlier version of this study (Bloom, Canning, and Malaney 1999) presents the theoretical basis for the multiple-regression analyses we perform. Here we rely on a more intuitive description of our framework.

In recent years, development economists have relied heavily on cross-country data to study the process and determinants of economic growth. Two key assumptions lie at the core of many of these studies. The first is that there is a ceiling on the level of income per worker that a country can attain. This ceiling, which is usually denoted as the country's steady-state level of income, depends on the country's characteristics, such as the extent of its natural resource base, the level of education of its population, the quality of its institutions, the features of its physical geography, and the soundness of its economic policies. Because these characteristics vary across countries, so too will the levels of income they can attain. The second assumption is that each country converges to its steady-state income level over time. Thus countries are continually tending to approach their ceiling levels of income, though at any time their actual incomes will differ from the attainable ceiling. In addition the ceiling itself may be moving in response to technical change and changes in any of its underlying determinants.

Of course, countries can have income levels above the ceiling. For example, the adoption of bad economic policies or a fall in the world price of a country's major export can cause the steady-state level of income to fall so that the economy is temporarily above the new steady state and experiences negative growth. In this sense the "ceiling" is not a strict upper limit on income. Rather, it defines the direction in which income levels will tend to move.

The model of economic growth just described has two powerful implications. First, it implies that the poorer a country is with respect to its steady state, the faster it is likely to grow. This implication is sometimes referred to as the income catch-up phenomenon. Second, the higher a country's ceiling level of income, the faster is its expected rate of growth for a given level of initial income. This phenomenon has been dubbed "conditional convergence."

Although economic models are usually formulated in terms of income per worker, they are generally tested with data on income per capita, development economists' standard measure of economic performance. Because a model is estimated with growth rates, as opposed to levels, of income, distinguishing between income per person of working age and income per capita makes no difference in stable populations (where the growth rate of the overall population is equal to that of the working-age population). However, the assumption of demographic stability is patently at odds with the data for most countries, including Asian countries at various stages of their demographic transition. Thus, following Bloom and Williamson (1998), we invoke the relationship between income per capita and income per worker; that is, income per capita equals income per worker multiplied by the ratio of workers to the population as a whole. Allowing also for the possibility that population growth and labor force growth may affect income in ways other than through pure accounting yields the multiple-regression equation that we rely upon to estimate the determinants of the growth of income per capita:

$$g_y = \alpha_0 + \alpha_1 y + \alpha_2 \log(L/P) + \alpha_3 g_L + \alpha_4 g_P + \alpha_5 X + \varepsilon, \tag{1}$$

where g_y refers to the growth rate of income per capita, y is the natural logarithm of the initial level of income per capita, $\log(L/P)$ is the natural logarithm of the number of workers per capita, and g_L and g_P are the growth rates of the working-age and the total populations, respectively, over the sample period. X is a vector of factors that may influence the ceiling level of income, and ε is a random error. The pure accounting framework places restrictions on the parameters that we can test—namely, that the effects of initial income per worker and workers per capita are equal and opposite, whereas the working-age and total population growth rates have coefficients of one and minus one respectively. According to this equation, the growth of per capita income depends on the levels of income per capita (which have a negative effect) and the numbers of workers per capita (positive effect) at the start of the sample period, on the growth rates of the total population (negative effect) and of the working-age population (positive effect), and on the factors that determine the ceiling level of income (positive effect for any factor that raises the ceiling). For reasons discussed earlier, we include among the last set of factors life expectancy and the density of the working-age population, both measured at the start of the sample period. The population density of the working-age population is arguably more relevant to economic growth than is the density of the total population. We enter into the equation separate density variables for coastal and inland areas because the effects of density may depend on access to world trade. These variables are based on data contained in the Geographic Information System, with inland areas defined as those more than 100 kilometers from the coast or from a navigable river that leads to the sea (Gallup, Sachs, and Mellinger 1999). Our specification deliberately omits saving and investment rates as explanatory variables, both because they may reflect an uncertain amount of demographic influence and because they are likely to be determined jointly with the growth of income per capita.

We report two sets of multiple-regression equations for the determinants of economic growth. In the first set we estimate the determinants of growth in a standard cross-country framework with data for 70 Asian and non-Asian countries for 1965–90. The period selected is constrained by data availability and the need to have some data from before the period (we use data for 1960–65) to use as instruments. We use these instrumental variables to correct for possible reverse causality between the growth rates of the total and working-age populations and economic growth. We treat all variables measured at the start of the sample period, before the growth has occurred, as immune from the problem of reverse causality. In the second set of equations we repeat the exercise using panel data for the five consecutive five-year periods spanned by the years 1965–90. That is, we seek to explain each five-year growth experience with data on conditions at the beginning of the period and demographic change during the period, again using an instrumental-variables approach to deal with possible reverse causation. This allows the level of initial income and the factors that influence the ceiling level of income (and therefore the rate of income growth) to vary over time. We also allow for average differences in the rate of income growth between the five-year periods, which could reflect differences in worldwide levels and rates of change of technical knowledge.

Cross-country results

Table 1 reports our cross-country estimates for 1965–90. (Summary statistics for the data used in the cross-country regressions are reported in Appendix Table 1; the countries included in the regressions and the regional assignments we use are listed in Appendix Table 2.) Column 1 of Table 1 reports results for an ordinary least squares (OLS) specification that is representative of the economic growth literature. It includes initial income per capita, schooling, openness to international trade, institutional quality, and such geographic factors as whether or not a country is located in the tropics and whether it is landlocked (Barro 1991; Barro and Sala-i-Martin 1995; Gallup, Sachs, and Mellinger 1999). The coefficient of initial income per capita is significantly negative, as the hypothesis of conditional convergence postulates. The other variables are assumed to determine the steady-state level of income.

Development economists have long argued that education is a prime determinant of long-run economic performance. We follow Barro and Sala-i-Martin (1995), whose analysis suggests that secondary schooling is the most important component of education. Sachs and Warner (1997) argue that the level of openness to trade is an important predictor of growth.

They suggest that trade plays an important role in the growth process because it encourages market competition, improves the efficiency of resource allocation within the economy, combats monopolies, and acts as a vehicle for the importation of new technology. The quality of institutions, as captured by the Knack and Keefer (1995) index, is another possible determinant of economic growth, with institutional quality being positively correlated with growth.

Geographic variables also appear to play an important role. The percentage of a country's land area that is in the tropics has a significant negative effect on economic growth. Studies (e.g., Bloom and Sachs 1998; Gallup, Sachs, and Mellinger 1999) have shown that tropical location affects various factors that can influence productivity. For example, the burden of several infectious diseases such as malaria and schistosomiasis is significantly higher in warm, humid climates. A strong link exists between climate and agricultural output (Gallup 1998). The cost of transportation, as determined by geography, is another salient factor, as illustrated by the negative (and marginally significant) effect of being landlocked.

Although each of these variables is widely acknowledged to play a role in the growth process, most of the standard growth literature has placed little emphasis on the role of demographic variables in economic growth, life expectancy being the exception. Column 2 of Table 1 reports the results of a regression that includes a full set of demographic variables. These include the growth rate of the total population, the growth rate of the working-age population, and the natural logarithm of the initial ratio of the working-age population to the total population. We also add the log of life expectancy in 1965 and coastal and inland population densities as demographic variables that may directly affect steady-state income levels.

To correct for possible reverse causality involving the growth rates of the working-age and total populations during 1965–90, we instrument these variables with the growth rates of the working-age and total populations during 1960–65 and the 1965 fertility and infant mortality rates. These instruments appear to be highly correlated with the population growth rates during 1965–90 and can be considered to be predetermined in the sense that they are measured no later than at the outset of the period of economic growth under study. The results of using these instrumental variables are shown in column 3 of Table 1.

There is a potential problem with using variables from before the period as instruments if income growth is correlated over time. In this case, income growth is correlated with past income growth, which may be correlated with past growth in our population variables. This is unlikely to be a serious problem, however, because in practice the growth rates of income per capita are almost completely uncorrelated over successive five-year periods (Easterly et al. 1993).

TABLE 1 Regression results explaining economic growth: Cross-country results, 70 countries, 1965–90 (Dependent variable: annual average growth rate of real GDP per capita in purchasing power parity terms)

Independent variable	Basic specification (OLS) (1)	Demographic specification (OLS) (2)	Instrumental variables (IV) (3)	Growth-accounting restriction (IV) (4)	Geographic specification (OLS) (5)	Geographic and demographic specification (IV) (6)
Constant	14.04 (5.41)	3.608 (0.81)	7.105 (1.29)	5.818 (1.90)	13.50 (5.40)	7.517 (1.39)
Log GDP per capita, 1965	-1.778 (5.05)	-2.045 (7.04)	-1.976 (6.62)		-1.757 (5.33)	-2.023 (7.03)
Log GDP per worker, 1965				-2.045 (7.26)		
Located in the tropics	-0.870 (1.80)	-2.045 (7.04)	-1.382 (4.58)	-1.397 (4.81)	-1.580 (2.82)	-1.398 (5.20)
Landlocked	-1.062 (2.53)	0.338 (0.86)	0.294 (0.80)	0.204 (0.61)	-0.496 (1.85)	0.168 (0.43)
Quality of institutions	0.248 (2.02)	0.201 (2.40)	0.158 (1.72)	0.187 (2.45)	0.387 (3.41)	0.169 (1.40)
Openness of economy	2.370 (5.17)	1.729 (4.70)	1.675 (5.35)	1.730 (6.11)	1.175 (2.02)	1.093 (2.72)
Log years of secondary schooling, 1965	0.491 (2.73)	0.017 (0.12)	-0.002 (0.01)	0.050 (0.43)	0.053 (0.39)	0.018 (0.13)
Growth in total population, 1965–90		-1.850 (2.03)	-2.590 (2.83)			-2.227 (2.20)
Growth in working-age population, 1965–90		2.178 (3.68)	2.925 (2.53)			2.343 (1.85)

	(1)	(2)	(3)	(4)	(5)	(6)
Difference in growth of working-age and total population			2.251			
			(4.59)			
Log ratio of working-age to total population, 1965	4.157	6.178		3.936		
	(1.36)	(1.05)		(0.70)		
Log of life expectancy, 1965	3.289	2.638	2.659	2.549		
	(3.43)	(2.28)	(2.87)	(2.41)		
Log of coastal population density, 1965	0.297	0.255	0.253	0.215		
	(3.10)	(2.58)	(3.11)	(2.25)		
Log of inland population density, 1965	-0.130	-0.121	-0.124	-0.053		
	(2.02)	(2.06)	(2.04)	(0.92)		
Africa					-1.290	-0.621
					(1.33)	(1.09)
Latin America					0.410	-0.358
					(0.53)	(0.74)
East Asia					3.554	0.899
					(5.14)	(1.29)
Southeast Asia					1.440	0.291
					(1.98)	(0.53)
South Asia					-0.700	-1.264
					(0.78)	(2.62)
Adjusted R^2	0.58	0.83	0.85	0.85	0.77	0.88
Number of observations	70	70	70	70	70	70

NOTES: "Purchasing power parity" means that incomes are adjusted by local prices to give comparable values of purchasing power for a common basket of goods across countries. Growth rates of the total population and the working-age population (and their differences) are instrumented with fertility in 1965 and growth rates of the total population and working-age population between 1960 and 1965. Heteroskedasticity-consistent t-statistics are reported in parentheses below the coefficient estimates.

In both columns 2 and 3, five of our demographic variables—life expectancy, total population growth, growth of the working-age population, coastal population density, and inland population density—are statistically significant, and their inclusion in the specification significantly improves its explanatory power (raising the total variance explained from less than 0.6 to more than 0.8). These results confirm the importance of demographic factors in the growth process.

One of the most robust results is the importance of life expectancy in predicting economic growth. Life expectancy can affect economic growth through several mechanisms. For example, as people live longer, they can be expected to save more to ensure that they have enough assets put aside for a longer period of old age (Lee, Mason, and Miller 2000). In addition, changes in the age distribution due to increased longevity can increase aggregate savings because of variations in saving behavior at different stages of the life cycle (Higgins 1998; Higgins and Williamson 1997; Kelley and Schmidt 1996; Modigliani 1986). Life expectancy also serves as a proxy for the health status of the population as a whole because declines in the mortality rate are related to declines in morbidity. A growing literature shows that a healthier work force is more productive (e.g., Bloom et al. 1998; Strauss and Thomas 1995, 1998). These effects are particularly strong in developing countries, where large proportions of the work force are involved in manual labor, which is heavily dependent on physical wellbeing.

Growth of the total population has a strong negative effect on economic growth, whereas growth of the working-age population has a strong positive effect. These results persist, and remain statistically significant, even when we use instrumental variables to control for reverse causation.

We also find that population density along the coast has a positive effect on economic growth, while population density inland has a negative effect. A possible explanation for the divergence is that coastal regions are better able to integrate their economies into the world economy and can capture the fruits of specialization and scale economies through international trade. Inland regions, particularly landlocked countries, face higher transport costs in reaching world markets and so have much tighter resource constraints. In countries where the population is predominantly inland, as in landlocked countries, high population density may put pressure on agricultural production and depress income levels. Burundi and Rwanda are two examples of landlocked countries with high population densities and low incomes. If a population has access to the sea and cheap sea trade routes, however, higher population density may allow greater specialization and exploitation of scale economies. Hong Kong and Singapore are examples of cities with high population density that have easy access to the sea and high incomes, due in large part to their reliance on external trade. By contrast, Bangladesh is the most densely populated country in the world, with three major rivers that run through it to the Bay of Bengal; but its economic performance is extremely poor.

Column 4 of Table 1 reports the results of imposing the restrictions implied by our growth-accounting framework. Under these restrictions we can replace the income-per-capita and workers-per-capita terms with a single income-per-worker term. In addition, only the difference in the growth rates of the working-age population and the total population should matter. An F-test of these two restrictions gives a value of $F(2) = 1.47$, and therefore they cannot be rejected. This result implies that we find no significant effect of balanced population growth—that is, when the labor force and total population are growing at the same rate. However, the further restriction that the coefficient on the difference in growth rates between the working-age population and the total population be equal to 1 is rejected by a test with $t = 2.56$. This suggests that reducing the birth rate and the dependency ratio has a significantly larger effect on economic growth rates than the pure accounting restrictions would suggest.

Columns 5 and 6 report the results of specifications that include dummy variables for Africa, Latin America, and the subregions of Asia (East Asia, Southeast Asia, and South Asia). When these dummies are added to the base specification in column 5, we find that although this specification is successful in explaining growth in both Africa and Latin America, both East and Southeast Asia have significant dummies. If we define the Asian economic "miracle" as that part of its growth rate that standard growth determinants cannot explain, we obtain figures for "miracle" growth of around 3.5 percent a year for East Asia and 1.5 percent a year for Southeast Asia. Growth regressions such as these often find a negative coefficient on the Africa dummy, but the inclusion of the geographic variables helps to explain Africa's poor performance and eliminate this unexplained residual (Bloom and Sachs 1998).

Adding demographic variables (column 6) explains almost all of East Asia's "miracle" growth. Once demographic variables are included, the East Asian "miracle" is less than 1 percent growth per year, while the "miracle" in Southeast Asia is less than 0.5 percent growth per year, and in neither case are these figures statistically significant. The only significant outlier in column 6 is South Asia, which underperformed the rest of the world's economies by about 1.3 percent in annual growth during the period, given its initial conditions and its demographic and other characteristics. The mystery in Asia may be not why East Asia did so well, but rather why South Asia performed so poorly.

Panel data results

Table 2 presents panel data results to test the robustness of our cross-country results. We are essentially running five cross-sectional regressions, one

TABLE 2 Regression results explaining economic growth: Panel study results, 70 countries, 1965–90 (Dependent variable: annual average percentage growth rate of real GDP per capita in purchasing power parity terms over five-year periods)

Independent variable	Basic specification (OLS) (1)	Demographic specification (OLS) (2)	Instrumental variables (IV) (3)	Growth-accounting restriction (IV) (4)	Geographic specification (OLS) (5)	Geographic and demographic specification (IV) (6)
Constant	12.76 (5.74)	−6.342 (1.03)	−3.804 (0.62)	−4.672 (0.85)	14.52 (4.81)	−1.009 (0.13)
Log GDP per capita in base year	−1.690 (5.78)	−2.280 (6.30)	−2.213 (6.12)		−1.933 (4.81)	−2.205 (5.36)
Log GDP per worker in base year				−2.253 (6.43)		
Located in the tropics	−1.085 (2.57)	−1.139 (2.63)	−1.270 (2.61)	−1.141 (2.68)	−1.083 (2.35)	−1.230 (2.50)
Landlocked	−0.358 (0.87)	−0.016 (0.04)	0.044 (0.12)	−0.048 (0.13)	0.108 (0.266)	0.079 (0.22)
Quality of institutions	0.249 (2.22)	0.237 (2.10)	0.211 (1.84)	0.230 (2.09)	0.392 (2.87)	0.244 (1.81)
Openness over 5-year period	2.455 (6.05)	2.058 (4.85)	2.069 (4.76)	2.047 (5.03)	1.738 (3.98)	1.825 (3.93)
Log years of secondary schooling in base year	0.724 (2.98)	0.016 (0.07)	−0.035 (0.15)	0.017 (0.08)	0.228 (0.93)	−0.067 (0.29)
Growth in total population over 5-year period		−0.980 (2.13)	−1.300 (2.39)			−1.188 (2.13)
Growth in working-age population over 5-year period		1.265 (3.34)	1.750 (3.47)			1.515 (2.66)
Difference in growth of working-age and total population				1.550 (3.29)		

Log ratio of working-age to total population in base year	4.094	6.144			4.317	
	(1.12)	(1.49)			(0.92)	
Log life expectancy in base year	6.274	5.734	5.681		4.834	
	(3.86)	(3.58)	(3.59)		(2.78)	
Population density in base year	0.167	0.153	0.147		0.066	
	(1.76)	(1.63)	(1.52)		(0.63)	
Africa				-2.191	-0.880	
				(3.48)	(1.34)	
Latin America				-0.065	-0.292	
				(0.131)	(0.56)	
East Asia				2.698	1.320	
				(4.28)	(1.44)	
Southeast Asia				0.558	0.126	
				(0.81)	(0.17)	
South Asia				-0.946	-0.974	
				(1.11)	(1.17)	
Dummy, 1965–70	2.099	2.537	2.642	2.536	1.535	2.332
	(5.41)	(6.85)	(7.30)	(7.017)	(3.89)	(5.61)
Dummy, 1970–75	1.592	1.735	1.739	1.670	1.173	1.536
	(3.55)	(4.26)	(4.40)	(4.13)	(2.71)	(3.77)
Dummy, 1975–80	1.319	1.311	1.278	1.246	0.997	1.136
	(3.16)	(3.16)	(3.14)	(3.06)	(2.43)	(2.71)
Dummy, 1980–85	-0.807	-0.880	-0.934	-0.933	-0.963	-0.997
	(2.21)	(2.46)	(2.61)	(2.61)	(2.76)	(2.76)
Adjusted R^2	0.30	0.39	0.38	0.39	0.37	0.39
Number of observations	391	391	391	391	391	391

NOTE: Purchasing power parity means that incomes are adjusted by local prices to give values that are comparable across countries in terms of purchasing power over a common basket of goods. Growth rates of the total population and working-age population (and their differences) in each five-year period are instrumented with their growth rates over the previous five years and fertility and infant mortality rates in the base year. Heteroskedasticity-consistent *t* statistics are reported in parentheses below the coefficient estimates.

for each five-year period between 1965 and 1990, and assuming common coefficients across those time periods. For explanatory variables we use initial conditions from the start of each five-year period and population growth rates over each period. We use the same set of explanatory variables as in Table 1, but include a set of time dummies to capture worldwide shocks to growth in each five-year period relative to the base period, 1985–90. We do not introduce country fixed effects because the necessary presence of the initial income level would result in inconsistent (biased) coefficient estimates. Although this problem can be overcome (Islam 1995), the techniques required involve instrumenting all the explanatory variables, with a consequent large loss of precision in the estimates.

Column 1 reports the base specification used in the first set of regressions. The results are similar to those in Table 1. Adding demographic variables in column 2 once again shows the importance of each of these factors, as most enter significantly into the regression equation (as they also do when we instrument them in column 3). Unfortunately, data on coastal versus inland population density are not available on a time-series basis, precluding their use in the panel study. Instead we use the overall density of the working-age population, which never turns out to be statistically significant in our regressions and may be a poor proxy for the disaggregated densities, which have opposite signs in the regressions reported in Table 1. (Kelley and Schmidt 2000 have re-estimated these regressions over a different sample of observations and find significant effects for density and the initial working-age ratio.)

Column 4 again imposes the accounting restrictions implied by our theoretical framework. Once more we accept the two equality restrictions, with an F-statistic of $F(2, 375) = 1.031$. In this case we also accept the restriction that the coefficient on the difference between the growth rates of the working-age population and total population is unity (t-statistic = 1.17). The panel data results indicate that the age-structure effects are close to those predicted by a simple accounting framework, and that the behavioral effects of demography come entirely from the effect of increased life expectancy on economic growth.

The difference in results between the 1965–90 cross-section and the panel data analyses, which persists even with identical specifications, deserves comment. We suspect that it masks the existence of feedback effects from income to demography and places some bounds on the time frame within which they occur. Over a 25-year period an increase in the differential population growth rate caused, say, by the introduction of some new contraceptive technology can increase income levels, leading to further reductions in fertility and increases in life expectancy that have appreciable effects on the dependency burden and provide a further boost to economic growth. A period of 25 years is long enough for demographically induced income growth to accelerate the process of demographic transition and the related process of economic growth. Five years may not be long enough for these causal mechanisms to work themselves through.

Including the dummy variables with the base specification in column 5 again shows East Asia to be a significant outlier, with a growth rate about 2.7 percent a year above that explained by the regression. When we add our (instrumental) demographic variables, however, about half of this "miraculous" growth, or some 1.4 percentage points, disappears. Indeed, when we include demographic variables, once again the East Asian dummy is not statistically significant, suggesting there was nothing miraculous about East Asia's income growth. In addition, a comparison of columns 4 and 5 indicates that the negative African dummy, which represents growth rates 2.2 percent a year lower than Africa's objective conditions would suggest, disappears when we add demographic variables. These results show that demographic factors have played a large role in both East Asia's economic "miracle" and sub-Saharan Africa's economic debacle.

The analysis presented here assumes that the effect of demography on economic growth is automatic. But there are strong reasons to believe that the beneficial effects of demographic transition may be lost in countries that have inappropriate economic policies. Bloom and Canning (2000a) examine this issue of the interaction between the demographic effects and policy variables and find considerable evidence that good policies are a precondition for enjoying a "demographic dividend."

This section has approached the issue of feedback effects indirectly by comparing the long-term and short-term effects of demographic factors on the pace of economic growth. Our interpretation is highly tentative, especially given the similarity of the OLS and the instrumental-variables estimates. (Hausman specification tests, for example, do not permit us to reject the exogeneity of the population growth rates in our regressions.) The next section provides some direct evidence concerning the effects of income on vital rates. That evidence leads us, unambiguously, to prefer this section's instrumental-variables results because they are, in principle, robust to reverse causation.

The effects of income
on life expectancy and fertility

In examining the effects of income on demographic characteristics, we focus on life expectancy and fertility rates. We do so in part to take advantage of the extensive literature on their determinants at both the household and national levels.

In the case of life expectancy, Fogel (1994) argues that declines in European mortality during the Industrial Revolution followed economic growth. Preston (1975 and 1980) attributes most of the decline in death rates observed around the world between 1930 and 1970 to such factors as advances in health care technology, and only a small portion to economic growth. Working with data from 1960 for developing countries, Pritchett and Summers (1996) find a significant effect of income and education in reducing infant mortality and argue that the relationship is causal, but they find no significant effect of income on life expectancy. It may seem plausible, even obvious, that economic growth leads to improved health and longevity, but the evidence is far from conclusive.

With respect to fertility, Becker and Barro (1988) argue that rising income leads to a higher opportunity cost of time and a reduction in the desired number of children. Caldwell (1982) argues that children in agricultural societies provide services, such as tending livestock, gathering fuelwood, and fetching water, thereby raising their parents' standard of living, and that the process of industrialization and economic development results in children becoming a net economic burden on their parents, especially as mobility increases and schooling becomes compulsory. This leaves only altruism as a motive for childbearing, and consequently family size falls. Wang et al. (1999) find effects of both income level and education rates, particularly female education rates, on fertility. There is also an ongoing debate about the relative importance of family planning programs versus economic development as determinants of fertility. Gertler and Molyneaux (1994), Pritchett (1994), and Schultz (1994) show that desired fertility, as determined by economic forces such as education levels and wage rates for women, plays a significant role in determining completed fertility, whereas family planning activity seems less important. Bongaarts (1994) contests some key components of this collection of studies, but these studies do suggest that fertility decline is at least partly influenced by economic growth, though the mechanism relating economic growth and fertility decisions may operate, in part, indirectly through other variables.

We foresee continuing discussion on the nature and strength of these linkages. Our immediate concern is not to resolve, or even contribute to, these longstanding debates. Rather, we use country-level data simply to examine the existence of any feedback from economic growth to fertility and life expectancy, particularly in the context of Asia, without delving into its precise structure.

We begin our analysis with life expectancy. Investigators have shown that many factors besides income affect health and life expectancy. Education levels (particularly female education levels), the number of physicians per capita, health expenditures per capita, and access to clean water and sanitation are but a few of the variables that explain cross-country differences in life expectancy (World Bank 1993). If we include these variables in a study of the proximate determinants of life expectancy, the estimated effect of the income level is the effect holding all these other factors constant. All these proximate determinants of life expectancy are themselves, to some extent, dependent on the income level and move with it. To estimate the total effect of changes in the income level on life expectancy, we follow Pritchett and Summers (1996) and exclude factors that affect life expectancy but may themselves be determined by the income level. This allows us to estimate both the direct and indirect effects of income per capita on life expectancy.

Our earlier admonitions about reverse causality apply with equal force to estimating the effect of income levels on demographic characteristics. We address this issue in a similar manner as before, using the well-established instrumental-variables regression approach to purge actual income of the component that is due to reverse causality. Ultimately the validity of this procedure depends on having a set of instrumental variables that are good predictors of income but are not linked to life expectancy. For this purpose we use a measure of the openness of the economy during the previous five years, the black-market premium on the currency exchange rate, the proportion of the country's land mass within 100 kilometers of the coast, a dichotomous indicator for landlocked countries, and the distance between the capital city and major world markets. These policy and geographic variables are correlated with income levels but have no obvious direct connections to health status. We avoid using as instruments such geographic variables as latitude or tropical location, which may be directly related to health status through climate. And unlike Pritchett and Summers (1996), we do not include the ratio of investment to income as an instrument. Our reservation is that the investment rate may respond to demographic factors, either through the attractiveness of investment when workers are healthier, or through longer life expectancy, generating savings for retirement.

Although the geographic variables seem to be good instruments, they vary across countries but not across time. This leaves only our policy variables as instruments of the time-series changes that drive the panel data results when we have fixed effects. There is no clear reason for a feedback from life expectancy (or fertility) to these policy variables; nevertheless we plan to find more convincing instruments for future work.

The effect of a change in income on life expectancy is likely to be felt only in the long term, because health status is related to many events and conditions experienced over a person's lifetime, particularly during youth, as well as to current income. A complex process of population selectivity is also involved, since the most frail members of a population will tend to die at early ages, leaving increasingly high concentrations of physically robust individuals alive (Manton and Stallard 1984). The short-run effect of changes in income on changes in life expectancy may mislead us about the long-run effect. To capture the long-run effect, we focus on estimating the relationship between life expectancy and income level, rather than the changes in each. We adopt a panel study approach, including a set of time-period indicators, to capture the effects of health advances and increased access to those advances over the 25 years (1965–90) under consideration. We also include indicator variables for each country (referred to as country fixed effects) to capture the effect on life expectancy of country-specific conditions, such as climate and weather patterns.

Table 3 reports the results of this analysis. Variables are expressed in natural logarithms so that the coefficients can be interpreted as measures of the percentage change in life expectancy associated with a unit change in each explanatory variable. In the case of income per worker, a unit change also corresponds to a 1 percent increase because this variable is expressed in units of natural logarithms. All the other variables are dichotomous, which means that they take on the value of one if a particular observation possesses the characteristic in question, and a value of zero otherwise. The coefficients for these variables thus can be interpreted as the percentage difference in life expectancy between observations with and without the particular characteristic.

As argued and documented above, the rate of growth of GDP per capita (i.e., our measure of economic growth) depends directly on the age structure of the population, and so one cannot regard it as an independent variable when explaining life expectancy and fertility. We therefore use GDP per worker as our independent variable. As in the previous section we report OLS estimates as a benchmark for the other results (column 1). Our estimates of cross-country instrumental variables, reported in column 2, suggest that a 10 percent rise in income per worker increases life expectancy by 1.9 percent. Since the standard error of this parameter estimate is small, the effect is significantly different from zero at all conventional test levels. The estimates also indicate that life expectancy rose an average of 5 percent from 1965 to 1990 for countries in the sample, above and beyond the increase due to income growth during the period.

Adding regional-indicator variables in column 3 suggests that life expectancy is some 9 percent higher in East Asia and 6 percent higher in Southeast Asia than we would expect, given their income levels. Africa, in contrast, has a life expectancy 9 percent lower than its income levels would suggest.

The positive income coefficients in regressions 1 and 2 indicate that the large income differences among countries in our sample are positively associated with differences in life expectancy. Introducing country fixed effects raises the subtly different question of whether changes in a country's income over time are associated with changes in that country's life expectancy. Here we find that the introduction of country fixed effects drives the income coefficient to zero and suggests that the roughly 15 percent in-

TABLE 3   Regression results indicating the effect of income on life expectancy at birth: 70 countries, 1965–90 (Dependent variable: log life expectancy)

Independent variable	Base specification, OLS (1)	Base specification, instrumental variables (2)	Geographic specification, instrumental variables (3)	Fixed effects, OLS (4)	Fixed effects, instrumental variables (5)
Constant	2.671	2.471	2.873	Fixed	Fixed
	(64.3)	(44.6)	(22.0)	effects	effects
Log GDP per worker	0.165	0.188	0.145	–0.002	–0.008
	(44.0)	(34.4)	(11.2)	(0.11)	(0.21)
Dummy, 1965	–0.059	–0.050	–0.072	–0.137	–0.141
	(3.28)	(2.74)	(4.05)	(11.0)	(7.23)
Dummy, 1970	–0.047	–0.041	–0.055	–0.099	–0.101
	(2.80)	(2.39)	(3.49)	(8.75)	(7.43)
Dummy, 1975	–0.044	–0.040	–0.047	–0.065	–0.067
	(2.72)	(2.39)	(3.19)	(6.16)	(6.46)
Dummy, 1980	–0.038	–0.035	–0.038	–0.034	–0.034
	(2.39)	(2.18)	(2.59)	(3.24)	(3.83)
Dummy, 1985	–0.006	–0.003	–0.006	–0.004	–0.004
	(0.39)	(0.21)	(0.43)	(0.37)	(0.45)
Africa			–0.091		
			(3.22)		
Latin America			–0.003		
			(0.25)		
South Asia			0.005		
			(0.16)		
Southeast Asia			0.061		
			(2.82)		
East Asia			0.089		
			(6.34)		
Adjusted R^2	0.76	0.76	0.81	0.94	0.94
Number of observations	569	569	569	569	569
Number of countries	107	107	107	107	107

NOTES: Log GDP per worker is instrumented with log black-market premium, log openness, log distance to major market, landlocked dummy, and percentage of land within 100 km of coast. Heteroskedasticity-consistent t statistics are reported in parentheses below the coefficient estimates.

crease in world life expectancy between 1965 and 1985 was entirely independent of income growth.

The fixed-effects results are somewhat puzzling insofar as they indicate that health improvements have not been any larger among those countries with higher income growth than among other countries. Some countries, such as China, Cuba, and Sri Lanka, have managed to achieve impressive levels of life expectancy at low levels of income. For other countries the effects of income changes on health perhaps reveal themselves only over time frames longer than 25 years. Technically our instruments may not fully capture time-series movements in income levels; but this seems unlikely, given that we find similar results using OLS and that our instruments do produce significant results when we explain fertility changes. Mortality rates, even among the old, may depend on nutrition levels and health care when young, so that health status responds slowly to income changes. Long lags in the link between income improvements and increases in life expectancy may explain our failure to find any significant effect in our fixed-effects analysis of panel data.

To study the effects of income on fertility (as measured by the total fertility rate), we follow exactly the same approach as for life expectancy. Our estimates are reported in Table 4. The instrumental-variables regression in column 2 suggests that 10 percent higher income is associated with 4.9 percent lower fertility. East Asia and Latin America stand out when regional indicator variables are added to the equation. East Asian fertility is 40 percent lower than we would expect given its income, whereas Latin American fertility is 25 percent higher.

The estimates also reveal a sharp downward trend in fertility, independent of the effect of rising incomes. For example, fertility was roughly 22 percent lower in 1990 than in 1965, with income levels held constant. Presumably this trend reflects increased knowledge about and access to contraceptives, changing attitudes toward family planning, higher levels of schooling and better job-market opportunities (especially for women), and rising female influence on household decisions.

In a fixed-effects framework the coefficient on income in column 5 indicates that a 10 percent rise in income produces a 2.2 percent fall in fertility. The standard error of the coefficient estimate with fixed effects is much higher because of the need to estimate 107 coefficients corresponding to the country indicator variables, but the estimated coefficient is still statistically significant at the 5 percent significance level. These results suggest that the negative effect of income on fertility is quite robust. Not only do countries with higher income levels have lower fertility, but also countries that increase their income levels over time reduce their fertility levels. These results hold when we use instrumental variables to safeguard against picking up feedback effects from fertility to income. The fixed-effects results also indicate a sharp (30 percent) worldwide reduction of fertility rates, independent of rising incomes.

A comprehensive study of the proximate causes of health and fertility would include the explanatory variables we have examined, as well as many

TABLE 4   Regression results indicating the effect of income on fertility: 70
countries, 1965–90 (Dependent variable: log total fertility rate)

Independent variable	Base specification, OLS (1)	Base specification, instrumental variables (2)	Geographic specification, instrumental variables (3)	Fixed effects, OLS (4)	Fixed effects, instrumental variables (5)
Constant	4.502 (40.3)	5.539 (35.2)	4.877 (9.47)	Fixed effects	Fixed effects
Log GDP per worker	−0.374 (30.5)	−0.491 (28.6)	−0.418 (8.07)	−0.196 (4.75)	−0.223 (2.44)
Dummy, 1965	0.260 (5.36)	0.219 (4.03)	0.233 (4.54)	0.315 (11.5)	0.301 (6.74)
Dummy, 1970	0.226 (4.66)	0.193 (3.80)	0.206 (4.43)	0.261 (12.2)	0.252 (8.37)
Dummy, 1975	0.198 (4.08)	0.173 (3.46)	0.182 (4.11)	0.202 (10.3)	0.198 (9.65)
Dummy, 1980	0.173 (3.65)	0.158 (3.27)	0.162 (3.72)	0.150 (7.91)	0.150 (9.21)
Dummy, 1985	0.097 (2.09)	0.084 (1.77)	0.087 (2.01)	0.075 (3.64)	0.075 (4.23)
Africa			0.002 (0.02)		
Latin America			0.251 (5.09)		
South Asia			−0.084 (0.79)		
Southeast Asia			−0.149 (1.50)		
East Asia			−0.391 (7.45)		
Adjusted R^2	0.60	0.60	0.66	0.95	0.95
Number of observations	569	569	569	569	569
Number of countries	107	107	107	107	107

NOTES: Log GDP per worker is instrumented with log black-market premium, log openness, log distance to major market, landlocked dummy, and percentage of land within 100 km of coast. Heteroskedasticity-consistent t statistics are reported in parentheses below the coefficient estimates.

others. Our concern, however, is limited to establishing whether variations
in income due to sources other than health and fertility, respectively, have
effects on health and fertility. With respect to health, our main finding is
that higher income is associated with better health when we look across

countries, though not within individual countries, over time. With respect to fertility, our main finding is that higher income leads to lower fertility across countries, and also for individual countries, over time. The results suggest a strong feedback from economic growth to demographic change, certainly with respect to fertility. The results also indicate that demographic characteristics in East Asia were particularly favorable for economic growth during 1965–90; the region had considerably higher levels of life expectancy than can be accounted for solely on the basis of income. The very sharp decline in fertility rates between 1965 and 1980 also appears to play an important role in this process.

Discussion

Perhaps the most striking feature of the global distribution of income is the remarkably wide gulf in income per capita between industrial and developing countries. For example, income per capita in the United States is roughly 50 times higher than that in Chad after adjustment is made for differences in purchasing power. Within Asia, income levels in Japan are around 13 times those found in Bangladesh. It is difficult to attribute such extreme gaps to differences in geography and physical environment, technological options, or underlying tastes and preferences for goods and services and other determinants of the quality of life. This difficulty has led to the generation of models of endogenous growth (e.g., Lucas 1990; Romer 1993) that attempt to explain large income differences as the result of a self-sustaining growth process involving two-way linkages between income and capital, both physical and human.

The interaction between demographic change and economic growth means that we must view the growth process as a system with causality running both ways. This interaction can also support an endogenous growth process. Becker, Murphy, and Tamura (1990) and Ehrlich and Lui (1991) construct theoretical models in which the interaction between fertility rates, mortality rates, and economic growth can give rise to self-sustaining economic growth. Once takeoff has been achieved, however, the sustained growth in these models rests on the assumption that there are no diminishing returns to capital (either physical or human), a condition that is difficult to substantiate empirically.

Our findings indicate that the interaction between demography and economic growth gives rise to the possibility of cumulative causation, but only for a limited period of time. Initial increases in life expectancy and reductions in fertility and in the youth dependency ratio can provide a strong boost to economic growth in developing countries. This growth in turn leads to further reductions in fertility rates, and perhaps to an increase in life expectancy. These demographic changes then set up another round of economic growth. This virtuous cycle, however, has a natural limit. Although decreases in fertility rates lower the youth dependency ratio in poor countries, they eventually produce a smaller working-age population. They do so when the elder dependency ratio—that is, the ratio of retirees (whose ranks are further swelled by increases in life expectancy) to workers—inevitably increases. The demographic transition promotes economic growth for a period, but eventually these strong dynamic effects subside. Even so, a higher level of steady-state income per capita may exist after the demographic transition has been completed than before, owing to the effect of longer life expectancy on education and saving rates.

Poverty traps arise naturally in this view of the world. Poor health and high fertility keep income down, which in turn impedes the process of demographic transition and perpetuates the state of low income. Breaking free of this trap requires some external stimulus, either to income, to health, or to fertility. A sufficiently large stimulus can catalyze a self-sustaining process of rapid economic growth and demographic change, which eventually settles down when the economy achieves high income levels, high life expectancy, and low fertility. This idea receives support from the work of Quah (1997), which shows that the global distribution of income is dominated by two distinct groups of countries, the poor and the rich, with few countries in between. Many theories (reviewed by Azariadis 1996) have been put forward to explain the bipolar distribution of countries by per capita income (or, more technically, the existence of multiple equilibria in income levels). Identifying the mechanisms that actually matter, however, is ultimately an empirical issue. Our evidence-based view is that the feedback relationships between demographic change and economic growth are strong enough to suggest that they play an important role in explaining income differences between nations.

An important implication of the systems approach we are advancing is that two factors determine outcomes: the external forces that tweak and trigger the system, and the linkages through which those stimuli are channeled. It follows that demographic change can be important for economic growth in two ways. First, reductions in fertility and mortality caused, for example, by the public provision of family planning and reproductive health services can have a direct effect on the age distribution, which in turn has a direct effect on income per capita. Second, if higher incomes should prove to be the best contraceptive, an initial boost in income can promote demographic change and further increases in income. The operation of a multiplier mechanism of this type can greatly magnify any initial increases in income and generate rapid (that is, endogenous) growth and a two-tier distribution of country income per capita. An important implication of this cumulative-causation framework is that even small stimuli ultimately can have a powerful effect on income if the linkages among population, capital, and income are sufficiently strong. Indeed, the nature and strength of the linkages determine whether the effect of a particular catalyst on, say, income is ultimately multiplied or dampened.

We can use our analysis for the period 1965–90 to help predict what the future may hold for Asia. Table 5 reports levels and changes in several key demographic variables that our results suggest are linked to economic growth. The figures clearly show that the "demographic dividend" that East Asia has enjoyed is beginning to dissipate. The dependency ratio in East Asia fell from 0.78 in 1965 to 0.48 in 1995, but the differential between the growth rates of the working-age population and the total population declined from 0.68 percentage points a year during 1965–90 to just 0.18 percentage points a year during 1990–95. We anticipate a further rise in the dependency ratio because of projected increases in longevity. The combination of these demographic changes and the change in East Asia's income levels—East Asia moved from being roughly at the world average in 1965 to twice the world average in 1995—strongly suggest a slowing of income growth.

The demographic characteristics of Southeast Asia today are remarkably similar to those of East Asia in 1965. Like East Asia, though a less

TABLE 5 Demographic variables affecting economic growth: World and Asian subregions, 1965 and 1995

Explanatory variable	World		East Asia		Southeast Asia		South Asia	
	1965	1995	1965	1995	1965	1995	1965	1995
Life expectancy (years)	52.3	64.3	63.2	74.5	49.9	63.7	46.0	59.8
Total fertility rate	4.95	2.96	4.37	1.84	6.00	3.59	6.27	4.73
Age dependency ratio	0.77	0.62	0.78	0.48	0.88	0.68	0.84	0.81
Labor force participation (proportion)	0.78	0.77	0.75	0.76	0.86	0.82	0.75	0.79
Growth in total population (%)	1.83	1.48	1.74	1.02	2.24	1.73	2.25	1.89
Growth in working-age population (%)	2.13	1.70	2.41	1.20	2.63	2.32	2.43	2.33
Growth in working-age population minus total population (%)	0.30	0.22	0.68	0.18	0.39	0.59	0.18	0.44
Real GDP per capita (US dollars)	2,856	5,077	2,296	9,777	1,164	3,110	989	1,536
Total years of education, working-age population	3.89	5.83	5.89	8.49	2.93	5.13	1.6	3.62

NOTES: Growth in total population and growth in working-age population are calculated for the years 1965–70 and 1990–95. The data for total years of education are for 1965 and 1990.
SOURCES: Demographic data are from United Nations (1994). GDP and school-enrollment data are from the Penn World Table (version 5.6) and include a smaller sample of countries (Summers and Heston 1991).

extreme case, Southeast Asia is an outlier in our demographic regressions, as shown in column 3 of Tables 3 and 4. The life expectancy of its population is higher and its fertility lower than its income level would otherwise suggest. Its working-age population is now growing 0.59 percentage points a year faster than its total population, indicating the prospect of a rapid decline in the current elder dependency ratio of 0.68. Given Southeast Asia's low income levels, relatively high stocks of human capital, and past success at improving labor productivity, the demographic effects suggest that in the coming decades Southeast Asia could well experience economic success on a par with that of East Asia.

The situation in South Asia is more difficult to judge. In both income and demography it is clearly at an earlier stage of development than East or Southeast Asia. Its life expectancy has improved and its fertility has declined somewhat, and Tables 3 and 4 imply that its demographic characteristics are in line with its income level. Current trends suggest a substantial decline in its dependency ratio in coming years, but given the region's history of slow productivity growth, whether it will be able to capitalize on this opportunity is unclear. Even given its demographic characteristics, the regression results in Table 1 suggest that during 1965–90 South Asia performed substantially worse than the rest of the world economy. Thus South Asia appears to demonstrate that the demographic transition is a necessary, but not sufficient, condition for rapid economic growth.[2]

Conclusion

This study establishes the existence of strong two-way linkages between demographic change and economic growth. These linkages suggest that a multiplier mechanism partly determines both demography and income. Within this framework, policy-induced changes in demographic or economic variables can promote a virtuous cycle of cumulative causation in which economic and demographic characteristics interact in a mutually reinforcing way. Even small initial changes can lead to a growth spurt that will continue until fertility rates stabilize at a low level. The same mechanism can also create the poverty traps that seem to have regions like Africa and South Asia in their grip.

The analysis presented in this chapter shows that demographic variables have played a major role in East Asia's economic success. Increases in life expectancy have had a large effect on incomes in the region. A rapid fertility decline, induced partly by the region's economic success, led to a substantial reduction in the youth dependency ratio, thereby helping to boost growth rates of income per capita. East Asia appears to have had exceptionally favorable demographic characteristics in the form of high life expectancy and low fertility, despite its initially low income level. Strong feedback from income growth to demographic change, mainly in the form of fertility decline, helped complete the virtuous cycle of rising incomes and falling birth rates that we believe represents a very important part of the so-called East Asian miracle.

Economic growth in East Asia will likely slow in the future because fertility rates will stabilize at their current low levels and the dependency ratio will rise as the population ages. By contrast, Southeast Asia appears primed for an acceleration of long-run economic growth driven by increasingly favorable demographic circumstances.

The presence of two-way causality between economic growth and the demographic transition means that care must be taken in interpreting correlations between demographic change and economic growth, even correlations that account for nondemographic influences on growth and non-income influences on demography. We must be careful to separate those components of both demographic change and economic growth that are determined within the system and those that are determined outside the system. We must also pay greater attention to the ways in which the interaction between economic growth and the demographic transition can give rise to cumulative causality and either a virtuous or a vicious cycle involving life expectancy, fertility, and income, perhaps along with other variables such as education and gender equity. The results presented here should be regarded as preliminary. Future studies should estimate the feedbacks between demographic change, capital accumulation, and economic growth as a fully specified interacting system.

APPENDIX TABLE 1   Variable definitions and selected descriptive statistics used in the analysis, 70 countries

Definition and source	Mean	Standard deviation	Minimum value	Maximum value
Average growth rate of GDP per capita (%), 1965–90 Source: Summers and Heston (1991)	1.93	1.83	–2.24	7.41
GDP per capita, 1965 (purchasing power parity in 1985 dollars) Source: Summers and Heston (1991)	3,430	2,986	412	11,638
Proportion of land area in the tropics Source: Gallup, Sachs, and Mellinger (1999)	0.50	0.49	0.00	1.00
Dichotomous variable (= 1 if the country is landlocked) Source: Gallup, Sachs, and Mellinger (1999)	0.13	0.34	0.00	1.00
Average population growth rate (%), 1965–90 Source: World Bank (1996)	1.92	1.04	0.17	4.27
Average growth rate of working-age population (%), 1965–90 Source: World Bank (1996)	2.18	1.07	0.25	4.20
Ratio of working age to total population, 1965 Source: World Bank (1996)	0.56	0.06	0.47	0.68
Average years of secondary schooling, population aged 15–65, in 1965 Source: Barro and Lee (1994)	0.81	0.76	0.01	3.51
Life expectancy at birth, 1965 Source: World Bank (1996)	58.7	11.7	33.5	74.1
Percentage of years economy is open, 1965–90 Source: Sachs and Warner (1995)	0.46	0.45	0.0	1.0
Index of the quality of government institutions (scale of 0 to 10) Source: Knack and Keefer (1995)	6.10	2.40	2.27	9.98
Working-age population density (per km^2) in coastal areas Source: Gallup, Sachs, and Mellinger (1999)	174.9	568.7	0.0	3,729.3
Working-age population density (per km^2) in the inland areas Source: Gallup, Sachs, and Mellinger (1999)	56.1	109.1	0.0	537.0

NOTE: For the list of countries included, see Appendix Table 2.

APPENDIX TABLE 2   Countries used in the cross-country regressions, by region

East Asia	Europe	Latin America and the Caribbean
Hong Kong	Austria	Argentina
Japan	Belgium	Bolivia
Republic of Korea	Denmark	Brazil
Singapore	Finland	Chile
Southeast Asia	France	Colombia
Indonesia	Germany (Fed. German	Costa Rica
Malaysia	Republic in 1965)	Dominican Republic
Philippines	Greece	Ecuador
Thailand	Ireland	El Salvador
South Asia	Italy	Guatemala
Bangladesh	Netherlands	Honduras
India	Norway	Jamaica
Pakistan	Portugal	Mexico
Sri Lanka	Spain	Nicaragua
Africa	Sweden	Paraguay
Cameroon	Switzerland	Peru
Gambia	United Kingdom	Trinidad and Tobago
Ghana	**Middle East**	Uruguay
Guinea Bissau	Israel	Venezuela
Kenya	Jordan	**Northern America**
Malawi	Syria	Canada
Mali	Tunisia	United States
Senegal	Turkey	**Oceania**
Sierra Leone		Australia
South Africa		New Zealand
Uganda		Papua New Guinea
Zambia		
Zimbabwe		

NOTE: A different set of countries is used in the panel regressions. These are available from the authors upon request.

Notes

We thank Eric Bettinger, David Evans, Bryan Graham, and Larry Rosenberg for assistance in preparing this chapter, and Allen Kelley and Robert Schmidt for valuable comments. We also thank the United States Agency for International Development (USAID) for financial support provided under the Consulting Assistance on Economic Reform II Project, contract number PCE-0405-C-00-5015-00. The views and interpretation in this chapter are our own and should not be attributed to USAID. Preparation of this chapter was also supported by a grant from the Economic Advisory Service of the World Health Organization.

1 In an effort to find a causal link from education to fertility in Taiwan, Cheng and Nwachukwu (1997) instead find evidence based on aggregate data that the causality runs the other way, from fertility to education.

2 That the demographic transition creates favorable conditions for, but does not guarantee, rapid economic growth is further illustrated by the financial and economic crisis that began in East and Southeast Asia in mid-1997. Although the immediate cause of the crisis was a massive outflow of foreign capital from a region that was heavily dependent on short-term debt, weaknesses inherent in domestic financial systems and the broader system of international finance undeniably contributed to the collapse, favorable demographic circumstances notwithstanding (Furman and Stiglitz 1998; Radelet and Sachs 1998).

References

Asian Development Bank. 1997. *Emerging Asia*. Manila.

Azariadis, Costas. 1996. "The economics of poverty traps," *Journal of Economic Growth* 1(4): 449–485.

Barlow, R. 1994. "Population growth and economic growth: Some more correlations," *Population and Development Review* 20(1): 153–165.

Barro, R. J. 1991. "Economic growth in a cross-section of countries," *Quarterly Journal of Economics* 106(2): 407–443.

Barro, R. J. and J.-W. Lee. 1994. "Sources of economic growth," *Carnegie-Rochester Conference Series on Public Policy* 40: 1–46.

Barro, R. J. and X. Sala-i-Martin. 1995. *Economic Growth*. New York: McGraw-Hill.

Becker, G. S. and R. J. Barro. 1988. "A reformulation of the economic theory of fertility," *Quarterly Journal of Economics* 103(1): 1–25.

Becker, G. S., K. M. Murphy, and R. Tamura. 1990. "Human capital, fertility, and economic growth," *Journal of Political Economy* 98(5, part 2): S12–S37.

Bloom, D. E. and D. Canning. 1999. "From demographic lift to economic liftoff: The case of Egypt," paper presented at the Conference on Growth beyond Stabilization: Prospects for Egypt. Cairo, 3–4 February.

———. 2000a. "Demographic change and economic growth: The role of cumulative causality," in *Population Does Matter: Demography, Growth, and Poverty in the Developing World*, eds. Nancy Birdsall, Allen C. Kelley, and Steven Sinding. New York: Oxford University Press, forthcoming.

———. 2000b. "The health and wealth of nations," *Science*, No. 287: 1207–1209, 18 February.

Bloom D. E., D. Canning, and P. N. Malaney. 1999. "Demographic change and economic growth in Asia," Center for International Development Working Paper No. 15, Harvard University, Cambridge, MA.

Bloom, D. E. and R. B. Freeman. 1986. "The effects of rapid population growth on labor supply and employment in developing countries," *Population and Development Review* 12(3): 381–414.

———. 1988. "Economic development and the timing and components of population growth," *Journal of Policy Modeling* 10(1): 57–81.

Bloom, D. E. and J. D. Sachs. 1998. "Geography, demography, and economic growth in Africa," *Brookings Papers on Economic Activity* 2: 207–273.

Bloom, D. E. and J. G. Williamson. 1997. "Demographic change and human resource development," in *Emerging Asia*, ed. Asian Development Bank. Manila: Asian Development Bank.

——— 1998. "Demographic transitions and economic miracles in emerging Asia," *World Bank Economic Review* 12(3): 419–456.

Bloom, D. E. et al. 1998. *Health, Health Policy, and Economic Outcomes*. Special report for the Health and Development Satellite Team of the World Health Organization. Cambridge, MA: Harvard Institute for International Development, Harvard University; and Washington, DC: World Bank.

Bongaarts, John. 1994. "The impact of population policies: Comment," *Population and Development Review* 20(3): 616–620.

Boserup, Ester. 1981. *Population and Technological Change: A Study of Long-Term Trends*. Chicago: Chicago University Press.

Brander, J. A. and S. Dowrick. 1994. "The role of fertility and population in economic growth: Empirical results from aggregate cross-national data," *Journal of Population Economics* 7(1): 1–25.

Caldwell, J. C. 1982. *Theory of Fertility Decline*. London: Academic Press.

Cheng, B. S. and S. L. S. Nwachukwu. 1997. "The effect of education on fertility in Taiwan: A time series analysis," *Economics Letters* 56(1): 95–99.

Coale, Ansley J. 1986. "Population trends and economic development," in *World Population and U.S. Policy: The Choices Ahead*, ed. Jane Menken. New York: W.W. Norton.

Coale, Ansley J. and Edgar M. Hoover. 1958. *Population Growth and Economic Development in Low-Income Countries*. Princeton, NJ: Princeton University Press.

Easterly, W. et al. 1993. "Good policy or good luck: Country growth-performance and temporary shocks," *Journal of Monetary Economics* 32(3): 459–483.

Ehrlich, Paul. 1968. *The Population Bomb*. New York: Ballantine.

Ehrlich, I. and F. T. Lui. 1991. "Intergenerational trade, longevity, and economic growth," *Journal of Political Economy* 99(5): 1029–1059.

Fogel, Robert W. 1994. "Economic growth, population theory, and physiology: The bearing of long-term processes on the making of economic policy," *American Economic Review* 84(3): 369–395.

Furman, J. and J. E. Stiglitz. 1998. "Economic crises: Evidence and insights from East Asia," *Brookings Papers on Economic Activity* 2: 1–135.

Gallup, J. L. 1998. "Agricultural productivity and geography," Working Paper Series. Cambridge, MA: Harvard Institute for International Development, Harvard University.

Gallup, J. L., J. D. Sachs, and A. Mellinger. 1999. "Geography and economic development," *International Regional Science Review* 22(2): 179–232.

Gertler, P. J. and J. W. Molyneaux. 1994. "How economic development and family planning programs combined to reduce Indonesian fertility," *Demography* 31(1): 33–63.

Hanushek, E. A. 1992. "The tradeoff between child quantity and quality," *Journal of Political Economy* 100(1): 84–117.

Higgins, Matthew. 1998. "Demography, national savings, and international capital flows," *International Economic Review* 39(2): 343–369.

Higgins, Matthew and Jeffrey G. Williamson. 1997. "Age structure dynamics in Asia and dependence of foreign capital," *Population and Development Review* 23(2): 261–293.

Islam, N. 1995. "Growth empirics: A panel data approach," *The Quarterly Journal of Economics* 110(4): 1127–1170.

Kelley, A. C. and R. M. Schmidt. 1995. "Aggregate population and economic growth correlations: The role of the components of demographic change," *Demography* 32(4): 543–555.

———. 1996. "Savings, dependency, and development," *Journal of Population Economics* 9(4): 365–386.

———. 2000. "Economic and demographic change: A synthesis of models, findings, and perspectives," in *Population Does Matter: Demography, Growth, and Poverty in the Developing World*, eds. Nancy Birdsall, Allen C. Kelley, and Steven Sinding. New York: Oxford University Press, forthcoming.

Knack, Stephen and Philip Keefer. 1995. "Institutions and economic performance: Cross-country tests using alternative institutional measures," *Economics and Politics* 7(3): 207–227.

Knodel, J., N. Havanon, and W. Sittitrai. 1990. "Family size and the education of children in the context of rapid fertility decline," *Population and Development Review* 16(1): 31–62.

Knodel, J. and M. Wongsith. 1991. "Family size and children's education in Thailand: Evidence from a national sample," *Demography* 28(1): 119–131.

Krugman, Paul. 1994. "The myth of Asia's miracle," *Foreign Affairs* 73(6): 62–78.

Kuznets, S. 1967. "Population and economic growth," *Proceedings of the American Philosophical Society* 111: 170–193.

Landes, David S. 1998. *The Wealth and Poverty of Nations: Why Some Are So Rich and Some So Poor*. New York: W. W. Norton.

Lee, Ronald D., Andrew Mason, and Timothy Miller. 2000. "Saving, wealth, and population," in *Population Does Matter: Demography, Growth, and Poverty in the Developing World*, eds. Nancy Birdsall, Allen C. Kelley, and Steven Sinding. New York: Oxford University Press, forthcoming.

Leff, R. D. 1969. "Dependency rates and savings rates," *American Economic Review* 59(5): 886–896.

Lucas, R. E. 1990. "Why doesn't capital flow from rich to poor countries?" *American Economic Review* 80(2): 92–96.

Malthus, T. R. 1798 [1986]. *An Essay on the Principle of Population*. London: W. Pickering.

Manton, K. G. and E. Stallard. 1984. *Recent Trends in Mortality Analysis*. Orlando, FL: Academic Press.

Mason, Andrew. 1988. "Saving, economic growth, and demographic change," *Population and Development Review* 14(1): 113–144.

Meltzer, David. 1995. "Mortality decline, the demographic transition, and economic growth," unpublished paper, Brigham and Women's Hospital and National Bureau of Economic Research, Cambridge, MA.

Modigliani, F. 1986. "Life-cycle, individual thrift, and the wealth of nations," *American Economic Review* 76(3): 297–313.

Preston, Samuel H. 1975. "The changing relation between mortality and the level of economic development," *Population Studies* 29(2): 231–248.

———. 1980. "Mortality declines in less developed countries," in *Population and Economic Change in Developing Countries*, ed. Richard Easterlin. Chicago: University of Chicago Press.

Pritchett, L. H. 1994. "Desired fertility and the impact of population policies," *Population and Development Review* 20(1): 1–55.

Pritchett, L. H. and L. H. Summers. 1996. "Wealthier is healthier," *Journal of Human Resources* 31(4): 841–868.

Quah, D. T. 1997. "Empirics for growth and distribution: Stratification, polarization, and convergence clubs," *Journal of Economic Growth* 2(1): 27–59.

Radelet, S. and J. D. Sachs. 1998. "The East Asian financial crisis: Diagnosis, remedies, prospects," *Brookings Papers on Economic Activity* 1: 1–74.

Rodrik, D. 1994. "King Kong meets Godzilla: The World Bank and the East Asian miracle," in *Miracle or Design? Lessons from the East Asian Experience*, eds. A. Fishlow et al. Policy Essay No. 11. Washington, DC: Overseas Development Council.

———. 1998. "TFPG controversies, institutions, and economic performance in East Asia," in *The Institutional Foundation of Economic Development in East Asia*, eds. Y. Hayami and M. Aoki. London: Macmillan.

Romer, P. M. 1993. "Idea gaps and object gaps in economic development," *Journal of Monetary Economics* 32(3): 543–573.

Rosenzweig, M. R. 1990. "Population growth and human capital investments: Theory and evidence," *Journal of Political Economy* 98(5, part 2): S38–S70.

Sachs, Jeffrey D. and Andrew Warner. 1995. "Economic reform and the process of global integration," *Brookings Papers on Economic Activity* 1: 1–118.

——— 1997. "Sources of slow growth in African economies," *Journal of African Economies* 6(3): 335–376.

Schultz, T. P. 1994. "Human capital, family planning, and their effects on population growth," *American Economic Review, Papers, and Proceedings* 84(2): 255–260.

Simon, Julian L. 1981. *The Ultimate Resource*. Princeton: Princeton University Press.

Strauss, J. and Duncan Thomas. 1995. "Health and labour productivity: Sorting out the relationships," in *Agricultural Competitiveness: Market Forces and Policy Choice. Proceedings of the Twenty-second International Conference of Agricultural Economists*, eds. G. H. Peters and D. D. Hedley. International Association of Agricultural Economists Series. Aldershot, UK: Dartmouth.

———. 1998. "Health, nutrition, and economic development," *Journal of Economic Literature* 36(2): 766–817.

Summers, R. and A. Heston. 1991. "The Penn World Table (Mark 5): An expanded set of international comparisons, 1950–1988," *Quarterly Journal of Economics* 106(2): 327–368.

United Nations. 1994. "World population prospects, 1950–2050 (the 1994 revision)," in *Demographic Indicators 1950–2050 (The 1994 Revision)*, electronic data. New York.

Wang, J. et al. 1999. *Measuring Country Performance on Health: Selected Indicators for 115 Countries*. Human Development Network, Health, Nutrition and Population Series. Washington, DC: World Bank.

Webb, S. and H. Zia. 1990. "Lower birth rates = higher savings in LDCs," *Finance and Development* 27(2): 12–14.

World Bank. 1993. *The East Asian Miracle: Economic Growth and Public Policy*. New York: Oxford University Press.

———. 1996. *World Development Indicators*. Washington, DC: World Bank.

Young, Alwyn. 1994. "Lessons from the East Asian NICS: A contrarian view," *European Economic Review* 38(3–4): 964–973.

———. 1995. "The tyranny of numbers: Confronting the statistical realities of the East Asian growth experience," *Quarterly Journal of Economics* 110(3): 641–680.

The Extension of Life
in Developed Countries
and Its Implications
for Social Policy in the
Twenty-first Century

ROBERT W. FOGEL

AS DEVELOPING COUNTRIES in East and Southeast Asia undergo the economic and social changes that accompany the advanced stage of the demographic transition, they will soon confront many of the same policy issues now faced by developed countries. One such issue is how to meet the demands of the increasing number of people who survive to old age. Although the approaches that Asian countries take to this problem will undoubtedly be informed by their own cultures and histories, it may be helpful to consider how the social, economic, and demographic trends in the West have shaped policy discussions in this matter.

The development of longitudinal household data sets is a major advance in the provision of sounder forecasts on the scope of retirement, pension, and health problems over the next one or two generations. The use of cross-sectional data sets to make longitudinal forecasts is an ingrained habit, not only in economics but also in the other social sciences and, although to a much lesser extent, even in the biomedical sciences. We will not adequately avoid the misleading inferences obtained from cross-sectional data until we develop a succession of longitudinal data sets covering several cohorts that are about a generation apart.

An adequate temporal separation between cohorts is necessary to permit the analysis of the effects of substantially different economic and biomedical regimens on the process of aging. Cross-sectional data do not reveal the long-term relationships between income, environmental change, and demand over the past century that caused the average length of retirement to increase fourfold, the proportion of a cohort that lives to retirement to increase sixfold, and the amount of leisure time available to those still in the labor force to increase nearly threefold.

The creation of an adequate succession of life cycle studies can be accelerated by making use of existing archival data. In the United States, data are potentially available for the construction of prospective life cycle samples for four birth cohorts: circa 1840, circa 1875, circa 1920, and circa 1950. The construction of a life cycle sample for the circa 1840 birth cohort, which is based on 40,000 men mustered into the Union Army, is now nearing completion. Some of the findings reported in this article are based on preliminary examinations of the Union Army data set.

A theoretical framework

The study of the causes of the long-term reduction in mortality points to a synergism between technological and physiological improvements. This synergism has produced a form of human evolution that is biological but not genetic, as well as rapid, culturally transmitted, and not necessarily stable. The process is continuing in both rich and developing countries. Costa and I call it "technophysio evolution" (Fogel and Costa 1997).

Unlike the genetic theory of evolution through natural selection, which applies to the whole history of life on earth, technophysio evolution applies only to the last 300 years of human history, and particularly to the last century. Despite its limited scope, technophysio evolution appears to be relevant to forecasting likely trends over the next century or so in longevity, the age at onset of chronic diseases, body size, and the efficiency and durability of vital organ systems (Fogel and Costa 1997). It also has a bearing on such pressing issues of public policy as the growth in population, in pension costs, and in health care costs.

The theory of technophysio evolution rests on the proposition that during the last 300 years, particularly during the last century, human beings have gained an unprecedented degree of control over their environment—a degree of control so great that it sets them apart not only from all other species, but also from all previous generations of *Homo sapiens*. This new degree of control has enabled our species, over this same 300-year interval, to increase its average body size by more than 50 percent, to augment its average longevity by more than 100 percent, and to greatly improve the robustness and capacity of vital organ systems.

Figure 1 shows how dramatic the change in our control of the environment has been since 1700. During its first 100,000 or so years, *Homo sapiens* increased numerically at an exceedingly slow rate. The discovery of agriculture about 11,000 years ago broke the tight constraint on the food supply imposed by a hunting and gathering technology, making it possible to release between 10 and 20 percent of the labor force from the direct production of food, and also giving rise to the first cities. The new technology of food production was so superior to the old one that it was possible to support a much higher rate of population increase than had existed prior to about 9000 BC. Yet, as Figure 1 shows, the advances in the technology of food production after the *second* Agricultural Revolution, which began in northwestern Europe about AD 1700, were far more dramatic than the earlier breakthrough. They included the enclosure of fields, the use of new fodder crops, the improvement of soils with marl (a fertilizer), and the flooding of meadows for more efficient production of grass for livestock. The innovations permitted population to increase at so high a rate that the line of population appears to rise almost vertically. The new technological breakthroughs in manufacturing, transportation, trade, communications, energy production, leisure-time services, and medical services were in many respects even more striking than those in agriculture. Figure 1 emphasizes the huge acceleration in both population and technological change during the twentieth century. The absolute increase in world population between 1900 and 2000 was about three times as great as the increase during the whole previous history of humankind.

FIGURE 1   Growth of the world population and some major events in the history of technology

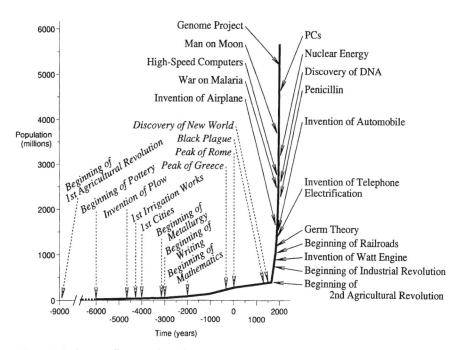

NOTE: "Beginning" usually means the earliest stage of the diffusion process that starts with the invention of a process or a machine and its general application to production.
SOURCES: Cipolla (1974); Clark (1971); Fagan (1977); McNeill (1971); and Piggott (1965). See also Allen (1992 and 1994), Slicher van Bath (1963), and Wrigley (1987).

The escape from chronic malnutrition

The most important aspect of technophysio evolution is the continuing con-
quest of chronic malnutrition, which was virtually universal three centuries ago. Even the wealthy English peerage had a diet during the sixteenth
and seventeenth centuries that was deleterious to health. Although abundant in calories and proteins, aristocratic diets were deficient in vitamins
and included large quantities of toxic substances, especially alcoholic bev-
erages and salt. A diet heavy in salt and alcohol probably increased the
incidence of liver, renal, gastrointestinal, and cardiovascular diseases among
peers who survived to middle age and may have contributed to their high
mortality rates at ages 40 and older. But it was in utero that dietary habits
of the peerage were most deadly, since ladies of the realm were apparently
consuming well over 3 ounces of absolute alcohol per day on average—
more than enough to produce a high incidence of birth defects (Fogel 1986).

Most people in 1700 were chronically malnourished not because their
diets abounded in toxic substances or were qualitatively deficient but because of severe deficiencies in dietary energy. Table 1 shows that in rich
countries today some 1,800 to 2,000 kilogram calories of energy are available for work to a typical adult male 20–39 years old. During the eighteenth century, however, France produced less than one-third the current
US amount of energy available for work, and England was not much better off. Only the United States provided potential energy for work equal to
or greater than current levels during the eighteenth and early nineteenth
centuries, although some of that energy was wasted because of the prevalence of diarrhea and other conditions that undermined the body's capacity to process nutrients.

One implication of these estimates of caloric availability is that mature adults of the eighteenth and much of the nineteenth century must
have been very small by current standards and less physically active. This
inference is supported by data on stature and weight that have been collected for European nations, which show that during the eighteenth and
nineteenth centuries Europeans were severely stunted, with mean heights
that generally fell below the fifth centile of the current Dutch or Norwegian standard. Patchy estimates suggest that average weights of males in
their 30s were in the range of 20 to 35 percent below current levels.

Recent studies have established the predictive power of height and
body mass with respect to morbidity and mortality at later ages. The results of two of these studies are summarized in Figures 2 and 3. Figure 2
presents a "Waaler surface" for mortality. Estimated from Norwegian data,
this surface relates the risk of death over an 18-year period to both height
and weight for males of ages 50–64 in 1963. Transecting the iso-mortality
map are lines that give the locus of each body mass index (BMI) with val-

TABLE 1 Energy available for work, per equivalent adult male, ages 20–39: France, England and Wales, and the United States, 1700–1980 (in kilogram calories per day)

Year	France	England and Wales	United States
1700[a]		720	2,313
1705	439		
1750		812	
1785	600		
1800		858	
1840			1,810
1850		1,014	
1870	1,671		
1880			2,709
1944			2,282
1975	2,136		
1980		1,793	1,956

[a]Prerevolutionary Virginia only.
SOURCE: Fogel and Floud (1999: Table 6).

ues between 16 and 34. The BMI is a measure of weight standardized for height and is computed as the ratio of weight in kilograms to height in meters squared (BMI = kg/m^2). The dark curve through the middle of the diagram gives the weights that minimize risk at each height. This figure shows that even when body weight is maintained at recommended levels (BMI in the range of 23 to 25), short men are at substantially greater risk of death than tall men. Also shown in this figure are estimates of heights and weights in France at four dates, indicating the large reductions in risk of death associated with improvement in stature and BMI (Fogel and Floud 1999).

Poor body builds also increase vulnerability to diseases, not just contagious diseases, but chronic diseases as well. The implication of combined stunting (low height-for-age) and low BMI for the prevalence of chronic diseases is illustrated by Figure 3, which presents a Waaler surface for morbidity estimated from the US National Health Interview Survey (NHIS) data for 1985–88. The coordinates in height–BMI of Union Army veterans who were aged 65 or older in 1910 and of veterans (mainly of World War II) who were the same ages during 1985–88 are also shown. These coordinates predict a decline of about 35 percent in the prevalence of chronic disease between the two cohorts, which is close to what actually occurred.

Table 2 compares the prevalence of chronic diseases among Union Army men aged 65 and older in 1910 with two surveys of veterans of the same ages in the 1980s. The table indicates that among the elderly, heart disease was 2.9 times as prevalent, musculoskeletal and respiratory dis-

FIGURE 2 Iso-mortality curves of relative risk for height and weight among Norwegian males aged 50–64 in 1963, with the estimated French height and weight plotted at four dates

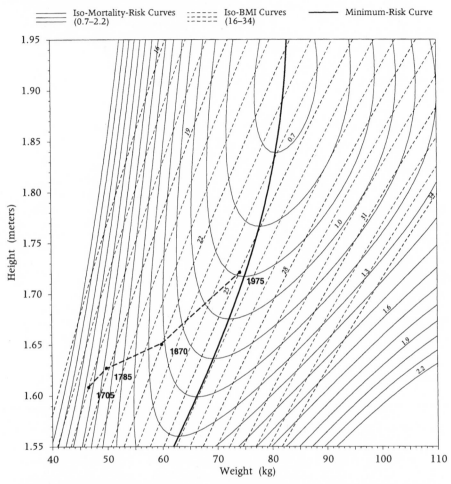

SOURCE: Fogel (1993, 1994b).

eases were 1.6 times as prevalent, and digestive diseases were 4.7 times as prevalent among veterans aged 65 or older in 1910 as in 1985–88. Young adults born between 1822 and 1845 who survived the deadly infectious diseases of childhood and adolescence were not freer of degenerative diseases than persons of the same ages today, as some have suggested, but more afflicted.

Variations in height and weight appear to be associated with variations in the chemical composition of the tissues that make up vital organs, in the quality of the electrical transmission across membranes, and in the functioning of the endocrine system and other vital systems. Nutritional status thus appears to be a critical link connecting improvements in technology to improvements in human physiology.

FIGURE 3 Health improvement predicted by the NHIS 1985–88 health surface

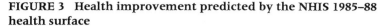

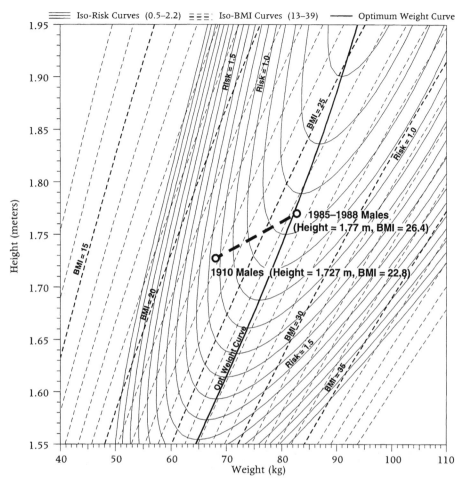

NOTE: All risks are measured in relation to the average risk of morbidity (calculated over all heights and weights) among white males, ages 45–64, included in the US National Health Interview Survey (NHIS) during 1985–88.
SOURCE: Kim (1993: Fig. 11).

Research on this question is developing rapidly, and some of the new findings are yet to be confirmed. The exact mechanisms by which malnutrition and trauma in utero or early childhood are transformed into organ dysfunctions are still unclear. What is agreed upon is that the basic structure of most organs is laid down early, and it is reasonable to infer that poorly developed organs may break down earlier than well-developed ones. The principal evidence so far is statistical, and despite agreement on certain specific dysfunctions there is no generally accepted theory of cellular aging (Tanner 1990 and 1993).

Bearing these caveats in mind, one can conveniently divide recent research on the connection between malnutrition and body size on the

TABLE 2   Prevalence of chronic conditions among Union Army
veterans in 1910, US veterans in 1983, and US veterans included in the
National Health Interview Survey (NHIS) during 1985–88 (each
veteran group ages 65 and older) (percentages reporting)

Chronic condition	Union Army veterans, 1910	US veterans		NHIS, 1985–88
		1983	Age-adjusted, 1983	
Musculoskeletal	67.7	47.9	47.2	42.5
Digestive	84.0	49.0	48.9	18.0
Hernia	34.5	27.3	26.7	6.6
Diarrhea	31.9	3.7	4.2	1.4
Genito-urinary	27.3	36.3	32.3	8.9
Central nervous, endocrine, metabolic, or blood	24.2	29.9	29.1	12.6
Circulatory[a]	90.1	42.9	39.9	40.0
Heart	76.0	38.5	39.9	26.6
Varicose veins	38.5	8.7	8.3	5.3
Hemorrhoids[b]	44.4			7.2
Respiratory	42.2	29.8	28.1	26.5

NOTES: Prevailing rates of Union Army veterans are based on examinations by physicians. Those for the 1980s
are based on veterans' reports of ever having had specified conditions. Those for veterans included in the US
National Health Interview Survey (NHIS) are based on self-reports of conditions existing during the past 12
months. Comparison of the NHIS rates with those obtained from physicians' examinations in the National
Health and Nutrition Examination Survey II indicates that the use of self-reported health conditions does not
introduce a significant bias into the comparison. See Fogel, Costa, and Kim (1993) for a more detailed discussion
of possible biases and their magnitudes.
[a]Among veterans in 1983 the prevalence of all types of circulatory diseases is underestimated because of
underreporting of hemorrhoids.
[b]The variable indicating whether the 1983 veteran ever had hemorrhoids is unreliable.
SOURCE: Fogel, Costa, and Kim (1993: Table 8).

one hand and the later onset of chronic diseases on the other into three
categories. The first category involves forms of malnutrition (including the
ingestion of toxic substances) that cause permanent, promptly visible physiological damage, as is seen in the impairment of the nervous systems of
fetuses as a result of excessive smoking or the consumption of alcohol by
pregnant women. It appears that protein calorie malnutrition (PCM) in
infancy and early childhood can lead to permanent impairment of central
nervous system function. Folate and iodine deficiency in utero and mod-
erate-to-severe iron deficiency during infancy also appear to cause permanent neurological damage (Chavez, Martinez, and Soberanes 1995; Czeizel
and Dudás 1992; Lozoff, Jimenez, and Wolf 1991; Martorell, Rivera, and
Kaplowitz 1990; Rosenberg 1992; Scrimshaw 1993; Scrimshaw and Gordon 1968).

Not all damage resulting from retarded development in utero or infancy and caused by malnutrition shows up immediately. In recent studies
Barker and his colleagues (Barker 1992 and 1994; Barker et al. 1991) have

reported that such conditions as coronary heart disease, hypertension, stroke, noninsulin-dependent diabetes, and autoimmune thyroiditis begin in utero or in infancy but do not become apparent until mid-adult or later ages. In these cases, individuals appear to be in good health and function well in the interim. However, early onset of the degenerative diseases of old age appears to be linked to inadequate cellular development early in life.

Certain physiological dysfunctions incurred by persons suffering from malnutrition can, in principle, be reversed by improved dietary intake, but they often persist because the cause of the malnutrition persists. If the malnutrition persists long enough, these conditions can become irreversible or fatal. This category of consequences includes the degradation of tissue structure, especially in such vital organs as the lungs, heart, and gastrointestinal tract. In the case of the gastrointestinal system, atrophy of the mucosal cells and intestinal villi results in decreased absorption of nutrients. Malnutrition also has been related to the impairment of immune functions, increased susceptibility to infections, poor wound healing, electrolyte imbalances, endocrine imbalances, and, in adults, dangerous cardiac arrhythmias and increased chronic rheumatoid disorders (McMahon and Bistrian 1990)

So far I have focused on the contribution of technological change to physiological improvement. The process has been synergistic, however, with improvement in nutrition and physiology contributing significantly to economic growth and technological progress. For example, technophysio evolution appears to account for about half of British economic growth over the past two centuries. Much of this gain resulted from improvement in human thermodynamic efficiency. The rate of converting human energy input into work output appears to have increased by about 50 percent since 1790 (Fogel 1994a).

Probable trends in morbidity and mortality rates

The current pace of technological change within and beyond the biomedical sciences, as well as the continuing increase in stature and the reduction in mortality and morbidity rates at older ages, suggests that technophysio evolution has not yet run its course. This conclusion is supported by recent evidence from the National Long-Term Care Surveys (NLTCS). They indicate that long-term prevalence rates of chronic disability among persons aged 65 and older declined by 1.3 percent per annum over the 12 years between 1982 and 1994 (Manton, Corder, and Stallard 1997). This rate of decline is quite similar to the annual rates of decline obtained from the comparison of the principal chronic conditions among veterans aged 65 and older in 1910 and in 1985–88 (see Table 2).

If one projects the rate of decline in chronic disabilities obtained from the NLTCS studies to 2040, the implied disability rate is only about 55 percent of the rate that prevailed in 1994. It has been argued that future improvements in human physiology are unlikely in rich nations because the increase in the mature stature of males has leveled off in several developed countries (Schmidt, Jorgensen, and Michaelson 1995). This finding does not necessarily imply that secular growth has ended or that stature no longer will be useful in forecasting trends in mortality. The United States and other countries have experienced renewed growth in final heights that followed periods of leveling-off and even periods of reversal (see Figure 4).

Although a biological theory suitable for establishing an upper limit on human height has not emerged yet, several factors suggest that average final heights will continue to increase in the United States. First, in recent years an increasing share of the gross increase in population, up to nearly

FIGURE 4 Trends in mean height and in life expectancy at age 10: Native-born, white males, United States, 1710–1970

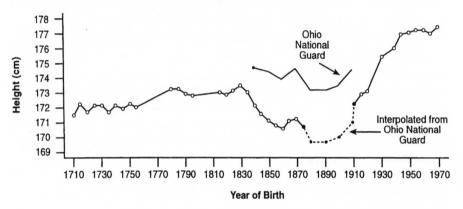

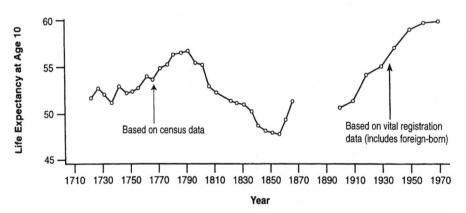

NOTE: Height is by birth cohort, whereas life expectancy at age 10 is by period.
SOURCES: Fogel (1986: Fig. 9.1); Costa and Steckel (1997: Fig. 2.1).

one-third, has been the result of immigration by persons with substantially lower average adult stature than natives of native parents. This factor accounts for part of the recent leveling-off in the increase in stature shown in Figure 4.

The more or less simultaneous leveling-off in height in several developed countries may be due to common environmental insults. One leading candidate is the spread of smoking among women of childbearing ages during the 1930s and 1940s. Several studies have shown that smoking by pregnant women not only retards fetal development but also is associated with the subsequent stunting of children during developmental ages and at maturity (Barker et al. 1991; Eskenazi and Bergmann 1995; Fogelman and Manor 1988; Gidding et al. 1995; Kaplan and Salonen 1990; Rantakallio 1988; Wheeler et al. 1995; Zarén, Lindmark, and Gebre-Medhin 1996).

Even if there is no further increase in stature at maturity in native-born persons of native-born parents, the cohort born in 1980 will be substantially taller at older ages than the cohorts currently at ages 60 and older, who were born mainly between 1905 and 1930 and who were shorter at maturity. Because mortality now is concentrated overwhelmingly at ages 60 and older, it is the increase in stature at these ages that is relevant for forecasting mortality declines (Kim 1996).

Figure 4 not only points up the instability of technophysio evolution, it also suggests the need to consider the specific factors influencing the physiological development of particular cohorts, while keeping in mind that despite the long-run trend, physiological improvement has not proceeded steadily in either Europe or the United States. Figure 4 summarizes the available data on US secular trends in stature and mortality since 1710 (Costa and Steckel 1997; Fogel 1986). The series on both stature and period life expectancy at age 10 contain striking cycles. Both series rise during most of the eighteenth century, attaining substantially greater heights and life expectations than prevailed in England during the same period. Life expectancy began to decline during the 1790s and continued to do so for about half a century. There may have been a slight decline in the heights of cohorts born between 1785 and 1820; but the sharp decline, which probably lasted about half a century, began with cohorts born around 1830. At the same time, cohort life expectancy at age 20 began an accelerated decline (Pope 1992). (Figure 4 shows period rather than cohort life expectancies because less complete information is available for cohort life expectancies.) A new rise in heights, the one with which we long have been familiar, probably began with cohorts born during the last decade of the nineteenth century and continued for about 60 years. Similar cycles in height occurred in Hungary, Sweden, and Britain.

Evidence on trends in BMI and morbidity is sparser, but the time pattern agrees with that of stature and mortality. BMI of 18-year-old cadets at

FIGURE 5   Mean body mass index by age group and year: United States, 1864–1991

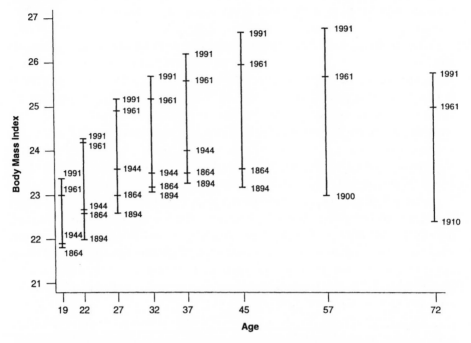

NOTE: The age groups, which are centered at the ticks, are ages 18–19, 20–24, 25–29, 30–34, 35–39, 40–49, 50–64, and 65–79. For some years the BMI is not available for a specific age group.
SOURCE: Costa and Steckel (1997: Fig. 2.4).

the Citadel, a US military academy, declined from the 1870s to the 1890s before rising by 1920 (Coclanis and Komlos 1995). Figure 5 shows declines in BMI between 1864 and 1894 among men of ages 20–24, 25–29, 30–34, 35–39, and 40–49. Prevalence rates for chronic conditions at older ages among cohorts who were born in the period 1840–49 were higher than those for cohorts born in the periods 1830–39 and 1820–29. At ages 65–74 men who were born in the period 1820–29 were significantly less likely than men born between 1840 and 1849 to suffer from rheumatism, hemorrhoids, respiratory disorders, hernias, and stomach disorders. They were significantly less likely to have respiratory and stomach disorders than were men born in the period 1830–39, who, in turn, were less likely than men born in the period 1840–49 to suffer from circulatory conditions (Costa and Steckel 1997). The stunting of the 1840–49 cohort relative to the 1830–39 and 1820–29 cohorts appears to be reflected in health outcomes at older ages.

Although the combination of factors tending to retard improvements in nutritional status and health varied from one country to another, one factor stands out more than any other: rapid urbanization. In both Europe and the United States the urban population grew far more rapidly during the nineteenth century than at any other time in history, exceeding the capacity of cities to supply clean water, remove waste, and contain the spread of infection (Bairoch 1988). The mortality rate appears to have been influenced both by the size of the city and by the rapidity of its growth rate. In the United States around 1830, cities with 50,000 or more persons had death rates more than twice as high as those of rural areas. Similar patterns have been observed for Europe. The exact threshold at which city size began to affect mortality rates varied with time, place, and circumstance; but in the United States during the mid-nineteenth century, cities of about 25,000 persons appear to have been the threshold of significant elevation in mortality (Fogel et al. 1978).

The implication of all these trends is that in making forecasts, one needs to take into account the specific physiological history of each cohort. Individuals who will turn 65 in 2040 have already reached physiological maturity. As both the "early indicators" and the Barker studies (Barker 1992 and 1994; Costa 1998) have shown, much information contained in their developmental history since birth can be used in forecasting the likely influences on their health and longevity at late ages.

Forecasting health care and pension costs

Does the probable future decline in the age-specific morbidity schedule imply that expenditures on health will be less as a percentage of income in 2040 than they are today? To answer that question it is necessary to forecast how the structure of various categories of consumption will change between now and 2040. Estimating the future burden of pensions also turns heavily on projections of the changing structure of consumption.

The crucial nature of the changing structure of consumption is often overlooked by economists who are concerned with the crises in the pay-as-you-go pension systems and in the state-funded health care programs that afflict all developed nations. The usual focus is on such issues as distortions in the prices of health services and of labor incentives or on the potential for raising taxes to cover looming deficits. Although these are important issues, they are secondary issues as far as their effect on the future structure of consumption is concerned.

The key variable in predicting the structure of consumption is income. The long-term relationship between income and consumption is grossly distorted, however, when cross-sections are used to estimate the relationship. In the case of the increased consumption of leisure, cross-sectional regressions yield a negative income elasticity of demand: in other words, cross-sectional regressions lead to the erroneous implication that the consumption of leisure will decline as income rises. Nor is this misleading result attenuated when cross-sections two decades apart are compared, although such a comparison introduces the influences of changes in cohorts. One problem is that some of the most important changes in the structure of consumption are not reflected in the major bodies of data on which economists have relied (for example, in the National Income Product Accounts). Another is that distortions arise when trends over successive life cycles are estimated from data sets that are essentially cross-sectional (such as the Current Population Survey and the Consumer Expenditure Survey). Even when longitudinal data are used as a basis for analysis, these data often pertain only to recent cohorts, which by themselves do not adequately capture secular changes in demand covering a reasonably long succession of cohorts.

A century ago the typical household in the more developed countries spent 80 percent or more of its income on food, clothing, and shelter. Today these commodities account for much less than half of household consumption. Many people are alarmed at this and other recent changes in the structure of consumption, particularly the reduced role of manufactured products, changes that they fear may presage economic and social decadence and portend a reversal in national fortunes. A similar state of mind was widespread at the end of the nineteenth century. But then the focus of concern was the decline of agriculture and the rise of industry. Those who identified the good life with agriculture were fearful of life in an urban and industrial age. Now it is life in a service society that promotes anxiety (Fogel 2000).

The decline in hours of work, the rise in unemployment, and the threatened "end of the job" also create anxiety, although there is another way of looking at these phenomena (Aronowitz and DiFazio 1994; Rifkin 1995). Table 3, line 5, shows the remarkable reduction in average daily work that has occurred for males in the US labor force over the past century (Fogel 1997a and 2000). The table also forecasts the future division of the average day, indicating that by 2040 more than half of the discretionary day will be devoted to leisure activities. The forecast is for a reduction of the work year from the current average of about 1,730 hours to just 1,400 hours, with the average work week down to 30 hours, paid holidays up to 30, and sick days at 14.

The workday of women in 1880 was somewhat longer, and in some respects may have been more arduous, than that of men. Evidence suggests that a female workday in 1880 may have run about 15 minutes longer than that of males, amounting to perhaps 8.75 hours per day, on the basis of a 365-day year, or about 3,200 hours annually (Davidson 1982: Chap. 9).

As a result of the mechanization of the household, smaller number of persons per household, and the marketing of prepared foods, the typical nonemployed married woman today spends about 3.4 hours per day engaged in housework. If she is employed, the figure for housework drops to

TABLE 3 Secular trends in time use: Estimated and projected average hourly division of the day of the average male household head, United States, circa 1880, 1995, and 2040

Activity	Circa 1880	1995	2040
Sleep	8.0	8.0	8.0
Meals and essential hygiene	2.0	2.0	2.0
Chores[a]	2.0	2.0	2.0
Travel to and from work[b]	1.0	1.0	0.5
Work[c]	8.5	4.7	3.8
Illness[d]	0.7	0.5	0.5
Subtotal	22.2	18.2	16.8
Residual for leisure activities[e]	1.8	5.8	7.2

NOTE: Calculations for all three periods are based on a 365-day work year.
[a]Includes chopping firewood, shoveling coal, making repairs in home and fences, maintaining tools, gardening, carting, weaving and sewing, and caring for children and the aged. Much of what was called "chores" is now called "do-it-yourself" activity and "sweat equity."
[b]In the case of farm laborers, travel is the walk from cottage to fields where work was conducted.
[c]Circa 1880: work is calculated on 3,109 annual hours. Other assumptions are a 64-hour work week, 7 holidays, and 18 sick days. 1995: calculated on 1,730 annual hours. Other assumptions are a 37.5-hour work week, 28 holidays, and 14 sick days. Circa 2040: calculated on 1,400 annual hours. Other assumptions are a 30-hour work week, 30 holidays, and 12 sick days.
[d]The numbers of sick days circa 1880 and in 1995 are based on US data and are applied to the 14 discretionary hours.
[e]Includes travel time to and from leisure-time activities. Circa 1880, seven holidays at 14 hours per day of discretionary time provide 0.3 hours of leisure per day on a 365-day basis. The corresponding figures for 1995 and 2040 are 1.1 hours and 1.2 hours per day, respectively.
SOURCE: Fogel (2000: Table 5.1).

2.1 hours; but women in the labor force average about 4.6 hours per day as employees. Hence when "work" is combined with "chores," men and women work roughly equal amounts per day, and both enjoy much more leisure than their predecessors did. The principal difference is that the gains for women have come exclusively from the reduction in hours of housework, whereas the gains for men have come from a reduction in the hours of employed work (Moffit 1968–92; Robinson 1988).

So far I have retained the common distinction between work and leisure, although these terms are already inaccurate and may soon be obsolete. This distinction was invented when most people were engaged in manual labor for 60 or 70 hours per week and was intended to contrast such labor with the elevated activities of the gentry or their American equivalent, Thorstein Veblen's "leisure class" (Veblen 1899 [1934]). Leisure is not a synonym for indolence, however, but rather a reference to desirable forms of effort or work. ("Work" is to be understood here in the physiological rather than the economic sense.) As George Bernard Shaw put it, "labor is doing what we must; leisure is doing what we like; rest is doing nothing whilst our bodies and our minds are recovering from their fatigue" (Shaw 1928 [1931]: 91).

To some extent at present, and more so in the future as the average work week declines toward 28 hours and voluntary retirement normally begins at age 55, these terms will lose their pejorative connotation. "Work" will increasingly mean activity under compulsion of earning income, regardless of whether the effort is manual or mental. And "leisure" will mean purely voluntary activity, as was characteristic of the English gentry or Veblen's American leisure class, although it may incidentally produce income. To avoid creating confusion, I reserve the word "work" for use in its physiological sense, an activity that requires energy above the basal metabolic rate and maintenance. Activity aimed primarily at earning a living I will call "earnwork." Purely voluntary activity, even if it incidentally generates payment, I will call "volwork."

It is not only daily and weekly hours of earnwork that have declined (line 5 in Table 3). The share of lifetime discretionary hours spent in earnwork has declined even more rapidly. Table 3 does not reflect the fact that the average age at which a person enters the labor force is about five years later today than it was in 1880, that the number of holidays during the work year has substantially increased, or that the expected average period of retirement for those who live to age 20 is about 15 years longer today than it was in 1880 (Lee 1996).

Thus, contrary to much public opinion, the lifetime discretionary hours spent at earning a living have declined by about one-third over the past century despite the large increase in the total amount of discretionary time over the average life span (Table 4). In 1880 four-fifths of discretionary time was spent at earning a living. Today the lion's share (59 percent) is spent doing what we like. Moreover, it appears probable that by 2040, close to 75 percent of discretionary time will be spent doing what we like, de-

TABLE 4   Estimated and projected lifetime distribution of discretionary time: United States, circa 1880, 1995, and 2040

Specified hours and years	Circa 1880	1995	2040
Lifetime hours			
Discretionary hours	225,900	298,500	321,900
Earnwork hours	182,100	122,400	75,900
Volwork hours	43,800	176,100	246,000
Years of life remaining after entering labor force	50.1	58.4	63.0
Expected years in the labor force	42.3	43.0	33.0

NOTE: Discretionary time excludes time required for sleep, eating, and vital hygiene, which is assumed to require an average of 10 hours per day. The availability of discretionary time is assumed to commence with the average age at entry into the labor force and includes chores, travel to and from earnwork, and earnwork. See discussion in text.
SOURCE: Fogel (2000: Table 5.2 and p. 317, n. 22).

spite a further substantial increase in discretionary time as a consequence of the continuing extension of the life span.

Why do so many people want to forgo earnwork, which would allow them to buy more food, clothing, housing, and other goods? The answer turns partly on the extraordinary technological change of the past century, which has not only greatly reduced the number of hours of labor the average individual needs to obtain his or her food supply, but has also made housing, clothing, and a vast array of consumer durables so cheap in real terms that the totality of material consumption requires many fewer hours of labor today than were required over a lifetime for food alone in 1880.

Indeed, we have become so rich that we are approaching saturation in the consumption, not only of necessities, but of goods recently thought to be luxuries, or goods that existed only as dreams of the future during the first third of the twentieth century. Today in the United States there are nearly two cars per household, on average. Virtually everyone who is old enough and well enough to drive a car has one. There are 2.2 television sets per household (0.8 per person). With some items, such as radios, we seem to have reached supersaturation, since there is now more than one radio per ear (5.6 per household). The level of saturation with many consumer durables is so high that even the poorest one-fifth of households is well endowed with them (US Bureau of the Census 1996: 623, 723; US Department of Labor, Bureau of Labor Statistics 1994).

Consequently, the era of the household accumulation of consumer durables, which sparked the growth of many manufacturing industries during the decades following World War II, is largely over in the United States. Most of the future purchases of consumer durables in the United States will be for replacement and for newly established households (Edmondson 1996; US Bureau of the Census 1994 and 1996: 623; US Department of Labor, Bureau of Labor Statistics 1994).

Table 5 shows how sharply the US distribution of consumption changed between 1875 and 1995. Food, clothing, and shelter, which accounted for about 74 percent of consumption (expanded to include the value of leisure time) in 1875, accounted for only 13 percent of expanded consumption in 1995. Leisure, on the other hand, rose from 18 percent of consumption to 67 percent. The expenditure category of "other," consisting mainly of utilities and services, rose only slightly from 6 to 7 percent of consumption, partly because of the great reduction in the cost of these services. On the one hand, as Table 5 shows, the long-term income elasticities of the demand for food and clothing are below 0.5 and the elasticity of the demand for shelter is close to but below 1.0. On the other, the elasticities of demand for leisure (volwork) and for medical services are well over 1.0. Even if these last two elasticities decline somewhat during the next 45 years, it is still likely that the burden of health care and retirement will require a sub-

TABLE 5   Long-term trend in the distribution of expanded consumption and in implied income elasticities of several consumption categories: United States, 1875 and 1995

Consumption class	Distribution of expanded consumption (percent)		Long-term income elasticity
	1875	1995	
Food	49	5	0.2
Clothing	12	2	0.3
Shelter	13	6	0.7
Health care	1	9	1.6
Education	1	5	1.6
Leisure	18	67	1.5
Other	6	7	1.1

NOTES: Expanded consumption is the sum of conventional consumption expenditures plus the imputed value of leisure time. Health care and education include government and employer expenditures plus out-of-pocket expenditures.
SOURCE: Fogel (2000: Table 5.3).

stantially larger share of gross domestic product than has been allowed in most recent forecasts.

More conventional forecasts have been compromised by the failure to take adequate account of the growth in the consumption of leisure, and by a failure to recognize differences in the time preference for leisure. People may decide to enjoy leisure while still in the labor force by varying daily, weekly, and annual hours of work. Or they can enjoy leisure in a block of time later in life by lowering the age of retirement. Different households have different time preferences for leisure, which depend partly on their uses of leisure and partly on their lifetime targets for levels of various categories of material consumption. On average, the consumption of leisure time after retirement has grown more rapidly than the consumption of leisure time before retirement. In 1880 only a quarter of lifetime volwork was performed after retirement. Today nearly half is performed after retirement.

Clearly, improvement in forecasting the problems of funding pensions requires a more refined economics of leisure than has so far been developed. The need for a new economics of leisure was signaled by the dismantling of standard working hours in recent decades. This process was spurred by the large-scale entry of women into the labor force after World War II (Goldin 1990). Many married women sought jobs that could be pursued part-time. And many preferred jobs that would permit them to work in blocks of time lasting several months, after which they could take several months off without losing the opportunity to return.

These new, flexible arrangements are desired by an increasing number of workers, both men and women, who want a life that is not overwhelmed by earnwork. Although money and social status matter to these workers, they are content with a lifestyle that places greater emphasis on such values as family life, shared time, spiritual values, and good health. A poll conducted in late 1995 reported that 48 percent of US adult earnworkers had either cut back on hours of work, declined a promotion, reduced their commitments, lowered material expectations, or moved to a place with a quieter life during the preceding five years (Marks 1995). What is at issue to such employees is time—time to enjoy the things they have, time to spend with their families, and time to discover the spiritual side of life (Shellenbarger 1997; *Wall Street Journal* 1996).

Although the average annual hours of earnwork undertaken by household heads have continued to decline over the past quarter-century, the combined hours of earnwork undertaken by households with husbands and wives present have increased by 24 percent since 1969 (Moffitt 1968–92; Robinson and Godbey 1997; US Bureau of the Census 1994; cf. Hochschild 1997; Schor 1991). These extra hours are concentrated in prime working ages, and they are one of the main ways by which couples are financing early retirement. The failure to take account of the possibility that households currently undertaking above-average hours of earnwork may not be forgoing leisure but only shifting their time preferences for leisure is one of the factors contributing to the misinterpretation of the social security problem.

What, then, is the virtue of increasing spending on retirement and health rather than on goods? It is the virtue of providing consumers in rich countries with what they want most. It is the virtue of not insisting that individuals increase earnwork an extra 10 hours a week or an extra 30,000 hours per lifetime in order to produce more food or durables than they want, just because such consumption will keep factories humming. The point is that leisure activities (including lifelong learning)—volwork—and health care are the growth industries of the late twentieth and the early twenty-first centuries. They will spark economic expansion during our age, just as agriculture did in the eighteenth and early nineteenth centuries, and as manufacturing, transportation, and utilities did in the late nineteenth and much of the twentieth centuries.

The growing demand for health care services is not due primarily to a distortion of the price system; rather, it is due mainly to a combination of the high income elasticity of the demand for health services and the increasing effectiveness of medical intervention. The increase in medical effectiveness since 1910 is strikingly demonstrated by comparing the first and last columns of the row for hernias in Table 2. Prior to World War II, hernias were generally permanent and often exceedingly painful. By the 1980s, however, about three-quarters of all veterans who had ever had hernias were cured of them. Similar progress over the seven decades is indicated by the row for genito-urinary conditions, which shows that three-quarters of those who ever had such conditions were cured of them (compare columns 3 and 4). Other areas where medical intervention has been highly effective include control of hypertension and reduction in the incidence of stroke, surgical removal of osteoarthritis, replacement of knee and hip joints, removal of cataracts, and chemotherapies that reduce the incidence of osteoporosis and heart disease (Manton 1993; Manton, Corder, and Stallard 1997). The success of medical interventions combined with rising incomes has led to a huge increase in the demand for medical services.

Can developed nations afford a substantial rise in immaterial consumption?

Today many people have time to enjoy those amenities of life that only the rich could afford in abundance a century ago. These amenities broaden the mind, enrich the soul, and relieve the monotony of much earnwork. They include travel, athletics, enjoyment of the performing arts, education, and shared time with the family.

Today people are increasingly concerned with the meaning of their lives. In 1880 earthly self-realization was not a salient issue for most individuals, whose days were taken up almost entirely with earning food, clothing, and shelter, and whose reward was promised in heaven. A half-century from now, perhaps even sooner, when increases in productivity make it possible to provide goods in abundance with half the labor required today, the consideration of life's meaning and other matters of self-realization may take up the bulk of discretionary time.

The forecasts embodied in Tables 3 and 4 imply that by 2040 those still in the labor force, as conventionally defined, will have more than 50 hours per week of leisure (volwork), that the average age at retirement (the beginning of full-time volwork or the end of regular earnwork) will begin about age 55, and that the average duration of full-time volwork will be about 35 years. Will developed nations have the resources to afford amounts of leisure that would once have been considered luxurious and also to provide high-quality health care for an additional seven or eight years of life?

On the assumption that the per capita income of those nations will continue to grow at a rate of 1.5 percent per annum, the resources to finance such expanded demands will be abundant. This is a modest growth rate, well below the long-term experience of the United States since World War II, and also well below the experience of the past decade and a half (Maddison 1991 and 1995). Consider a typical American household of two children established in 1995 in which the head is aged 20 and the spouse, working part-time, earns 36 percent of the income of the head (Fogel 2000: Chap. 5). Such a couple could accumulate the savings necessary to retire at age 55, with a pension paying 60 percent of their peak life cycle earnings, by putting aside 14.7 percent of annual earnings from the year that the head and spouse enter the labor force. That pension would permit them at age 55 to maintain their preretirement standard of living, with a real income that would rank them among the richest fifth of householders today.

By putting aside an additional 9.4 percent of income, the couple could buy high-quality medical insurance that would cover the entire family until their children entered the labor force, and also cover the parents' medical needs between the time they retired and age 83 (assumed to be the average age at death in their cohort). Saving an additional 7.8 percent of income would permit the parents to finance the education of their children for 16 years—that is, through the bachelor's degree at a good university.

What I have described is a provident fund of the type recently introduced or under consideration in some of the high-performing Asian economies (Iyer 1993; Poortvliet and Laine 1995). I have assumed that the savings would be invested in conservatively managed funds, such as Teachers Insurance and Annuity Association/College Retirement Equities Fund (TIAA-CREF), which most American universities subscribe to for their faculties. These pension funds might be managed by the government, by private firms, or as joint ventures. The only requirement would be that the funds are invested in a balanced portfolio of government and private securities that yielded a respectable rate of return and were kept insulated from irrelevant political pressures. As in TIAA-CREF, individuals might be permitted modest latitude in choosing among investment opportunities.

The point of the example is that prospective real resources are adequate to finance early retirement, expanded high-quality education, and an increasing level of high-quality medical care. Despite an allowance for a 1.3 percent decline per annum in age-specific morbidity rates, it is likely that health expenditures will continue to rise as a share of gross domestic product (GDP). Changes in age structure, combined with a high income elasticity of demand for health care, probably will raise the share of health expenditures to around 20 percent of GDP by 2040.

After saving in a provident fund, the typical working household will still have 68 percent of a substantially larger income than is typical today to spend on other forms of consumption. Since current levels of food, clothing, and shelter will require a decreasing number of hours of work during the family's life cycle, dropping to about 20 percent of earnwork hours just before retirement, families will be able to increase their expenditures on health care and still also increase their rate of accumulation in consumer durables and housing, or increase their expenditures on such consumables as travel, entertainment, and education, or reduce their hours of earnwork, or retire before age 55.

Embedded in my simulation is a suggestion for modernizing current government systems of taxation and expenditure. Close to half of what are called taxes are actually deferred income or forced savings. In these cases the government does not collect money for its own benefit but merely acts as an intermediary to ensure that money needed by individuals for later use (such as retirement) is set aside for the stated purpose and then delivered to households when needed. The particular form of intermediation exercised by the US government, however, is quite peculiar. Instead of setting up an account in the name of the individual doing the saving, the government transfers the funds to a person who earlier deferred consumption. At the same time it promises the current taxpayer that when he or she is ready to retire, the government will find new taxpayers to provide the promised funds. Under normal circumstances governments of developed countries provide this form of intermediation quite efficiently. The cost of administering the US Social Security system, for example, is less than 0.6 percent of expenditures (US Social Security Administration 1997).

In the United States the increased demand for health care and longer periods of retirement will require raising the income tax from current levels of about 15 percent of payrolls to around 25 percent, because by 2030 only two people will be paying into Social Security and Medicare for every one person receiving benefits. Such a tax is economically feasible, since if the economy grows at only 1.5 percent per capita annually, the average income of workers will be about 56 percent higher in real terms before payroll taxes and about 38 percent higher after payroll taxes. In other words, providing undiminished benefits through the current government plan will actually leave future taxpayers with post-tax real incomes substantially higher than they are today.

But is such a plan politically feasible? Could politicians persuade workers today to accept an additional tax burden equal to 10 to 15 percent of their earnings by arguing that the income of individuals after the new tax will still leave them with a third more income than people had a generation ago? Such reminders of how much better off people are today do little to assuage the public's anger at appearing to be overtaxed. The search for a more transparent system of funding retirement and health care is therefore a search for a plan that will not cause a catastrophic political reaction either today or in 2030.

The problem with current systems, aside from the fact that they give the impression that personal savings are actually taxes, is that their operation is subject to heavy political buffeting. Rates of return on the savings for deferred income are highly variable, partly because of flaws in the original design of the systems, and are often far lower than they would have been had they been invested in a fund similar to TIAA-CREF. Moreover, the current systems are affected by variations in fertility and mortality rates, which have created financial crises and thrown into doubt governments' promises that they will be able to provide the money supposedly set aside for later retirement income, health care, or education. The crisis, then, is not in a nation's resources for providing extended retirement, improved health care, and extended education, but in the exceedingly clumsy system for financing these services.

I have focused this analysis on the typical (median- or average-income) household to demonstrate that the economies of developed nations have the prospective resources to permit early retirement, expanded education, and expanded medical care. Unfortunately, the income of some households is so low that saving 32 percent of earnings would not provide a provident fund large enough to permit decent retirement, health care, and education for those households. This is not a problem of inadequate national resources but of inequity. Such inequities can continue to be addressed by redistributing income from high-income to poor households through taxes and subsidies. Correcting these inequities, in any event, does not require restricting spending on retirement or health care.

The wealthier nations are increasingly moving into an era that provides unprecedented opportunities for individual self-realization. Self-realization in turn requires good health and extensive leisure. The process of technophysio evolution is satisfying these conditions. Self-realization also requires, however, an answer to the question that persons with leisure have contemplated for more than 2000 years. How do individuals realize their fullest potential? Technophysio evolution is making it possible to extend this quest from a minute fraction of the population to nearly all of it. Although retired persons will have more time to pursue this quest, even those still in the labor force will have sufficient leisure to seek self-realization either within their professional occupations or outside of them (Laslett 1991; Lenk 1994). One implication of this analysis is that decisionmakers both in government and in the private sector now need to review existing policies for their bearing on the timely growth of institutions that will satisfy an expanding demand for volwork.

Note

This chapter draws upon joint research reported in several earlier studies (Floud, Wachter, and Gregory 1990; Fogel 1992, 1993, 1994a, 1994b, 1996, 1997a, and 1997b; Fogel and Floud 1999; Fogel and Costa 1997; Fogel, Costa, and Kim 1993; Kim 1996; Lee 1996) and in two books (Costa 1998 and Fogel 2000). Research for this chapter was supported by the National Institutes of Health (Grant AG10120), the National Science Foundation (Grant SES-9114981), and the Charles R. Walgreen Foundation. I thank the University of Chicago Press for permission to make use of material in Fogel (2000) and John M. Kim for permission to use the Waaler surface reproduced above as Figure 3. I am grateful for editorial suggestions by Susan Jones.

References

Allen, Robert C. 1992. *Enclosure and the Yeoman: The Agricultural Development of the South Midlands, 1450–1850*. Oxford: Oxford University Press.

———. 1994. "Agriculture during the industrial revolution," in *The Economic History of Britain Since 1700*, eds. Roderick Floud and Donald McCloskey, 2nd ed., Vol. 1. Cambridge: Cambridge University Press, pp. 96–122.

Aronowitz, Stanley and William DiFazio. 1994. *The Jobless Future: Sci-tech and the Dogma of Work*. Minneapolis: University of Minnesota Press.

Bairoch, Paul. 1988. *Cities and Economic Development from the Dawn of History to the Present*, trans. C. Brauder. Chicago: University of Chicago Press.

Barker, D. J. P. (ed.). 1992. *Fetal and Infant Origins of Adult Disease*. London: British Medical Journal.

———. 1994. *Mothers, Babies and Disease in Later Life*. London: BMJ Publishing Group.

Barker, D. J. P. et al. 1991. "Relation of birth weight and childhood respiratory infection to adult lung function and death from chronic obstructive airways disease," *British Medical Journal* 303(6804): 671–675.

Chávez, Adolfo, Celia Martínez, and Beatriz Soberanes. 1995. "The effect of malnutrition on human development: A 24-year study of well-nourished children living in a poor Mexican village," in *Community Based Longitudinal Studies of the Impact of Early Malnutrition on Child Health and Development: Classical Examples from Guatemala, Haiti and Mexico*, ed. Nevin S. Scrimshaw. Boston: International Nutritional Foundation for Developing Countries, pp. 79–124.

Cipolla, Carlo M. 1974. *The Economic History of World Population*, 6th ed. Harmondsworth, Middlesex: Penguin.

Clark, Grahame. 1971. *World Prehistory: An Outline*. Cambridge: Cambridge University Press.

Coclanis, Peter A. and John Komlos. 1995. "Nutrition and economic development in post-reconstruction South Carolina: An anthropometric history," *Social Science History* 19(1): 91–116.

Costa, Dora L. 1998. *The Evolution of Retirement: An American Economic History, 1880–1990*. Chicago: University of Chicago Press.

Costa, Dora L. and Richard H. Steckel. 1997. "Long-term trends in health, welfare, and economic growth in the United States," in *Health and Welfare during Industrialization*, eds. Richard H. Steckel and Roderick Floud. Chicago: University of Chicago Press, pp. 47–89.

Czeizel, Andrew E. and István Dudás. 1992. "Prevention of the first occurrence of neural-tube defects by periconceptional vitamin supplementation," *New England Journal of Medicine* 327(26): 1832–1835.

Davidson, Caroline. 1982. *A Woman's Work Is Never Done: A History of Housework in the British Isles, 1650–1950*. London: Chatto and Windus.

Edmondson, Brad. 1996. "Who needs two cars?" *American Demographics* 18(12): 14–15.

Eskenazi, Brenda and Jackie J. Bergmann. 1995. "Passive and active maternal smoking during pregnancy, as measured by serum cotinine, and postnatal smoke exposure. I. Effects on physical growth at age 5 years," *American Journal of Epidemiology* 56(9 suppl.): S10–S18.

Fagan, Brian M. 1977. *People of the Earth*, 2nd ed. Boston: Little, Brown and Co.

Floud, Roderick, Kenneth W. Wachter, and Annabel Gregory. 1990. *Height, Health, and History: Nutritional Status in the United Kingdom, 1750–1980*. Cambridge: Cambridge University Press.

Fogel, Robert W. 1986. "Nutrition and the decline in mortality since 1700: Some preliminary findings," in *Long-Term Factors in American Economic Growth*, eds. Stanley L. Engerman and Robert E. Gallman. Chicago: University of Chicago Press, pp. 439–555.

———. 1992. "Second thoughts on the European escape from hunger: Famines, chronic malnutrition, and mortality rates," in *Nutrition and Poverty*, ed. S. R. Osmani. Oxford: Clarendon Press, pp. 243–286.

————. 1993. "New sources and new techniques for the study of secular trends in nutritional status, health, mortality and the process of aging," *Historical Methods* 26(1): 5–43.

————. 1994a. "Economic growth, population theory, and physiology: The bearing of long-term processes on the making of economic policy," *American Economic Review* 84(3): 369–395.

————. 1994b. "The relevance of Malthus for the study of mortality today: Long-run influences on health, mortality, labour force participation, and population growth," in *Population, Economic Development, and the Environment,* eds. Kerstin Lindahl-Kiessling and Hans Landberg. Oxford: Oxford University Press, pp. 231–284.

————. 1996. "The escape from hunger and premature death, 1700–2100: Europe, America and the Third World." The 1996 Ellen McArthur Lectures, presented at Cambridge University, 12–20 November.

————. 1997a. "Economic and social structure for an ageing population," Philosophical Transactions of the Royal Society of London, Series B, *Biological Sciences* 352(1363): 1905–1917.

————. 1997b. "New findings on secular trends in nutrition and mortality: Some implications for population theory," in *Handbook of Population and Family Economics,* eds. M. R. Rosenzweig and O. Stark. Amsterdam: Elsevier Science, pp. 435–486.

————. 2000. *The Fourth Great Awakening and the Future of Egalitarianism.* Chicago: University of Chicago Press.

Fogel, Robert W. and Dora L. Costa. 1997. "A theory of technophysio evolution, with some implications for forecasting population, health care costs, and pension costs," *Demography* 34(1): 49–66.

Fogel, Robert W., Dora L. Costa, and John M. Kim. 1993. "Secular trends in the distribution of chronic conditions and disabilities at young adult and late ages, 1860–1988: Some preliminary findings." Paper presented at the National Bureau of Economic Research (NBER) Summer Institute, Economics of Aging Program, 26–28 July, Cambridge, MA.

Fogel, Robert W. and Roderick Floud. 1999. "A theory of multiple equilibria between populations and food supplies: Nutrition, mortality and economic growth in France, Britain and the United States, 1700–1980." Typescript, Center for Population Economics, University of Chicago.

Fogel, Robert W. et al. 1978. "The economics of mortality in North America, 1650–1910: A description of a research project," *Historical Methods* 11(2): 75–108.

Fogelman, K. R. and O. Manor. 1988. "Smoking in pregnancy and development into early adulthood," *British Medical Journal* 297(6658): 1233–1236.

Gidding, Samuel S. et al. 1995. "Cardiac function in smokers and nonsmokers: The CARDIA Study. The Coronary Artery Risk Development in Young Adults Study," *Journal of the American College of Cardiology* 26(1): 211–216.

Goldin, Claudia. 1990. *Understanding the Gender Gap: An Economic History of American Women.* New York: Oxford University Press.

Hochschild, Arlie R. 1997. *The Time Bind: When Work Becomes Home and Home Becomes Work.* New York: Basic Books.

Iyer, Subramaniam N. 1993. "Pension reform in developing countries," *International Labour Review* 132(2): 187–207.

Kaplan, George A. and Jukka T. Salonen. 1990. "Socioeconomic conditions in childhood and ischaemic heart disease during middle age," *British Medical Journal* 301(6761): 1121–1123.

Kim, John M. 1993. "Economic and biomedical implications of Waaler surfaces: A new perspective on height, weight, mortality, and morbidity." Unpublished manuscript. Center for Population Economics, University of Chicago.

————. 1996. "Waaler surfaces: The economics of nutrition, body build, and health." Ph.D. dissertation, University of Chicago.

Laslett, Peter. 1991. *A Fresh Map of Life.* Cambridge, MA: Harvard University Press.

Lee, Chulhee. 1996. "Essays on retirement and wealth accumulation in the United States, 1850–1990." Ph.D. dissertation, University of Chicago.

Lenk, Hans. 1994. "Value changes and the achieving society: A social-philosophical perspective," in *OECD Societies in Transition: The Future of Work and Leisure*. Paris: Organization for Economic Co-operation and Development, pp. 81–94.

Lozoff, Betsy, Elias Jimenez, and Abraham W. Wolf. 1991. "Long-term developmental outcome of infants with iron deficiency," *New England Journal of Medicine* 325(10): 687–695.

Maddison, Angus. 1991. *Dynamic Forces in Capitalist Development*. Oxford: Oxford University Press.

———. 1995. *Monitoring the World Economy, 1820–1992*. Paris: Organization for Economic Co-operation and Development (OECD).

Manton, Kenneth G. 1993. "Biomedical research and changing concepts of disease and aging: Implications for long-term forecasts for elderly populations," in *Forecasting the Health of Elderly Populations*, eds. Kenneth G. Manton, Burton H. Singer, and Richard M. Suzman. New York: Springer, pp. 319–365.

Manton, Kenneth G., Larry Corder, and Eric Stallard. 1997. "Chronic disability trends in elderly United States populations: 1982–1994," *Proceedings of the National Academy of Sciences, USA* 96(6): 2593–2598.

Marks, John. 1995. "Time out," *U.S. News and World Report*, 11 December, pp. 85–96.

Martorell, R., J. Rivera, and H. Kaplowitz. 1990. "Consequences of stunting in early childhood for adult body size in rural Guatemala," *Annales Nestlé* 48: 85–92.

McMahon, M. Molly, and Bruce R. Bistrian. 1990. "The physiology of nutritional assessment and therapy in protein-calorie malnutrition," *Disease-a-Month* 36(7): 373–417.

McNeill, William. 1971. *A World History*, 2nd ed. New York: Oxford University Press.

Moffitt, R. 1968–92. *Current Population Surveys: March Individual Level Extract, 1968–1992*. Inter-University Consortium for Political and Social Research, No. 6171. On-line documentation at http://www.icpsr.umich.edu.

Piggott, Stuart. 1965. *Ancient Europe from the Beginnings of Agriculture to Classical Antiquity*. Chicago: Aldine.

Poortvliet, William G. and Thomas P. Laine. 1995. "A global trend: Privatization and reform of social security pension plans," *Benefits Quarterly* 11(3): 63–84.

Pope, Clayne L. 1992. "Adult mortality in America before 1900: A view from family histories," in *Strategic Factors in Nineteenth-Century American Economic History: A Volume to Honor Robert W. Fogel*, eds. Claudia Goldin and Hugh Rockoff. Chicago: University of Chicago Press, pp. 267–296.

Rantakallio, Paula. 1988. "The longitudinal study of the northern Finland birth cohort of 1966," *Paediatric and Perinatal Epidemiology* 2(1): 59–88.

Rifkin, Jeremy. 1995. *The End of Work: The Decline of the Global Labor Force and the Dawn of the Post-market Era*. New York: G. P. Putnam's Sons.

Robinson, John P. 1988. "Who's doing the housework?" *American Demographics* 10(12): 24–28, 63.

Robinson, John P. and Geoffrey Godbey. 1997. *Time for Life: The Surprising Ways Americans Use Their Time*. University Park: Pennsylvania State University.

Rosenberg, Irwin H. 1992. "Folic acid and neural-tube defects—Time for action?" *New England Journal of Medicine* 327(26): 1875–1877.

Schmidt, I. M., M. H. Jorgenson, and K. F. Michaelson. 1995. "Height of conscripts in Europe: Is postneonatal mortality a predictor?" *Annals of Human Biology* 22(1): 57–67.

Schor, Juliet. 1991. *The Overworked American: The Unexpected Decline of Leisure*. New York: Basic Books.

Scrimshaw, Nevin S. 1993. "Malnutrition, brain development, learning and behavior," Twentieth Kamla Puri Sabharwal Memorial Lecture, presented at Lady Irwin College, New Delhi, 23 November.

Scrimshaw, Nevin S. and J. S. Gordon (eds.). 1968. *Malnutrition, Learning and Behavior.* Cambridge, MA: Massachusetts Institute of Technology (MIT) Press.

Shaw, George Bernard. 1928 [1931]. *The Intelligent Woman's Guide to Socialism and Capitalism. The Collected Works of Bernard Shaw,* Vol. 20. Ayot St. Lawrence edition. New York: Wm. H. Wise.

Shellenbarger, Sue. 1997. "New job hunters ask recruiters, 'Is there a life after work?'" *Wall Street Journal,* 29 January, p. B1.

Slicher van Bath, B. H. 1963. *The Agrarian History of Western Europe, A.D. 500–1850,* trans. Olive Ordish. London: Edward Arnold.

Tanner, J. M. 1990. *Foetus into Man: Physical Growth from Conception to Maturity,* rev. ed. Cambridge, MA: Harvard University Press.

———. 1993. "Review of D. J. P. Barker's *Fetal and Infant Origins of Adult Disease,"* *Annals of Human Biology* 20(5): 508–509.

US Bureau of the Census. 1994. *Current Population Survey: March 1994.* Inter-University Consortium for Political and Social Research, No. 6461. Washington, DC. On-line documentation at http://www.icpsr.umich.edu.

———. 1996. *Statistical Abstract of the United States,* 116th ed. Washington, DC: Government Printing Office.

US Department of Labor, Bureau of Labor Statistics. 1994. *Consumer Expenditure Survey, Interview Survey, 1994.* Inter-University Consortium for Political and Social Research, No. 6710. Washington, DC. On-line documentation at http://www.icpsr.umich.edu.

US Social Security Administration. 1997. *Annual Report.* Washington, DC: Government Printing Office.

Veblen, Thorstein. 1899 [1934]. *The Theory of the Leisure Class: An Economic Study of Institutions.* New York: Modern Library.

Wall Street Journal. 1996. "The overloaded American: Too many things to do, too little time to do them." 8 March, Sec. R.

Wheeler, Timothy, Timothy Chard, Frederick Anthony, and Clive Osmond. 1995. "Relationships between the uterine environment and maternal plasma placental protein 14 in early pregnancy," *Human Reproduction* 10(10): 2700–2704.

Wrigley, E. A. 1987. "Urban growth and agricultural change: England and the Continent in the early modern period," in E. A. Wrigley, *People, Cities and Wealth: The Transformation of Traditional Society.* Oxford: Basil Blackwell, pp. 157–193.

Zarén, B., G. Lindmark, and M. Gebre-Medhin. 1996. "Maternal smoking and body composition of the newborn." *Acta Paediatrica* 85(2): 213–219.

MARY ARENDS-KUENNING is Assistant Professor of Agricultural and Consumer Economics, University of Illinois, Urbana-Champaign.

DWAYNE BENJAMIN is Professor of Economics, University of Toronto.

DAVID E. BLOOM is Clarence James Gamble Professor of Economics and Demography, School of Public Health, Harvard University.

LOREN BRANDT is Professor of Economics, University of Toronto.

DAVID CANNING is Professor of Economics, Queen's University of Belfast.

KUO-MEI CHEN is Research Assistant, Institute of Economics, Academia Sinica, Taipei, Taiwan.

LII-TARN CHEN is Associate Research Fellow, Institute of Economics, Academia Sinica, Taipei, Taiwan.

C. Y. CYRUS CHU is Distinguished Research Fellow, Institute of Economics, Academia Sinica, Taipei, Taiwan.

CHING-FAN CHUNG is Research Fellow, Institute of Economics, Academia Sinica, Taipei, Taiwan.

ANGUS DEATON is Dwight D. Eisenhower Professor of Economics and International Affairs, Princeton University.

ROBERT W. FOGEL is Director of the Graduate School of Business, Center for Population Economics, and Charles R. Walgreen Distinguished Service Professor of American Institutions, The University of Chicago. He is also Co-director of the Program on Cohort Studies, National Bureau of Economic Research, Cambridge, Massachusetts.

PAUL J. GERTLER is Professor of Economic Analysis and Policy, Haas School of Business, and Professor of Health Services Finance, School of Public Health, University of California at Berkeley.

CHARLES HIRSCHMAN is Boeing International Professor, Department of Sociology, University of Washington, Seattle.

SHENG-CHENG HU is Research Fellow and Director, Institute of Economics, Academia Sinica, Taipei, Taiwan.

RONALD LEE is Professor in the Departments of Demography and Economics, University of California at Berkeley.

PIA N. MALANEY is Research Associate, Center for International Development, Harvard University.

ANDREW MASON is Professor and Chair, Department of Economics, University of Hawaii at Manoa, and Senior Fellow, East-West Center, Honolulu.

CEM METE is Postdoctoral Fellow, Economic Growth Center, Yale University.

TIMOTHY MILLER is a Researcher in the Department of Demography, University of California at Berkeley.

JOHN W. MOLYNEAUX is an Economist at RAND, Santa Monica.

MARK R. MONTGOMERY is Associate Professor of Economics, State University of New York at Stony Brook, and Senior Associate, Policy Research Division, Population Council.

CHRISTINA PAXSON is Professor of Economics and Public Affairs, Princeton University.

DUDLEY L. POSTON, JR., is Professor of Sociology and the George T. and Gladys H. Abell Professor of Liberal Arts, Texas A&M University.

SCOTT ROZELLE is Associate Professor, Department of Agricultural and Resource Economics, University of California at Davis.

I-JU TSAI is Assistant Professor of Economics, Institute of Economics, Academia Sinica, Taipei, Taiwan.

YIH-JIN YOUNG is Assistant Professor, Department of Sociology, Nassau Community College, Garden City, NY.